Get the eBook FREE!

(PDF, ePub, Kindle, and liveBook all included)

We believe that once you buy a book from us, you should be able to read it in any format we have available. To get electronic versions of this book at no additional cost to you, purchase and then register this book at the Manning website.

Go to https://www.manning.com/freebook and follow the instructions to complete your pBook registration.

That's it!
Thanks from Manning!

Blazor in Action

Blazor in Action

CHRIS SAINTY

MANNING
SHELTER ISLAND

For online information and ordering of this and other Manning books, please visit
www.manning.com. The publisher offers discounts on this book when ordered in quantity.
For more information, please contact

> Special Sales Department
> Manning Publications Co.
> 20 Baldwin Road
> PO Box 761
> Shelter Island, NY 11964
> Email: orders@manning.com

Manning Publications Co.	Development editors:	Toni Arritola and Kristen Watterson
20 Baldwin Road	Technical development editor:	Andrew West
PO Box 761	Review editor:	Aleksandar Dragosavljević
Shelter Island, NY 11964	Production editor:	Andy Marinkovich
	Copy editor:	Carrie Andrews
	Proofreader:	Keri Hales
	Technical proofreader:	Karthikeyarajan Rajendran
	Typesetter and cover designer:	Marija Tudor

ISBN 9781617298646
Printed and bound by CPI Group (UK) Ltd, Croydon, CR0 4YY

This book is dedicated to my son, Archie.

contents

preface   x
acknowledgments   xii
about this book   xiv
about the author   xvii
about the cover illustration   xviii

1 Starting your Blazor journey   1

1.1   Why choose Blazor for new applications?   2

1.2   Components, a better way to build UI   3

What is a component?   3 ▪ The benefits of a component-based UI   4 ▪ Anatomy of a Blazor component   4

1.3   Blazor, a platform for building modern UIs with C#   5

Understanding hosting models   6 ▪ Blazor WebAssembly   7 Blazor Server   11 ▪ Other hosting models   16

2 Your first Blazor app   18

2.1   Setting up the application   19

Blazor WebAssembly template configurations   20 ▪ Creating the application   21

2.2   Building and running the application   24

2.3   Key components of a Blazor application   25

Index.html   25 ▪ Program.cs   27 ▪ App.razor   29 wwwroot folder and _Imports.razor   30

vi

2.4   Writing your first components   30

*Organizing files using feature folders   31 ▪ Setting up
styling   34 ▪ Defining the layout   36 ▪ The Blazing
Trails home page   38*

3 Working with Blazor's component model   49

3.1   Structuring components   51

Single file   51 ▪ Partial class   52

3.2   Component life cycle methods   54

*The first render   57 ▪ The life cycle with async   58
Dispose: The extra life cycle method   60*

3.3   Working with parent and child components   62

*Passing values from a parent to a child   64 ▪ Passing data
from a child to a parent   68*

3.4   Styling components   71

*Global styling   72 ▪ Scoped styling   73 ▪ Using CSS
preprocessors   76*

4 Routing   84

4.1   Introducing client-side routing   85

Blazor's router   85 ▪ Defining page components   88

4.2   Navigating between pages programmatically   89

4.3   Passing data between pages using route parameters   92

4.4   Handling multiple routes with a single component   96

4.5   Working with query strings   101

*Setting query-string values   101 ▪ Retrieving query-string values
using SupplyParameterFromQuery   103*

5 Forms and validation—Part 1: Fundamentals   108

5.1   Super-charging forms with components   110

*Creating the model   111 ▪ Basic EditForm configuration   112
Collecting data with input components   115 ▪ Creating
inputs on demand   120*

5.2   Validating the model   123

*Configuring validation rules with Fluent Validation   123
Configuring Blazor to use Fluent Validation   125*

5.3   Submitting data to the server   130

*Adding MediatR to the Blazor project   132 ▪ Creating a request
and handler to post the form data to the API   132
Setting up the endpoint   136*

6   **Forms and validation—Part 2: Beyond the basics   140**

6.1   Customizing validation CSS classes   141

*Creating a FieldCssClassProvider   141 ▪ Using custom
FieldCssClassProviders with EditForm   143*

6.2   Building custom input components with InputBase   145

*Inheriting from InputBase<T>   145 ▪ Styling the custom
component   148 ▪ Using the custom input component   149*

6.3   Working with files   151

*Configuring the InputFile component   151 ▪ Uploading files when
the form is submitted   153*

6.4   Updating the form to allow editing   159

*Separating the trail form into a standalone component   159
Refactoring AddTrailPage.razor   161 ▪ Adding the edit trail
feature   165 ▪ Testing the edit functionality   177*

7   **Creating more reusable components   180**

7.1   Defining templates   181
7.2   Enhancing templates with generics   185
7.3   Sharing components with Razor class libraries   189

8   **Integrating with JavaScript libraries   194**

8.1   Creating a JavaScript module and accessing it via a
component   195

*Testing out the RouteMap component   199 ▪ Calling JavaScript
functions from C# and returning a response   200*

8.2   Calling C# methods from JavaScript   203
8.3   Integrating the RouteMap component with the
TrailForm   206
8.4   Displaying the RouteMap on the TrailDetails drawer   214

9   **Securing Blazor applications   221**

9.1   Integrating with an identity provider: Auth0   223

*Registering applications with Auth0   224 ▪ Customizing tokens
from Auth0   224 ▪ Configuring Blazor WebAssembly to use*

Auth0   225 ▪ Configuring ASP.NET Core WebAPI
to use Auth0   229

9.2   Displaying different UI fragments based on authentication
status   230
Updating the Home feature   233

9.3   Prevent unauthorized users accessing a page   238
Securing API endpoints   239 ▪ Calling secure API endpoints from
Blazor   241

9.4   Authorizing users by role   245
Adding roles in Auth0   245 ▪ Consuming Auth0 roles in Blazor
WebAssembly   247 ▪ Implementing role-based logic   249

10 Managing state   253

10.1   Simple state management using an in-memory store   254
Creating and registering a state store   254 ▪ Saving data entered
on the form to AppState   255

10.2   Improving the AppState design to handle more state   258

10.3   Creating persistent state with browser local storage   260
Defining an additional state store   261 ▪ Adding and removing
trails from the favorites list   264 ▪ Displaying the current number
of favorite trails   265 ▪ Reorganizing and refactoring   266
Showing favorited trails on the favorite trails page   268
Initializing AppState   270

11 Testing your Blazor application   272

11.1   Introducing bUnit   273

11.2   Adding a bUnit test project   274

11.3   Testing components with bUnit   277
Testing rendered markup   278 ▪ Triggering event handlers   281
Faking authentication and authorization   283 ▪ Emulating
JavaScript interactions   285 ▪ Testing multiple components   287

appendix A   Adding an ASP.NET Core backend to a Blazor WebAssembly
app   291
appendix B   Updating existing areas to use the API   305

index   315

preface

I've been an ASP.NET developer for over 17 years now. I love working with ASP.NET Core and the C# language. But there was always an element missing for me. . . .

Since I was young, I've enjoyed building web UIs. When I was 15, my best friend and I decided to build a website about the *Quake* games we enjoyed playing. He built the backend while I built the UI. I remember spending hours and days creating nested tables and inline styles to create the look we wanted for the site. This seems torturous now, but I really loved it at the time. Throughout my resulting career, I've really enjoyed building the client-side experience, but this has always taken me away from C# and ASP.NET Core. Instead, I've learned JavaScript and various frameworks and tooling that are popular in that ecosystem. While I enjoyed JavaScript, I really wanted to be using my favorite language, C#, when building client-side web applications.

Then one day in February 2018, I stumbled across a video of Steve Sanderson at NDC Oslo 2017 (https://youtu.be/MiLAE6HMr10). In this talk, he presented an experiment he had built that took a portable .NET run time called Dot Net Anywhere and compiled it to a format called WebAssembly. He used this as a base to create a framework that allowed client-side web applications to be built using Razor (a mix of C#, HTML, and CSS) that ran entirely in the browser. He called it Blazor.

The first experimental preview of Blazor was released by Microsoft on March 22, 2018, with new previews almost every month. I followed along with each preview, trying out the new features and writing blog posts about my experiences. On April 18, 2019, Daniel Roth published a blog post announcing that it was moving out of the experimental phase and Microsoft had committed to ship it as a supported web UI framework. Finally, the missing element!

Since that blog post, Blazor has gone from strength to strength. Additional hosting models have been added, allowing Blazor to run in more places. With .NET 6, we've seen some of the biggest leaps forward with the framework. AOT (ahead-of-time) mode has been introduced, producing huge performance improvements for Blazor WebAssembly applications. The evolution of Xamarin, .NET MAUI, allows Blazor to move out of the browser and be used to create cross-platform desktop and mobile applications.

This book is the result of my journey with Blazor from that first time watching Steve's NDC Oslo presentation to building production applications today. To date, I've published over 75 blog posts about Blazor on my personal blog and have written many for other publications. Blazor also gave me a passion for public speaking, first at .NET user groups and eventually at international conferences. I even got to give a talk on Blazor at NDC Oslo in room 7, the same room that Steve was in when he first presented his experiment a few years earlier.

acknowledgments

This book has been one of the hardest projects of my life, and while it has my name on the cover, it was only possible with the help of many other people. I'd like to take this opportunity to say a huge thank-you to those people.

First and foremost, I want to thank my wife, Robyn. You have been my rock throughout the last year and a half. You have had to deal with me at my worst during this time, but your unwavering support and encouragement made me believe that I could finish this. I will always be grateful for that, and I love you very much.

I'd also like to thank my whole family for their support and encouragement—especially my dad, who talked me out of quitting at one point when I completely lost faith.

Next, I'd like to thank some amazing people at Manning without whom this book would not exist. Brian Sawyer recruited me, convinced me to write a proposal, and convinced me that I could pull it off! Kristen Watterson, my developmental editor for almost the entire project, helped shape the book into what it is today. Toni Arritola stepped in at the eleventh hour to get the book over the line. Andrew West, my technical developmental editor, made sure my code made sense and actually worked. Finally, Karthikeyarajan Rajendran did a great job with the final technical proofread of the book. Thanks also to the production team at Manning for all their hard work in producing this book.

Also, a special thanks to all the reviewers for their comments and feedback: Al Pezewski, Alberto Acerbis, Ashwini Gupta, Bruno Sonnino, Grant Colley, Jason Hales, Jeff Smith, Jim Wilson, John Rhodes, Kalyan Chanumolu, Marcin Sęk, Mark Chalkley, Mike Ted, Pedro Seromenho, Richard Michaels, Rohit Sharma, Ron Lease, Rui Ribeiro, Steve Goodman, Tanya Wilke, Thomas Gueth, and Wayne Mather—you made this a better book.

Finally, I'd like to thank Steve Sanderson, Daniel Roth, and the whole ASP.NET Core team at Microsoft. You've created something really special with Blazor, and it's literally changed my life. I'm now an author, international speaker, and Microsoft MVP all because of Blazor. Thank you.

about this book

Blazor in Action has been written to take you from being a beginner to being proficient and confident building Blazor applications. Initially, the book covers high-level concepts such as hosting models and components before drilling down into specific features of the framework, such as routing, forms and validation, and templated components.

To help imbed the various concepts and features, you'll build a real application—Blazing Trails—chapter by chapter. By the end of the book, you'll have a complete reference app you can refer to anytime.

Who should read this book

This book is aimed at developers who have a basic understanding of .NET, C#, and web technologies (HTML, JavaScript, and CSS). If you've been building web applications using Razor Pages or MVC, then the learning curve will feel quite shallow. If you've been building apps using ASP.NET Core Web APIs and a JavaScript framework such as React, Vue.js, or Angular, then you'll be in an even better position.

How this book is organized: A road map

This book is organized into 11 chapters and 2 appendices.

- Chapter 1 introduces Blazor, component-based UIs, and hosting models. It covers what Blazor is and the reasons why you might choose to use it, as well as how components are a better way to build UIs and how Blazor has embraced this approach. It also covers what hosting models are and discusses the advantages and tradeoffs they each have.

- Chapter 2 begins the journey of building the Blazing Trails application. Initially it covers choosing the right project template for a new Blazor application, as well as how to build and run it. Then it walks through the key parts of a Blazor application. It concludes by talking about file organization using feature folders and how to write your first components.

- Chapter 3 dives deeper into Blazor's component model. It discusses how to structure components, what life cycle methods are and what order they execute in, and how to work with parent and child components. It also covers styling components and using CSS preprocessors with Blazor.

- Chapter 4 looks at client-side routing, showing how to define page components and navigate between them. It also tackles more advanced topics such as passing data in the URL and navigating programmatically.

- Chapter 5 is the first of two chapters covering forms and validation. In this chapter, fundamentals such as using Blazor's built-in form components, validating user input, and submitting data to a server are tackled.

- Chapter 6 builds on the previous chapter, covering more advanced topics such as creating custom form components, working with files, and adapting a form to handle editing existing data.

- Chapter 7 explores how to make components more reusable. It introduces templated components and how they can be further enhanced using generics.

- Chapter 8 shows how to use JavaScript interop to integrate existing JavaScript libraries into a Blazor application. It also covers techniques that allow C# code to call into JavaScript code and JavaScript code to call into C#.

- Chapter 9 tackles securing Blazor applications by showing how to integrate with an identity provider called Auth0.

- Chapter 10 looks at state management and implements an in-memory state store. It tackles state store design and how to store state using the browser's local storage APIs.

- Chapter 11 covers testing components using the bUnit testing framework. Five key scenarios are covered: testing rendered markup, triggering event handlers from test code, faking authentication and authorization, emulating JavaScript interop, and testing multiple components together.

- Appendices A and B cover code refactoring required as the example application grows. Appendix A covers adding a ASP.NET Core Web API to the solution. If you're building the example app along with book, appendix A should be completed between chapters 4 and 5. Appendix B walks through refactoring the rest of the application to use the Web API introduced in appendix A. Appendix B should be followed after completing chapter 6 and before starting chapter 7.

About the code

This book contains many examples of source code, both in numbered listings and in line with normal text. In both cases, source code is formatted in a `fixed-width font` `like this` to separate it from ordinary text. Sometimes code is also in bold to highlight code that has changed from previous steps in the chapter, such as when a new feature adds to an existing line of code.

In many cases, the original source code has been reformatted. We've added line breaks and reworked indentation to accommodate the available page space in the book. In rare cases, even this was not enough, and listings include line-continuation markers (➥). Additionally, comments in the source code have often been removed from the listings when the code is described in the text. Code annotations accompany many of the listings, highlighting important concepts.

You can get executable snippets of code from the liveBook (online) version of this book at https://livebook.manning.com/book/blazor-in-action. Source code is also available for chapters 2–11 in my GitHub repository at https://github.com/chrissainty/blazor-in-action. The code added in the two appendices are incorporated into the chapters they precede.

All the code in this book was built using the .NET 6 SDK and Visual Studio 2022. However, other tools such as Visual Studio Code and the .NET CLI or JetBrains Rider will run the code as well.

liveBook discussion forum

Purchase of *Blazor in Action* includes free access to liveBook, Manning's online reading platform. Using liveBook's exclusive discussion features, you can attach comments to the book globally or to specific sections or paragraphs. It's a snap to make notes for yourself, ask and answer technical questions, and receive help from the author and other users. To access the forum, go to https://livebook.manning.com/book/blazor-in-action/discussion. You can also learn more about Manning's forums and the rules of conduct at https://livebook.manning.com/discussion.

Manning's commitment to its readers is to provide a venue where a meaningful dialogue between individual readers and between readers and the author can take place. It is not a commitment to any specific amount of participation on the part of the author, whose contribution to the forum remains voluntary (and unpaid). We suggest you try asking the author some challenging questions lest his interest stray! The forum and the archives of previous discussions will be accessible from the publisher's website as long as the book is in print.

about the author

CHRIS SAINTY is a web developer with over 17 years of experience. He has been using Blazor since the first experimental preview back in March 2018 and was one of the first people to start blogging about it. Chris has published over 75 blog posts on Blazor on his own blog, while also writing guest posts for *Visual Studio Magazine*, Progress Telerik, and Stack Overflow. He is also an active open source developer and currently maintains some of the most popular Blazor NuGet packages covering integration with browser local storage APIs to UI components such as modals and toasts. Away from the keyboard, Chris is a seasoned conference speaker and has talked about Blazor at events all over the world. These contributions have also earned him the Microsoft MVP (Most Valuable Professional) Award.

about the cover illustration

The figure on the cover of *Blazor in Action* is "Homme de Oonolaska," or "Oonolaska Man," taken from a collection by Jacques Grasset de Saint-Sauveur, published in 1797. Each illustration is finely drawn and colored by hand.

In those days, it was easy to identify where people lived and what their trade or station in life was just by their dress. Manning celebrates the inventiveness and initiative of the computer business with book covers based on the rich diversity of regional culture centuries ago, brought back to life by pictures from collections such as this one.

Starting your Blazor journey

This chapter covers
- Reasons to choose Blazor for your next application
- Why components are a better way to build UIs
- Hosting models for Blazor

We live in exciting times, as .NET developers' lives have never been better. We can create apps for any operating system, be it Windows, Linux, iOS, Android, or macOS, and of course, we can build amazing web-based applications with ASP.NET MVC, Razor Pages, and Web API, which have allowed us to create robust scalable and reliable systems for years.

However, there has long been a missing piece to the puzzle. One thing all of ASP.NET's web solutions have in common is that they are server based. We've never been able to leverage the power of C# and .NET to write client-side web applications; this has always been the domain of JavaScript—but not anymore.

In this chapter, I'm going to introduce you to a revolutionary client-side framework called *Blazor*. Built on web standards, Blazor allows us to write rich, engaging user interfaces using C# and .NET. We'll explore how Blazor can make your

1

development process more efficient and raise your productivity levels, especially if you're using .NET on the server as well. We'll cover hosting models, an important concept to understand when starting out with Blazor. Next, we'll begin to explore components and the benefits of using them to build UIs. Finally, we'll discuss the reasons why you should consider Blazor for your next project.

1.1 Why choose Blazor for new applications?

Arguably, the hardest part of starting a new project in recent times has been selecting the tech stack—there are just so many choices available. This is especially true in the frontend world. We must pick a framework (Angular, React, Vue.js), pick a language (TypeScript, CoffeeScript, Dart), and pick a build tool (webpack, Parcel, Browserify). If a team is new to this ecosystem, it can seem an almost impossible task to try and work out which combination of technologies will help make the project a success; it's even hard for teams with experience!

Let's cover some of the top reasons for choosing Blazor for your next project and how Blazor can help you avoid some of the issues I've just mentioned.

- *C#, a modern and feature-rich language*—Blazor is powered by C#, the eighth most popular language, according to the 2021 Stack Overflow Developer Survey (http://mng.bz/p240). It's powerful, easy to learn, and versatile. While C# is an object-oriented language, it's adopting more and more abilities to enable a more functional approach, if you prefer. Static typing helps developers catch errors at build time, making the development life cycle faster and more efficient. It's also been around for a long time, currently in its tenth version. It's stable, well designed, and well supported.
- *Great tooling*—The .NET community has been fortunate to have some amazing tooling. Visual Studio is an extremely powerful, feature-rich, and extensible IDE (integrated development environment). It's also 100% free for individuals, open source work, or non-enterprise teams of up to five people. If you prefer something more lightweight, then there is Visual Studio Code (VS Code), one of the most popular code editors today. Both Visual Studio and VS Code are available cross-platform. Visual Studio is available on Windows and macOS, and VS Code is available on Windows, macOS, and Linux. There is also a great third-party IDE by JetBrains called *Rider*, which is cross-platform running on Windows, macOS, and Linux.
- *.NET Ecosystem*—While many new frameworks need to wait for an ecosystem to build up around them, Blazor can tap into the existing .NET ecosystem. At the time of writing, Blazor applications target .NET 6 and can, in theory, use any compatible NuGet package. I say "in theory," as some packages perform actions that aren't allowed in a WebAssembly scenario, such as modifying the filesystem.
- *Unopinionated*—While other frameworks stipulate how applications must be written, Blazor does not. There are no preferred patterns or practices for Blazor

development; you can write applications using the ones you're familiar and comfortable with. If you like MVVM (model-view-viewmodel), go for it. If you prefer using Redux, have at it. The choice is yours.

- *Shallow learning curve*—If you're an existing .NET developer, then the learning curve for Blazor is quite shallow. Razor, C#, dependency injection, and project structure will all look familiar to you, and with Blazor being unopinionated around patterns, you can just use what you're familiar and productive with. All this means you can focus on writing features more quickly, rather than learning the framework.

- *Code sharing*—If you're using C# on the server, then Blazor makes an excellent pairing. One of the most frustrating problems with different client and server languages is the inability to reuse code. Models or data transfer objects (DTOs) must be duplicated between server and client; they need to be kept updated, in sync. This could be a manual process or automated using some kind of code generation, but this is just another thing to set up and maintain. With Blazor, everything is C#. Any shared code can be placed in a common .NET class library and shared easily between server and client.

- *Open source*—As with many projects at Microsoft, Blazor is fully open source and the code is freely available on GitHub for you to browse, download, or fork your own copy. The team works in the open and is guided by developer requests and feedback. You can even contribute if you wish.

1.2   Components, a better way to build UI

Blazor, as with many modern frontend frameworks, uses the concept of components to build the UI. Everything is a component—pages, parts of a page, layouts. There are various types of components in Blazor, as well as multiple ways to design them, all of which will be explored in future chapters. But learning to think in terms of components is essential for writing Blazor applications.

1.2.1   What is a component?

Think of a component as a building block. You put these building blocks together to form your application. These building blocks can be as big or as small as you decide; however, building an entire UI as a single component isn't a good idea. Components really show their benefit when used as a way to divide up logical areas of a UI. Let's look at an example of a user interface structured as components (figure 1.1).

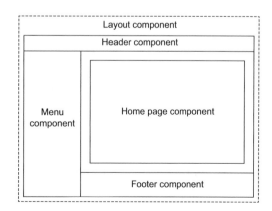

Figure 1.1   Example of a layout divided into components

Each area of the interface is a component, and each one has a certain responsibility. You may also notice that there is a hierarchy forming. The layout component sits at the top of the tree; the menu, header, home page, and footer are all child components of the layout component. These child components could, and probably would, have child components of their own. For example, the header component could contain a logo component and a search component (figure 1.2).

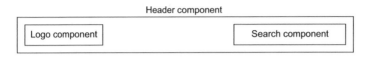

Figure 1.2   Example of nesting components to form a component tree

1.2.2   *The benefits of a component-based UI*

Many UIs have repeating elements in them. A great advantage to using components is that you can define an element in a component and then reuse the component wherever the element repeats. This can drastically cut down on the amount of repeated code in an application. It also makes the maintainability of the application much better— if the design of that element changes, you need only to update it in a single place.

To cater to more advanced scenarios, components can define their own APIs, allowing data and events to be passed in and out. Imagine a line-of-business application. It's probably safe to assume that within that app there are many places data is displayed in table format. One approach is to create each table as its own component; however, this means we would end up with a lot of components that display data in a table. A better approach is to define a single component that takes in a data set as a *parameter* and then displays it in a table. Now we have a single component for displaying data in a table that we can reuse all over the application. We can also add features to this component, such as sorting or paging. As we do, this functionality is automatically available to all the tables in the application, as they are all reusing the same component.

While often self-contained, it's possible to have components work together to create a more complex UI. For example, let's take the data table scenario we just talked about, which could be a single component but could potentially be quite large. Another approach is to divide it into several smaller components, each performing a certain job. We could have a table header component, a table body component, and even a table cell component. Each of these components is performing a specific job, but they are still part of the overall table component.

1.2.3   *Anatomy of a Blazor component*

Now that we have a better idea of what components are in a general sense, let's look at an example of a component in Blazor. For this, we'll grab a component from the Blazor project template. Figure 1.3 shows an example of a component from Blazor's standard project template, `Counter.razor`.

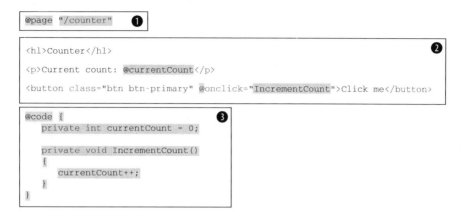

```
@page "/counter"      ❶

<h1>Counter</h1>                                              ❷
<p>Current count: @currentCount</p>
<button class="btn btn-primary" @onclick="IncrementCount">Click me</button>

@code {                   ❸
    private int currentCount = 0;

    private void IncrementCount()
    {
        currentCount++;
    }
}
```

Figure 1.3   The sections of a component in Blazor

This particular component is known as a *routable component*, as it has a *page directive* declared at the top. Routable components are essentially a page in the application. When the user navigates to the /counter route in the application, this component will be loaded by the Blazor router. It displays a simple counter with a button, and when the user clicks the button, the count is incremented by one and the new value displayed to the user.

While understanding the code isn't important at this point, we can understand the structure of the component. Figure 1.3 is divided up into three sections; each has a certain responsibility.

- *Section 1*—Used to define directives, add using statements, inject dependencies, or any other general configuration that applies to the whole component.
- *Section 2*—Defines the markup of the component; this is written using the Razor language, a mix of C# and HTML. Here we define the visual elements that make up the component.
- *Section 3*—The code block. This is used to define the logic of the component. It is possible to write any valid C# code into this section. You can define fields, properties, or even entire classes if you wish.

We'll be covering components in much greater detail throughout the rest of this book, so we'll leave it there for now. But this has given you a taste of what a component in Blazor looks like and how it is composed.

1.3   Blazor, a platform for building modern UIs with C#

Blazor is a fully featured framework for building modern client-side applications using the power of C# and .NET. This allows developers to build engaging applications that work across nearly any platform, including web, mobile, and desktop.

Blazor is an alternative to JavaScript frameworks and libraries such as Angular, Vue.js, and React. If you've had experience working with any of these, then you'll probably start spotting familiar concepts. The most notable influence is the ability to build UIs with components, a concept all these technologies share and something we'll explore in more detail later in this chapter.

Because Blazor is built on top of web standards, it doesn't require the end user to have .NET installed on their machines or any kind of browser plug-in or extension. In fact, with Blazor WebAssembly applications, we don't even need .NET running on the server; this flavor of Blazor can be hosted as simple static files.

Being built on .NET means we have access to the vibrant ecosystem of packages available on NuGet. We have best-in-class tooling with Visual Studio, VS Code, and Jet-Brains Rider. Also, with .NET being cross-platform, we can develop our Blazor applications on whatever our preferred platform is, be that Windows, macOS, or Linux.

While this book is going to focus on Blazor for web application development, I want to highlight that Blazor's programming model can also be used to build cross-platform desktop applications. With .NET 6, Blazor Hybrid was introduced. Built on top of the new .NET Multi-platform App UI (aka MAUI) framework, it works in a similar way to Electron applications. Content from a Blazor application is rendered via a BlazorWebView control. This offers a lot of choice in how these applications are structured. Developers can use Blazor and web technologies to construct the entire UI—except for the chrome, the outermost container for the application that includes the title bar. Or they can target only a specific piece of the interface to be written with Blazor and host that alongside native controls.

It doesn't stop there. There has been a long-running experimental project called *Mobile Blazor Bindings* (http://mng.bz/OGOO). This is a collaboration between the ASP.NET Core team and the .NET MAUI team to investigate the potential and demand for using Blazor's programming model to build native mobile applications! This really makes Blazor a compelling technology to learn, as once understood, it could allow developers to build UIs for almost any platform or device.

Hopefully, you can already see that Blazor is an exciting technology with a lot of potential. But there is a key concept that is important to understand before we go any further—that of hosting models. Let's tackle that next.

1.3.1 *Understanding hosting models*

When first getting started with Blazor, you will immediately come across hosting models. Essentially, hosting models are where a Blazor application is run. Currently, Blazor has two web-specific hosting models—Blazor WebAssembly and Blazor Server. Regardless of which model you choose for your application, the component model is the same, meaning components are written the same way and can be interchanged between either hosting model (figure 1.4).

Figure 1.4 shows an abstract representation of Blazor's architecture with the separation between the app and component model and the various hosting models. One of the interesting aspects of Blazor is the potential of other hosting models being made available over time. This allows Blazor to run in more places and be used to create more types of UIs.

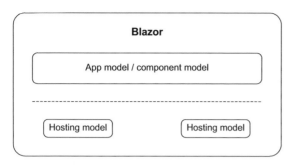

Figure 1.4 Blazor has a separation between hosting models and its app/ component model. This means components written for one hosting model can be used with another.

1.3.2 *Blazor WebAssembly*

Blazor WebAssembly allows your application to run entirely inside the client's browser, making it a direct alternative to JavaScript SPA (single-page application) frameworks. To help you understand how this hosting model works, we'll walk through the process of initializing a Blazor WebAssembly application (figure 1.5).

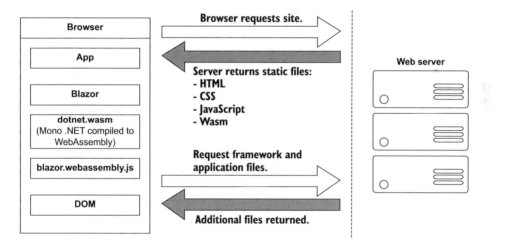

Figure 1.5 Boot-up of a Blazor WebAssembly application showing the interactions between the client's browser and the web server

The process begins when a request is made by the browser to the web server. The web server will return a set of files needed to load the application. These include the host page for the application, usually called index.html; any static assets required by the application, such as images; CSS and JavaScript, as well as a special JavaScript file called *blazor.webassembly.js.*

In the Blazor WebAssembly hosting model, part of the Blazor framework resides in JavaScript and is contained in the blazor.webassembly.js file. This part of the framework does three main things:

- Loads and initializes the Blazor application in the browser
- Provides direct DOM (Document Object Model) manipulation so Blazor can perform UI updates
- Provides APIs for JavaScript interop scenarios, which we'll discuss in detail in later chapters

At this point, you may be wondering why we have a JavaScript file. One of the big selling points of Blazor is the ability to write UI logic using C# instead of JavaScript, right? Yes, that's true. But as of right now, WebAssembly has a large limitation: it can't alter the DOM or call Web APIs directly. These features are planned and being worked on for the next phase of WebAssembly, but until they land, JavaScript is the only way to perform these tasks.

It's possible that in the future this file will no longer be required. This will depend on how fast features are added to WebAssembly and adopted by browsers. But for now, it's an essential part of the framework.

Now that we've cleared that up, let's get back to booting the Blazor app. I want to point out that the files returned from the server are all static files; they haven't required any server-side compilation or manipulation. This means that they can be hosted on any service that offers static hosting. There is no requirement for a .NET run time to be present on the server. For the first time, this opens up free hosting options such as GitHub pages to .NET developers (this applies to standalone Blazor WebAssembly applications only).

Once the browser has received all the initial files from the web server, it can process them and construct the DOM. Next, blazor.webassembly.js is executed. This performs many actions, but in the context of starting a Blazor WebAssembly app, it downloads a file called *blazor.boot.json*. This file contains an inventory of all the framework and application files that are required to run the app. Once it's downloaded, it is used to download the remaining files needed to run the application.

Most of these files are normal .NET assemblies; there is nothing special about them, and they could be run on any compatible .NET run time. But there's also another type of file that is downloaded called *dotnet.wasm*. This file is a complete .NET run time that has been compiled to WebAssembly.

WebAssembly

WebAssembly is a low-level, assembly-like language that can be run in modern web browsers with near-native performance. Although it's possible to write WebAssembly directly, it's more commonly used as a compilation target for higher level languages such as C/C++ and Rust. It's designed to run alongside JavaScript, allowing JavaScript to call in to WebAssembly and vice versa. WebAssembly also operates in the same security sandbox as JavaScript applications. Visit https://webassembly.org for detailed information on WebAssembly.

By default, only the .NET run time is compiled to WebAssembly—the framework and application files are standard .NET assemblies. However, in .NET 6, an AOT (ahead-of-time) mode was introduced that allows developers to compile their applications to WebAssembly. The benefit of this is much improved performance for CPU-intensive code. Using AOT, CPU-intensive code compiled to WebAssembly will be many times more performant than the interpreted approach used by default. However, there's a tradeoff, and that's size. AOT-compiled code is around two times bigger than the standard assemblies, meaning a much larger overall download size for the application.

Once the blazor.boot.json file has been downloaded and the files listed in it have been downloaded, it's time for the application to be run. The WebAssembly .NET run time is initialized, which in turn loads the Blazor framework and, finally, the application itself. At this point, we have a running Blazor application that exists entirely inside the client's browser. Aside from requesting additional data (if applicable), there's no further reliance on the server.

CALCULATING UI UPDATES

We now understand how a Blazor WebAssembly application boots up. But how do UI updates get calculated? Just as we did for the initialization process, we're going to follow a scenario to understand how this happens and what Blazor does (figure 1.6).

For our scenario, we have a Blazor WebAssembly application with two pages containing only a header: Home and Counter, respectively. The user is on the home page of the application and will click the link to go to the Counter page. We'll follow the

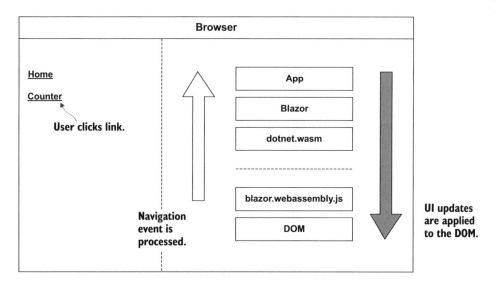

Figure 1.6   The process of client-side navigation in Blazor WebAssembly, from clicking a link to the application of UI updates

process Blazor goes through to update the UI while navigating from the Home page to the Counter page.

When the user clicks on the Counter link, the navigation event is intercepted by Blazor's JavaScript run time (blazor.webassembly.js). This event is then passed over to the Blazor framework running on the WebAssembly run time (dotnet.wasm) and is processed by Blazor's router component.

The router checks its routing table for any routable components that match the route the user has attempted to navigate to. In our case, it will find a match with the Counter component, a new instance of that component will be created, and the relevant life cycle methods will be executed.

Once complete, Blazor will work out the minimum number of changes that are required to update the DOM to match that of the Counter component. When this is complete, those changes will be passed back down to the Blazor JavaScript run time, which will then apply those changes to the physical DOM. At this point, the UI will update and the user will be on the Counter page.

All of this has happened client side in the user browser. There was no need for a server during any point in this process. It's fair to say that in a real-world application, you would probably make a call out to a server at some point in this process. This usually happens during the execution of the life cycle methods of the component being navigated to in order to load some initial data for the component. But this would depend on the individual application.

BENEFITS AND TRADEOFFS

Now that we know a bit more about how the Blazor WebAssembly hosting model works, let's talk about the benefits and tradeoffs of choosing this model. Let's start with the benefits:

- *Applications run on the client*—This means that there is much less load on the server, so you can offload much of the work to the client. This could lead to significant cost savings on server infrastructure and improve the scalability of an application.
- *Can work in offline scenarios*—As the app runs entirely inside the browser, there's no need for a persistent connection to the server, making applications more tolerant to unstable network connections. It's also trivial to enable progressive web application (PWA) functionality. In fact, Blazor WebAssembly has this as an option you can select when creating your application.
- *Deployed as static files*—As Blazor WebAssembly apps are just static files, they can be deployed anywhere static hosting is available. This opens up some options that historically have never been available to .NET developers. Services such as GitHub pages, Netlify, Azure Blob Storage, AWS (Amazon Web Services) S3 buckets, and Azure Static Web Apps are all options for hosting standalone Blazor WebAssembly applications. The cost of deploying static files is relatively less compared to hosting web applications in each of the leading Cloud providers.

- *Code sharing*—Potentially one of the greatest benefits with Blazor WebAssembly is if you're using C# on the server. You can now use the same C# objects on your client as you use on the server. The days of keeping TypeScript models in sync with their C# equivalent and vice versa are over.

Of course, nothing is a silver bullet, so let's understand some tradeoffs of this model:

- *Payload*—When compared to some JavaScript applications, the initial download size of Blazor apps can be much bigger (although this is improving with every release). A minimal Blazor app can be produced that weighs in at about 1 MB when published; however, other apps could be significantly larger. Every application is different, and there is no standard size for a Blazor app. This is a one-time cost, though, as the run time and many of the framework assemblies are cached on the first load, meaning subsequent loads can be as small as a few KB.
- *Load time*—A knock-on effect of the payload size can be load time. If the user is on a poor internet connection, the amount of time required to download the initial files will be longer, which will delay the start of the application, leaving the user with a loading message of some kind. This can be offset slightly by using server-side prerendering; however, while this will give the user something more interesting to look at initially, the app still won't be interactive until all files have been downloaded and initialized. Server-side prerendering for Blazor WebAssembly apps also requires an ASP.NET Core element on the server, which negates any free hosting options.
- *Restricted run time*—This is arguably not a tradeoff as such, but for existing .NET developers who are used to having relatively free rein over the machine their apps run on, it's something to be aware of. WebAssembly applications run in the same browser sandbox as JavaScript applications. This means, for example, that you will not be allowed to reach out to the users' machine and do things such as access the local file system.
- *Code security*—Just as with JavaScript applications, your code is downloaded and run in the browser. Therefore, the user has access to your applications DLLs. This means you should not include any code that contains intellectual property in a Blazor WebAssembly application. Any valuable code should be kept on the server as part of an API.

To summarize, Blazor WebAssembly is the hosting model to choose if you're looking to replace a JavaScript SPA framework such as Angular, React, or Vue.js. While there are a few tradeoffs to consider, there are some substantial benefits to choosing this model.

1.3.3 Blazor Server

Now that we've seen how Blazor WebAssembly works, let's turn our attention to the Server hosting model and see how it differs. Blazor Server was the first production-supported hosting model for Blazor, being released around 8 months before the WebAssembly version. As we did with the previous model, we'll walk through initializing a Blazor Server application to help you understand how things work (figure 1.7).

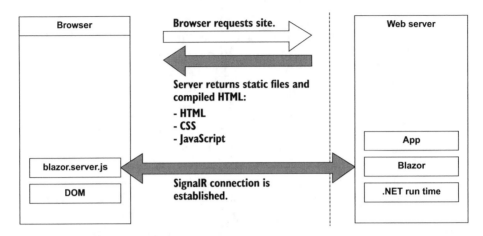

Figure 1.7   Boot-up process of a Blazor Server application

The process begins with a request to load the site from the browser. When this request hits the web server, two things could happen: the app is started up, or if the app is already running, a new session is established. Why would the app already be running? Unlike Blazor WebAssembly, which behaves more like a desktop application with each user having their own instance, Blazor Server runs one instance of the app that all users connect to. Therefore, the app could already be running, and the new request just establishes a new session. Each user has their own instance of the app, which runs locally on their machine. Blazor Server is different—only one instance of the application runs on the server, but it can support many clients. Therefore, the app could already be running, and the new request would just establish a new session.

The request is then processed by the application, and the initial payload is sent back to the browser. This includes static assets such as CSS and JavaScript files and images. There is also the initial HTML, but this is compiled rather than the static HTML we saw in Blazor WebAssembly. This is because the hosting page for a Blazor Server application is a *Razor Page* rather than a static HTML page in the WebAssembly model. The advantage of this is it allows Blazor Server applications to use server-side prerendering out of the box. In fact, this feature is enabled by default when you create this type of Blazor application.

Once the initial payload is returned to the browser, the files are processed and the DOM is created—then a file called *blazor.server.js* is executed. The job of this run time is to establish a SignalR connection back to the Blazor application running on the server. At this point, the application is fully booted and ready for user interaction.

SignalR

SignalR is an open source library from Microsoft that allows developers to add real-time functionality to their applications. Clients connect to a server via a hub, and the server then pushes updates to the clients in real time using WebSockets (with fallback to other technologies when required). A common example of using SignalR is to create real-time chat applications.

While SignalR is used in Blazor to transport events and UI updates back and forth between client and server, it's considered an implementation detail of the framework and not something a developer working with Blazor Server would need to configure or interact with. Visit https://dotnet.microsoft.com/apps/aspnet/signalr for detailed information on SignalR.

CALCULATING UI UPDATES

What happens when a user interacts with the application? We saw earlier that in Blazor WebAssembly the events are processed right there in the browser along with calculating any UI updates and applying them to the DOM. But that can't happen here, as the application is running on the server.

We'll follow the same scenario as we did with Blazor WebAssembly. We have a Blazor Server application with two pages containing only the headers Home and Counter, respectively. The user is on the Home page of the application and will click a link to go to the Counter page. We'll follow the process Blazor goes through to update the UI while navigating from the Home page to the Counter page (figure 1.8).

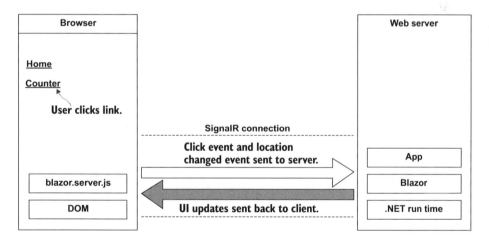

Figure 1.8   Process of updating the UI in Blazor Server

The user clicks the link in the menu, and the click event is intercepted by Blazor's run time on the client. The run time then processes the event to understand what has happened. In this case, there are two things—a mouse click event and a navigation event, due to it being a hyperlink that was clicked. These two events are then bundled up and sent back to the server over the SignalR connection that was established when the application started.

On the server, the message sent from the client is unpacked and processed. The Blazor framework then calls any application code necessary. In this case, it would instantiate an instance of the Counter page component and execute the relevant life cycle methods.

Once this process is complete, Blazor will work out the minimum number of changes needed to make the current page transform to the Counter page and then send these back to the client via the SignalR connection. Just to be clear, Blazor will not send back an entirely new page to the client. It will send back only the minimum number of instructions needed to update the current DOM to match the Counter page. In our case, the only difference is the heading. Blazor will send back a single instruction to change the text in the heading from Home to Counter. Nothing else will be changed.

Once back on the client, the changes are unpacked and the required changes are applied to the physical DOM. From the user's perspective, they appear to have navigated to a new page in the application, the Counter page. But they are still on the same physical page; it just has a different header.

You may have spotted this already, but the overall process isn't any different to how Blazor WebAssembly worked; it's just been stretched out a bit over that SignalR connection. Blazor Server is just as much an SPA as Angular, Vue.js, or Blazor WebAssembly. It just happens to run its logic and calculate UI updates on the server instead of the client. In fact, I bet if you were presented with two identical applications, one written in Blazor Server and one in Blazor WebAssembly, you wouldn't be able to tell the difference between them, as a user.

PERFORMANCE

Before we discuss the benefits and tradeoffs for this model, I want to quickly mention performance. With all the network chatter that goes on in this hosting model, you might have wondered whether this will scale particularly well.

In 2019, the ASP.NET Core team did some testing to establish the performance levels of Blazor Server apps. They set up an application in Azure and tested it on differently-powered virtual machines, checking the number of *active* users the application could support. Here are the results:

- *Standard D1 v2 instance (1 vCPU and 3.5 GB memory)*—Over *5,000* concurrent users
- *Standard D3 v2 instance (4 vCPU and 14 GB memory)*—Over *20,000* concurrent users

As you can see, Blazor Server is no slouch when it comes to performance. The main factor the team found that affects the number of clients that can be supported is memory. This makes sense, as the server needs to keep track of all the clients that are connected to it—the more clients there are, the more information needs to be stored in memory.

The other major finding from testing was how network latency affected the application. As all interactions are sent back to the server for processing, latency can have a large impact on usability. If the server is located 250 milliseconds (ms) away from the client, then each interaction is going to take at least 500 ms to be processed, as it must travel to the server (250 ms), then be processed, then travel back again (250 ms).

Testing found that when the latency went above 200 ms, then the UI began to feel sluggish and less responsive. As a rough rule, you always want your users to be on the same continent as the server. If you want to have a globally available Blazor Server application, then you need to have your app evenly distributed across the world, aiming to keep all clients within 200 ms of a server.

BENEFITS AND TRADEOFFS

As we did before, let's look at the benefits and tradeoffs of choosing a Blazor Server application.

- *Small payload*—As the application is running on the server as opposed to the client, the initial download is significantly smaller. Depending on static assets such as CSS and images, a Blazor Server application can be as small as 100–200 KB.
- *Fast load time*—With a much smaller payload, the application loads much faster. The server-side prerendering also helps, as the user never sees a loading message.
- *Access to the full run time*—The application code is executing on the server on top of the full .NET run time. This means you can do things such as access the server's file system if necessary without hitting any security restrictions.
- *Code security*—If you have code that is proprietary, and you don't want people being able to download and interrogate it, then Blazor Server is a good choice. The application code is all executed on the server, and only the UI updates are sent to the client. This means your code is never exposed to the client in any way.

There are some good benefits to Blazor Server, but what do the tradeoffs look like?

- *Heavy server load*—Where Blazor WebAssembly allows us to utilize the power of the client, Blazor Server does the complete opposite. Almost all of the work is now being performed by the server. This means you might need a larger investment in your infrastructure to support Blazor Server apps. Depending on the size of the application, load balancing may also be required to correctly manage the SignalR-based sessions used by Blazor Sever.
- *Doesn't work offline*—Where Blazor WebAssembly takes offline working in stride, Blazor Server does not. The SignalR connection is the lifeline of the application, and without it, the client can't function at all. By default, this results in an overlay with a message saying the client is attempting to re-establish the connection. If this fails, the user has to refresh the browser to restart the application.
- *Latency*—Due to its design, Blazor Server apps are sensitive to latency issues. Every interaction the user has with the application must be sent back to the server for processing and await any updates that need to be applied. If there is a high latency in the connection between client and server, a noticeable lag manifests in the UI and actions quickly feel sluggish. In real numbers, a latency above 200 ms will start causing these issues.

- *Requires a stable connection*—Continuing on from the need for low latency and tying in with the inability to work offline, Blazor Server apps need to have a stable internet connection. If the connection is intermittent in any way, the user will continually see the reconnecting overlay in their application, which quickly becomes very disruptive. An obvious scenario where this could occur is when a user is on a mobile device, which has intermittent connection.

In summary, if you're looking for a fast-loading application and you have users with a fast and stable network connection, then Blazor Server is a great choice. You're also getting code security thrown in when choosing this hosting model.

1.3.4   *Other hosting models*

Before we wrap up this chapter, I want to make you aware of two other hosting models—Blazor Hybrid and Blazor Mobile Bindings. I won't go into great detail on these, as they are not the focus of this book, but knowing they exist illustrates the scope of what can be built with Blazor.

BLAZOR HYBRID

Blazor Hybrid is built on technology from the .NET MAUI framework and allows developers to use Blazor to write cross-platform desktop applications. Components are written using C#, HTML, and CSS, just as with Blazor WebAssembly and Blazor Server, and are rendered using a control called BlazorWebView. The following listing shows an example of a component that runs in a Blazor Hybrid application.

> Listing 1.1   A component that runs on Blazor Hybrid

```
<div>
    <p>Current count: @currentCount</p>
    <button @onclick="IncrementCount">Click me</button>
</div>

@code {
    private int currentCount = 0;

    private void IncrementCount()
    {
        currentCount++;
    }
}
```

A big benefit of Blazor Hybrid is that it can run components that can also run in Blazor WebAssembly or Blazor Server. The code shown in listing 1.1 can execute on all three hosting models without any modification.

MOBILE BLAZOR BINDINGS

Mobile Blazor Bindings is an experimental hosting model and takes a different approach to authoring components. Components for this hosting model must be written using native controls. The following listing contains the same component as listing 1.1 but is rewritten for the Mobile Blazor Bindings hosting model.

Listing 1.2   A component that runs on Mobile Blazor Bindings

```
<StackLayout>
    <Label> Current count: @currentCount </Label>
    <Button OnClick="@IncrementCount">Click me</Button>
</StackLayout>

@code {
    private int currentCount = 0;

    private void IncrementCount()
    {
        currentCount++;
    }
}
```

As you can see, the programming model is the same between the two code samples. The logic in the code block is unchanged; it's just C# after all. The only difference is in the markup, where web technologies have been swapped for native mobile controls. This means that we can't swap components around between web-based hosting models and native hosting models. However, once we've mastered Blazor's programming model, we can easily use that knowledge to create other types of UIs.

Summary

This chapter has been an introduction to the Blazor framework. We've touched on many great features of Blazor and introduced quite a few concepts that probably don't make much sense right now. Don't worry; in the coming chapters will explore all these and more, in detail. For now, here's a summary of what we've covered:

- Blazor allows developers to use the power of C# and .NET to create rich interactive UIs without the need for JavaScript.
- Blazor is an SPA framework that can run entirely inside the browser via WebAssembly, an open web standard, or on the server utilizing a SignalR connection to link the client's browser with the application.
- Blazor WebAssembly can be used with any existing server technology. However, there are real benefits when using it with an ASP.NET Core backend, as code can easily be shared via a .NET class library.
- Applications are written using components. Components allow us to create self-contained pieces of UI that can work alone or in combination with each other.

Your first Blazor app

After reading chapter 1, you should have a good idea of what Blazor is and how it works. You should also now understand the concept of hosting models and have some compelling reasons why you might want to choose Blazor for your next project. But so far, we've only talked in theory. We still need to get our hands dirty building something with Blazor, and that's going to happen in this chapter.

We're going to create the application that we'll be building throughout the rest of the book—Blazing Trails! The app will allow walkers to discover new routes to explore, as well as add and update routes of their own. As we build this app, you will learn about the key features of Blazor, things such as routing, forms and validation, and authentication.

In this chapter, we begin by looking at the available templates provided by Microsoft to create a new application. Templates are a great way to get started quickly, and they provide all the primary building blocks we need for a working application. Once we understand the options, we'll then choose a template as the base for our Blazing Trails app. We'll build and run the template so we can get a feel for how it behaves; then we'll strip out all the unnecessary parts, leaving us with only the key components. We'll write our first components, and by the end of the chapter, we will have an app that looks like figure 2.1.

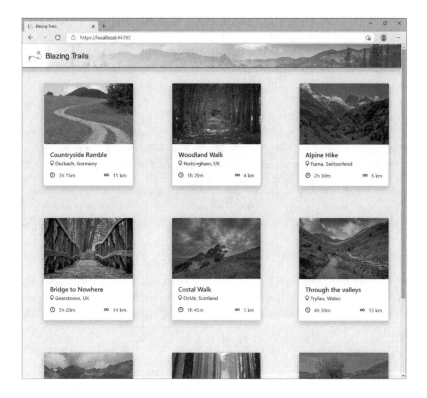

Figure 2.1   A preview of the Blazing Trails application we will build in this chapter

2.1   Setting up the application

In other frameworks, setting up a new application involves creating everything manually, from scratch. While this has the benefit of creating only what is necessary, it can be a tedious and repetitive process. Generally speaking, .NET applications aren't created this way. Many, if not all, start life being generated from a template. Using a template has many advantages:

- Developers can have a working application in seconds.
- Boilerplate code is taken care of and doesn't need to be written for every new application.
- The template serves as a working example of using the framework.
- The process is repeatable. Using a template will give you the same starting point time and time again.

Blazor comes with two templates that can be used to create new applications. When choosing a template, we're essentially making the choice of which hosting model we want to use, either Blazor Server or Blazor WebAssembly. In fact, the two available templates are named *Blazor Server* and *Blazor WebAssembly*, which makes knowing the hosting model they use straightforward. In this book, we're going to be using Blazor WebAssembly to build our Blazing Trails application, so that is the template type we'll focus on in this chapter.

> **What if I want to use Blazor Server?**
>
> If you're interested in the Blazor Server hosting model instead, don't worry, this book will still be just as useful to you. As I mentioned in chapter 1, hosting models only dictate where the code runs, not its behavior. Therefore, you will be able to follow along with everything in this book using the Blazor Server template. On odd occasions there will be slight differences in configuration between Blazor WebAssembly and Blazor Server apps, and I will call those out at the relevant time.

2.1.1   *Blazor WebAssembly template configurations*

Before we create the application, I want to talk about the configuration options available for the Blazor WebAssembly template. This template is the more complex of the two available because you can configure it in two modes, *hosted* or *standalone* (figure 2.2).

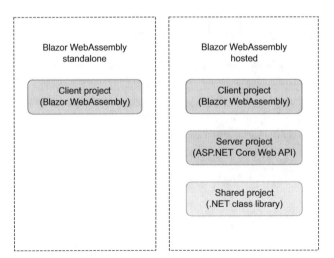

Figure 2.2   **The left side shows the project created when configuring the template in standalone mode. The right side shows the projects created when configuring the template in hosted mode.**

In the standalone mode, which is the default configuration, you will end up with a single Blazor WebAssembly project in the solution. This template is great if you're looking to build an application that doesn't need any kind of backend or server element to it or if you already have an existing API.

Hosted mode is a little bit more complex. If you enable the ASP.NET Core Hosted option when creating the template, you will end up with three projects in the solution:

- *Client Project*—Blazor WebAssembly
- *Server Project*—ASP.NET Core Web API
- *Shared Project*—.NET class library

In this configuration, you are getting a full-stack .NET application—a fully functioning backend (ASP.NET Core Web API), a place to put code that is shared between the frontend and backend project (.NET class library), and the frontend project (Blazor WebAssembly).

I want to highlight that using this configuration does require a .NET run time to be installed on the host server. Recall from chapter 1, an advantage of using Blazor WebAssembly is that it doesn't require a .NET run time on the server. That benefit doesn't apply when you're using the hosted configuration. This is because there is a full ASP.NET Core web API project in the solution that does need a .NET run time on the server to function.

Now that we understand our options, which are we going to choose for our Blazing Trails application? Well, to get started, we're going to choose the simpler standalone configuration. By the end of the book, we will have an application that is essentially the same as the hosted template, but to learn the most about Blazor, we'll build up to it over the coming chapters.

2.1.2 Creating the application

There are two ways to create a new application using a template, the .NET CLI (command-line interface) or an IDE (integrated development environment) such as Visual Studio or JetBrains Rider. From my experience, most .NET developers tend to prefer using an IDE to create their applications. Throughout this book, I will be using Visual Studio for Windows. But you can easily follow along using the .NET CLI and an editor such as VS Code. To create the application, open Visual Studio and take the following steps (figure 2.3). There may be slight differences in wording or order of screens on other IDEs:

1 File > New Project.
2 From the project templates list, select Blazor WebAssembly App.
3 The next screen allows us to set the name of the project and the solution, as well as where the files will be saved on disk. Enter the details as per figure 2.3, and then click Create to move to the next step.
4 The second configuration screen allows us to specify some additional settings for the solution. At this point, we can take the default settings that are shown in figure 2.4.

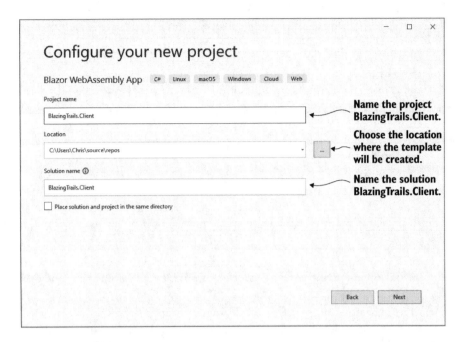

Figure 2.3   The first application configuration dialog. This allows the name of the project and solution to be specified along with where the final application files will be created.

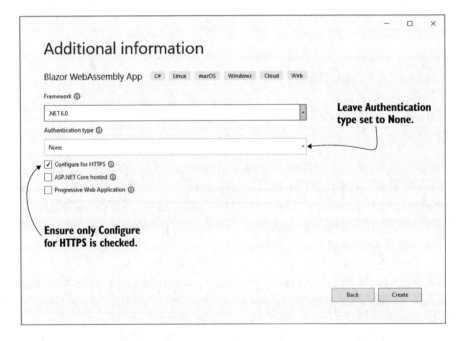

Figure 2.4   The second application configuration dialog. This allows additional information about the solution to be configured.

5   After a few seconds, Visual Studio will generate the application using the template and settings we've specified. Once this is done, you will see the project files, as shown in figure 2.5.

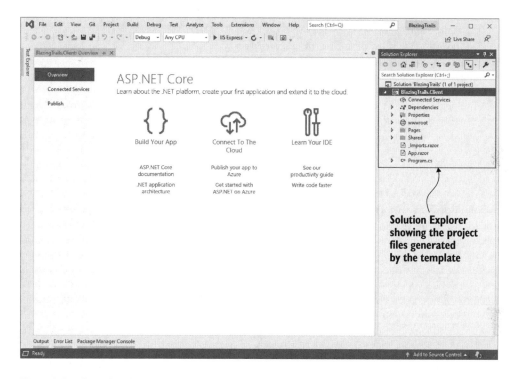

Figure 2.5   Visual Studio showing the files generated from the template inside of the solution explorer window

Using the .NET CLI

If you prefer using the command line, then you can create the same application using the .NET CLI. In order to replicate the exact structure we did with the IDE, you will need to run the following commands:

```
dotnet new blazorwasm -o BlazingTrails/BlazingTrails.Client
dotnet new sln -n BlazingTrails
dotnet sln add BlazingTrails\BlazingTrails.Client
```

This will create a new application with the same configuration and folder structure we set up using Visual Studio. We are telling the .NET CLI to create a new Blazor Web-Assembly application and output the result of that command into the folder specified with the -o switch. We're then creating a new solution and adding the Blazor Web-Assembly project to that solution.

At this point, you've created your first Blazor application. Congratulations! Now that we have our shiny new application, let's look at how we can build and run it.

2.2   *Building and running the application*

When it comes to running .NET applications, there are three steps that need to happen:

1 Restore any packages (also referred to as *dependencies*).
2 Compile or build the application.
3 Fire up a web server and serve the application.

In previous versions of .NET, these steps needed to be performed manually, so you would need to first restore any packages, then build the code, and finally run the app. However, this is no longer the case. We can now jump straight to running the application, and either Visual Studio or the .NET CLI will take care of performing the first two steps, if they're required.

However, it's always good to understand how to manually perform these steps yourself if the need arises. When using Visual Studio, you can restore packages by right-clicking on the solution and selecting Restore NuGet Packages from the Context menu. If you're using the .NET CLI, then you can execute the `dotnet restore` command.

To perform a build from Visual Studio, select Build > Build Solution from the top menu. You can also use a keyboard shortcut to perform the same task: Ctrl+Shift+B. From the .NET CLI, you can use the `dotnet build` command. Performing a build will also perform a package restore, if it's required, both when using Visual Studio or the CLI. So, having to manually restore packages shouldn't be an issue.

All that's left is to run the application. From Visual Studio, this can be done in several ways. First, you can click the Play button found in the main toolbar. You can also use a keyboard shortcut, which is F5. Finally, you can select Debug > Start Debugging from the top menu. Any of the above will run the application, and Visual Studio will fire up a browser and load the application automatically.

Depending on the type of applications you've created and run before, you could see an extra step that asks if you want to trust the development SSL certificate. Answering yes to this will install the development certificate on your machine, and this allows the application to be run over https rather than http. I would recommend trusting and installing the development SSL certificate—running sites over https is best practice, even in development, as it mimics the live environment.

If you've followed these steps, you should see the application running as shown in figure 2.6. If you're using the CLI to run your application, then you can execute the `dotnet watch` command. This is a much better choice than the standard `dotnet run` command, as it will not only automatically start the browser, but it will also watch the source files in the project for changes and apply those changes via the hot reload feature that shipped with .NET 6. This means most simple edits, such as applying new CSS classes or changing markup, will be applied almost instantly without losing the state of the application—a huge productivity boost.

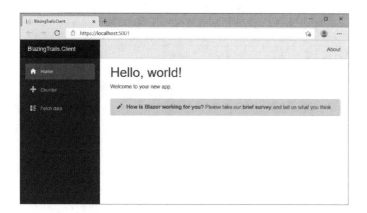

**Figure 2.6   The initial
page of the application
generated using the Blazor
WebAssembly template**

Welcome to your first Blazor app! There are three pages provided by the template: the Home page, the Counter page, and the Fetch Data page. Figure 2.6 shows the Home page. The Counter page displays a simple counter with a button that can be clicked to increment the count. The Fetch Data page displays a list of weather forecast data in a table that is loaded from an external source (a JSON file in the standalone template).

Feel free to click around and get a feel for what it's like to use it. Once you're familiar with the application, we'll move on and look at the key components that make up the application.

2.3   *Key components of a Blazor application*

While the template has generated several files, not all of them are important to understand. In this section, we're going to look at the key files you should understand, what they do, and why they're important. Then we're going to remove all the other files from our project to give us a clean base ready to start building Blazing Trails.

2.3.1   *Index.html*

Index.html is one of the most important components of a Blazor WebAssembly application. It can be found in the wwwroot directory of the project, and it's the host page for the Blazor application. See figure 2.7 for a breakdown of the key elements.

The key element in the index.html file is the link to the Blazor JavaScript run time (blazor.webassembly.js), found near the bottom of the page. As we saw in chapter 1, this is the file that downloads the .NET WebAssembly-based run time, as well as the application and any of its dependencies. Once this is complete, it also initializes the run time, which loads and runs the application.

When the application runs, its content needs to be outputted somewhere on the page; by default, this is outputted to a `div` with the ID of `app`. The fact that the element is a `div` isn't important; it could be any HTML element—within reason. It's the `id="app"` that is important. This is configurable and is set up in the Program.cs file, which we'll look at in a second. Any default content that exists in the tag will be

```
<!DOCTYPE html>
<html>

<head>
    <meta charset="utf-8" />
    <meta name="viewport" content="width=device-width, initial-scale=1.0, maximum-scale=1.0, user-scalable=no" />
    <title>BlazingTrails.Client</title>
    <base href="/" />
    <link href="css/bootstrap/bootstrap.min.css" rel="stylesheet" />
    <link href="css/app.css" rel="stylesheet" />
    <link href="BlazingTrails.Client.styles.css" rel="stylesheet" />
</head>

<body>
    <div id="app">Loading...</div>

    <div id="blazor-error-ui">
        An unhandled error has occurred.
        <a href="" class="reload">Reload</a>
        <a class="dismiss">X</a>
    </div>
    <script src="_framework/blazor.webassembly.js"></script>
</body>

</html>
```

The base tag is used by Blazor's router to understand which routes it should handle.

This div is where the Blazor application will load.

This div is displayed automatically by Blazor when an unhandled exception occurs.

Blazor's JavaScript run time downloads and initializes the application.

Figure 2.7   Breakdown of the key elements in the index.html page of a Blazor WebAssembly application

replaced at run time with the output from the application. This has a useful benefit: initial content can be used as a placeholder, which will be displayed to the user until the application is ready. An example of this is shown in figure 2.7, where a loading message is displayed.

If an unhandled exception is ever caused inside the application, then Blazor will display a special UI that signals to the user that something has gone wrong. This is defined here in the index.html. This can be customized however you like, but the containing element must have an id attribute with the value blazor-error-ui. The default message, shown in figure 2.8, states there has been a problem and offers the user a button that will cause a full page reload, essentially restarting the application. This is the only safe option at this point, as the application will be in an unknown state.

The final key piece to the index.html file is the base tag. This is an important tag when it comes to client-side routing—something we'll talk about in greater detail in chapter 4. This tag is important because it tells Blazor's router which URLs, or routes, are in scope for it to handle. If this tag is missing or configured incorrectly, then you may see some unexpected or unpredictable behavior when navigating your application. By default, the tag is configured with a value of /. This means that the application is running at the root of the domain—for example, www.blazingtrails.com—and the router should handle all navigation requests within that domain. However, if the application is running as a subapplication—for example, www.blazorapps.com/blazingtrails—then the base tag needs to reflect this with a value of /blazing-trails/. This means the router will handle only navigation requests that start with /blazingtrails/. It's important to make sure the value you enter for the base tag ends with a /. If this is missed, the browser will remove any value until it finds a /. For example, /blazingtrails/ will be used as-is, and /blazingtrails will become /.

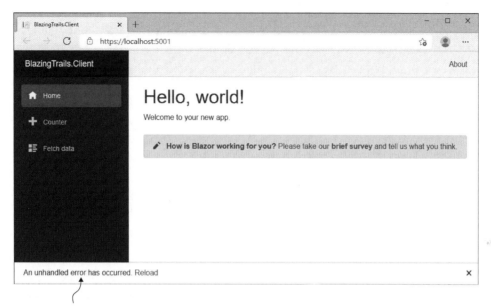

**Default error UI displayed by Blazor
when an unhandled exception occurs**

Figure 2.8   The default error UI displayed by Blazor when an unhandled exception occurs in
the application. The user is presented with the option to reload the application to get back to a
working state.

2.3.2   *Program.cs*

Just like other ASP.NET Core applications, Blazor apps start off as .NET console apps.
What makes them a Blazor application is the type of host they run. In the case of
Blazor WebAssembly, it runs a `WebAssemblyHost`. The purpose of the code contained in this file is to configure and create that host. Figure 2.9 shows the default configuration of the `Program` class.

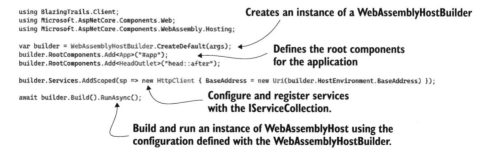

Figure 2.9   The default Program class for a Blazor WebAssembly application, found in the
Program.cs file

Beginning with .NET 6, by default, the Program.cs file uses a new syntax called *top-level statements* (originally introduced in C# 9). Essentially, this removes a lot of the boilerplate from the file with the goal of lowering the barrier of entry into the .NET ecosystem. This means there is no longer a namespace definition or a `Program` class with a static `Main` method. We can just start writing code, and everything just works. As you might have guessed, under the hood, the compiler is still generating a `Program` class with a static `Main` method; we just don't need to worry about it now. You can learn more about top-level statements on the Microsoft Docs site (http://mng.bz/nNE4).

There are two critical pieces of configuration happening in figure 2.9: the root components for the application are defined, and any services are configured and added to the `IServiceCollection`. When defining the root components, we are giving the builder two pieces of information—the type of components and where they should be injected into the host page.

By default, the template comes with two root elements defined. The first registers the `App` component. This is the entry point to the application, and we'll be looking at this next. The second is the `HeadOutlet` component. This is new in .NET 6 and enables us to make modifications to the `head` element in the host page—things like updating the page title or setting meta tags.

Blazor needs to know where these root components will be placed in the host page. The argument the `builder.RootComponents.Add` method takes is a CSS selector, which is used to identify the target element where the component will be injected. Specific elements or elements with a specific ID can be targeted—for example, `#root-component` or any other valid CSS selector. To learn more about CSS selectors, visit www.w3schools.com/cssref/css_selectors.asp.

The next line shows the `HttpClient` being configured and registered with the `IServiceCollection`, making it available to classes and components via dependency injection (DI). Blazor uses the same DI container as other ASP.NET Core apps and allows registering of services using one of three lifetimes:

- *Transient*—A new instance is provided each time it's requested from the service container. Given a single request, if two objects needed an instance of a transient service, they would each receive a different instance.
- *Scoped*—A new instance is created once per request. Within a request, you will always get the same instance of the service across the application.
- *Singleton*—An instance is created the first time it's requested from the service container, or when the `Program.Main` method is run, and an instance is specified with the registration. The same instance is used to fulfill every request for the lifetime of the application.

While it uses the same system for DI, the scopes behave a little differently in Blazor applications. For Blazor WebAssembly, Scoped and Singleton behave the same. This is because there is no request in a Blazor WebAssembly application. It is downloaded and executed in the client browser. As there is no request for the Scoped lifetime to bind to, any Scoped services will live for the lifetime of the application—making them the same as Singleton services.

The last thing the `Main` method does is take all the configurations specified with the `WebAssemblyHostBuilder` and call its `Build` method. This will create an instance of a `WebAssemblyHost`, which is the heart of your Blazor app. It contains all the application configurations and services needed to run your app.

Where's the Startup class?

If you've worked with other ASP.NET Core applications in the past, you may be asking yourself why we're configuring services inside of Program.cs and not inside the `Startup` class. The answer is because the `Startup` class no longer exists in the default templates.

Beginning with .NET 6, the default ASP.NET Core templates no longer specify a Program.cs file and a Startup.cs file. This is because the templates now use top-level statements by default and push all configuration into a single Program.cs file.

However, Blazor WebAssembly dropped the `Startup` class back in .NET Core 3.1 because it wasn't necessary. The `Startup` class contained two methods, `ConfigureServices` and `Configure`. The first of these, `ConfigureServices`, was used to configure and register services with the service container. `Configure` was used to configure the middleware pipeline for the application.

However, in Blazor WebAssembly, there is no middleware, as there is no request. Blazor WebAssembly (or any SPA framework, for that matter) acts far more like a desktop application than a traditional server-based web app. Once it's loaded, it processes interactions locally in the user's browser and only makes requests back to the server for additional data.

This means that the `Configure` method was not needed in the `Startup` class, which only leaves the `ConfigureServices` method. The Blazor team felt it was not necessary to have two files with only a single method inside them, so they moved the service registration over to the `Program.Main` method and removed the `Startup` class.

2.3.3   App.razor

This is the root component for a Blazor application, and we saw how this was configured in the `Program.cs` file in the previous section. This doesn't have to be the case; however, you can configure a different component to be the root component if you wish. Or you can even have multiple root components. You just need to update the configuration in the `Program.Main` method.

The `App` component contains a vital component for building multipage applications—the `Router` component. This component is responsible for managing all aspects of client-side routing. When an application first starts up, the router will use reflection to scan the application's assemblies for any routable components (we'll talk about these in more detail in chapter 4, but they're essentially pages). It then stores information about them in a routing table. Whenever a link is clicked or navigation is triggered programmatically, the router will look at the requested route and try to find a match in the routing table. If a match is found, then it will load that component; otherwise it will load a Not Found template, which is specified inside the Router component.

We're going to cover the Router component in detail in chapter 4, so don't worry if this all sounds a bit confusing right now. It's just important to know that the Router component resides inside the App component and is responsible for handling the routing in the application.

2.3.4   *wwwroot folder and _Imports.razor*

I'm going to cover both of these files in this section, as there is not a huge amount to say about them. In fact, the _Imports.razor file is one component that is not required to run a Blazor application—but having one does make things easier.

By convention, all ASP.NET Core applications have a wwwroot folder, which is used to store public static assets. This is the place where you can put things such as images, CSS files, JavaScript files, or any other static files you need. Anything you put in this folder will be published with your application and available at run time. As I mentioned earlier, this is also where the index.html file is kept.

The _Imports.razor file is optional when building a Blazor application. However, it's useful to have at least one of these files. Its job is to store using statements. The benefit is that those using statements are made available to all the components in the file's directory and any subdirectories. This saves you having to add common using statements to every component in your application.

As I alluded to, you can have multiple _Import.razor files throughout your project. This allows us to specify using statements that apply only to a certain set of components based on the file structure. For example, if we had a structure of BlazingTrails > Features > Home and we wanted a set of using statements to be applied only to components in the Home folder, we could add an _Imports.razor file to that folder and add the using statements we require. These would then only be applied to components in the Home folder.

2.4   *Writing your first components*

We've had a look at the app created by the template, and we've covered each of the key files and, at a high level, what they do. Now it's time to write some code of our own. As I said at the start of the chapter, we're going to build the foundations of the Blazing Trails application, which is shown in figure 2.10.

First, we will talk about how the application files are going to be organized. Second, we'll remove all the unneeded files that were generated by the template. This will give us a clean base to start building from. Finally, we'll define several new components to create what you see in figure 2.10: a layout component, a page component, and a couple of regular components. Sounds fun? Let's get going!

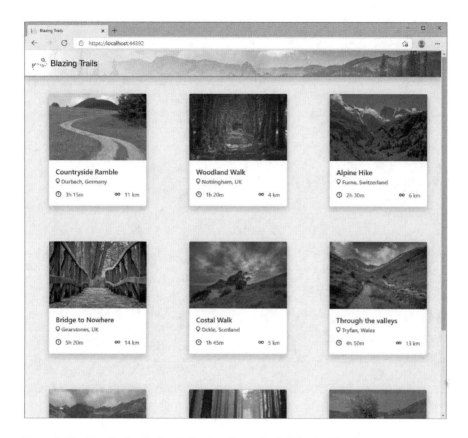

Figure 2.10 The Blazing Trails application that we're building in this chapter

2.4.1 Organizing files using feature folders

Before we start adding our own code, we need to remove all the unnecessary files generated by the template. By default, the app structure used by the template divides files by responsibility. There's a Pages folder for routable components, and there's a Shared folder for anything that is used in multiple places or is a global concern. This kind of separation doesn't scale well and makes adding or changing functionality much more difficult, as files end up being spread out all over the place. Instead, we're going to use a structure called *feature folders* to organize our application.

When using feature folders, all the files relating to that feature are stored in the same place. This has two major benefits. First, when you go to work on a particular feature, all the files you need are in the same place, making everything easier to understand and more discoverable. Second, it scales well. Every time you add a new feature to the app, you just add a new folder and everything goes in there. You can also arrange each feature with subfeatures if they contain a lot of files. Figure 2.11 shows an example of both structures side by side.

Pages

  Account.razor

  ProductList.razor

  Product.razor

  ShoppingBasket.razor

Components

  AccountDetails.razor

  AccountSummary.razor

  AddressList.razor

  ItemSummary.razor

  ProductDetails.razor

  ProductStockAndPrice.razor

  ShoppingBasketItemSummary.razor

  ShoppingBasketPaymentOptions.razor

  ShoppingBasketDeliveryOptions.razor

Shared

  Button.razor

  Table.razor

Features

  Account

    AccountPage.razor

    Summary.razor

    Details.razor

    AddressList.razor

  ProductList

    ProductListPage.razor

    ItemSummary.razor

  Product

    ProductPage.razor

    Details.razor

    StockAndPrice.razor

  ShoppingBasket

    ShoppingBasketPage.razor

    ItemSummary.razor

    PaymentOptions.razor

    DeliveryOptions.razor

  Shared

    Button.razor

    Table.razor

Figure 2.11   A side-by-side comparison of organizing files by responsibility/type or by feature. The list on the left shows files organized by responsibility/type, while the list on the right shows the same files organized by feature.

In figure 2.11, I've only shown components, but you should put any files that relate to that feature in the folder—C# classes, TypeScript files, CSS files, anything at all. Static assets such as images are the only exception to this. These need to be placed in the wwwroot folder; otherwise they will not be available at run time, as static files are served only from that folder. However, you can mirror your feature folder structure in the wwwroot folder if you wish.

The other little thing I like to do when using this organization system with Blazor is to append any routable component with the word *Page*. When a feature has several other components in it, it's almost impossible to identify the routable component easily. The only real way to know is to open the file and check for the @page directive at the top. By adding page to the end, it makes this obvious at a glance and saves having to go poking around in various files.

Now that I've hopefully convinced you of the value of using feature folders, we're going to start to put them into practice. We're going to remove a load of the files from our Blazing Trails application to give us a fresh slate to start building. Then we will start adding new features using the feature folder structure.

Start by deleting the Pages and Shared folders along with their contents. Then delete the Sample-Data folder from the wwwroot folder. Also delete most of the contents of the app.css; just leave the import statement for the open iconic styles and the class called `#blazor-error-ui` and `#blazor-error-ui  .dismiss`. We also need to delete the last `using` statement from the _Imports.razor file, `@using Blazing-Trails.Client.Shared`.

We have removed all the bits we don't need, so the project should now look like figure 2.12. It also won't build, but don't worry; we're going to add a few things, and then we can get back to a working build.

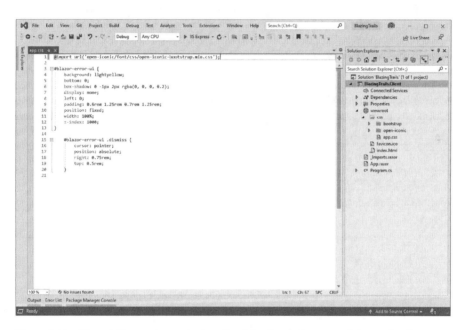

Figure 2.12   The solution explorer panel on the right shows the state of the application once all the unneeded files have been removed. The main panel shows the app.css once the boilerplate CSS classes have been stripped out.

Add a new folder at the root of the project called *Features*. Inside that folder, add a folder called *Layout* and another called *Home*. Inside Layout, add a new Razor component called `MainLayout.razor`. Inside Home, add a new Razor component called `HomePage.razor`. Once you've done that, head back over to the _Imports.razor and add the following `using` statements:

```
@using BlazingTrails.Client.Features.Home
@using BlazingTrails.Client.Features.Layout
```

At this point, your solution should look like figure 2.13.

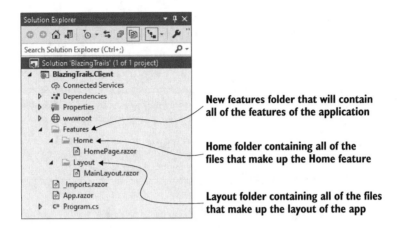

Figure 2.13   The new structure of the project using feature folders

You can now build the application, and you shouldn't see any build errors. However, you can't run the application just yet—there would be an error. We still have a few things to configure. Next, we're going to briefly look at styling before moving on and defining the layout for Blazing Trails.

2.4.2   *Setting up styling*

The Blazor templates ship with a CSS framework called Bootstrap. As this is a popular choice among developers for styling applications, and as it's already included, we're going to use it for Blazing Trails. (You can visit the Bootstrap docs site to learn more about how the framework works and the full range of features it offers: http://mng .bz/J26a.)

I've created some custom images to brand the application. There is a logo (logo.png) and a background for the navbar (navbar-bg.jpg). These can be found on the GitHub repo that accompanies this book (https://github.com/chrissainty/blazor -in-action) and will need to be placed in a new folder under wwwroot called *Images.* Feel free to use your own images if you prefer. Keeping the same names means all the code in this book will just work. If you do change the names, just make sure to update the code in the relevant places.

Before we move on to layouts, we're going to add some custom styles to the app.css file. By adding the styles here, they will affect the whole application. These styles will customize the look of some common elements, such as links and buttons, as well as the navbar. Open the app.css in the wwwroot > css folder. Then copy in the code from the following listing.

Listing 2.1   app.css

```css
:root {
  --brand: #448922;
  --brand-hover: #5da030;
}
```

**CSS variables are used to save you
from repeating the brand color
codes. This also makes updating the
color in the future much easier.**

```css
body {
  background-color: #f9f9f9;
}

a {
  color: var(--brand);
  text-decoration: underline;
}

a:hover {
  color: var(--brand-hover);
  text-decoration: none;
}

.navbar {
  border-bottom: 2px solid var(--brand);
  background: linear-gradient(90deg, rgba(255,255,255,1) 5%,
  ➥rgba(255,255,255,0) 100%), url("../images/navbar-bg.jpg") no-repeat
  ➥center;
  background-size: cover;
}

.btn-primary {
  background-color: var(--brand);
  border-color: var(--brand);
}

.btn-primary:hover {
  background-color: var(--brand-hover);
  border-color: var(--brand-hover);
}

.btn-outline-primary {
  border-color: var(--brand);
  color: var(--brand);
}

.btn-outline-primary:hover {
  background-color: var(--brand);
  border-color: var(--brand);
}

.grid {
    display: grid;
    grid-template-columns: repeat(3, 288px);
    column-gap: 123px;
    row-gap: 75px;
}
```

I won't go into detail on what each style is doing, but I will point out one nice feature available in CSS called *CSS variables*. These allow us to define variables that can be used throughout an application's style sheet. Using variables means we have to specify things like brand colors only once. They also make future branding changes much easier to complete.

The final thing we'll do regarding styling is to make some adjustments to the index.html page. First, we'll add a reference to Bootstrap Icons (https://icons .getbootstrap.com/). This free icon set is from the creators of Bootstrap and look great. In order to use them, we'll add the following line to the head element of the index.html page in wwwroot:

```
<link href="https://cdn.jsdelivr.net/npm/bootstrap-icons@1.4.1/font/
    bootstrap-icons.css" rel="stylesheet">
```

This line can be pasted directly under the existing link to the bootstrap.min.css file. This link will pull in the Bootstrap Icons CSS file from their content delivery network (CDN). If you'd prefer to use a local file instead of a CDN, you can find out how to download one from the link I provided to the Bootstrap Icons site.

Second, we're going to update the title of the tag from `BlazingTrails.Client` to `Blazing Trails`. The updated tag should look like this:

```
<title>Blazing Trails</title>
```

The third and last change we're going to make is to remove the following stylesheet reference:

```
<link href="BlazingTrails.Client.styles.css" rel="stylesheet" />
```

This is used for scoped CSS, a topic we'll cover in chapter 3. When we do, we'll add this back in. But for now, we're going to remove it, as it will cause an error in the browser console. Now that our basic styling is in place, let's move on and set up our layout.

2.4.3   *Defining the layout*

Blazor borrows the concept of a layout from other parts of ASP.NET Core. Essentially it allows us to define common UIs, which is required by multiple pages. Things such as the header, footer, and navigation menu are all examples of things you might put in your layout. We also add a reference to a parameter called `Body` where we want page content to be rendered. This comes from a special base class that all layouts in Blazor must inherit from called `LayoutComponentBase`. Figure 2.14 shows an example of what might be defined in a layout along with where the rendered page content would be displayed.

You don't have to stick with a single layout for your whole application; you can have multiple layouts for different parts of your app. So, if you wanted a particular layout for the public-facing pages but a different one for the admin pages, you can do

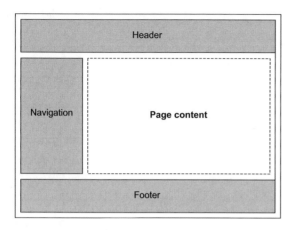

Figure 2.14 An example layout defining shared UI. Any page that uses this layout will have its content rendered in the center panel marked `Page Content`.

that. In Blazor, the default layout is defined within the `Router` component (figure 2.15), which can be found in `App.razor`. This will automatically be applied to all pages in the application.

```
<Router AppAssembly="@typeof(App).Assembly">
    <Found Context="routeData">
        <RouteView RouteData="@routeData" DefaultLayout="@typeof(MainLayout)" />
        <FocusOnNavigate RouteData="@routeData" Selector="h1" />
    </Found>
    <NotFound>
        <PageTitle>Not found</PageTitle>
        <LayoutView Layout="@typeof(MainLayout)">
            <p role="alert">Sorry, there's nothing at this address.</p>
        </LayoutView>
    </NotFound>
</Router>
```

The default layout is defined by passing the type of the component you wish to use.

Figure 2.15 Shows where the default layout is defined on the `Router` component. This layout will automatically be applied to all pages in the application.

If you want to use a different layout on certain pages, you can specify an alternative by applying the `@layout` directive. This goes at the top of the page, and you pass the name of the component you wish to use. For example, if we had an alternative layout called *AdminLayout*, our layout directive would look like this: `@layout AdminLayout`.

Now that we understand what a layout is and why they're useful, let's get on with defining the initial layout for Blazing Trails. We're going to update the `MainLayout` component. To begin, we will do two things. First, we'll use the `@inherits` directive to inherit from the `LayoutComponentBase` class. This marks this component as a layout component and will give us access to the `Body` parameter. Second, we'll define where our page content is rendered using the `Body` parameter. Listing 2.2 shows what the `MainLayout` should look like.

Listing 2.2   MainLayout component for Blazing Trails

```
@inherits LayoutComponentBase          ◁——┐ Defines the component
                                            │ as a layout component
<main class="container mt-5 mb-5">
    @Body                              ◁——┐ Marks the location where page
</main>                                     │ content is rendered in the layout
```

The only thing missing from our layout now is the header. We'll define this as a separate component, and as it's part of the overall Layout feature, it will go in the Layout feature folder next to the `MainLayout` component. As we did before, add a new Razor component called `Header.razor` and then we'll add the markup shown in listing 2.3, which adds a Bootstrap navbar displaying the text *Blazing Trails*.

Listing 2.3   Header component defining a Bootstrap navbar

```
<nav class="navbar mb-5 shadow">
    <a class="navbar-brand" href="/">
        <img src="/images/logo.png">
    </a>
</nav>
```

That's all we need in the `Header` component. We can now add that to the `Main-Layout` by declaring it as we would any normal HTML element. The final code for the `MainLayout` is shown in the next listing.

Listing 2.4   Completed MainLayout component

```
@inherits LayoutComponentBase

<Header />                             ◁——┐ This is a reference to the Header component. Note
                                            the capital H. Component references are case-
<main class="container mt-5 mb-5">          sensitive in Blazor and should start with a capital
    @Body                                   letter to avoid collisions with regular HTML elements.
</main>
```

That's it for the layout. If you try to run the application at this point, you will be able to see the header we've just created but there will be a message saying "Sorry, there's nothing at this address." That's because we haven't defined any routable components (pages) yet. Let's do that next and create the home page for Blazing Trails.

2.4.4   *The Blazing Trails home page*

In this section, we will create and load some test data (trails) for the application, and we will create a card component to display each trail within the test data. By the end of the chapter, we will have the application we saw at the start of this chapter. We already created the `HomePage` component in section 2.4.1, but it still has the boilerplate code that comes with a new component. We need to update this code to make the component routable. Once we do that, we'll define a class that represents a trail. We can then define some test data to use to build out the rest of the UI. Finally, we'll load the test data into the HomePage and loop over it to display the various trails via a reusable TrailCard component that we'll create. Sound good? Let's get cracking!

As we talked about earlier, to make a component routable, we need to use the @page directive and a route template that specifies the route it will be responsible for. At the top of the HomePage.razor file, add the directive along with a route template:

```
@page "/"
```

When a route template contains only a forward slash (/), it tells the router that this is the root page of the application. You can run the application at this point to check that the HomePage's content is being displayed. You should see the same header as before with the text HomePage displayed (figure 2.16).

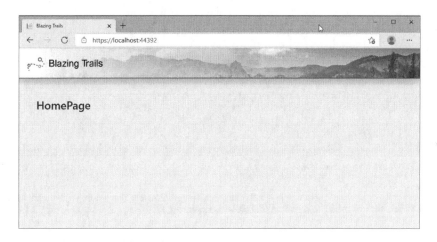

Figure 2.16 The current state of the Blazing Trails application displaying the Header component and HomePage component with its default text

We need a way of representing a trail in our code. To do that, we will add a new class called Trail to the Home feature folder. It will contain the various data points for a trail, things like its name, length, and the time it takes to complete it. We'll also include a second class called RouteInstruction in the file. This class represents a waypoint on the route to help guide other walkers. I like to include closely related classes in the same file, as it makes working with them much easier. Listing 2.5 shows the contents of the Trail.cs file.

Listing 2.5 Trail.cs

```
public class Trail
{
    public int Id { get; set; }
```

```
    public string Name { get; set; } = "";
    public string Description { get; set; } = "";
    public string Image { get; set; } = "";
    public string Location { get; set; } = "";
    public int TimeInMinutes { get; set; }
    public string TimeFormatted => $"{TimeInMinutes / 60}h {TimeInMinutes % 60}m";
    public int Length { get; set; }
    public IEnumerable<RouteInstruction> Route { get; set; } =
      Array.Empty<RouteInstruction>();
}

public class RouteInstruction
{
    public int Stage { get; set; }
    public string Description { get; set; } = "";
}
```

Now that we have a definition for a trail, we'll define some test data to use. Currently, our app doesn't have a backend—there is no API we can call to retrieve or save data. To simulate making an http call to load data from an API, we'll define our test data in a JSON file. This is a great way to develop frontend applications that don't currently have a useable server element. We can use the `HttpClient` to load the data from the JSON file in the same way we'd load data from an API. Then once the server element is established, the http call just needs to be updated to point at the API endpoint instead of the JSON file.

In the wwwroot folder, create a directory called `trails`. Inside that folder, add a new JSON file called *trail-data.json* with the code shown in the following listing.

Listing 2.6   trail-data.json: Contains trail test data

```
[
    {
    "id": 1,
    "image": "trails/1.jpg",          ◁—┘  This shows the location of the
    "name": "Countryside Ramble",            trail image relative to the root
    "location": "Durbach, Germany",          of the application at run time.
    "timeInMinutes": 195,             ◁—┘  This is the time it takes to walk
    "length": 11,                            the trail as total minutes.
    "description": "A really nice walk in some very scenic countryside.",
    "route": [                    ◁—┐  This is an array of route
      {                               instructions for the trail.
        "stage": 1,
        "description": "Follow the path to the fork and go left."
      },
      {
        "stage": 2,
        "description": "Cross the bridge and turn right."
      },
      {
        "stage": 3,
        "description": "The trail finishes at the end of the valley."
      }
```

```
    ]
  },
  {
    "id": 2,
    "image": "trails/2.jpg",
    "name": "Woodland Walk",
    "location": "Nottingham, UK",
    "timeInMinutes": 80,
    "length": 4,
    "description": "Lots of tall trees and bubbling streams.
    ➡A very calming hike.",
    "route": [
      {
        "stage": 1,
        "description": "The walk is one big loop. Just keep following the
        ➡signs."
      }
    ]
}]
```

I've only included two trails in this code snippet, but feel free to add as many trails as you wish to the file. The companion code for this chapter on GitHub (https:// github.com/chrissainty/blazor-in-action/tree/main/chapter-02) will contain many more trails, so feel free to copy that if you prefer.

For the images, I've just downloaded some free ones from Pixabay (https://pixabay .com) and added them to the wwwroot > Trails folder.

With our test data in place, we'll return to the `HomePage` component, where we need to load it. We're going to load the data using the `HttpClient`, but to use it we need to get an instance of it using dependency injection. Blazor makes this easy by providing an `inject` directive: `@inject [TYPE] [NAME]`, where `[Type]` is the type of the object we want and `[Name]` is the name we'll use to work with that instance in our component. Under the page directive, add `@inject HttpClient Http`, which will give us an instance of the `HttpClient` to work with.

The inject directive: What's going on under the hood?

The inject directive allows us to quickly and easily inject instances of objects, registered with the service container in `Program.cs`, into our components. But the directive is just some syntactic sugar saving us a chunk of typing.

Blazor uses property injection for its components. What the inject directive compiles down to is a property decorated with an attribute called `Inject`. So, if we use our `Inject` directive above as an example, it ends up compiled to this:

```
[Inject]
public HttpClient Http { get; set; }
```

In fact, you could write this code in the `@code` block at the bottom of the component and not use the `Inject` directive at all if you prefer. It's just a lot more typing!

Before we can use the `HttpClient`, we need somewhere to store the results returned by the call. Our JSON test data is an array of trails, and as we're not going to modify what's returned, just listing it out, we can create a private field of type `IEnumerable<Trail>`. This is done in the `@code` block of the component as shown in the following listing.

Listing 2.7   **HomePage with injected HttpClient and trails field**

```
@page "/"
@inject HttpClient Http

<h3>HomePage</h3>

@code {

    private IEnumerable<Trail> _trails;

}
```

The Page directive defines the route this component is responsible for.

The Inject directive is used to get instances of objects from the dependency injection container.

The Private field holds trail data.

Now that we have somewhere to store our test data, we can make the call to retrieve it. A great place to do this kind of thing is the `OnInitialized` life cycle method. This method is provided by `ComponentBase`—which all Blazor components inherit from—and it's one of three primary life cycle methods. The other two are `OnParametersSet` and `OnAfterRender`—they all have async versions as well. `OnInitialized` is run only once in the component's lifetime, making it perfect for loading initial data like we need to. We'll be covering component life cycle methods in detail in chapter 3, so don't worry if you have questions right now.

To retrieve the data from the JSON file, we can make a GET request just like we would if we were reaching out to an API. However, instead of passing the address of the API in the call, we pass the relative location of the JSON file. As the file is in the wwwroot folder, it will be available as a static asset at run time, just like the CSS file. This means the path we need to pass in the GET request is `"trails/trail-data.json"`.

A great productivity enhancement that ships with Blazor is the addition of some extension methods for the `HttpClient`:

- `GetFromJsonAsync<T>`
- `PostAsJsonAsync`
- `PutAsJsonAsync`

Under the hood, these methods are using the `System.Text.Json` library. The first method will deserialize a successful response containing a JSON payload to a type (`T`) we specify. The second and third will serialize an object to JSON to be sent to the server. All three of these methods do this in a single line. No more having to manually serialize and deserialize objects or check for success codes. This makes everything much cleaner and removes a lot of boilerplate.

When using these new methods, be aware that when a nonsuccess code is returned from the server, they'll throw an exception of type `HttpRequestException`. This means that it's generally a good practice to wrap these calls in a `try catch` statement so nonsuccess codes can be handled gracefully. The final code for the `HomePage` components `@code` block is shown in the following listing.

Listing 2.8 Final code block for the HomePage component

```
@code {
    private IEnumerable<Trail> _trails;                    ◁─┐  The private field holds
                                                               the results returned
                                                               from the http call.
    protected override async Task OnInitializedAsync()
    {
        try
        {                                                  The http call loads test data
                                                           from the trail-data.json file.
            _trails = await Http.GetFromJsonAsync
              ➾<IEnumerable<Trail>>("trails/trail-data.json");    ◁─
        }
        catch (HttpRequestException ex)             ◁─┐  The Catch block handles
        {                                              nonsuccess responses
            Console.WriteLine($"There was a problem     from the http call.
            ➾loading trail data: {ex.Message}");
        }
    }
}
```

You may have noticed that Visual Studio (or whichever IDE you're using) is indicating a problem with the `_trails` field and the call to load the trail data (figure 2.17) by displaying a green wavy line under those sections.

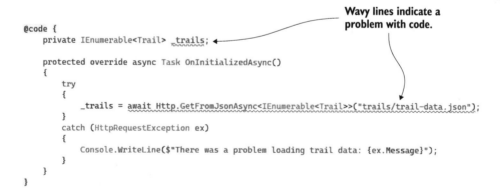

Figure 2.17 Wavy lines under sections of code indicate that there is a problem with the code that needs to be resolved.

We're seeing these warnings because of a change in the default project settings from .NET 6—nullable references types (NRTs) (http://mng.bz/v6Or) are enabled by default. This feature is designed to help us make the flow of nulls explicit in our code. Essentially, it makes us deal with nulls properly.

The warning we see for the `_trails` field is the compiler telling us that it's a non-nullable type and hasn't been given a default value or initialized in a constructor. This means we could try to use it and its value could be null. The `GetFromJsonAsync` method can return a null value; the warning here is telling us that so we can act appropriately. The fix for these warnings is to make the `_trails` field nullable by using the `?` operator:

```
private IEnumerable<Trail>? _trails;
```

We've now declared that we know this field may be null, and you will see the warnings have disappeared. If you're new to NRTs, this might take a little getting used to. But dealing with nulls properly will help us write better and more stable applications.

Great! We now have our data being loaded into our component, but we need to do something with it. It would be nice to display a message to the user to let them know when we're loading the data—just in case it takes a while. Then once we have the data, we need to display it using cards shown in figure 2.18.

We can use a simple `if` statement in our markup to check the value of the `_trails` field. If it's null, then we can surmise that the data is still being loaded,

Figure 2.18   Cards are used to display each trail and its associated information.

excluding an error scenario, of course. If the value is not null, then we have some data, and we can go ahead and display it (see the following listing).

Listing 2.9 HomePage.razor: Markup for the HomePage component

```
<PageTitle>Blazing Trails</PageTitle>          ◁──┐ The PageTitle component is used to set the
                                                   │ page title displayed in the browser tab.
@if (_trails == null)          ◁──┐ This checks to see if
{                                  │ data has been loaded.
    <p>Loading trails...</p>
}
else
{
    <div class="grid">                            ┌─ Once data is loaded, loop over it
        @foreach (var trail in _trails)       ◁──┘ and create a card for each trail.
        {
            <div class="card shadow" style="width: 18rem;">
                <img src="@trail.Image" class="card-img-top"
                ➥alt="@trail.Name">
                <div class="card-body">
                    <h5 class="card-title">@trail.Name</h5>
                    <h6 class="card-subtitle mb-3 text-muted">
                        <span class="oi oi-map-marker"></span>
                        @trail.Location
                    </h6>
                    <div class="d-flex justify-content-between">
                        <span>
                            <span class="oi oi-clock mr-2"></span>
                            @trail.TimeFormatted
                        </span>
                        <span>
                            <span class="oi oi-infinity mr-2"></span>
                            @trail.Length km
                        </span>
                    </div>
                </div>
            </div>
        }
    </div>
}
```

We've used another cool feature of Blazor in the code here—the `PageTitle` component. It's used to change the title of the page in the browser tab—something that has been difficult to achieve in Blazor before .NET 6. The title element of a web page is held in the head element of the host page, outside the scope of the Blazor app. To manipulate a page title in previous versions of Blazor, we needed to use some Java-Script interop or maybe find a NuGet package someone in the community had built.

At this point, you should be able to build the app and run it. If all has gone to plan, you should see the trails displayed on the home page. Now, we could finish here but there's one little refactor I think we should do first.

You may have noticed there's a fair amount of code for creating the trail card in listing 2.9. While it's all perfectly valid as is, wouldn't it be nice to encapsulate it all in a component instead? This would make the code in the `HomePage` component much easier to read.

Create a new component called `TrailCard.razor` in the Home feature folder. Then replace the boilerplate code with the markup for the card from the `HomePage`.

That was pretty painless. But now we have a problem. How do we get access to the current trail data? The answer is *parameters*.

We can pass data into components via parameters. Think of these as the public API for a component, and they work one way, from parent to child. We can define them in the code block by creating a public property and decorating it with the `Parameter` attribute. We pass data into them from the parent using attributes on the component tag.

For our `TrailCard` component, we'll create a parameter that will allow us to pass in the current trail from the parent. We can then update the Razor code to use this parameter. See the following listing for the completed `TrailCard` component.

Listing 2.10   TrailCard.razor

```
<div class="card shadow" style="width: 18rem;">
    <img src="@Trail.Image" class="card-img-top" alt="@Trail.Name">
    <div class="card-body">
        <h5 class="card-title">@Trail.Name</h5>
        <h6 class="card-subtitle mb-3 text-muted">
            <span class="oi oi-map-marker"></span>
            @Trail.Location
        </h6>
        <div class="d-flex justify-content-between">
            <span>
                <span class="oi oi-clock mr-2"></span>
                @Trail.TimeFormatted
            </span>
            <span>
                <span class="oi oi-infinity mr-2"></span>
                @Trail.Length km
            </span>
        </div>
    </div>
</div>

@code {
    [Parameter, EditorRequired]                            Defines a required
    public Trail Trail { get; set; } = default!;    ◁──   component parameter
}
```

In addition to using the `Parameter` attribute, we've also added another attribute called `EditorRequired`. This was introduced in .NET 6, and we can use it to indicate that a parameter is required. If we try to use the `TrailCard` component now, without passing a trail to the `Trail` parameter, we'll get a warning.

As we talked about earlier, due to nullable reference types being enabled, we need to handle the potential nullability of the parameter. There are two approaches for this: mark the parameter as nullable or give it a default value. Which option we use will depend on the situation, but in this case, we're going to choose the latter in combination with the *null forgiving operator* (!).

The null forgiving operator allows us to tell the compiler that a value isn't null or won't be null. It's very useful for situations where the compiler can't work this out for itself, which does happen every so often. In the case of a required component parameter (that's also a reference type), it's reasonable to assume that the value of the parameter won't be null other than through us as developers doing something a bit strange. Therefore, initializing it using the default keyword and the null forgiving operator is a clean option. We won't have to write any additional null checking code in our markup or methods when using the parameter, and if at run time the parameter's value was null, we would see a clear error that would allow us to debug the issue.

All that's left now is to update the `HomePage` component to use the new `Trail-Card` component. The final code for the `HomePage` component is shown in the following listing.

Listing 2.11   The HomePage component updated to use the TrailCard

```
@page "/"                        The Page directive marks the component as a routable component
@inject HttpClient Http          with the route template stating which route it's responsible for.

@if (_trails == null)            The Inject directive allows services
{                                to be injected into the component
    <p>Loading trails...</p>     from the service container.

}                                The If block checks if the _trails
else                             field is null and displays a loading
{                                message until it has a value.

    <div class="grid">                      The Foreach loop iterates over the
        @foreach (var trail in _trails)     trails contained in the _trails field.
        {
            <TrailCard Trail="trail" />      The Child component defines a TrailCard
        }                                    component and passes in the current trail via
    </div>                                   the Trail parameter defined on the TrailCard.
}

@code {                                      This Private field holds
    private IEnumerable<Trail>? _trails;     the current trails.

    protected override async Task OnInitializedAsync()
    {
        try                                             HttpClient is used to
        {                                               load test data from
            _trails = await Http.GetFromJsonAsync       a local JSON file.
            ➡<IEnumerable<Trail>>("trails/trail-data.json");
        }
        catch (HttpRequestException ex)
        {
            Console.WriteLine($"There was a problem loading trail data:
            ➡{ex.Message}");
        }                                      The Catch block allows
    }                                          handling of errors from
}                                              the http call gracefully.
```

Congratulations, we've just built the first small part of Blazing Trails!

Summary

We've covered a lot of topics in this chapter, so don't worry if you're feeling a little overwhelmed. Throughout the rest of the book, we'll dive deep into everything we've touched on, and by the time we finish Blazing Trails, you'll be a Blazor pro!

- Blazor comes with two templates—Blazor Server and Blazor WebAssembly—that help you get started building applications faster.
- Blazor WebAssembly is the more complex template with two configurations, standalone and hosted. Standalone generates a single Blazor WebAssembly project, which is useful when you have an existing backend, or your application doesn't require a backend. Hosted provides a full stack application with an ASP.NET Core backend, Blazor frontend, and a .NET class library for shared code.
- Blazor applications can be created with either an IDE such as Visual Studio or from the command line using the .NET CLI.
- Building your application will automatically restore any dependencies it requires.
- Blazor applications use a host page that contains the HTML element where the Blazor app will be rendered, as well as a link to the Blazor JavaScript run time.
- Blazor WebAssembly applications don't have a `Startup` class, only a `Program` class, due to not having a middleware pipeline. Service configuration and registration are moved to `Program.cs`.
- For Blazor WebAssembly, `Program.cs` is used to create and run an instance of `WebAssemblyHost`. This is done via the `WebAssemblyHostBuilder`. We use the builder to configure the various aspects of our Blazor application, such as its root components and service container.
- `App.razor` is the default root component and contains the `Router` component. All other components will be rendered as children of `App`.
- Feature folders can offer a number of benefits when organizing the files in your application. Everything that's related to a feature is in one place, making updates and maintenance easier.
- Layout components are a great way to define common UI, which would be repeated on every page, such as headers and navigation menus.
- Values can be passed into components via parameters, which can be thought of as the API for a component. Parameters must be public properties; they cannot be private.

Working with Blazor's component model

This chapter covers

- Exploring options for structuring components
- Looking at life cycle methods
- Handling DOM events
- Passing values between components
- Styling components

The fundamental building blocks of Blazor applications are components. Almost everything you do will directly or indirectly work with them. In order to build great applications, you must know how to harness their power. You've already had a taste of using them in chapter 2. In this chapter, we're going to look at them in much more detail.

Components define a piece of UI, which can be something as small as a button or as large as an entire page. Components can also contain other components. They encapsulate any data that a piece of UI requires to function. They allow a piece of UI to be reused across an application or even shared across multiple applications—something we'll look at in chapter 7.

Data can be passed into a component using parameters. Parameters define the public API of a component. The syntax for passing data into a component using parameters is the same as defining attributes on a standard HTML element—with a key-value pair. The key is the parameter name, and the value is the data you wish to pass to the component.

The data a component contains is more commonly referred to as its *state*. Methods on a component define its logic. These methods manipulate and control that state via the handling of events.

Components can be styled via traditional global styling or via scoped styles. Scoped styles allow the component to define its own CSS classes without fear of colliding with other styles in the application. It's even possible to use CSS preprocessors such as Sass (https://sass-lang.com/) with scoped styling.

To help us put all of this into real-world context, we'll be adding a cool new slide-out drawer feature to Blazing Trails (figure 3.1).

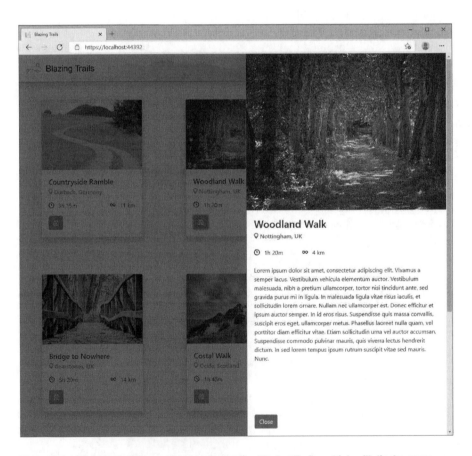

Figure 3.1   We'll be building a slide-out drawer for Blazing Trails, which will display more detailed information about the selected trail.

The drawer will slide out from the right-hand side of the page. To trigger the drawer, we'll add a button to the `TrailCard` component we built in chapter 2. The drawer will display more detailed information about the selected trail. When the user clicks the Close button on the drawer, it will cleanly slide back out of view.

Hopefully that has piqued your interest! But first we need to do a bit of ground-work. Let's get started!

3.1 Structuring components

As you will find with almost every part of Blazor, there are multiple ways of doing things. The Blazor team have been very deliberate with making the framework unopinionated so developers can build applications the way that works best for them. One example of this is in how components are structured.

It is possible to define a component in a single .razor file that contains both its markup and logic. But it is also possible to separate a component into a .razor file that defines the markup and a C# class that defines the logic.

3.1.1 Single file

When using a single file approach, unsurprisingly, all markup and logic for a component is defined in a single file. The primary advantage of this approach is that it allows you to work with everything in one place. This can really help with productivity, as you don't need to keep swapping back and forth between multiple files.

Single file is the default when creating new components. The following listing shows a component that uses the single file format.

Listing 3.1   A component defined using a single file approach

```
@page "/"                          Directives are declared
@inject HttpClient Http            at the top of the file.

@if (_trails == null)
{
    <p>Loading trails...</p>
}
else
{
    <div class="grid">             Markup is declared after
        @foreach (var trail in _trails)   the directive section.
        {
            <TrailCard Trail="trail" />
        }
    </div>
}


@code {
    private IEnumerable<Trail>? _trails;         The component logic
                                                 is declared inside of a
    protected override async Task OnInitializedAsync()   code block.
    {
```

```
try
{
    _trails = await Http.GetFromJsonAsync
      <IEnumerable<Trail>>("trails/trail-data.json");
}
catch (HttpRequestException ex)
{
    Console.WriteLine($"There was a problem
     loading trail data: {ex.Message}");
}
}

}
```

The component logic
is declared inside of a
code block.

The code here should look familiar—this is the Blazing Trails `HomePage` component we created in chapter 2. The entire component is defined in a single .razor file with the markup coming first and the logic coming second, defined in the code block.

This is my preferred approach for structuring components, as I really like having everything in a single file—it allows me to work faster since I don't have to switch files. But there is another benefit that I find useful: monitoring component size.

When building applications, it's easy to create very large components that are doing lots of things. However, just like when creating regular C# classes, you should try to keep your components focused, with a single purpose. One way I use to gauge this is the size of my component files. When I find I'm constantly scrolling up and down a file adding markup and logic, it's an indication that my component may be doing too much and I should be thinking about splitting it out into additional components with more focused responsibility. This isn't a clear-cut method, however; there are times when a component may be quite large but still has only one responsibility, but it at least makes me think about it.

One argument that I often hear against this method is that markup and logic should be separated because otherwise we're mixing concerns. I disagree with this view. The logic in a component should be logic that operates over the markup and drives the function of the component. Business logic has no place in components. If you take this view, then the logic and markup are intertwined—one can't exist without the other. Thus, separating them seems to fall into the same category as organizing an application's files by type rather than feature. And as I explained in chapter 2, this is inefficient and hinders productivity.

3.1.2 *Partial class*

Another approach is to split the markup and logic of a component into two separate files. The markup of the component is kept in the .razor file, and the logic is added to a C# class. In earlier versions of Blazor, it was only possible to apply this approach using inheritance, as there was no support for the *partial* keyword. This is no longer the case.

Let's take a look at the `HomePage` component refactored to use this approach. Listing 3.2 shows the component's markup.

Listing 3.2   HomePage.razor: The markup

```
@page "/"        <--- Directives section

@if (_trails == null)
{
    <p>Loading trails...</p>
}
else
{
    <div class="grid">
        @foreach (var trail in _trails)
        {
            <TrailCard Trail="trail" />
        }
    </div>
}
```

Only markup is included in the razor file.

Now here's the logic for the component, shown next.

Listing 3.3   HomePage.razor.cs: The logic

```
using Microsoft.AspNetCore.Components;
using System.Net.Http.Json;

namespace BlazingTrails.Client.Features.Home;

public partial class HomePage
{
    private IEnumerable<Trail>? _trails;

    [Inject] public HttpClient Http { get; set; } = default!;

    protected override async Task OnInitializedAsync()
    {
        try
        {
            _trails = await Http.GetFromJsonAsync<IEnumerable<Trail>>
            ("trails/trail-data.json");
        }
        catch (HttpRequestException ex)
        {
            Console.WriteLine($"There was a problem loading trail data:
            {ex.Message}");
        }
    }
}
```

The class is marked as partial.

Blazor uses property injection for dependencies. This is achieved in a class by using the Inject attribute.

Methods that were previously in the code block are declared in the class.

As you can see, using this technique, you can make the two elements of the component separate. You should also note the naming of the files, HomePage.razor and HomePage.razor.cs. If you're using Visual Studio to build your applications, following this naming convention will produce a nested effect (figure 3.2).

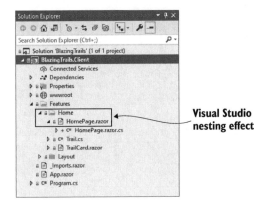

Visual Studio
nesting effect

Figure 3.2   Naming a partial class the same as
the markup portion of the component will produce
a nested effect when using Visual Studio.

This makes it easier to work with the component, as the files are always grouped together in the UI. It also keeps the number of files being displayed in the IDE to a minimum, as you can simply hide any partial classes you're not currently interested in.

The major benefit of separating the markup and logic of the component is the development experience. Again, in the single file approach, the razor editor is not as fully featured as when working with regular C# class files. By separating out the logic to a C# class file, developers can access all the editor features they're used to.

The drawback of this approach is that you now have two files to manage when you're working with a component. This can end up with lots of switching back and forth, as you will need to be in the logic file when adding methods or other members to the component. Then you will need to be in the markup file to add any UI, hook up event handlers, and so on.

Which approach you choose for building your applications is largely a personal choice based on which method you find most productive. As I said earlier, my preference is single file; it's the structure that makes me the most productive—it's also the structure that we will be using throughout this book.

3.2   Component life cycle methods

Just as in other component-based frameworks, components in Blazor have a life cycle: they're created, they exist for a period, and then they're destroyed. Figure 3.3 represents all the major parts of a component's life cycle.

Depending on what an application is doing, it may need to perform actions at certain points during this life cycle—for example, load initial data for the component to display when it is first created, or update the UI when a parameter has a certain value from the parent. Blazor supports this by giving us access to the component life cycle at specific points, which are

1 `OnInitialized/OnInitializedAsync`

2 `OnParametersSet/OnParametersSetAsync`

3 `OnAfterRender/OnAfterRenderAsync`

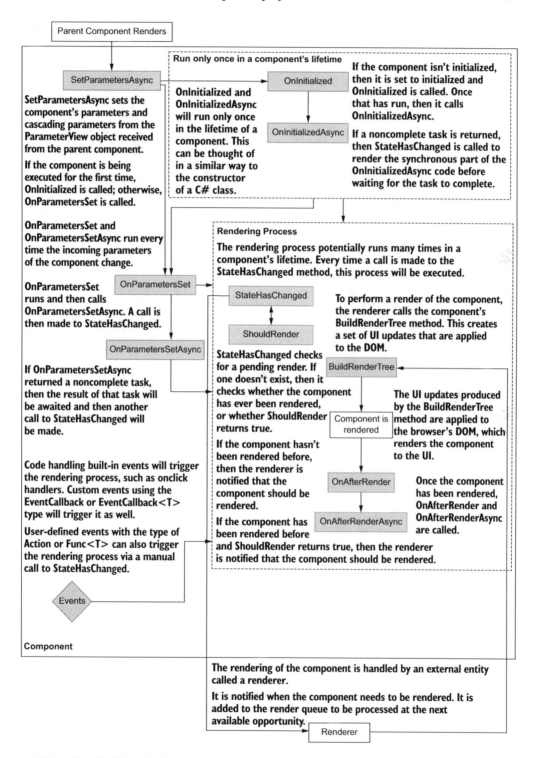

Figure 3.3 The life cycle of a component

The life cycle methods are provided by the `ComponentBase` class, which all components inherit from. Each method has a synchronous and asynchronous version. The synchronous version is always called before the asynchronous version.

To help visualize the life cycle, we will create a component that will log messages to the browser console when each method is run. The code is shown in listing 3.4.

NOTE If you run the following component in a Blazor Server app, the output will be in the output window in Visual Studio.

Listing 3.4 Lifecycle.razor logs the component life cycle methods

```
<h1>Componet Lifecycle</h1>
<p>Check the browser console for details...</p>

@code {

    public override async Task SetParametersAsync
    ➥(ParameterView parameters)
    {
        Console.WriteLine("SetParametersAsync - Begin");
        await base.SetParametersAsync(parameters);
        Console.WriteLine("SetParametersAsync - End");
    }

    protected override void OnInitialized()
        => Console.WriteLine("OnInitialized");

    protected override async Task OnInitializedAsync()
        => Console.WriteLine("OnInitializedAsync");

    protected override void OnParametersSet()
        => Console.WriteLine("OnParametersSet");

    protected override async Task OnParametersSetAsync()
        => Console.WriteLine("OnParametersSetAsync");

    protected override void OnAfterRender
    ➥(bool firstRender)
        => Console.WriteLine(
        ➥$"OnAfterRender (First render: {firstRender})");

    protected override async Task OnAfterRenderAsync
    ➥(bool firstRender)
        => Console.WriteLine(
        ➥$"OnAfterRenderAsync (First render: {firstRender})");
}
```

Each life cycle method is overridden and will print its name to the browser console when it runs.

Figure 3.4 shows the life cycle output printed to the browser console when the component is run for the first time. Let's walk through that process first.

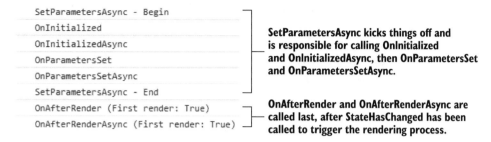

Figure 3.4 Shows the order each life cycle method is called in

3.2.1 *The first render*

During the first render, all the component's life cycle methods will be called. During subsequent renders, only a subset of the methods will run.

The process starts with `SetParametersAsync` being called. This is the only life cycle method that requires us to call the base method; if we don't, then the component will fail to load. This is because the base method does two essential things:

- *Sets the values for any parameters the component defines*—This happens both the first time the component is rendered and whenever parameters could have changed.
- *Calls the correct life cycle methods*—This depends on whether the component is running for the first time or not.

If we removed the call to the base method, the output in the browser console would look like this:

```
SetParametersAsync - Begin
SetParametersAsync - End
```

> **NOTE** `SetParametersAsync` is not a life cycle method that is often used by developers. Commonly, it is just `OnInitialized`, `OnParametersSet`, and `OnAfterRender`. In advanced scenarios, you may choose to override `Set-ParametersAsync` and not call the base method of `SetParametersAsync`. Doing so would allow complete control over the component's initialization and subsequent updates. This can be a useful tool when creating highly performant components; however, that is out of scope for this book.

During a first render, the component hasn't been initialized. This means that `On-Initialized` and `OnInitializedAsync` will be called first—it is also the only time they will run. This pair of methods is the only one that runs once in a component's lifetime. You can think of these as constructors for your component. It makes them a great place to make API calls—for example, to get the initial data the component will display.

Once the `OnInitialized` methods have run, `OnParametersSet` and `On-ParametersSetAsync` are called. These methods allow developers to perform actions whenever a component's parameters change. In the case of a first render, the component's parameters have been set to their initial values.

The final methods to run are `OnAfterRender` and `OnAfterRenderAsync`. These methods both take a Boolean value indicating if this is the first time the component has been rendered. On the initial render, the value of `firstRender` will be set to `true`; for every render after, it will be `false`:

```
void OnAfterRender(bool firstRender)
Task OnAfterRenderAsync(bool firstRender)
```

This is useful because it allows one-time operations to be performed when a component is first rendered, but not on subsequent renders. The primary use of the `OnAfterRender` methods is to perform JavaScript interop (chapter 8) and other DOM-related operations, such as setting the focus on an element.

3.2.2   *The life cycle with async*

One key point about the render we just covered is that it ran synchronously. In the `Lifecycle` component, there are no awaited calls in any of the async life cycle methods, meaning each method ran in sequence. However, when async calls are added, then things look a bit different. To demonstrate this, let's update the `OnInitializedAsync` method in the `Lifecycle.razor` component to make an async call.

```
protected override async Task OnInitializedAsync()
{
    Console.WriteLine("OnInitializedAsync - Begin");
    await Task.Delay(300);
    Console.WriteLine("OnInitializedAsync - End");
}
```

If we run the app again and check the browser console, we'll see the output shown in figure 3.5.

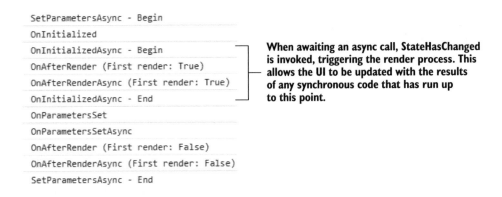

Figure 3.5   While awaiting the result of the asynchronous operation, the component is rendered.

Well, that's a bit different! While Blazor was awaiting the async call, the component was rendered. It was then rendered a second time after the `OnParametersSet` methods, as before. This is because Blazor checks to see if an awaitable task is returned from `OnInitializedAsync`. If there is, it calls `StateHasChanged` to render the component with the results of any of the synchronous code that has been run so far, while awaiting the completion of the task. This behavior is also true for async calls made in `OnParametersSetAsync`.

When dealing with multiple asynchronous calls, rendering may not behave quite as you'd expect. To demonstrate this, let's look at another example shown in the following listing.

Listing 3.5 A component that makes multiple asynchronous calls

```
@foreach (var word in _greeting)
{
    <p>@word</p>
}

@code {

    List<string> _greeting = new List<string>();

    protected override async Task OnInitializedAsync()
    {
        _greeting.Add("Welcome");          ⟵┐  The first word is added
                                              │  to the greeting list.
        await Task.Delay(1000);
        _greeting.Add("to");               ⟵┐  The second word is added
                                              │  to the greeting list.
        await Task.Delay(1000);
        _greeting.Add("Blazor in Action"); ⟵
    }
}
```

An async call is made. ⟶ (points to `await Task.Delay(1000);`)

Another async call is made. (points to `await Task.Delay(1000);`)

The final words are added to the greeting list. (points to `_greeting.Add("Blazor in Action");`)

This component is simulating making multiple asynchronous calls in its `OnInitializedAsync` life cycle method. As each call returns, new words are added to the greeting list, which is then printed out via a `foreach` statement.

What would you expect to be displayed? Perhaps `Welcome`, then after 1 second, the next word `to` would be added, then after another second the final words `Blazor in Action` would appear? That would be a fair answer, but you'd be wrong. What happens is this: the word `Welcome` is displayed, then after 2 seconds the words `to Blazor in Action` are added (figure 3.6).

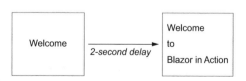

Figure 3.6 Initially the word `Welcome` is displayed on the page, and 2 seconds later the words `to Blazor in Action` are displayed.

Why does this happen? The code up to the first awaited method is executed, and, as we just learned, a call is made to `StateHasChanged` at this point to render the results of any synchronous code while awaiting that task. This explains the render of the word `Welcome` but not why the word `to` isn't rendered after the first awaited call.

The reason for this is that Blazor doesn't understand our code. There is no way for it to know that it should render after we add `to` to the greeting list. Instead, the code continues to execute until the end of the method, and at this point, Blazor can perform a new render of the component.

If we want the UI to update after each word is added to the list, then we must manually call `StateHasChanged` to inform Blazor that the UI should be updated:

```
await Task.Delay(1000);
_greeting.Add("to");
StateHasChanged();
```

With this update to the code, if we reload the page, we should see the words appear in the sequence shown in figure 3.7.

Figure 3.7   By telling Blazor when to update the UI, the words are rendered as they are added to the list.

By telling Blazor when the UI needs to be updated, we've achieved the desired result of the words being rendered as they're added to the list.

3.2.3   *Dispose: The extra life cycle method*

There is another life cycle method that we can use, but this one is optional and it's not built in to the `ComponentBase` class: `Dispose`. This method is used for the same purposes in Blazor as in other C# applications: to clean up resources. This method is essential when creating components that subscribe to events, as failing to unsubscribe from events before a component is destroyed will cause a memory leak.

In order to access this method, a component must implement the `IDisposable` interface. To do this, we can use the `@implements` directive, shown in the following listing.

Listing 3.6   Lifecycle.razor implementing `IDisposable`

```
@implements IDisposable          The implements directive allows
                                 components to implement the
<h1>Component Lifecycle</h1>     specified interface.
<p>Check the browser console for details...</p>
```

```
@code {

    // Other methods ommitted for brevity

    public void Dispose()
        => Console.WriteLine($"Dispose");
}
```

The implements directive allows components to implement the specified interface.

To see the effect of this new life cycle method, we need to navigate away from the component. This will remove it from the DOM and invoke the `Dispose` method. When we do this, we see the output shown in figure 3.8 in the console.

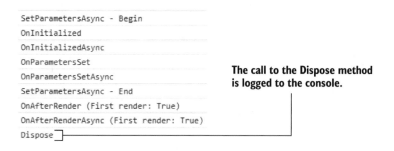

```
SetParametersAsync - Begin
OnInitialized
OnInitializedAsync
OnParametersSet
OnParametersSetAsync
SetParametersAsync - End
OnAfterRender (First render: True)
OnAfterRenderAsync (First render: True)
Dispose
```

The call to the Dispose method is logged to the console.

Figure 3.8 After implementing `IDisposable`, Blazor will automatically call our component's `Dispose` method when the component is destroyed.

Blazor understands the `IDisposable` interface. When it detects its presence on a component, it will call the `Dispose` method at the correct point when destroying the component instance.

Since .NET 5, Blazor also supports the `IAsyncDisposable` interface. This allows disposal of resources asynchronously, which is useful when using JavaScript interop. We'll talk more about this in chapter 8. But for now, note that `IDisposable` and `IAsyncDisposable` can't both be implemented on the same component. If both are implemented, then only the async version will run (see the following listing).

Listing 3.7 Lifecycle.razor: `IDisposable` and `IAsyncDisposable`

```
@implements IDisposable
@implements IAsyncDisposable

<h1>Componet Lifecycle</h1>
<p>Check the browser console for details...</p>

@code {

    // Other methods ommitted for brevity

    public void Dispose()
        => Console.WriteLine($"Dispose");
```

Both IDisposable and IAsyncDisposable have been implemented.

```
public async ValueTask DisposeAsync()
    => Console.WriteLine($"DisposeAsync");
}
```

Both IDisposable and IAsyncDisposable have been implemented.

Reloading the component and navigating away as before, to trigger the `Dispose` methods, produces the output shown in figure 3.9 in the browser console.

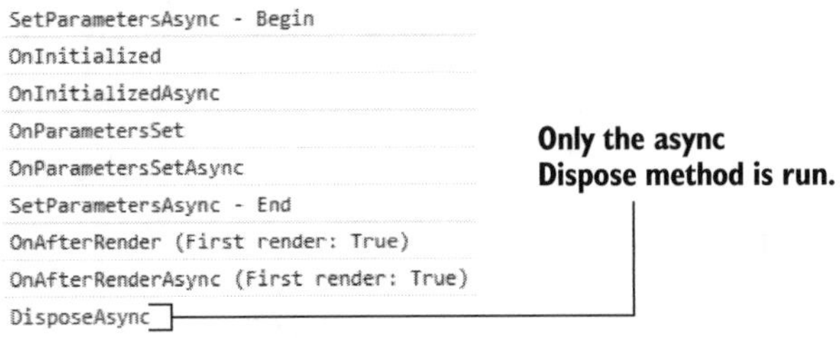

```
SetParametersAsync - Begin
OnInitialized
OnInitializedAsync
OnParametersSet
OnParametersSetAsync
SetParametersAsync - End
OnAfterRender (First render: True)
OnAfterRenderAsync (First render: True)
DisposeAsync
```

Only the async Dispose method is run.

Figure 3.9   When both `IDisposable` and `IAsyncDisposable` are implemented, Blazor will only call the async `Dispose` methods.

As you can see, only the async `Dispose` methods have been called and the synchronous methods have been ignored.

3.3   *Working with parent and child components*

A great analogy for components is LEGO blocks. Each LEGO block is a self-contained unit, but the real fun comes when you plug the blocks together to build something bigger and better. This is the same for components. They can be useful on their own, but they are more powerful when used together.

When using multiple components, you will soon end up with components that contain other components. These are known as *parent and child components*. These components will sometimes need to communicate with each other, such as for passing data and firing and handling events. In Blazor, we achieve this using *component parameters*.

Component parameters are declared on a child component, which forms that component's API. A parent component can then pass data to the child using that API. But component parameters can also be used to define events on the child that the parent can handle. This allows data to be passed from the child back up to the parent. To help bring this to life, we're going to add a new feature to Blazing Trails, shown in figure 3.10.

We'll add a View button to the `TrailCard` that, when clicked, will slide open a drawer on the right side of the application. This drawer will display more detailed information about the selected trail. For this to work, we need to have three different components communicate and pass data. Figure 3.11 illustrates their relationship.

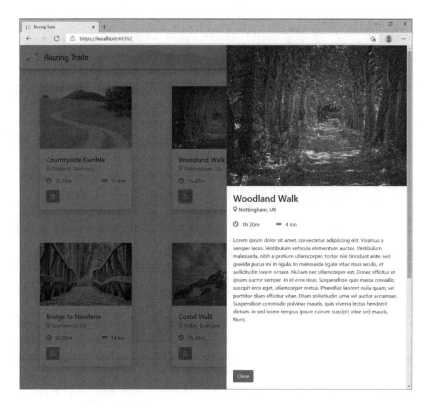

Figure 3.10   Clicking the View button on a trail will slide open a new drawer component, which displays more information about the selected trail.

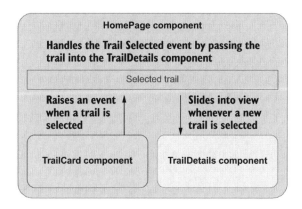

Figure 3.11   The `HomePage` component handles any trail-selected events from the `TrailCard` component. It records the selected trail and passes it to the `TrailDetails` component. When this happens, the `TrailDetails` card will slide into view, displaying the selected trail.

The `HomePage` component will coordinate the operation. It will handle any `On-Selected` events from the `TrailCard` component. When an `OnSelected` event is raised, the `HomePage` component will record the selected trail and pass it into the

TrailDetails component. Inside the TrailDetails component, whenever the trail value changes, it will trigger the drawer to activate and slide into view.

3.3.1 *Passing values from a parent to a child*

To build our new drawer, we need to create a component that takes in a trail and then displays its information. We will use a component parameter to create its API.

THE TRAILDETAILS COMPONENT

The TrailDetails component, shown in listing 3.8, will display the selected trail, which is passed in via a component parameter. We're going to create this component in the Home feature folder.

Listing 3.8   TrailDetails.razor: Displays trail data

```
<div class="drawer-wrapper @(_isOpen ? "slide" : "")">
    <div class="drawer-mask"></div>
    <div class="drawer">
        @if (_activeTrail is not null)
        {
            <div class="drawer-content">
                <img src="@_activeTrail.Image" />
                <div class="trail-details">
                    <h3>@_activeTrail.Name</h3>
                    <h6 class="mb-3 text-muted">
                        <span class="oi oi-map-marker"></span>
                        @_activeTrail.Location
                    </h6>
                    <div class="mt-4">
                        <span class="mr-5">
                            <span class="oi oi-clock mr-2"></span>
                            @_activeTrail.TimeFormatted
                        </span>
                        <span>
                            <span class="oi oi-infinity mr-2"></span>
                            @_activeTrail.Length km
                        </span>
                    </div>
                    <p class="mt-4">@_activeTrail.Description</p>
                </div>
            </div>
            <div class="drawer-controls">
                <button class="btn btn-secondary"
                        @onclick="Close">Close</button>
            </div>
        }
    </div>
</div>

@code {
    private bool _isOpen;
    private Trail? _activeTrail;
```

```
[Parameter, EditorRequired]
public Trail? Trail { get; set; }                    ◁──┐  A component parameter is defined as
                                                          │  a public property, which is decorated
protected override void OnParametersSet()                │  with the Parameter attribute.
{
    if (Trail != null)
    {
        _activeTrail = Trail;
        _isOpen = true;
    }
}

private void Close()
{
    _activeTrail = null;
    _isOpen = false;
}
}
```

A component parameter is defined as a public property that is decorated with the `Parameter` attribute. We can even mark certain parameters as required using the `EditorRequired` attribute with the `Parameter` attribute, as we have in the `Trail-Details` component. Blazor uses this attribute to find component parameters during the execution of the `SetParametersAsync` life cycle method we looked at earlier in the chapter. During this life cycle method, the parameter values are set via reflection.

We're using the `OnParametersSet` life cycle method to trigger the drawer sliding into view. As we learned earlier, this life cycle method is run every time the component's parameters change. This makes it perfect for our scenario, as we can use it to trigger opening the drawer.

Opening and closing the drawer is done using CSS. When a new trail is passed in, the `_isOpen` field is set to `true`. This triggers the logic at the top of the component to render the slide CSS class.

```
<div class="drawer-wrapper @(_isOpen ? "slide" : "")">
```

In the app.css file (found in the wwwroot > css folder), we need to add the styles shown in the following listing to the bottom of the file.

Listing 3.9 App.css: Styles for the `TrailDetails` component

```
.drawer-mask {
    visibility: hidden;
    position: fixed;
    overflow: hidden;
    top: 0;
    right: 0;
    left: 0;
    bottom: 0;
    z-index: 99;
    background-color: #000000;
    opacity: 0;
```

```
        transition: opacity 0.3s ease, visibility 0.3s ease;
}

.drawer-wrapper.slide > .drawer-mask {
    opacity: .5;
    visibility: visible;
}

.drawer {
    display: flex;
    flex-direction: column;
    position: fixed;
    top: 0;
    right: 0;
    bottom: 0;
    width: 35em;
    overflow-y: auto;
    overflow-x: hidden;
    background-color: white;
    border-left: 0.063em solid gray;
    z-index: 100;
    transform: translateX(110%);
    transition: transform 0.3s ease, width 0.3s ease;
}
```

> The translateX function positions the drawer off the right-hand side of the screen by 110% of its width, making it appear closed.

```
.drawer-wrapper.slide > .drawer {
    transform: translateX(0);
}
```

> When the .slide class is applied in the TrailDetails component, translateX is used again to position the drawer into view.

```
.drawer-content {
    display: flex;
    flex: 1;
    flex-direction: column;
}

.trail-details {
    padding: 20px;
}

.drawer-controls {
    padding: 20px;
    background-color: #ffffff;
}
```

The two key parts of the styles here are the `transform: translateX` properties on the `.drawer` and `.drawer-wrapper.slide > .drawer` classes. Without these properties, the drawer would sit in its open position, in full view. Figure 3.12 shows the effect of the properties on the drawer.

The transform property on the `.drawer` class repositions the drawer off the right-hand side of the screen by 110% of its width. The transform property on the `.drawer-wrapper.slide > .drawer` class repositions it back to its default, bringing it into view.

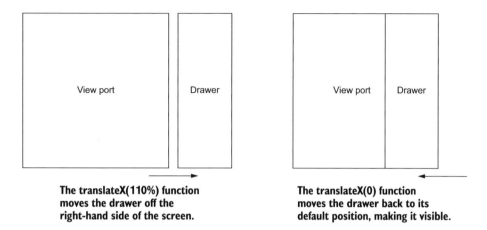

The translateX(110%) function moves the drawer off the right-hand side of the screen.

The translateX(0) function moves the drawer back to its default position, making it visible.

Figure 3.12   By default, the drawer is positioned off the right-hand side of the screen using the `translateX` CSS function. When the .slide class is applied, `translateX` is used again to reposition the drawer back to its standard placement, making it visible.

UPDATING THE HOMEPAGE COMPONENT

To pass the trail into the `TrailDetails` component, we use attributes when defining the component in the parent. The parent for us is the `HomePage` component. The following listing shows the `HomePage` component updated with the `TrailDetails` component.

Listing 3.10   HomePage.razor: Defining a child component

```
@page "/"
@inject HttpClient Http

@if (_trails == null)
{
    <p>Loading trails...</p>
}
else
{
    <TrailDetails Trail="_selectedTrail" />          ◁─┐ Data is passed to component
    <div class="grid">                                 │ parameters using attributes
        @foreach (var trail in _trails)                │ on the element.
        {
            <TrailCard Trail="trail" />
        }
    </div>
}

@code {
    private IEnumerable<Trail>? _trails;
    private Trail? _selectedTrail;
```

```
protected override async Task OnInitializedAsync()
{
    try
    {
        _trails = await Http.GetFromJsonAsync<IEnumerable<Trail>>
        ➥("trails/trail-data.json");
    }
    catch (HttpRequestException ex)
    {
        Console.WriteLine($"There was a problem loading trail data:
        ➥{ex.Message}");
    }
}
}
```

In the `HomePage` component, we have defined a field called `_selectedTrail`, which will store the selected trail. We then pass this into the `TrailDetails` component using an attribute-style syntax:

```
<TrailDetails Trail="_selectedTrail" />
```

The attribute name matches the component parameter we defined on the `Trail-Details` component. It is important that the case also matches; otherwise, Blazor will consider it a regular HTML attribute and ignore it. If you're using an IDE, such as Visual Studio for Windows or macOS, or JetBrains Rider, you will receive IntelliSense to help you do this. VS Code also has IntelliSense support for Blazor via the C# extension.

3.3.2   *Passing data from a child to a parent*

We have successfully used a component parameter to define the API of the `Trail-Details` component, but we can't see the fruits of our labor yet. In order to see something happen onscreen, we need to select a trail to display. This can be done by passing that information up from the `TrailCard` component to the `HomePage` component. To do this, we will use component parameters to define an event on the `TrailCard`. This event will pass the selected trail; the `HomePage` component can then handle this event and pass the trail to the `TrailDetails` component to display.

> **NOTE**   Events in Blazor are not true events in the .NET sense; they are just delegates. This goes for Blazor's built-in DOM events system and events defined by developers using component parameters. This also means there can only ever be one handler for any given event at any given time.

The following listing shows the updated code for the `TrailCard` component.

Listing 3.11   TrailCard.razor: Defining a component event

```
<div class="card shadow" style="width: 18rem;">
    <img src="@Trail.Image" class="card-img-top" alt="@Trail.Name">
    <div class="card-body">
```

```
        // other markup omitted for brevity
        <button class="btn btn-primary" title="View"
    ➥@onclick="@(() => OnSelected?.Invoke(Trail))">      ◁──┐ The delegate is
            <i class="bi bi-binoculars"></i>                     invoked, passing in
        </button>                                                the current trail.
    </div>
</div>

@code {
    [Parameter, EditorRequired]
    public Trail Trail { get; set; } = default!;
    [Parameter, EditorRequired]
    public Action<Trail> OnSelected { get; set; }   ◁──┐ Events are defined
}                                                         using delegate types of
                                                          either Action or Func.
```

We define the event as a delegate of type `Action<Trail>`. This allows us to pass the trail that this `TrailCard` is displaying back to the parent component. This happens when the View button is clicked. We handle the button's click event using Blazor's `@onclick` event.

> **Handling DOM Events**
>
> Blazor has its own events system that wraps the standard DOM events, allowing us to work with them natively, in C#. To handle an event, we use the following syntax on an element:
>
> ```
> @onEVENTNAME="HANDLER"
> ```
>
> EVENTNAME is the name of the event you wish to handle, and HANDLER is the name of the method that will be invoked to handle the event. Blazor will also pass an event argument to the `Handler` method, which is appropriate for the event. For example, if we wanted to handle the `keydown` event on an input, we could do so like this:
>
> ```
> <input @onkeydown="HandleKeydown" />
> ```
>
> Then in the code block, we can define the Handler like this:
>
> ```
> private void HandleKeydown(KeyboardEventArgs args)
> {
>     Console.WriteLine(args.Key);
> }
> ```
>
> Blazor will pass in the `KeyboardEventArgs` when it invokes the `Handler` method, and we can then access metadata about the event. In the preceding example, we are printing out the key that was pressed to the console.
>
> For a full list of event arguments and the events they are for, check out the official docs at http://mng.bz/M5Wo.

With the `TrailCard` updated, all that's left to do is handle the event in the `HomePage` component. First, we need to add a method to the code block, which will be called whenever an event is raised:

```
private void HandleTrailSelected(Trail trail)
{
    _selectedTrail = trail;
    StateHasChanged();
}
```

This method accepts the selected trail and assigns it to the `_selectedTrail` field. However, in order to see anything happen, we must call `StateHasChanged`. This lets Blazor know that we need the UI to update. We must do this manually because Blazor can't know the intent of our code. It has no idea that our custom event should trigger a re-render of the UI.

There are some cases where this manual control over re-renders is preferred; however, in most cases this is just an extra line of code that must be added to achieve the desired effect. There is another way. We can use a different type to define our event on the `TrailCard` called `EventCallback`. By using this type for our event, Blazor will automatically call `StateHasChanged` on the component that handles the event, removing the need to manually call it.

To take advantage of this, we can update the component parameter on `TrailCard` and update how the event is invoked, as shown in the following listing.

Listing 3.12   TrailCard.razor: Updates to use `EventCallback`

```
<div class="card" style="width: 18rem;">
    <img src="@Trail.Image" class="card-img-top" alt="@Trail.Name">
    <div class="card-body">
        // other markup omitted for brevity
        <button class="btn btn-primary" @onclick="
        @(async () => await OnSelected.InvokeAsync(Trail))">
        View</button>                    ◁─── When using EventCallback, a null check is not
    </div>                                    required. It also supports async handlers; therefore,
</div>                                        we must invoke the event asynchronously.

@code {
    [Parameter, EditorRequired]                          The component
    public Trail Trail { get; set; } = default!;         parameter is
    [Parameter]                                          now typed as
    public EventCallback<Trail> OnSelected { get; set; } ◁─── EventCallback<Trail>.
}
```

Then we can simply remove the `StateHasChanged` call from our handler in the `HomePage` component. In fact, as it's now just a single line, we can remove the braces and use C#'s expression body syntax to make things really neat:

```
private void HandleTrailSelected(Trail trail)
    => _selectedTrail = trail;
```

The final update is to assign the `HandleTrailSelected` method to the `OnSelected` event in the `HomePage` component. We do this the same way we did to pass the selected trail into the `TrailDetails` component—using attributes:

```
<TrailCard Trail="trail" OnSelected="HandleTrailSelected" />
```

At this point, we can run the application and test things out. Figure 3.13 shows the running app.

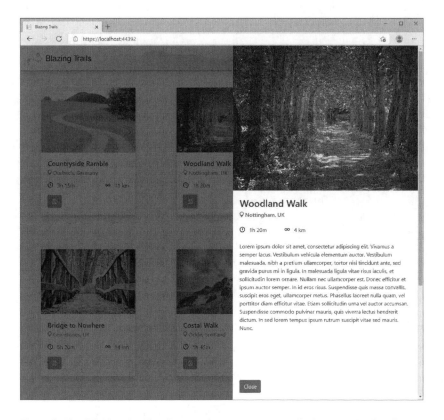

Figure 3.13 Clicking the View button of any `TrailCard` displays the details of that trail in the `TrailDetails` component.

If all has gone to plan, then clicking the View button should trigger the drawer and display the trail. Clicking the Close button at the bottom of the drawer will close it and allow a new trail to be selected.

3.4 Styling components

The styling is an important element to building any application, and it is a powerful tool in delivering great UX. Look at the drawer we just built—the ability for it to slide in and out of the viewport was achieved using CSS, not C#. There are two approaches to styling components in Blazor:

- Global styling
- Scoped styling

As you would expect, global styles are classes that are declared on the global scope and can apply to any element that uses that class name or meets the selector for that class. Scoped styles are the opposite. A stylesheet is created for a specific component, and any classes defined in it are made unique to that component using a unique identifier produced during the build process.

No matter which of these approaches you take to style your application, it is possible to combine it with CSS preprocessors. CSS preprocessors like Sass allow CSS to be written in a more modular and maintainable way, taking advantage of features such as variables and functions.

3.4.1   *Global styling*

Global styling is the default method when building applications. This is how we have been styling Blazing Trails up to this point. To apply global styling, one or more stylesheets are added to the host page, which, by default, is index.html in Blazor WebAssembly and _Host.cshtml in Blazor Server. The styles defined in those stylesheets are then available throughout the application.

Global styles are fantastic for creating a consistent look and feel across an application—for example, if all buttons needed to be blue with certain font size and rounded corners. This can be defined once in a global style and would apply to all buttons in the app:

```
button {
    font-size: 1rem;
    background-color: blue;
    border-radius: .25rem
}
```

This makes global styles an incredibly powerful tool, because if we wanted to change how the buttons (or any aspect of the applications design) looked, we can change the styles in one place, and the application is immediately updated.

This global scope of styles can also cause some issues when developing larger applications. For example, if we wanted a certain button to be green with square corners rather than the global blue style, we would need to add another style to the stylesheet. We would then need to apply the style to the particular button. That doesn't seem too bad, but think of this happening many times over—you end up with a stylesheet that is full of one-off styles or niche styles. You could say this is down to bad design or lack of maintenance—which would be fair—but it still doesn't stop it from happening.

Making changes to global styles can also be cumbersome. Constantly scrolling up and down a stylesheet with hundreds of lines of style classes can become tedious, especially when changes need to be made in multiple places.

There are mitigations for this, of course. Using a CSS preprocessor like Sass (syntactically awesome style sheets) allows the global styles to be broken up and kept next to the component they are for in the project structure. This makes working with them much easier and more efficient. There is also another option that has come about with the rise of SPA frameworks—scoped CSS.

3.4.2   Scoped styling

Scoped styling allows a developer to create styles that affect only a certain component in the application. In Blazor applications, this is done by creating a stylesheet with the same name as the component. During the build process, Blazor generates unique IDs for each component and then the styles for that component are rescoped using each ID.

To get a feel for this, let's rework the styles for the `TrailDetails` component we just built to use scoped CSS. To do this, we first need to create a new stylesheet called `TrailDetails.razor.css`, then take all the styles we added to app.css for the `TrailDetails` component and move them to this file.

It is important that we name the file this way; otherwise Blazor won't pick it up and associate its styles with the `TrailDetails` component. If you're using Visual Studio, a nice effect of this naming convention is the file nesting in Solution Explorer, shown in figure 3.14.

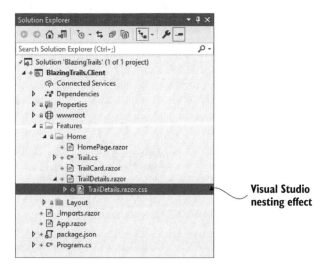

Figure 3.14   Giving files the same name with a different extension causes a nesting effect in Visual Studio.

When using scoped CSS, there will be a lot of stylesheets dotted around the application. Adding each and every one of them to the host page would be tedious and difficult to maintain. So, what Blazor does as part of the build process is bundle all the styles from the various stylesheets into a single stylesheet. This means we just need to reference that one stylesheet in our host page. The file has a naming convention of `[ProjectName].styles.css`. As our project is called `BlazingTrails.Client`, the file will be called `BlazingTrails.Client.styles.css`. Listing 3.13 demonstrates where to reference the file.

> **NOTE** If you've created a new project using .NET 5 or later, this reference will be included automatically for you. You only need to manually add this when upgrading from pre-.NET 5 projects.

Listing 3.13 Referencing scoped styles in index.html

```
<!DOCTYPE html>
<html>

<head>
    <meta charset="utf-8" />
    <meta name="viewport" content="width=device-width, initial-scale=1.0,
    ➥maximum-scale=1.0, user-scalable=no" />
    <title>BlazingTrails.Client</title>
    <base href="/" />
    <link href="css/bootstrap/bootstrap.min.css" rel="stylesheet" />
    <link href="css/app.css" rel="stylesheet" />
    <link href="BlazingTrails.Client.styles.css"
    ➥rel="stylesheet" />                          ⟵⎤  Scoped styles are referenced via a single
</head>                                               │  stylesheet that is named after the host
                                                      │  project appended with styles.css.
```

If we run the project and select a trail to open the drawer, we can use the browser's dev tools to look at the HTML and styles produced. Figure 3.15 shows what this looks like.

```
▼<div class="drawer-wrapper slide" b-jxhz4zizxo>
    <!--!-->
    <div class="drawer-mask" b-jxhz4zizxo></div>                     During the build, Blazor has created
  ▼<div class="drawer" b-jxhz4zizxo>                                 a unique ID for this component and
    ▼<div class="drawer-content" b-jxhz4zizxo>                       applied it as an attribute to all of
      ▶<div class="trail-image" b-jxhz4zizxo>…</div>                 the HTML elements within it.
        <!--!-->
      ▶<div class="trail-details" b-jxhz4zizxo>…</div>
      </div>
        <!--!-->
    ▶<div class="drawer-controls  b-jxhz4zizxo …</div>
    </div>
  </div>
</div>
```

Figure 3.15 Inspecting the HTML of the application in a browser shows a unique ID applied to each HTML element belonging to the `TrailDetails` component.

As shown in figure 3.15, each HTML element belonging to the `TrailDetails` component now has a unique attribute applied to it. This attribute follows the format of `b-[uniqueID]`. If we then select an element to inspect its styles, figure 3.16 shows how this ID is used to scope those styles.

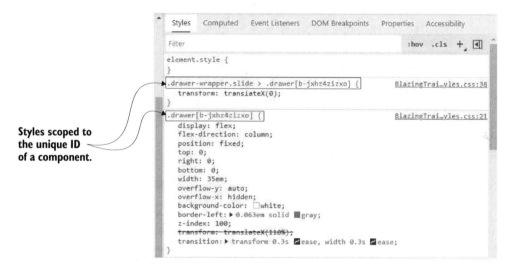

Styles scoped to the unique ID of a component.

Figure 3.16 **Blazor rewrites the styles in the component's stylesheet using the unique ID it generates for the component.**

Each selector for the styles in the TrailDetails.razor.css file has been rewritten to use the unique ID Blazor generated for the component. Doing this is what scopes the style to that component and stops the style affecting another element in another component.

GLOBAL STYLES CAN STILL HAVE AN EFFECT

If you use scoped styles and nothing else in your application, then what I'm about to say isn't an issue. However, if you have some global styles and some scoped styles, then you may still run into problems.

To give an example, let's say we had the following CSS class called `.drawer` in our global CSS file, in addition to the one we have in the `TrailDetails` component's scoped stylesheet:

```
.drawer {
    border: 5px solid lawngreen;
}
```

This class would still affect the `.drawer` class in the `TrailDetails` component. If we run the application, figure 3.17 shows what things would look like.

The border from the global .drawer class is still being applied to the component, even though it's using scoped styling.

Figure 3.17   **The green border style from the global `.drawer` class has been applied, even though the `TrailDetails` component is using scoped CSS.**

As you can see, using scoped styles doesn't make components immune from the standard behavior of CSS. This is something to think about when deciding how to style your components; mixing global and scoped styles could make things more complicated.

3.4.3   *Using CSS preprocessors*

Whether you choose to use global styles, scoped styles, or a mix of both, you can still leverage the power of CSS preprocessors. These work similarly to the way Type-Script does for JavaScript—as a superset language. They provide access to a richer feature set than CSS provides alone, at the cost of having to perform some kind of build action.

There are many options out there when it comes to CSS preprocessors, but the main players are:

- Less (Leaner Style Sheets; http://lesscss.org/)
- Sass (https://sass-lang.com/)
- Stylus (https://stylus-lang.com/)

They all provide similar feature sets, which offer the following enhancements over regular CSS, just with different syntaxes:

- *Mixins*—Reusable groups of styles
- *Variables*—Works the same way as variables in C# (this has now been added to standard CSS but doesn't work in older browsers, whereas the preprocessor versions do)
- *Nesting*—The ability to define the scope of a style by writing it within another

- *Import*—Allows us to organize large CSS files into smaller, more focused files and then import common aspects such as variables

Choosing a preprocessor largely comes down to which syntax you prefer. My favorite preprocessor is SCSS (https://sass-lang.com/). It has a syntax very similar to regular CSS, which makes everything easy to read. It has also been around for a very long time, so there's lots of documentation and blog posts out there to help if you get stuck.

INTEGRATING A CSS PREPROCESSOR

I'm going to show you how to integrate SCSS into a Blazor app, specifically when using scoped CSS. There are two ways we can integrate SCSS into our application: using JavaScript tools or using .NET tools. While there are a few options out there for integrating CSS preprocessors without using any JavaScript tooling (at least not directly), in my opinion none of them work as well or as reliably as the JavaScript options. But don't fear, I'll show you a method that requires the minimal amount of interaction with those tools.

If you're adamant that you don't want to use any JavaScript tools in your application, then check out either of the following options:

- Web Compiler from Mads Kristensen (http://mng.bz/woQa). This hasn't had any meaningful updates for a couple of years, but it does still appear to work.
- WebCompiler by excubo-ag (https://github.com/excubo-ag/WebCompiler). This is forked from Mads's Web Compiler and looks like a promising project. It uses a .NET CLI tool to perform the compilation of SCSS files and ties in with MSBuild. However, it currently only supports SCSS. This means if you are using a different preprocessor, such as Less or Stylus, you are out of luck. Configuration is a bit difficult, and there is limited documentation.

The option I prefer, and the one I'll show you, is to use a mix of NPM (Node package manager) and MSBuild. This requires having an up-to-date version of Node.js installed (download at https://nodejs.org/). The version I'm using is 16.13.1 and is the latest LTS (long-term service) version.

We will use a tool called Dart Sass (https://sass-lang.com/dart-sass), which we can install as an NPM package called Sass (https://www.npmjs.com/package/sass). We're then going to use MSBuild to call this tool during the build process, specifically at the start of the build process. This is important, as we need to compile our SCSS files to CSS before Blazor's compiler runs so it can pick up the compiled CSS files and bundle them into the single [ProjectName].style.css file we talked about earlier.

What is an NPM package?

As a .NET developer, you can view NPM (Node package manager) packages as the JavaScript equivalent of NuGet packages.

These packages are kept in an online repository at www.npmjs.org/ and are installable via the NPM CLI tool, which is installed as part of Node.js.

We need some SCSS to compile, so we'll add a new file called TrailDetails.razor.scss with the code shown in the following listing.

Listing 3.14   TrailDetails.razor.scss

```scss
.drawer-mask {
    visibility: hidden;
    position: fixed;
    overflow: hidden;
    top: 0;
    right: 0;
    left: 0;
    bottom: 0;
    z-index: 99;
    background-color: #000000;
    opacity: 0;
    transition: opacity 0.3s ease, visibility 0.3s ease;
}

.drawer-wrapper.slide {
    .drawer-mask {
        opacity: .5;
        visibility: visible;
    }

    .drawer {
        transform: translateX(0);
    }
}
```

This is the nesting feature from SCSS.

```scss
.drawer {
    display: flex;
    flex-direction: column;
    position: fixed;
    top: 0;
    right: 0;
    bottom: 0;
    width: 35em;
    overflow-y: auto;
    overflow-x: hidden;
    background-color: white;
    border-left: 0.063em solid gray;
    z-index: 100;
    transform: translateX(110%);
    transition: transform 0.3s ease, width 0.3s ease;
}

.drawer-content {
    display: flex;
    flex: 1;
    flex-direction: column;
}

.trail-details {
    padding: 20px;
}
```

```
.drawer-controls {
    padding: 20px;
    background-color: #ffffff;
}
```

This new SCSS version of the `TrailDetails` styles has only one slight modification: it's using the nesting feature from SCSS. It will allow us to confirm that the compilation steps worked and that the SCSS generates CSS.

In the root of BlazingTrails.Client, we will create a new file called package.json and add the lines of code shown in the following listing.

Listing 3.15   Package.json

```
{
    "scripts": {
        "sass": "sass"      ◁── The custom script sass calls the sass command-line tool.
    },
    "devDependencies": {
        "sass": "1.44.0"    ◁── This is the declaration of the build time dependency on the sass package.
    }
}
```

This file does two things: it specifies the Sass package as a development time dependency of our application, and it exposes a script that will allow us to call Sass from MSBuild.

The other updates we need to make are in the csproj file for our app. We will define a set of build targets that MSBuild will run through on each build before the application is compiled (figure 3.18).

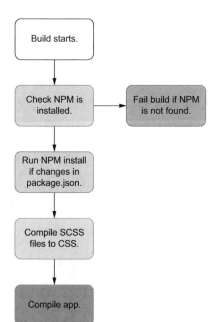

Figure 3.18   On each build, a check will be run to make sure NPM is installed. If it's not, then the build will fail. Next, if any changes have been made to the project.json file, like updating a package version, then `npm install` will be run. Finally, any SCSS files will be compiled to CSS before the application is compiled.

The first target will check if NPM is installed on the system and fail the build if it's not found. If NPM is present, then a check will be made for any changes to the package.json file. If any changes are detected, then `npm install` is run to make any updates. Once that is complete, we'll run the Sass compiler to compile any SCSS files to CSS. Listing 3.16 shows the configuration in the csproj file.

NOTE   Be sure to double-check the following changes to the csproj file. Errors may result in build errors or changes to SCSS files not being picked up.

Listing 3.16   BlazingTrails.Client.csproj

```xml
<Project Sdk="Microsoft.NET.Sdk.BlazorWebAssembly">

  <PropertyGroup>
    <TargetFramework>net6.0</TargetFramework>
    <Nullable>enable</Nullable>
    <ImplicitUsings>enable</ImplicitUsings>
    <NpmLastInstall>node_modules/.last-install
    ⇒</NpmLastInstall>
  </PropertyGroup>

  <ItemGroup>
    <PackageReference Include="Microsoft.AspNetCore.Components.WebAssembly"
    ⇒Version="6.0.0" />
    <PackageReference Include="Microsoft.AspNetCore.Components.WebAssembly.
    ⇒DevServer" Version="6.0.0" PrivateAssets="all" />
  </ItemGroup>

  <ItemGroup>
    <Watch Include="**/*.scss" />
    <None Update="**/*.css" Watch="false" />
  </ItemGroup>

  <Target Name="CheckForNpm" BeforeTargets="RunNpmInstall">
    <Exec Command="npm --version"
    ⇒ContinueOnError="true">
      <Output TaskParameter="ExitCode"
      ⇒PropertyName="ErrorCode" />
    </Exec>
    <Error Condition="'$(ErrorCode)' != '0'"
    ⇒Text="NPM is required to build this project." />
  </Target>

  <Target Name="RunNpmInstall"
  ⇒BeforeTargets="CompileScopedScss" Inputs="package.json"
  ⇒Outputs="$(NpmLastInstall)">
    <Exec Command="npm install" />
    <Touch Files="$(NpmLastInstall)"
    ⇒AlwaysCreate="true" />
  </Target>

  <Target Name="CompileScopedScss"
  ⇒BeforeTargets="Compile">
```

Defines a file that is used to record the last time an NPM install was performed

If running the app using dotnet watch, this tells the watch command to only rebuild the app when changes are made to SCSS files and not the CSS file. Without this, we end up in an infinite loop.

Runs the command npm --version to check if NPM is installed. If a nonzero error code is returned, then NPM is not installed and an error is shown on the build.

Run npm install but only when package.json is newer than NpmLastInstall specified in the PropertyGroup. This means npm install will only be run when something has changed and not on every build.

```
<ItemGroup>
  <ScopedScssFiles
  ➥Include="Features/**/*.razor.scss" />
</ItemGroup>
```

> The ItemGroup searches for all scoped SCSS files inside the Features folder.

```
<Exec Command="npm run sass --
➥%(ScopedScssFiles.Identity)
➥%(relativedir)%(filename).css" />    ◄
</Target>
```

> This runs the sass npm package to compile any SCSS files to CSS via the script defined in the package.json file.

```
</Project>
```

First, we added a new item group. This isn't related to running the CSS preprocessing, but it solves an issue that appears when running the app using `dotnet watch`. This instructs the `watch` command to respond only to changes in SCSS files and not CSS files. Without this, developers running the app from the command line would end up in an infinite loop.

Next, we added a `Target` element called `CheckForNpm`. This runs first and will do exactly what its name describes. It executes the command `npm --version`, then checks if the error code is something other than 0. A 0 indicates that the command was run successfully. If it's not 0, then an error is thrown and the build will fail (figure 3.19).

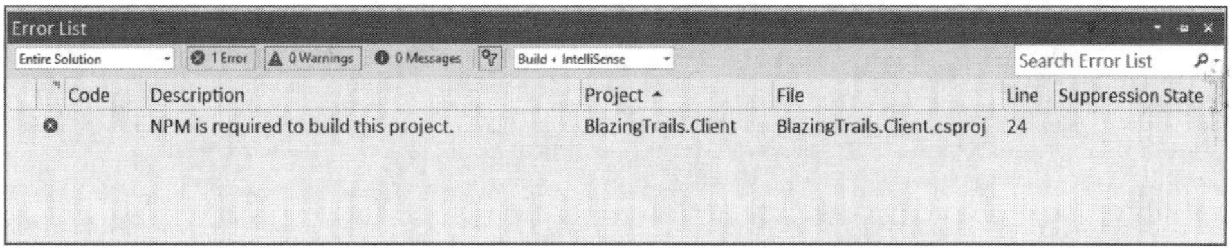

Figure 3.19 If NPM is not installed, the build will fail and produce the above error.

The second target, `RunNpmInstall`, is a conditional target and will run only if there is no node_modules folder, or the package.json has been updated in some way. This condition is checked by comparing the last modified timestamp from the package .json file (input) and the `NpmLastInstall` (output). `NpmLastInstall` is a property that is defined in the `PropertyGroup` section, and it contains the path to a file, `node_modules/.last-install`. This file is either created or written to any time it doesn't exist or whenever an update is made to package.json.

Finally, we come to the third target, `CompileScopedCSS`. This is the target that compiles any SCSS file into CSS. The list of files it compiles comes from the `ItemGroup` we added. It scans the application and retrieves a list of all the SCSS files that are in the Features folder.

With those changes in place, we can run a build for the application. The result is shown in figure 3.20.

**Checks for
NPM target**

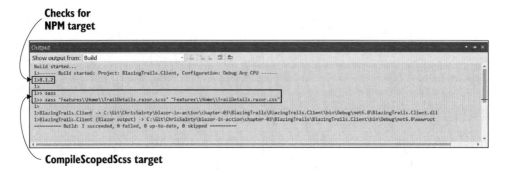

CompileScopedScss target

Figure 3.20   The build output shows each of the targets we defined being run before the main build happens.

Studying the build log, we can see two of the targets we added being run. The version number of NPM is output to the log by the first target. Then we see the Sass script being executed and our TrailDetails.razor.scss file being compiled into CSS. Depending on what version of Node you have installed, you may see some output from the `npm install` command as well. Figure 3.21 shows the compiled CSS file produced from the build process.

The new CSS file

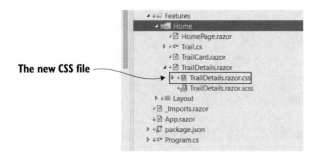

Figure 3.21   The newly generated CSS file produced during the build process

If we check the Home feature folder, there should be a new CSS file there, as shown in figure 3.21.

Summary

- Components can be structured in different ways: they can be defined in a single file containing both markup and logic, or they can be defined in two different files, one containing markup and the other the logic.
- Components have multiple life cycle methods that can be hooked into to perform actions at defined points on that life cycle.

- The three commonly used life cycle methods are `OnInitialized/On-InitializedAsync`, `OnParametersSet/OnParametersSetAsync`, and `OnAfterRender/OnAfterRenderAsync`.
- The `OnInitialized/OnInitializedAsync` method runs only once in the lifetime of a component. The other methods can run multiple times.
- Components can implement `IDisposable` or `IAsyncDisposable` to get access to an extra life cycle method, `Dispose/DisposeAsync`.
- Parent components can pass data into child components using component parameters.
- Component parameters form the public API of a component.
- Events can be defined as component parameters, which allow data to be passed from child to parent.
- Events defined using component parameters are just delegates.
- A parent handling a child component's event, defined as either `Action/Action<T>` or `Func/Func<T>`, must call `StateHasChanged` manually to trigger any required UI updates.
- Child components can define their events using the type `EventCallback` or `EventCallback<T>`, which will automatically call `StateHasChanged` on the parent component once the handler has been run.
- Components can be styled using global CSS, scoped CSS, or a mix of both.
- Scoped styles are created by defining a stylesheet with the naming convention `[ComponentName].razor.css`.
- If mixing global and scoped styles, it's important to remember that global styles can still affect components using scoped CSS.
- It's possible to use CSS preprocessors such as SCSS with Blazor's scoped CSS feature.

Routing

4

This chapter covers

- Distinguishing traditional routing from client-side routing
- Defining page components
- Triggering navigation programmatically
- Passing data via the URL
- Working with query strings

Routing, or navigation, is a fundamental concept when building web applications. Traditionally, moving from one page to another was a case of loading an entirely new, physical HTML page from the server. In more modern server-based frameworks such as MVC or Razor Pages, those pages are dynamically compiled on the server before being sent to the client, but the process is still the same. However, in single-page applications, things work a little differently.

As always, to help you learn about the concepts we're going to uncover in this chapter, we'll be building a new feature into Blazing Trails. Figure 4.1 shows how the feature will look once we're done.

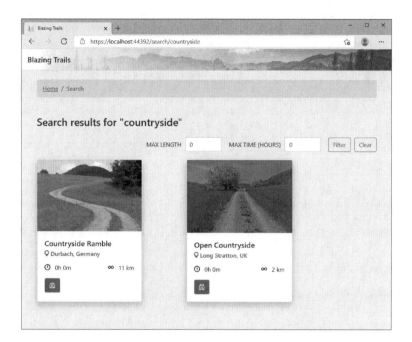

Figure 4.1   The new search feature we'll be building in this chapter

This time around, we'll be adding a search function to the app. This is going to allow the user to search for a trail by name or location. We'll use routing to navigate from the home page to the search page programmatically, passing the search term via the URL. Once on the search page, we'll extract it and then find any trails that match the term.

We'll also build the ability to filter any results. We'll explore a couple of ways to do this using multiple route templates and query strings that will allow the user to bookmark the search, including any filters, and be able to directly reload the results.

4.1   Introducing client-side routing

Client-side routing differs substantially from traditional navigation in server-based web applications. To navigate to another page in traditional multipage apps, a request is made to the server for the new page. The new page is then downloaded to the browser, and the browser renders it. With SPAs, generally speaking, all of the pages reside on the client and navigating between them is handled by a client-side router.

4.1.1   Blazor's router

In Blazor, the router is just another component, and you can find it inside the App component (App.razor). Listing 4.1 shows the Router component.

Listing 4.1   The router component found in the App.razor file

The router uses reflection to scan for page components. The AppAssembly parameter is used to tell the router where to scan.

The Found template is where page components that match a requested route are loaded.

```
<Router AppAssembly="@typeof(Program).Assembly">
    <Found Context="routeData">
        <RouteView RouteData="@routeData"
                   DefaultLayout="@typeof(MainLayout)" />
        <FocusOnNavigate RouteData="@routeData" Selector="h1" />
    </Found>
    <NotFound>
        <PageTitle>Not found</PageTitle>
        <LayoutView Layout="@typeof(MainLayout)">
            <p>Sorry, there's nothing at this address.</p>
        </LayoutView>
    </NotFound>
</Router>
```

The NotFound template is shown when the router can't find a match for the requested route in its routing table.

When a Blazor app first loads, the `Router` component uses reflection to scan the application's assemblies to find *routable components*, or what I prefer to call *page components*. These are components that have a special directive declared in them called `@page`. It knows what assembly to scan via the `AppAssembly` parameter. In larger applications, it's possible that page components could be in multiple assemblies. In this case, the `Router` component has an `AdditionalAssemblies` parameter that can be defined that takes an `IEnumerable<Assembly>`.

The `@page` directive allows us to specify what route the component will be loaded for. The router then stores the type of the component and the route it handles in a routing table. The router then listens for navigation events via the process described in figure 4.2.

When a link is clicked, a navigation event is triggered. Blazor has infrastructure that lives in the JavaScript world, and one of the things that code does is intercept various events, including navigation events.

The URL that the link points to is passed to a JavaScript service called `NavigationManager`; this service performs several checks to verify that the event should be handled by client-side routing. These checks include ensuring

- Blazor's router is active.
- No modifier keys were pressed, such as Shift or Control, which would signal the user wanted to open the link in a new tab/window.
- No target attribute was present on the link. Again, this would signal that the link should be opened in another tab/window. The only exception to this is a target of `_self`; this means open in the current tab/window.
- The link falls within the scope of the base tag defined in the host page of the Blazor app.

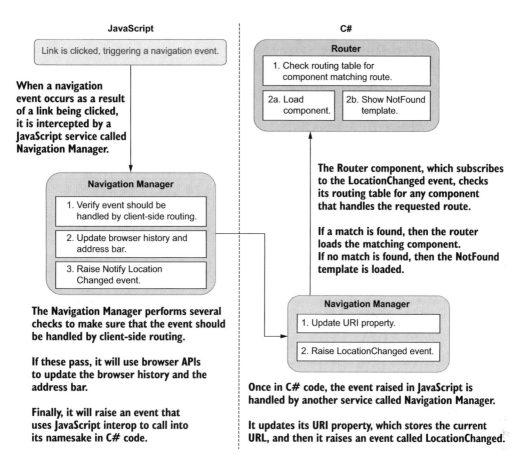

JavaScript

Link is clicked, triggering a navigation event.

When a navigation event occurs as a result of a link being clicked, it is intercepted by a JavaScript service called Navigation Manager.

Navigation Manager

1. Verify event should be handled by client-side routing.

2. Update browser history and address bar.

3. Raise Notify Location Changed event.

The Navigation Manager performs several checks to make sure that the event should be handled by client-side routing.

If these pass, it will use browser APIs to update the browser history and the address bar.

Finally, it will raise an event that uses JavaScript interop to call into its namesake in C# code.

C#

Router

1. Check routing table for component matching route.

2a. Load component.   2b. Show NotFound template.

The Router component, which subscribes to the LocationChanged event, checks its routing table for any component that handles the requested route.

If a match is found, then the router loads the matching component. If no match is found, then the NotFound template is loaded.

Navigation Manager

1. Update URI property.

2. Raise LocationChanged event.

Once in C# code, the event raised in JavaScript is handled by another service called Navigation Manager.

It updates its URI property, which stores the current URL, and then it raises an event called LocationChanged.

Figure 4.2   The process of a link being clicked through to a page component being loaded that handles the requested route specified in the link

If all these checks pass, then the browser's history will be updated along with the Uniform Resource Identifier (URI). This enables features such as the browser's Forward and Back buttons to function and the appearance of traditional full-page navigation. The final step the service takes is to raise an event that triggers some JavaScript interop. This event is picked up by a service with the same name, `Navigation-Manager`, that lives in the C# world.

When the C# `NavigationManager` receives the event, it updates its URI property. This property stores the current URL so components can access it if required. It then triggers an event called `LocationChanged`. Blazor's router subscribes to this event, and when it fires, the router checks the URI property of the `NavigationManager` against its routing table to find a match. If one is found, then the component is loaded; otherwise a `NotFound` template is rendered.

4.1.2   *Defining page components*

Page components are regular components that declare a specific directive—the @page directive. It has two parts, the directive name and the route template, and when declared looks like this:

```
@page "/my-awesome-page"
```

The route template is the section in quotes. This defines the URL that the component will handle—it must always start with a forward slash (/); otherwise you will receive a compiler error. Also, route templates must be unique. Be careful not to declare the same route template on multiple components, as this will result in a run-time error. As we'll see later, it's perfectly fine to have a single component declare multiple @page directives and handle multiple routes.

To begin building our new search feature for Blazing Trails, let's add a new page component to the application. Add a new Razor component in the Features > Home folder called SearchPage.razor with the code shown in the following listing.

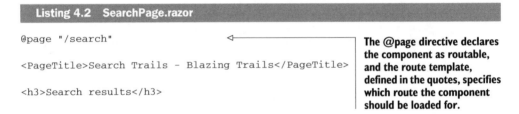

Listing 4.2   SearchPage.razor

```
@page "/search"                              ◁————————————    The @page directive declares
                                                             the component as routable,
<PageTitle>Search Trails - Blazing Trails</PageTitle>        and the route template,
                                                             defined in the quotes, specifies
<h3>Search results</h3>                                      which route the component
                                                             should be loaded for.
```

As you can see in this listing, defining page components is quite simple. The @page directive is added at the top of the page, and then the route that the component should handle is specified using the route template in quotes.

As I mentioned previously, the route template must be in quotes and must start with a /. If this is missing, then you will get a build error from the compiler.

You can now build the app and run it. You will need to type in the address of the search page manually, as we haven't linked to it yet. Figure 4.3 shows how the new page looks.

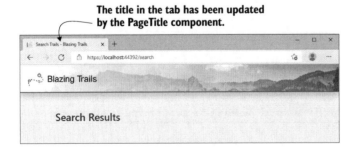

Figure 4.3   Our app's new search page

This isn't very inspiring right now, but in the next section we'll create the search box that will link to this page.

4.2 Navigating between pages programmatically

One of the first things we learn when building web pages is how to link one page to another using hyperlinks. This method is still a staple of modern SPA applications and works exactly as it would in a traditional server-based app, but there are many scenarios where programmatic navigation is required.

In Blazor, programmatic navigation is achieved via the `NavigationManager` `.NavigateTo()` method. We'll use this to redirect users after they've entered their search term. But first, we need to create a new component in the Home feature folder called `TrailSearch.razor`. This component will house the search box and logic for redirecting to the `SearchPage`. The following listing shows the code.

Listing 4.3 TrailSearch.razor

```
@inject NavigationManager NavManager    ◁── An instance of the NavigationManager
                                             is injected using the @inject directive.
<div class="jumbotron">
    <h1 class="display-4 text-center">Welcome to Blazing Trails</h1>
    <p class="lead text-center">Find the most beautiful hiking trails
    ↪using our blazing fast search!</p>
    <p class="mt-4">
        <input @onkeydown="SearchForTrail"    The @bind directive allows two-way binding
               @bind="_searchTerm"             in Blazor. Here we're binding the text the
               @bind:event="oninput"      ◁── user inputs to the _searchTerm field.
               type="text"
               placeholder="Search for a trail..."
               class="form-control form-control-lg" />
    </p>
</div>

@code {
    private string _searchTerm = "";

    private void SearchForTrail(KeyboardEventArgs args)
    {
        if (args.Key != "Enter") return;
        NavManager.NavigateTo($"/search/{_searchTerm}");
    }
}
```

The SearchForTrail method is called every time a keydown event is fired.

Update the _searchTerm field whenever the oninput event fires, essentially when a new character is entered.

Return if the key pressed wasn't the Enter key.

Use NavigationManager.NavigateTo to programmatically navigate to the search page, passing the search term entered by the user.

From the user's perspective, they are going to enter their search phrase into the search box and then press Enter to trigger the search. To achieve this, we're injecting an instance of the `NavigationManager`, which we use in the `SearchForTrail` method to redirect the user to the search page.

The other point of interest here is the `@bind` directive. We'll see more of this in chapter 5 when we talk about forms and validation, but this is how we perform two-way binding in Blazor. Here we're binding the value typed into the input to the _search-Term field:

```
@bind="_searchTerm"
```

By default, this binding happens when the control loses focus. In our case, the control never loses focus, so when the SearchForTrail method is called, the value of _searchTerm would still be null. To fix this, we've changed the event the bind directive uses to update the bound value:

```
@bind:event="oninput"
```

Instead of the default onchange event, we're using the oninput event, which updates the _searchTerm field every time a new character is typed into the input. Now, when the SearchForTrail method is called, the _searchTerm field is populated correctly.

We're also going to add some scoped styles for the TrailSearch component. Add a new SCSS file in the Home folder called *TrailSearch.razor.scss*, and add the code shown in the following listing.

Listing 4.4   TrailSearch.razor.scss

```
.jumbotron {
    background: none;

    input {
        border: 2px solid var(--brand);
    }
}
```

This will remove the default background color of the Bootstrap jumbotron. It also adds a border to the search input.

We just need to add our new TrailSearch component to the HomePage. The following listing shows a subsection of the HomePage component where the Trail-Search should be added.

Listing 4.5   HomePage.razor with the new TrailSearch component

```
<TrailDetails Trail="_selectedTrail" />

<TrailSearch />                    ⟵──┐  The TrailSearch component is referenced
<div class="grid">                       directly under the TrailDetails component.
    @foreach (var trail in _trails)
    {
        <TrailCard Trail="trail" OnSelected="HandleTrailSelected" />
    }
</div>
```

Once the HomePage component is updated, we can run the application to check everything is working as expected (figure 4.4).

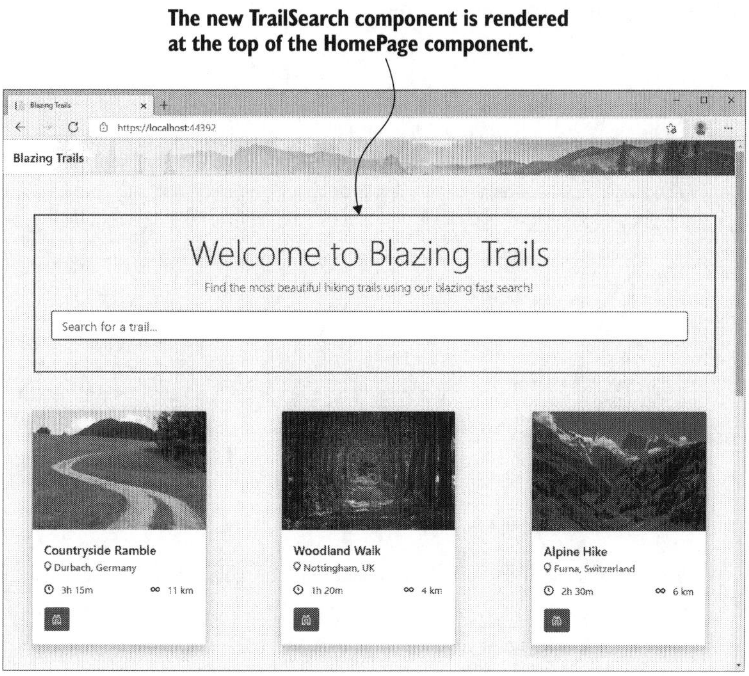

**The new TrailSearch component is rendered
at the top of the HomePage component.**

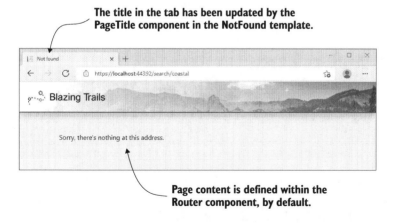

Figure 4.4   The home page updated with the new `TrailSearch` component.

Initially everything is looking great. The `TrailSearch` is rendering as expected, but
if we type in a search phase and press Return, we see a message stating there's nothing
at this address (figure 4.5).

**The title in the tab has been updated by the
PageTitle component in the NotFound template.**

**Page content is defined within the
Router component, by default.**

**Figure 4.5   Navigating to the search page shows a message indicating that
there is no component handling this route.**

This message is produced by Blazor's router and is configurable in the `NotFound` template section, shown in the following listing.

Listing 4.6   The router component's NotFound template

```
<Router AppAssembly="@typeof(Program).Assembly">
    <Found Context="routeData">
        <RouteView RouteData="@routeData"
                   DefaultLayout="@typeof(MainLayout)" />
        <FocusOnNavigate RouteData="@routeData" Selector="h1" />
    </Found>
    <NotFound>                            ◁──────  The NotFound template
        <PageTitle>Not found</PageTitle>          defines what is shown when
        <LayoutView Layout="@typeof(MainLayout)">  no component can be found
            <p>Sorry, there's nothing at this      to handle a given route.
              address.</p>     ◁─────  This is the default message
        </LayoutView>                    shown for an invalid route.
    </NotFound>
</Router>
```

The router's `NotFound` template can be used to customize what is shown when a route doesn't have a component to handle it. By default, the router is configured to display some HTML with the message "Sorry, there's nothing at this address." But you could change this to display a component instead of arbitrary HTML if you prefer.

We're seeing this because our `SearchPage` has the following route template:

```
@page "/search"
```

But we're passing the search term as part of the URL, `"/search/coastal"`. Blazor matches routes to components by breaking down the URL into segments and then doing a string comparison on each segment. In this case there would be two segments:

- Search
- Coastal

The router also does this when it stores the route template of a page component. Our `SearchPage`'s route template has only one segment:

- Search

When the router compares the requested route to the one stored in its routing table, they don't match, as the count is wrong. But even if the count matched, the next check is a string comparison and we can't have every possible term a user might search on in a route template. This is where route parameters come into play. Let's look at those next.

4.3   *Passing data between pages using route parameters*

When navigating between pages, there are times we want to pass arbitrary data as part of the URL—a case in point being our trail search needing to pass the search term to the search page. We can do this by using a special feature of route templates called *template parameters.*

Template parameters are sections of a route that are dynamic, rather than static text. You can think of them in the same way as arguments on a method. They are placeholders for a value that will be supplied later. They are paired with a component parameter that matches the name of the route parameter. When the component is executed, the value in the segment of the route defined by the route parameter is passed into the component parameter so we can access it in code.

The following listing shows the `SearchPage` component updated with a route parameter to capture the search term.

Listing 4.7   SearchPage.razor: Route template with route parameter

```
@page "/search/{SearchTerm}"

<h3>Search results for "@SearchTerm"</h3>

@code {
    [Parameter]
    public string SearchTerm { get; set; } = default!;
}
```

Route parameters are defined using curly braces in a route segment.

A component parameter matching the name of the route parameter is required to capture its value.

We've defined the second section of the route template to be a route parameter called `SearchTerm`. Route parameters are defined inside a route segment by using curly braces (`{}`); there can be only one per segment. We've also declared a component parameter with a name that matches that of the route parameter—the match is case-insensitive. We've also initialized the new parameter to its default value and applied the null forgiving operator. This is because it can't be null. If there is no search term in the URL, then Blazor's router won't match the component and it won't be loaded.

To prove that everything is working, the page heading has been updated to show the search term. If we run the app, type in a search term, and press Enter, we should now see the `SearchPage` displaying the term we searched for (figure 4.6).

The search term is now displayed in the header.

Figure 4.6   Typing a search term now correctly loads the `SearchPage` component and displays the term that was searched for.

Everything is now working as expected, and we can access the search term programmatically. Next we can add the logic so the search page displays matching trails. Listing 4.8 shows the updated code for `SearchPage.razor`.

Listing 4.8 Loading trails that match the search term

```
@page "/search/{searchterm}"
@inject HttpClient Http
@inject NavigationManager NavManager

<nav aria-label="breadcrumb">
    <ol class="breadcrumb">
        <li class="breadcrumb-item">
            <a href="/">Home</a>
        </li>
        <li class="breadcrumb-item active"
        ➥aria-current="page">Search</li>
    </ol>
</nav>

<h3 class="mt-5 mb-4">Search results for "@SearchTerm"</h3>

@if (_searchResults == null)
{
    <p>Loading search results...</p>
}
else
{
    <TrailDetails Trail="_selectedTrail" />
    <div class="grid">
        @foreach (var trail in _searchResults)
        {
            <TrailCard Trail="trail" OnSelected="HandleTrailSelected" />
        }
    </div>
}

@code {
    private IEnumerable<Trail>? _searchResults;
    private Trail? _selectedTrail;

    [Parameter] public string SearchTerm { get; set; } = default!;

    protected override async Task OnInitializedAsync()
    {
        try
        {
            var allTrails = await Http.GetFromJsonAsync
            ➥<IEnumerable<Trail>>("trails/trail-data.json");
            _searchResults = allTrails!
            ➥.Where(x => x.Name.Contains(SearchTerm,
            ➥StringComparison.CurrentCultureIgnoreCase) ||
            ➥x.Location.Contains(SearchTerm,
            ➥StringComparison.CurrentCultureIgnoreCase));
        }
        catch (HttpRequestException ex)
        {
            Console.WriteLine($"There was a problem loading trail data:
            ➥{ex.Message}");
        }
    }
```

Breadcrumbs allow navigation back to the home page.

When the component is loaded, it will get all the trails from the dummy data file and find any that have a name or location that contains the search term.

Technically, the call to GetFromJsonAsync returns a null. However, we have specific test data so we can safely ignore the potential null using the null forgiving operator.

```
    private void HandleTrailSelected(Trail trail)
        => _selectedTrail = trail;
}
```

While we've added a fair amount of code, most of it is familiar. The markup for displaying trails is essentially the same as we used on the `HomePage`. We've also included the `TrailDetails` component so the user can still click on a trail to view its details.

One extra feature is the breadcrumb section at the top of the page. This is to allow easy navigation back to the home page without having to use the browser's Back button. Another slight change is the logic in `OnInitializedAsync`, which loads the trails. We're now using a bit of Linq to filter the trails down to only those that contain the search term in either their name or location. Running the app and typing in a search term should now show any trails that match the term (figure 4.7).

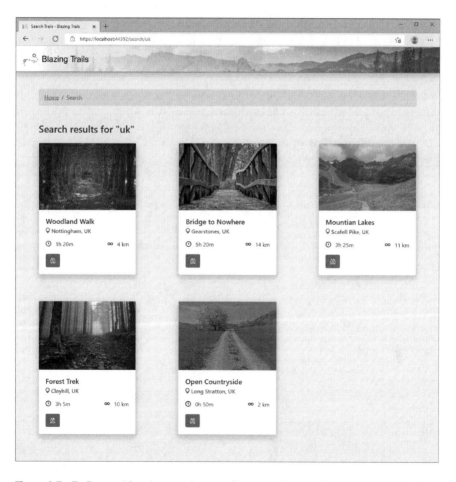

Figure 4.7 Trails matching the search term will now be displayed in a similar style to the home page.

Things are looking rather good for our search page. It now correctly displays trails that match the search term. But wouldn't it be nice if we could also filter the results on the trail's length? This seems like a useful addition to our search, and it would also give us a chance to look at multiple routes and route constraints.

4.4   *Handling multiple routes with a single component*

It's possible to have a single component be responsible for multiple routes. This can be useful for several reasons—for example, if you're moving to a new URL structure and you need to support both the old and new versions for a period. Another example is functionality reuse, and this is what we will implement next.

We're going to add a max length filter to our search results page. This will allow the user to limit search results to trails that have a length less than or equal to its value. We could filter the results using a method on the component and not update the URL at all; this would be quite simple. However, this approach wouldn't allow the users of Blazing Trails to bookmark their search filters.

Instead, we'll add a second route to the SearchPage component that will contain the max length filter. Then, if a filter is entered, we will redirect the user to the same page using the second route. We can then reuse all the existing functionality with a small addition to handle the max length filter.

First, we'll add an additional page directive to the SearchPage and a component parameter to store its value. See the following listing.

> **Listing 4.9   SearchPage.razor: Shows multiple @page directives**

```
@page "/search/{SearchTerm}"
@page "/search/{SearchTerm}/maxlength/{MaxLength:int}"      ◄─────┐  Shows the
                                                                  │  original @page
// Other code omitted                                             │  directive and
                                                                  │  matching
@code {                                                           │  component
    [Parameter]                                                   │  parameter
    public string SearchTerm { get; set; } = default!;            │
                                                              ◄───┘
    [Parameter]                                                      Shows the new @page
    public int? MaxLength { get; set; }                        ◄──── directive and matching
                                                                     component parameter
    // Other code omitted
}
```

There is a subtle but significant difference in the definition of the second @page directive's route template. Where the MaxLength route parameter is defined, there is some additional syntax: :int. This is called a *route constraint*.

Route constraints are important when dealing with route parameters that need to be worked with as a nonstring type. By default, all route parameters are considered strings by Blazor. This is a sensible default, as URLs are strings; therefore, values that are passed in the URL must be able to be represented as a string. But in our case, we need to work with `MaxLength` as an integer in our code.

We can tell Blazor that the value in that route parameter must be converted to an integer by using the `:int` route constraint. Once a route constraint has been applied, it becomes part of the checks Blazor performs to match a route.

Given our route template, if we try to load the page using the following route, `/search/uk/maxlength/ten`, Blazor would not consider this a match, as `ten` can't be converted to an integer value. However, the route `/search/uk/maxlength/10` would match, as `10` is a valid integer.

For a full list of all route constraints supported by the framework, you can check the following page on the official docs (http://mng.bz/d2xg).

With the additional route in place, we can turn our attention to adding the code needed for filtering. We'll create the search filter as a new component called `Search-Filter.razor` in the Home feature folder. The following listing shows the code.

Listing 4.10   SearchFilter.razor

```
@inject NavigationManager NavManager

<div class="filters">
    <label for="maxLength">Max Length</label>
    <input id="maxLength"
           type="number"
           class="form-control"
           @bind="_maxLength" />          ◁──┐ The value entered by the user is
                                              │ bound to the _maxLength field.
    <button class="btn btn-outline-primary"
            @onclick="FilterSearchResults">   ◁──┐ Clicking the Filter button executes
        Filter                                   │ the FilterSearchResults method.
    </button>
    <button class="btn btn-outline-secondary"
            @onclick="ClearSearchFilter">     ◁──┐ Clearing an existing filter is handled
        Clear                                    │ by the ClearSearchFilter method.
    </button>
</div>

@code {
    private int _maxLength;

    [Parameter, EditorRequired]
    public string SearchTerm { get; set; } = default!;    To filter the search
                                                          result, we navigate
    private void FilterSearchResults()                    to the second route
        => NavManager.NavigateTo(                         we defined for the
        ➥$"/search/{SearchTerm}/maxlength/{_maxLength}");  ◁── component.

    private void ClearSearchFilter()
    {
        _maxLength = 0;
```

```
        NavManager.NavigateTo($"/search/{SearchTerm}");
    }
}
```

To clear the filter, we navigate to the original route.

The `SearchFilter` component uses an HTML input to record the desired max trail length from the user. When the Filter button is clicked, the `NavigationManager`
`.NavigateTo` method is used to redirect the user to the second route we added to the `SearchPage` component. To do this, the `SearchFilter` component needs to know the search term, so we're specifying that as a component parameter to be supplied by the `SearchPage`. To clear a filter, the Clear button redirects the user to the original route.

We will also add a few styles to make the search filter sit to the right of the page. Let's add a new Sass file called *SearchFilter.razor.scss* into the Home feature folder with the styles shown in the following listing.

Listing 4.11   SearchFilter.razor.scss: SearchFilter styling

```scss
.filters {
    display: flex;
    margin-bottom: 20px;
    align-items: baseline;
    justify-content: flex-end;

    label {
        text-transform: uppercase;
        margin-right: 10px;
    }

    input {
        margin-right: 20px;
        width: 100px;
    }

    button:first-of-type {
        margin-right: 10px;
    }
}
```

With the styles in place, we just need to reference the `SearchFilter` component in the `SearchPage`. We'll add it just under the page header:

```
<h3 class="mt-5 mb-4">Search results for "@SearchTerm"</h3>
<SearchFilter SearchTerm="@SearchTerm" />
```

Running the app now should produce the UI shown in figure 4.8.

The last task we have is to implement the filtering functionality (listing 4.12). Notice that entering a max length and pressing filter will update the URL, but the search results are not updated.

The new SearchFilter component

Figure 4.8   The new `SearchFilter` component rendered into the `SearchPage`

Listing 4.12   SearchPage.razor: Logic to filter search results

```
private IEnumerable<Trail> _cachedSearchResults
= Array.Empty<Trail>();                           ⟵─┐ Stores a copy of the
                                                      │ unfiltered search results
// Other code omitted

protected override async Task OnInitializedAsync()
{
    try
    {
        var allTrails = await Http.GetFromJsonAsync
        <IEnumerable<Trail>>("trails/trail-data.json");
        _searchResults = allTrails!.Where(x => x.Name.Contains(SearchTerm,
        StringComparison.CurrentCultureIgnoreCase)
        || x.Location.Contains(SearchTerm,
        StringComparison.CurrentCultureIgnoreCase));
        _cachedSearchResults = _searchResults;      ⟵─┐ Stores a copy of the
    }                                                  │ unfiltered search results
    catch (HttpRequestException ex)
    {
        Console.WriteLine($"There was a problem loading trail data:
        {ex.Message}");
    }
}

protected override void OnParametersSet()
{
    if (_cachedSearchResults.Any()         │ Check for cached search results and a filter value;
        && MaxLength.HasValue)             │ if both are present, then filter the results.
```

```
{
    _searchResults = _cachedSearchResults
    ➥.Where(x => x.Length <= MaxLength.Value);
}
else if (_cachedSearchResults.Any()      | If there are cached search results but no filter,
        && MaxLength is null)             | then reset the results to the unfiltered set.
{
    _searchResults = _cachedSearchResults;
}
}
```

Looking at this code, you might be asking why we are doing the filtering in the `OnParametersSet` life cycle method and not in the `OnInitialized` life cycle method. Let me explain.

When we enter a filter, the URL is updated but the `SearchPage` component is not destroyed and re-created. When changing routes, Blazor performs a diff just like it would with any other UI update. In our case, we're navigating to the same component that is already rendered, so nothing in the UI needs to change.

As we learned in chapter 3, the `OnInitialized` life cycle method executes only once in a component's life cycle. Therefore, it won't execute when we add a filter. This means our filter code must go somewhere else. The correct life cycle method is `OnParametersSet`—this will get executed every time the filter is updated.

Our `SearchPage` component is now complete. Users can search for trails and then filter the results based on how far they wish to hike and even bookmark the results for easy access another time. Figure 4.9 shows the `SearchPage` with an active filter.

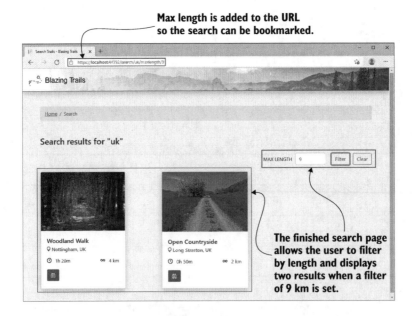

Figure 4.9   The finished `SearchPage` component with an active max length filter applied

In the last section of this chapter, I want to show you an alternative approach to our filter feature. Instead of using multiple routes, we can use query strings. Query strings are not supported by Blazor out of the box and require some extra configuration to use correctly, but they are a common feature of web applications, and knowing how to work with them in Blazor is a useful skill.

4.5 *Working with query strings*

Query strings have been an integral part of web applications since the early days of web development. A *query string* is an instance or collection of key-value pairs at the end of a URL. An example query string looks like this:

```
www.blazor.net?blazor=awesome
```

The query string starts with a question mark (?), then comes the key-value pair separated by an equals sign (=). Query strings can be a good option when you want to work with multiple optional values. Take our search filter feature: using a route to store the max length is fine, but imagine we added an additional filter, max time. This means we need to update our filter route to the following:

```
@page "/search/{SearchTerm}/maxlength/{MaxLength:int}/maxtime/{Hours:int}"
```

Route matching only works when all segments are present, so if the user selects only max hours, what do we do about max length? We could give it a default value of 0 and update our logic to check for zero instead of null. Or we could add another route to the page that contained max time but not max length.

Either of these would solve the issue, but what happens if we added another and another? This solution just doesn't scale with lots of optional values.

With query strings, we can include as many or as few key-value pairs as we wish. Because query strings sit outside of Blazor's routing system, we don't need to declare lots of route templates to cover all combinations of values.

Before .NET 6, working with query strings in Blazor was a completely manual process—there was nothing built into the framework to help us. However, with .NET 6, two important features were added that make working with query strings a breeze: the `SupplyParameterFromQuery` attribute and the query-string helper methods on `NavigationManager`. We will use these features to help improve the design of our trail search filters.

4.5.1 *Setting query-string values*

We're going to add an additional filter to our search that allows the user to filter trails based on how long they take to walk in hours. We'll call this `max time`. This means that users will be able to filter results based on either max length, max time, or both.

We'll start in the `SearchFilter` component and add a new field to store the max time as well as a new label and HTML input to record it (listing 4.13).

Listing 4.13   SearchFilter.razor: New max time field

```
//Other code omitted

<label for="maxLength">Max Length</label>
<input id="maxLength"
       type="number"
       class="form-control"
       @bind="_maxLength" />
<label for="maxTime">Max Time (hours)</label>
<input id="maxTime"
       type="number"
       class="form-control"
       @bind="_maxTime" />

//Other code omitted

@code {
    private int _maxLength;
    private int _maxTime;

    // Other code omitted
}
```

The new HTML input is bound to the _maxTime field.

With the ability to record the max time from the user, we can update the Filter-SearchResults method to add our filters as query-string values instead of route parameters. We'll take advantage of the new query-string helpers introduced in .NET 6 to do this. The following listing shows the new FilterSearchResults method.

Listing 4.14   `FilterSearchResults` adding filters as query strings

```
private void FilterSearchResults()
{
    var uriWithQuerystring =
    NavManager.GetUriWithQueryParameters(
    new Dictionary<string, object?>()
    {
        [nameof(SearchPage.MaxLength)] =
        _maxLength == 0 ? null : _maxLength,
        [nameof(SearchPage.MaxTime)] =
        _maxTime == 0 ? null : _maxTime
    });

    NavManager.NavigateTo(uriWithQuerystring);
}
```

Constructs a URI containing the key-value pairs provided as a query string

If the value of a key is null, the method will omit the entry from the query string.

Navigates to the URI with the query string

We use the GetUriWithQueryParameters method to construct a new URI containing a query string. There are two overloads of this method. The one we're using will return the current URI with the supplied key-value pairs attached as a query string. The other overload takes two arguments, a URI and a dictionary. It returns a new URI using the supplied URI as the base with the query string attached.

There is also a singular version of this method available called `GetUriWith-QueryParameter`. This method takes a name and a value and returns the current URI with the supplied name and value as a query string.

The `GetUriWithQueryParameters` method takes a dictionary, and depending on the value of a key, it will include or omit that value from the query string. In our code, if either `_maxLength` or `_maxTime` are 0, we don't want to include that entry on the query string. By setting their value to null, they will be ignored when the query string is built.

Once we have our URI with a query string, we can navigate to it using the `NavigationManager.NavigateTo` method. One other piece of housekeeping we must do is add the new `_maxTime` field to the `ClearSearchFilter` method. This can be added just underneath the existing `_maxLength` field:

```
maxTime = 0;
```

Before we can run the app, we need to update the `SearchPage`. You'll notice that when we added the key-value pairs to the dictionary we passed into the `GetUriWith-QueryParameters` method, we used `nameof()` to define the name of the keys— referencing two properties on the `SearchPage`. This is a great technique to avoid magic strings; however, we need to add the `MaxTime` property, as it currently doesn't exist. We also need to make another small change while we're there.

4.5.2   *Retrieving query-string values using SupplyParameterFromQuery*

Our `SearchFilter` component is now constructing a URI with the relevant values contained in a query string. But how are we going to retrieve those values in the `SearchPage` so we can do something with them? Well, we're going to use parameters decorated with a special attribute called `SupplyParameterFromQuery`. When we create a parameter on a component and add this attribute, Blazor will attempt to set the value of the property based on a query string with a matching name. This is why using the `nameof()` technique is so useful: it ensures that the key name used in the query string always matches that of the destination parameter.

Let's update the `SearchPage`'s `MaxLength` parameter with the `Supply-ParameterFromQuery` attribute and add the new `MaxTime` parameter while we're at it. The resulting code should look like this:

```
[Parameter, SupplyParameterFromQuery] public int? MaxLength { get; set; }
[Parameter, SupplyParameterFromQuery] public int? MaxTime { get; set; }
```

Note that we're still including the `Parameter` attribute. The `SupplyParameter-FromQuery` attribute works with the `Parameter` attribute. If both aren't added, the property won't be set.

Now that we can receive the values from the query string, we can do something with them. We're going to add a new method, `UpdateFilters`, that will filter the search results based on the values of `MaxLength` and `MaxTime` (listing 4.15).

Listing 4.15   SearchPage.razor: `UpdateFilters` method

```
private void UpdateFilters()
{
    var filters = new List<Func<Trail, bool>>();

    if (MaxLength is not null && MaxLength > 0)
    {
        filters.Add(x => x.Length <= MaxLength);
    }
    if (MaxTime is not null && MaxTime > 0)
    {
        filters.Add(x => x.TimeInMinutes
        <= MaxTime * 60);
    }
    if (filters.Any())
    {
        _searchResults = _cachedSearchResults
        .Where(trail => filters.All(filter => filter(trail)));
    }
    else
    {
        _searchResults = _cachedSearchResults;
    }
}
```

The filters variable will hold a list of lambda expressions based on which search filters are present.

If a max length filter is defined, add the lambda to filter it to the filters list.

If a max time filter is defined, add the lambda to filter it to the filters list.

Otherwise, use the unfiltered cached search results.

If there are any filters, filter the cached search results using them.

The `UpdateFilters` method builds up a list of lambda expressions that are used to filter the cached search results. We check if a filter is defined (it's not null and has a value greater than 0) and add lambdas only for the filters that are present. If no filters are present, then we use the cached search results, as-is.

We now need to call the `UpdateFilters` method at the appropriate time. As query-string values are handled in the same way as any other parameters, when they change, the `OnParametersSet` life cycle method will be called. This means that we can update the current `OnParametersSet` implementation to just call the `Update-Filters` method.

```
protected override void OnParametersSet()
        => UpdateFilters();
```

We can now run the app and test out our search filters. Figure 4.10 shows the result of entering some values into the filters.

As we can see, the values entered into the search filters are now being added to the URL as a query string. The code we wrote is pulling those values out and filtering the original results list so only the trails matching our criteria are displayed.

There is one slight issue with our code. If you copy the URL and open the same address in another tab, you'll notice the values in the search filter inputs are not being set to those in the query string, even though the results are showing correctly (figure 4.11).

Setting the search filters and clicking Filter
updates the page with the filter values
added to the URL as a query string.

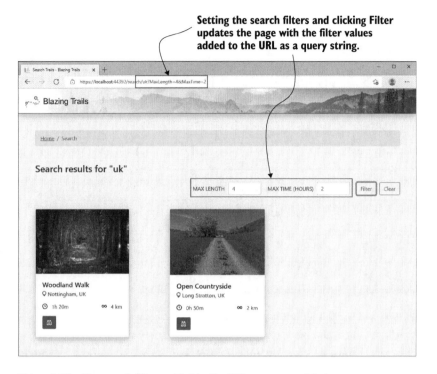

**Figure 4.10 The search filters added to the URL as a query string once
the Filter button is clicked**

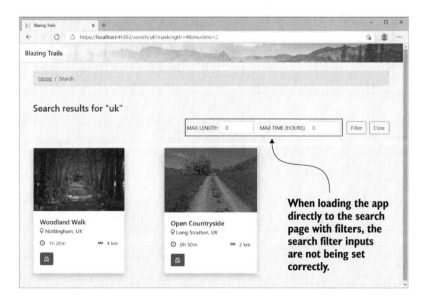

When loading the app
directly to the search
page with filters, the
search filter inputs
are not being set
correctly.

**Figure 4.11 When loading the app directly to the search page with filters, the
search inputs are not set correctly.**

To fix this, we need to pass in any existing search filters from the `SearchPage` to the `SearchFilter`. Let's add a new parameter for each of the filters to the Search-Filter component:

```
[Parameter] public int? MaxLength { get; set; }
[Parameter] public int? MaxTime { get; set; }
```

We can then initialize the values of the existing _maxLength and _maxTime fields to the value of the new parameters. As the parameters could be null, we'll use the null-coalescing operator, which will use the value of the parameter if it's not null or 0. We'll do this in `OnInitialized`:

```
protected override void OnInitialized()
{
    _maxLength = MaxLength ?? 0;
    _maxTime = MaxTime ?? 0;
}
```

Now we just need to update the `SearchPage` to pass in the `MaxLength` and `MaxTime` values to the `SearchFilter` component:

```
<SearchFilter SearchTerm="@SearchTerm" MaxLength="MaxLength"
    MaxTime="MaxTime" />
```

With that work complete, we can run the app again and check if everything is working as expected (figure 4.12).

Figure 4.12   The search filter values are now initialized correctly when navigating directly to the search page with filters.

As you can see, the search filters are now correctly being set to the values contained in the query string when loading the page directly.

Summary

- Navigation in Blazor is handled by a client-side router, which is a component.
- By default, the router component resides in the `App` component at the top of the app component tree.
- Pages in Blazor are just components that contain a special directive called `@page`.
- It is possible to define multiple page directives on a single component and have it load for more than one route.
- The page directive requires a route to be defined, which the component will handle.
- Reflection is used by the router to find pages; these are then stored in a table in memory by the router.
- When a route is requested, the router looks up which component handles the requested route. If a match for the route isn't found, then the markup defined in the router's `NotFound` template is displayed.
- Developers can trigger navigation programmatically using the `Navigation-Manager` service.
- The `NavigationManager` class exposes an event called `LocationChanged`, which is triggered whenever a navigation occurs. This can be subscribed to by developers to run custom actions.
- Simple data, such as IDs, can be passed between pages via route parameters.
- Route parameters are strings by default, and route constraints must be used if the developer wants to work with them as a different type; for example an `int`.
- Query string parameters can be added to the URL via the `GetUriWithQuery-Parameters` or `GetUriWithQueryParameter` methods available on the `NavigationManager` class.
- Page components can access query-string parameters in the URL by defining parameters that match the name of each query parameter, decorated with the `SupplyParameterFromQuery` attribute.

Forms and validation—
Part 1: Fundamentals

This chapter covers

- Creating forms using the `EditForm` component
- Capturing user input with built-in Blazor components
- Validating forms

This is the first of two chapters covering forms and validation in Blazor. In this first chapter, we will build a basic form that will allow us to add new trails into the app. In the next chapter, we'll add to our work, introducing more advanced features. Over the course of these chapters, we'll learn about all the great built-in components Blazor gives us, as well as the many extension points we can use to customize the various elements of our forms.

By the end of this chapter, we'll have built our first form with Blazor (figure 5.1). In order to do this, we'll need to validate the data collected using a library called Fluent Validation (https://fluentvalidation.net/) and persist it to a new API.

> **NOTE** If you're following along building the example application, you will need to complete appendix A before starting this chapter.

Figure 5.1 The finished add trail form we will be building throughout this chapter

With the ability to create trails via a form, we need to make some changes to the architecture of the application. Specifically, we'll be introducing an API into the solution along with a shared class library. The updated architecture of the application is shown in figure 5.2.

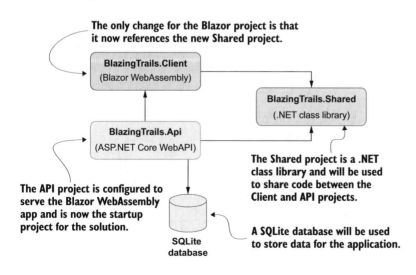

Figure 5.2 The new architecture for the Blazing Trails application. The API project will now serve the Blazor application and becomes the startup project for our solution. The Shared project will be used to share code between the API and Client projects. Any data will be stored in an SQLite database.

You may recognize this project structure from chapter 2, when we covered the templates available when creating new Blazor applications. This new project structure mirrors that of the Blazor WebAssembly ASP.NET Core Hosted template. The steps to add these new projects and configure them can be found in appendix A.

5.1 Super-charging forms with components

With Blazor, it's possible to work with HTML forms directly. However, that is not ideal. While collecting the data entered by the user and handling the form submit event is easy enough, there is still one major piece of functionality missing: validation. Validation is the main reason for using the form components provided by Blazor over a standard HTML form. Figure 5.3 gives an overview of the forms and validation system in Blazor.

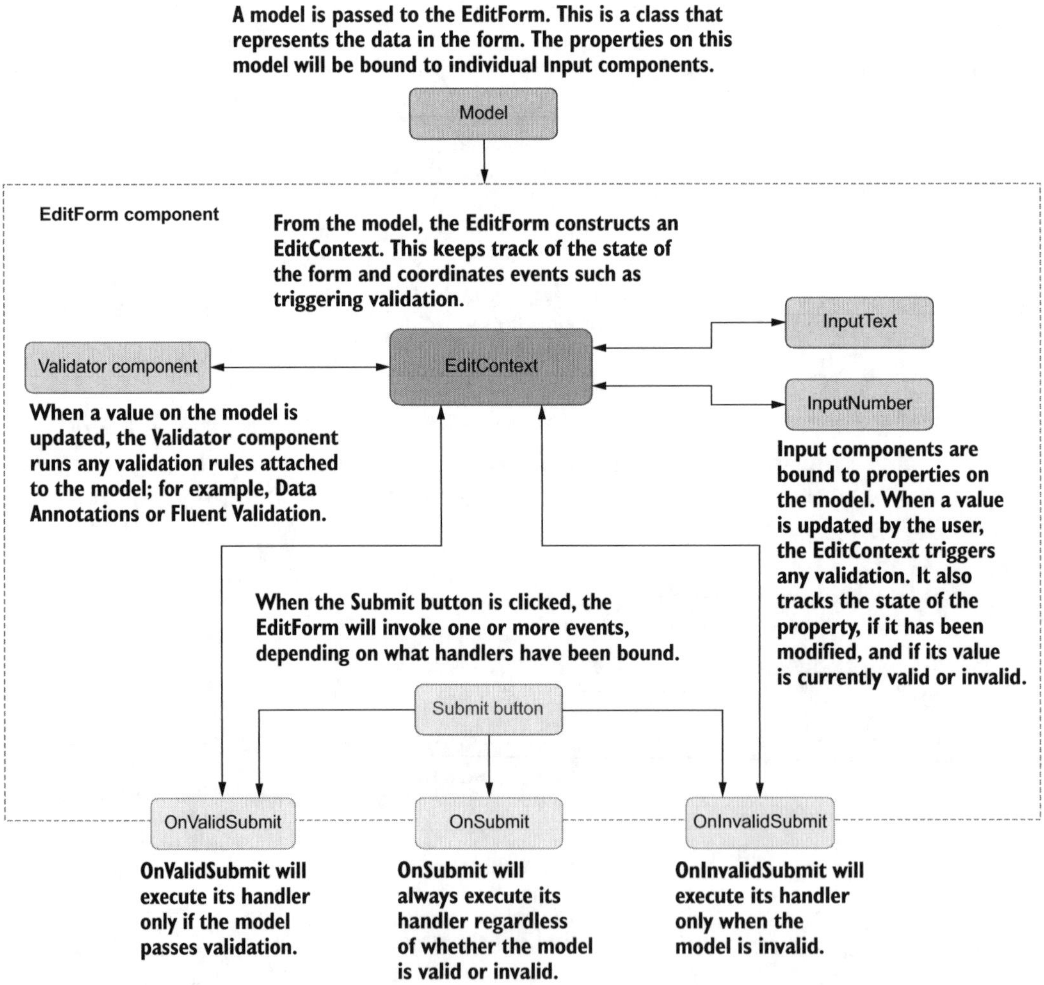

Figure 5.3 An overview of the various components and services that make up Blazor's forms and validation system

The primary component is `EditForm`—a drop-in replacement for an HTML form element. Inside this, we add a validator component and various input components along with a standard HTML Submit button.

We pass a model into the `EditForm`, which is an instance of a class that represents the data we want to collect with the form. Internally, the `EditForm` component constructs an `EditContext`—this is the brain of the form's system. It keeps track of all the input components and the state of the model. Whenever a value is updated on the model, it will trigger validation via a validator component. Blazor ships with a validator component called `DataAnnotationsValidator`, which allows the validation of models using the Data Annotations. Different validator components can be used to support different validation systems—more on this later.

The `EditForm` offers three events for handling form submits. The `OnSubmit` event is the same as the standard submit event on an HTML form. It will be invoked whenever the Submit button is clicked, and the handler is responsible for making sure the model is valid. The `OnValidSubmit` event is my personal favorite. This event is triggered when the Submit button is clicked but with a key difference: the `EditForm` will check with the `EditContext` first to make sure the model is valid. The handler will be called only when the model is valid. This makes writing the handler much simpler, as no validation code needs to be written. The final event is `OnInvalidSubmit`. As you can probably guess, this works in the opposite way to the `OnValidSubmit` event. It will only be invoked when the form is submitted but the model is invalid.

Now we've covered what is going on under the covers, at a high level. It's time to start building so we can see everything in action and really understand the nitty-gritty of it all.

Before we can start looking at the components, we first need to create our model—a class that represents the trail data we need to collect from the form. Once we create our form, we will bind the properties of this class to the various input components allowing us to capture the data entered.

We are going to create this class in the new BlazingTrails.Shared project. By creating it here, we can access it from both our Client and API projects, meaning that any updates can be done in a single place. We'll also add our validation here, so both the server and client will use the same validation rules.

5.1.1 Creating the model

In the shared project, create a new folder called *Features*, and inside that, add a new folder called *ManageTrails*. We are replicating the feature folder structure from our Blazor app to make working across the different projects easier by extending the feature folder organization pattern into a feature slice or vertical slice architecture. Our features will now span across the Web, Shared, and API projects. Inside this new folder, we will add a new class called `TrailDto`. This class is shown in the listing 5.1.

Listing 5.1   TrailDto.cs

```
public class TrailDto                    ◁──┐  The TrailDto class will be bound to our
{                                            │  form to collect values entered by the user.
    public int Id { get; set; }
    public string Name { get; set; } = "";
    public string Description { get; set; } = "";
    public string Location { get; set; } = "";
    public int TimeInMinutes { get; set; }
    public int Length { get; set; }
    public List<RouteInstruction> Route { get; set; } =
    ➥new List<RouteInstruction>();

    public class RouteInstruction         ◁──┐  RouteInstruction
    {                                         │  is a nested class.
        public int Stage { get; set; }
        public string Description { get; set; } = "";
    }
}
```

There is nothing special about this class right now, but later in the chapter, we will come back and make some modifications when we add in validation. The only thing to note is the use of a nested class called `RouteInstruction`. I like to use this technique when working with classes that are dependent, because it helps to reinforce the relationship and makes maintenance easier as everything is in one file.

5.1.2   *Basic EditForm configuration*

Now that we have our model, we can get on with creating the form itself. Back in the BlazingTrails.Client project, we will add a new feature folder called *ManageTrails*, mirroring what we did in the Shared project.

Inside this new folder, we will create a new component and call it _Imports. razor. Inside this new component, we will delete the contents and add a single line:

```
@using BlazingTrails.Shared.Features.ManageTrails
```

By declaring namespaces in a _Import.razor file, they are automatically added to any files (classes, records, components, etc.) within that folder—or its subfolders.

Next, we will add another component called `AddTrailPage.razor`. This page will contain the form for adding new trails to the application. The following listing shows the initial code for the component.

Listing 5.2   AddTrailPage.razor

```
@page "/add-trail"

<PageTitle>Add Trail - Blazing Trails</PageTitle>

<nav aria-label="breadcrumb">
    <ol class="breadcrumb">
        <li class="breadcrumb-item"><a href="/">Home</a></li>
```

```
        <li class="breadcrumb-item active" aria-current="page">
          ⮕Add Trail</li>
      </ol>
</nav>

<h3 class="mt-5 mb-4">Add a trail</h3>

<EditForm Model="_trail" OnValidSubmit="SubmitForm">      ⮜

    <div class="mt-4 mb-5">
        <div class="row">
            <div class="offset-4 col-8 text-right">
                <button class="btn btn-outline-secondary"
                        type="button"
                        @onclick="@(() => _trail =
                        ⮕new TrailDto())">Reset</button>
                <button class="btn btn-primary"
                        type="submit">Submit</button>
            </div>
        </div>
    </div>

</EditForm>
@code {
    private TrailDto _trail = new TrailDto();

    private async Task SubmitForm()      ⮜
    {
        // TODO: Submit data to API
    }
}
```

The EditForm component is used to define a Blazor form. As a minimum, a model and a submit action must be defined.

The Reset button clears the form by creating a new instance of the TrailDto class.

Clicking the Submit button will invoke the OnValidSubmit event and call the SubmitForm method.

A new instance of the TrailDto class is created when the component is initialized and assigned to the EditForm's Model parameter. Input components in the form will be bound to its properties.

The SubmitForm method is called whenever the EditForm's OnValidSubmit event is invoked.

Most of the code in the top half of the markup section will look familiar from the other pages we've worked on. In the bottom half is where things are a little more interesting. We can see the initial setup for our form. As we learned earlier, to use the EditForm component, we need to give it two things: a model and a method to call when the form is submitted.

The model is used internally to understand what validation rules exist and the current state of the model (i.e., whether it is valid or invalid). We will go deeper into this later in the chapter when discussing validation.

The other setup parameter we must provide is the submit handler. Again, as we saw earlier, there are three different submit events exposed by the EditForm:

1 OnSubmit
2 OnValidSubmit
3 OnInvalidSubmit

We're using the OnValidSubmit event, as the handler will be called only after validation has run and the model is valid.

There are also a couple of buttons at the end of the form. The Reset button does exactly what it says on the tin and will reset the form. As all the data recorded by the form is stored in the model, clearing the form is as simple as creating a new instance of the form model. The `Submit` button is no different to the Submit button in a regular HTML form. The only key thing to remember here is setting the button's type to `submit`.

> **TIP** When working with nonsubmit buttons in Blazor forms, explicitly set their type attribute to `button`. If you don't, they'll trigger the form to submit, as the default type for a button is `submit`.

That is the basic setup of our form completed. However, before we move on and start adding inputs to our form, we'll create a new component in the ManageTrails folder called `FormSection.razor`.

You'll notice in figure 5.4 that there are three sections to the form: Basic Details, Difficulty, and Route Instructions. This markup is repeated three times for each section with only the title and help text changing, which makes it a candidate for a component.

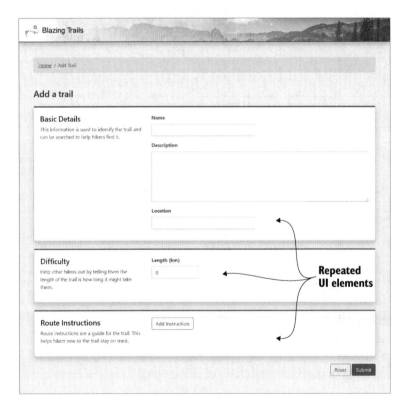

Figure 5.4   There are three repeated UI elements on the form representing the three sections. This kind of repetition is often a great time to implement a component.

I find forms are a prime location for repeated markup that can be refactored into components. The following listing shows the code for the `FormSection` component.

Listing 5.3 FormSection.razor

```
<div class="card card-brand mb-4 shadow">
    <div class="card-body">
        <div class="row">
            <div class="col-4">
                <h4>@Title</h4>
                <p class="text-secondary">@HelpText</p>
            </div>
            <div class="col-8">
                @ChildContent
            </div>
        </div>
    </div>
</div>

@code {
    [Parameter, EditorRequired]
    public string Title { get; set; } = default!;
    [Parameter, EditorRequired]
    public string HelpText { get; set; } = default!;
    [Parameter, EditorRequired]
    public RenderFragment ChildContent { get; set; }
    ➡= default!;
}
```

Shows the section title

Shows the section help text

Shows the content to be displayed

The `FormSection` component defines three parameters. The first is the section's `Title`, the second is the `HelpText`, and the third is `ChildContent`. By defining this simple component now, we've saved a lot of repeated markup on our form, making maintenance in the future much easier. We also need to add a SCSS file for the styles for the `FormSection`. The following listing shows the code.

Listing 5.4 FormSection.razor.scss

```
.card-brand {
    border-top: 4px solid var(--brand);
}
```

The `.card-brand` class is responsible for adding the thick green border to the top of the card.

5.1.3 Collecting data with input components

We now turn our attention to input components. Out of the box, Blazor ships with component versions of the standard HTML form input elements. Table 5.1 shows a list of HTML input elements and their Blazor equivalent.

Table 5.1 HTML input elements and their Blazor equivalent

HTML input control	Blazor input component
`<input>` or `<input type="text" />`	`<InputText />`
`<textarea>`	`<InputTextArea />`
`<input type="number">`	`<InputNumber />`
`<select>`	`<InputSelect>`
`<input type="date">`	`<InputDate />`
`<input type="checkbox">`	`<InputCheckbox />`
`<input type="radio">`	`<InputRadio />` and `<InputRadioGroup>`
`<input type="file">`	`<InputFile />`

Except for `InputFile`, which we'll cover in the next chapter, to use any of these input components we just need to bind them to a property on the form model using the `@bind` directive.

Figure 5.5 shows the finished Basic Details section we'll be building next, which uses the `InputText` and `InputTextArea` components. Listing 5.5 shows the markup for the section and should be placed inside the opening `EditForm` tag we added earlier. For each of the `Input` components, you can see the `@bind` directive being used to associate the component with a property on the model. It has a slightly different

Figure 5.5 The current state of the Basic Details section of the form

syntax to what we've seen before, as when binding to a component, we must specify the parameter we're binding to. All the `Input` components shipped with Blazor expose a `Value` parameter, hence `@bind-Value`.

Listing 5.5 The markup for the Basic Details section of the form

```
<FormSection Title="Basic Details"
             HelpText="This information is used to
            ➥identify the trail and can be searched to help hikers
            ➥find it.">
    <div class="row">
        <div class="col-6">
            <div class="form-group">
                <label for="trailName"
               ➥class="font-weight-bold text-secondary">Name</label>
                <InputText @bind-Value="_trail.Name"
               ➥class="form-control" id="trailName" />
            </div>
        </div>
    </div>

    <div class="row">
        <div class="col">
            <div class="form-group">
                <label for="trailDescription"
               ➥class="font-weight-bold text-secondary">Description</label>
                <InputTextArea
               ➥@bind-Value="_trail.Description" rows="6"
               ➥class="form-control" id="trailDescription" />
            </div>
        </div>
    </div>

    <div class="row">
        <div class="col-6">
            <div class="form-group">
                <label for="trailLocation"
               ➥class="font-weight-bold text-secondary">Location</label>
                <InputText @bind-Value="_trail.Location"
               ➥class="form-control" id="trailLocation" />
            </div>
        </div>
    </div>
</FormSection>
```

> The new FormSection component defines the section title and help text.

> An InputText component is used to collect the trail name.

> An InputTextArea component collects the trail description.

> Another InputText collects the trail's location.

By using the `FormSection` component, we have already saved ourselves a load of markup, which is great! We're using the form group CSS classes and markup from Bootstrap to style each field of the form. The group is made up of a label and input component. The input components are bound to properties on the model using the `@bind` directive—which we used previously in chapter 4 when we built our search feature. However, we use a slightly different format when binding to input components. In chapter 4, we used the `@bind` directive using this format:

```
@bind="_someValue"
```

Now we're using it like this:

```
@bind-Value="_someValue"
```

This is because we are now performing two-way binding on a component rather than an HTML element. When binding to a component, we must specify the property on the component we wish to bind to. In the case of Blazor's input components, that property is called `Value`—note the capital *V*. We're going to look at the `bind` directive in detail when we create our own custom input component in the next chapter, so if you still have questions, hold that thought.

Before we move on to the other section, we have another opportunity for a refactor—I really meant it when I said forms are a prime area for refactoring!

Looking at the form components we just added, there is a lot of repetition again. The markup for the layout of each row is repeated with only a single difference between them, the width—defined with the `col` and `col-*` classes. Let's tidy that up.

We'll create a new component called `FormFieldSet.razor` in the ManageTrails feature folder, then add the code shown in the following listing.

Listing 5.6   FormFieldSet.razor

```
<div class="row">
    <div class="@Width">                          ◁
        <div class="form-group">          ◁
            @ChildContent
        </div>                                The label and input
    </div>                              component will be passed
</div>                                     in as child content.
                                                              The width of the row
@code {                                                       can be passed in, but
    [Parameter, EditorRequired]                               there is a default
    public RenderFragment ChildContent { get; set; }          value provided.
    ➥= default!;                          ◁
    [Parameter]
    public string Width { get; set; }
    ➥= "col";                           ◁
}
```

The `FormFieldSet` component allows us to remove that repeated markup from our page. The only difference between rows is the length of the row, so by making that value a parameter, we can pass it in. However, to make life even easier, we can default its value to `col`, which is essentially full width. Now we only need to specify a width on components that aren't full width. Let's update the Basic Details section we just added to use the `FormFieldSet` component. The following listing shows the updated code.

Listing 5.7   Basic Details section using `FormFieldSet`

```
<FormSection Title="Basic Details"
             HelpText="This information is used to identify the
             ➥trail and can be searched to help hikers find it.">
```

```
<FormFieldSet Width="col-6">                                          ◁
    <label for="trailName" class="font-weight-bold text-secondary">Name</
    ➥label>
    <InputText @bind-Value="_trail.Name" class="form-control"
    ➥id="trailName" />                          Uses the FormFieldSet component
</FormFieldSet>                                       specifying a width class

<FormFieldSet>                                                        ◁
    <label for="trailDescription"
    ➥class="font-weight-bold text-secondary">Description</label>
    <InputTextArea @bind-Value="_trail.Description" rows="6"
    ➥class="form-control" id="trailDescription" />
</FormFieldSet>                                  Uses the FormFieldSet component
                                                 without a custom width specified
<FormFieldSet Width="col-6">
    <label for="trailLocation"
    ➥class="font-weight-bold text-secondary">Location</label>
    <InputText @bind-Value="_trail.Location" class="form-control"
    ➥id="trailLocation" />
</FormFieldSet>

</FormSection>
```

I think you'll agree: the code now looks much cleaner and is much easier to scan through. If you want, you can run the app and check out the progress so far.

Let's add in the next section. This should be really quick with all the great work we've done so far. Figure 5.6 shows the state of the form once the Difficulty section is complete.

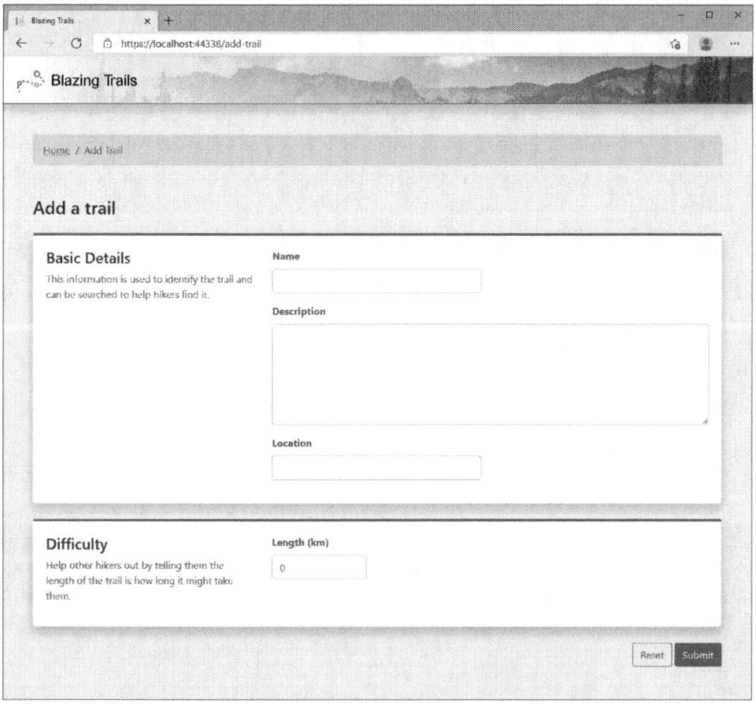

Figure 5.6 The current state of the form with the Basic Details and Difficulty sections added

The following listing shows the code for the Difficulty section.

Listing 5.8   The difficulty section of the add trail form

```
<FormSection Title="Difficulty"                       The section is defined using the
          HelpText="Help other hikers out by              FormSection component.
             telling them the length of the trail is how long it
             might take them.">

    <FormFieldSet Width="col-3">          The FormFieldSet component is used to
        <label for="trailLength"          contain the form elements in a row.
          class="font-weight-bold text-secondary">Length (km)</label>
        <InputNumber @bind-Value="_trail.Length"
          class="form-control" id="trailLength" />     The InputNumber
    </FormFieldSet>                                      component is used to collect
                                                         the length of the trail.
</FormSection>
```

By using the components we created earlier, we've been able to create this new section quickly and easily with really clean markup. For now, we only have a single input component that collects the length of the trail from the user.

We now have the first two sections of our form in place, and we have used our first Blazor form components, `InputText`, `InputTextArea`, and `InputNumber`. All that's left for us to do is build the route instructions section.

5.1.4   Creating inputs on demand

At some point, you will need to allow the user to create inputs on demand. In our case, this is route instructions. A route instruction is a guide, a waypoint that helps hikers find their way around the trail. Depending on the length of the trail, there could be any number of route instructions—there is no way for us to know up front how many inputs to give the user. We need to build the form in a way that allows the user to dynamically add route instructions as they see fit.

On the surface this can seem a bit daunting, but it's relatively simple to achieve. We will use a simple `foreach` loop over the collection of route instructions we defined on the form model at the start of the chapter:

```
public List<RouteInstruction> Route { get; set; } = new
    List<RouteInstruction>();
```

Figure 5.7 shows how the finished code is going to work. When a user clicks the Add Instruction button, a row will appear with a stage number and a description for them to fill in.

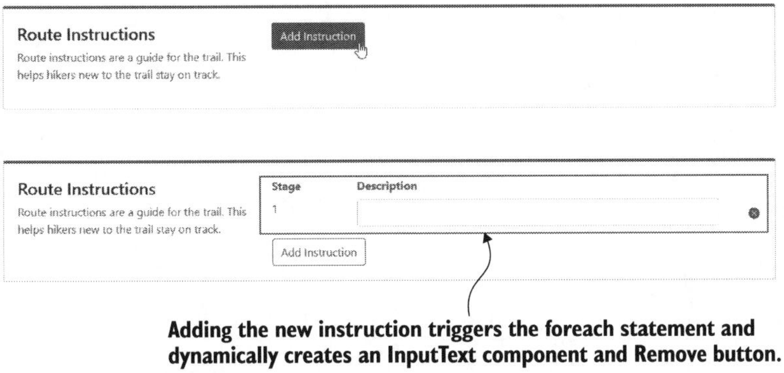

Adding the new instruction triggers the foreach statement and
dynamically creates an InputText component and Remove button.

**Figure 5.7   Clicking Add Instruction adds a new `RouteInstruction` to the
`Route` list on the form model. This triggers a re-render of the UI, which outputs
the dynamically created `InputText` component as well as a button to remove
the instruction from the list if it was added by mistake or is no longer required.**

The following listing shows the code for this section of the form.

Listing 5.9   The route instructions section of the add trail form

**The i variable keeps track of the number of route instructions
and is used to set the stage property on each RouteInstruction.
The stage is used to order the route instructions.**

```
<FormSection Title="Route Instructions"
            HelpText="Route instructions are a guide for the trail.
            This helps hikers new to the trail stay on track.">
    @{ var i = 0; }
    @foreach (var routeInstruction in _trail.Route)
    {
        i++;
        routeInstruction.Stage = i;


        <div class="row">
            <div class="col-2">
                <div class="form-group">
                    <label class="font-weight-bold text-secondary">
                    Stage</label>
                    <p>@routeInstruction.Stage</p>
                </div>
            </div>
            <div class="col">
                <div class="form-group">
                    <label for="routeInstructionDescription"
                    class="font-weight-bold text-secondary">Description</
                    label>
                    <InputText
                    @bind-Value="routeInstruction.Description"
```

**The foreach loop is used
to iterate over the route
instructions on the trail.**

**The stage
number is output**

The description for the route instruction instance is bound to an InputText.

```
                    ⤷class="form-control"
                        ⤷id="routeInstructionDescription" />
                </div>
            </div>
            <div class="col-1 d-flex mt-3">
                <button
                    ⤷@onclick="@(() => _trail.Route.Remove(routeInstruction))"
                    ⤷class="btn btn-link" type="button">
                    <svg width="1em" height="1em" viewBox="0 0 16 16"
                        ⤷class="bi bi-x-circle-fill text-danger"
                        ⤷ fill="currentColor"
                        ⤷xmlns="http://www.w3.org/2000/svg">
                        <path fill-rule="evenodd" d="M16 8A8 8 0 1 1 0
                            ⤷8a8 8 0 0 1 16 0zM5.354 4.646a.5.5 0 1
                            ⤷0-.708.708L7.293 81-2.647 2.646a.5.5
                            ⤷0 0 0 .708.708L8 8.70712.646 2.647a.5.5 0 0 0
                            ⤷.708-.708L8.707 812.647-2.646a.5.5 0 0
                            ⤷0-.708-.708L8 7.293 5.354 4.646z" />
                    </svg>
                </button>
            </div>
        </div>
    }

    <div class="row">
        <div class="col">
            <button class="btn btn-outline-primary"
                ⤷type="button"
                ⤷@onclick="@(() => _trail.Route.Add(
                ⤷new TrailDto.RouteInstruction()))">Add Instruction
                ⤷</button>
        </div>
    </div>
</FormSection>
```

Clicking this button will remove a route instruction from the list. Blazor will automatically re-render the UI and remove the relevant form controls for that entry.

Clicking the Add Instruction button will add a new route instruction to the list. This triggers Blazor to iterate the collection and output the contents of the foreach loop, enabling the user to enter the details of that instruction.

There are two key parts to the code in listing 5.9, the `foreach` loop and the Add Instruction button at the end of the `FormSection`. The Add Instruction button is the key to kicking off the process. When clicked, it will add a new `RouteInstruction` instance to the `Route` list. This changes the state of the `Route` property, triggering a re-render. As there is now an item in the list, the code inside the `foreach` block is executed and the relevant form inputs will be output on the UI.

From this point, the user can keep clicking the Add Instruction button to create as many instructions as they wish to define for the trail. If at any point they add one too many, or they want to remove an instruction for whatever reason, they can click the Remove button at the end of the description input. This will remove that specific entry from the `Route` list, and the stage numbers will automatically recalculate to keep the instructions in sequence.

Our form is now looking rather good! We can record all the various pieces of information about a trail and create as many route instructions as necessary. The next step is to add in validation. After all, our form won't be much good if we can't validate what has been entered!

5.2 *Validating the model*

Validation is the most important part of building forms. Without validation, the system can end up containing all kinds of rubbish data. Out of the box, Blazor includes a few components to help us do this. They are

- `DataAnnotationsValidator`
- `ValidationSummary`
- `ValidationMessage`

The `DataAnnotationsValidator` component allows Blazor forms to work with the Data Annotations validation system, which is the default for ASP.NET Core applications. This system works by decorating properties on a model with attributes that define the validation rules. For example, to make a text property `required`, we would do the following:

```
[Required]
public string Name { get; set;}
```

The `ValidationSummary` component displays all validation messages for a model. This can be useful when you want to have all the validation messages for a form grouped together in one place.

Finally, the `ValidationMessage` component displays a validation message for a specific property on the model. This allows a validation message to be displayed directly under, or next to, an input component, making it easy for the user to see where the problem is.

As with most things in Blazor, there is no restriction on which validation system you can use. So, if Data Annotations isn't your thing, you can easily swap to a different validation system. Personally, I like to use Fluent Validation (https://fluentvalidation .net/). I generally prefer the fluent syntax for defining validation rules. I also find creating more complex validation logic is much simpler with Fluent Validation than with Data Annotations. Therefore, we'll be using Fluent Validation for Blazing Trails.

5.2.1 *Configuring validation rules with Fluent Validation*

Before we start adding validation components to our form, we're going to set up our API and Shared projects to use Fluent Validation. We'll start by setting up our API. Then we'll move on to the Shared project and configure the validation rules on our model, `TrailDto`.

First, we need to install a NuGet package in the API project. Add the following package reference to the project file (alternatively, the package can be added through the Manage NuGet package GUI):

```
<PackageReference Include="FluentValidation.AspNetCore" Version="10.3.3" />
```

Once this is done, update the call to `builder.Services.AddControllers` to the following in `Program.cs`:

```
builder.Services.AddControllers().AddFluentValidation(fv =>
    fv.RegisterValidatorsFromAssembly(Assembly.Load("BlazingTrails.Shared")));
```

This will add the necessary services for Fluent Validation to run. To save us manually registering every validator for our application, we've used the `RegisterValidators-FromAssembly` configuration option. This lets us specify an assembly to scan that contains the validators for our application. The library will then register them for us. That's all we need to do on the API project. Now let's turn our attention to the Shared project.

As with the API project, we need to install the Fluent Validation NuGet package. Add the following package reference into the `.csproj` for the Shared project:

```
<PackageReference Include="FluentValidation" Version="10.3.3" />
```

With the package installed, we can open the `TrailDto` class and add a using statement to it:

```
using FluentValidation;
```

To set up the validation rules, we need to define a validator class for our `TrailDto`. Some people prefer to do this in a separate file, but I prefer to keep them together, as it makes maintenance easier. After the `TrailDto` class ends, add the class shown in the following listing.

Listing 5.10   `TrailValidator` class inside the TrailDto.cs file

```
public class TrailValidator :
  AbstractValidator<TrailDto>
{
    public TrailValidator()
    {
        RuleFor(x => x.Name).NotEmpty()
  .WithMessage("Please enter a name");
        RuleFor(x => x.Description).NotEmpty()
  .WithMessage("Please enter a description");
        RuleFor(x => x.Location).NotEmpty()
  .WithMessage("Please enter a location");
        RuleFor(x => x.Length).GreaterThan(0)
  .WithMessage("Please enter a length");
        RuleFor(x => x.Route).NotEmpty()
  .WithMessage("Please add a route instruction");
    }
}
```

Validation classes must inherit from the AbstractValidator<T> class, T being the class to be validated.

Validation rules are defined in the constructor of the validation class.

Validation rules are defined using a fluent syntax, hence the name. Each rule defines the property it's for, the criteria, and the error message to show if the criteria isn't met.

Defining a validator class means inheriting from the `AbstractValidator<T>` base class. The type parameter `T` is the class to be validated—in our case, that's `TrailDto`. We define the validation rules inside the constructor using the `RuleFor` method. This takes a lambda expression defining which property is to be validated. We then chain methods together to state what makes the property valid and what error message to show if it's not. Let's take the `Name` property rule as an example:

```
RuleFor(x => x.Name).NotEmpty().WithMessage("Please enter a name");
```

This rule states that the `Name` property can't be empty, and the `NotEmpty()` method covers several scenarios. As `Name` is a string, it will check that it's not null, an empty string, or whitespace. If any of these checks fail, the error message specified in the `WithMessage()` method will be returned.

The rules we've defined will make sure that the `TrailDto` is valid, but we also need to do the same for the `RouteInstruction` nested class. The validator class for this is shown in the following listing, which can be added below the `TrailValidator` class in the same file.

> **Listing 5.11 `RouteInstructionValidator` class inside `TrailDto.cs`**

```
public class RouteInstructionValidator :
➥AbstractValidator<TrailDto.RouteInstruction>     ◁──┐
{
    public RouteInstructionValidator()            ◁──────
    {
        RuleFor(x => x.Stage).NotEmpty()
        ➥.WithMessage("Please enter a stage");
        RuleFor(x => x.Description).NotEmpty()
        ➥.WithMessage("Please enter a description");
    }
}
```

The validator inherits from **AbstractValidator<T> as before, but this time T is the RouteInstruction class.**

Validation rules are defined in the constructor as before.

These are validation rules for the RouteInstruction class.

For the `RouteInstructionValidator`, we've defined a couple of rules to ensure both `Stage` and `Description` have a value. Other than that, everything is the same as the previous validator.

With the `RouteInstruction` validator in place, we have one last piece of configuration to do. We need to wire up the `RouteInstructionValidator` in the `TrailValidator`. At the end of the `TrailValidator` constructor, we'll add the following line:

```
RuleForEach(x => x.Route).SetValidator(new RouteInstructionValidator());
```

This tells the `TrailValidator` that for each entry in the `Route` collection, it should use the rules defined in the `RouteInstructionValidator` to validate the model. This will ensure that we can validate and display error messages for each dynamically created route instruction on the form.

5.2.2 Configuring Blazor to use Fluent Validation

Now we have the validation rules set up for the `TrailDto`, we need to tell Blazor how to understand and process them. To do this, we will install a package into the Client project, which is going to do all the heavy lifting for us. It's called `Blazored.Fluent-Validation` (https://github.com/blazored/fluentvalidation).

This package is one of my open source projects. It contains one component called `FluentValidationsValidator`, which, when included in an `EditForm` component, will allow the form model to be validated according to any Fluent Validation rules. To set up the Client project, we're going to add a package reference to the csproj file.

```
<PackageReference Include="Blazored.FluentValidation" Version="2.0.1" />
```

Then we will add the following `using` statement to the `_Imports.razor` at the root of the project.

```
@using Blazored.FluentValidation
```

We are now ready to add the validation components to our form. The first thing we'll do is tell the `EditForm` component that we want the model to be validated with Fluent Validation. To do this, we add the `FluentValidationsValidator` component somewhere between the opening and closing tags of the `EditForm`. I prefer to add it right at the top, directly under the opening `EditForm` tag.

```
<EditForm Model="_trail" OnValidSubmit="SubmitForm">
    <FluentValidationValidator />
```

We now need to add a `ValidationMessage` component under each of the existing inputs on the form. The following listing shows the updated Basic Details section.

Listing 5.12   Basic Details section with `ValidationFor` components

```
<FormFieldSet Width="col-6">
    <label for="trailName"
    ➥class="font-weight-bold text-secondary">Name</label>
    <InputText @bind-Value="_trail.Name"
    ➥class="form-control" id="trailName" />
    <ValidationMessage For="@(() => _trail.Name)" />          ◄┐
</FormFieldSet>

<FormFieldSet>
    <label for="trailDescription"
    ➥class="font-weight-bold text-secondary">Description</label>
    <InputTextArea @bind-Value="_trail.Description" rows="6"
    ➥class="form-control" id="trailDescription" />
    <ValidationMessage
    ➥For="@(() => _trail.Description)" />                     ◄─┤  Each input
</FormFieldSet>                                                     has a
                                                                   corresponding
<FormFieldSet Width="col-6">                                       Validation-
    <label for="trailLocation"                                     Message
    ➥class="font-weight-bold text-secondary">Location</label>      component.
    <InputText @bind-Value="_trail.Location"
    ➥class="form-control" id="trailLocation" />
    <ValidationMessage
    ➥For="@(() => _trail.Location)" />                       ◄─┘

</FormFieldSet>
```

The `ValidationMessage` component requires a single parameter to be set, called `For`. The `For` parameter takes an expression specifying which property on the model it should show validation messages for.

Now that we have some validation components in place, we can run the application and see what happens. Figure 5.8 shows the Basic Details section of the form and the result of clicking the Submit button without filling in any fields.

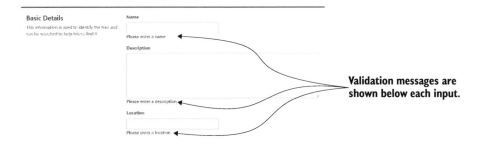

Figure 5.8   Validation messages are shown under each of the input components.

As you can see, the validation messages we specified on the `TrailValidator` class are now appearing in the UI. But there is more going on here than meets the eye. If we use the browser developer tools to inspect the HTML of the page, we can see another effect of validation (figure 5.9).

```
▼<div class="form-group">
    <!--!-->
    <label for="trailName" class="font-weight-bold text-secondary">Name</label>
    <!--!-->
    <input id="trailName" class="form-control invalid" aria-invalid>
    <!--!-->
    <!--!-->
    <div class="validation-message">Please enter a name</div>
  </div>
```

An invalid class has been applied to the input.

Figure 5.9   HTML for the `FormFieldSet` containing the name of the trail. An invalid CSS class has been applied to the input element.

The HTML is of the `FormFieldSet` containing the trail name and shows that the input element has a CSS class called `invalid` applied to it. This was applied because of Blazor's validation system. To help toward accessibility, an `aria` attribute was also applied, `aria-invalid`.

As we learned early in the chapter, the `EditContext` keeps track of the state of the form. It knows the state of each property on the model at any given time. When validation is executed, the input component bound to a property is updated with CSS classes that represent that property's state. Those classes are:

- `valid`
- `invalid`
- `modified`

We can use these classes to style inputs based on their validation state, and that's exactly what we're going to do now.

I suggest putting validation styling in a global CSS file, as it's almost always the same across an application. This avoids a lot of repetition compared to using scoped CSS. In the app.css file, in the wwwroot > css folder, we will add the styles shown in the following listing to the top of the file.

Listing 5.13   Validation styles

```css
.validation-message {
    color: red;
}
```
Text for the validation-message class will be red. This class is used by the validation message component.

```css
input.invalid,
textarea.invalid,
select.invalid {
    border-color: red;
}
```
Any input, textarea, or select element with a class of invalid will have a red border.

```css
input.valid.modified,
text.valid.modified,
select.valid.modified {
    border-color: green;
}
```
Any input, textarea, or select element with a class of valid AND modified will have a border of green.

As we saw previously, the validation message component renders the validation message we specified in our `validator` class. It outputs the message in a div with a class of `validation-message`. The first CSS class specifies that any text shown in an element with that class will have red text.

The next two classes deal with the three state classes that are applied to input components. The first makes sure that any form element with a class of `invalid` has a red border. The second adds a green border to any form element that has both the `modified` and `valid` classes. We specify both classes here, as when the form is first rendered, all input components start with the `valid` class applied. If we didn't do this, all components would have a green border when the form first loads.

If we run the application now and submit the form without entering any values, we should see our new styles in action. We can then enter a valid value and see the valid styling applied (figure 5.10).

Valid fields are now styled with a border using the color specified in the valid CSS class. When a field is invalid, it's styled with a border using the color specified in the

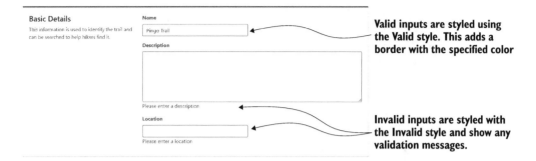

Figure 5.10 **Valid fields are styled using the `valid` class. They receive a border with the color specified in the CSS class. Invalid fields are styled with a border using the color specified in the invalid CSS class. They also show any validation messages underneath the input.**

invalid CSS class. Invalid fields also display any validation messages underneath the input. This now makes it much easier to see the state of the form at a glance.

All that is left for us to do before we tackle sending our form data to the server is add in the `ValidationMessage` components to the remaining sections of the form. The following listing shows the updated Difficulty section.

Listing 5.14   Updated Difficulty section with validation

```
<FormFieldSet Width="col-3">
    <label for="trailLength"
    ➥class="font-weight-bold text-secondary">Length (km)</label>
    <InputNumber @bind-Value="_trail.Length" class="form-control"
    ➥id="trailLength" />
    <ValidationMessage For="@(() => _trail.Length)" />    ◁──┐  This is the ValidationMessage
</FormFieldSet>                                                  component for the Length
                                                                property.
```

Just as we did with the Basic Details section, we've added in a `ValidationMessage` component and specified that it should show validation messages for the `Length` property. The last section is the Route Instructions shown in the following listing.

Listing 5.15   Updated Route Instructions section with validation

```
@{ var i = 0; }
@foreach (var routeInstruction in _trail.Route)
{
    // Code omitted for brevity
    <div class="col">
        <div class="form-group">
            <label for="routeInstructionDescription"
            ➥class="font-weight-bold text-secondary">Description</label>
            <InputText @bind-Value="routeInstruction.Description"
            ➥class="form-control" id="routeInstructionDescription" />
```

```
            <ValidationMessage
              ⇒For="@(() => routeInstruction.Description)" />              ◄──┐
        </div>
    </div>
    // Code omitted for brevity
}
<div class="row">
    <div class="col">
        <button class="btn btn-outline-primary" type="button"
          ⇒@onclick="@(() => _trail.Route.Add(new
          ⇒  TrailDto.RouteInstruction()))">
          ⇒Add Instruction</button>
        <ValidationMessage
          ⇒For="@(() => _trail.Route)" />                    ◄────────────────┐
    </div>
</div>
```

> **The ValidationMessage is used as before, except it is bound to the current route instruction in the foreach loop.**

> **Each route instruction in the collection is validated independently. But we also have a rule to make sure there is at least one route instruction in the collection. This ValidationMessage component will display the error message if that rule is not met.**

There is a little more going on in the Route Instructions section than the other two. In this section, we have two sets of `ValidationMessage` components. The first is inside the `foreach` loop and is bound using the iteration variable `routeInstruction`, rather than binding via the model as we've done previously. The second is outside the `foreach` and is bound to the `Route` collection. This is so if the user fails to add any route instructions, we can show a validation message stating that at least one instruction must be added.

With our form built and validation in place, the last thing we must do is submit our form data to the server and store it. We will tackle this in the next section.

5.3   *Submitting data to the server*

We have a form that allows us to capture data from the user, and we have validation in place to stop invalid data getting into the system. The last thing we need to do is to persist that data to our new API. To do this, we'll employ a couple of libraries that I'm a big fan of.

The first is called *MediatR* (https://github.com/jbogard/MediatR) by Jimmy Bogard. MediatR is an in-process messaging library that implements the mediator pattern (https://en.wikipedia.org/wiki/Mediator_pattern). Essentially, requests are constructed and passed to the mediator, which then passes them to a handler. MediatR uses dependency injection to connect requests with handlers. This makes things very flexible and easy to test. The main advantage of using MediatR is the ability to have loose coupling between components and server interactions.

The second is called *ApiEndpoints* (https://github.com/ardalis/ApiEndpoints) by Steve Smith (aka Ardalis). I love this project, as it solves an issue I've had for an awfully long time: controllers. Whether it's MVC or API controllers, they've always felt wrong. Steve Smith sums it up perfectly in the readme of the ApiEndpoints repo:

> *MVC Controllers are essentially an antipattern. They're dinosaurs. They are collections of methods that never call one another and rarely operate on the same state. They're not cohesive. They tend to become bloated and to grow out of control. Their private methods, if any, are usually only called by a single public method.*
>
> —Steve Smith, creator of ApiEndpoints

ApiEndpoints solves this by allowing us to define an endpoint as a class with a single method to handle the incoming request. This allows us to avoid all the issues that surround controllers and build clear and easy-to-maintain endpoints in our APIs. The overview of how we will interact with the server is shown in figure 5.11.

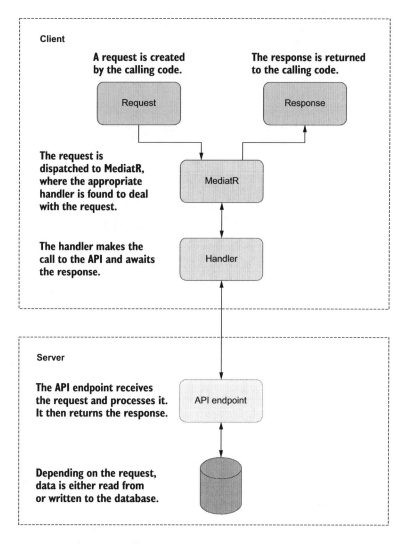

Figure 5.11   Overview of how the client will interact with the server using the MediatR and ApiEndpoints libraries

Taking our form as the example, we will create a request to post the data to the API and pass this request to MediatR. MediatR will route our request to a handler, which will process the request and make the API call. On the server, an API endpoint will receive the request and process it. In this case, it will save the data into a database, and if there are no issues, it will return a success response—otherwise an error response will be returned. This response will travel back until it reaches the calling code.

We're going to start at the Blazor end and set up MediatR; then we'll create our first request and handler. Finally, we'll move to the server and set up the endpoint.

5.3.1 Adding MediatR to the Blazor project

To add MediatR to Blazor, we need to add two NuGet packages to the csproj file called `MediatR` and `MediatR.Extensions.Microsoft.DependencyInjection`.

```
<PackageReference Include="MediatR" Version="9.0.0" />
<PackageReference Include="MediatR.Extensions.Microsoft.DependencyInjection"
    Version="9.0.0" />
```

Then we need to add MediatR to the service collection. To do this, we add a line into the `Program.Main` method in the Program.cs file.

```
builder.Services.AddMediatR(typeof(Program).Assembly);
```

This line adds MediatR to the service collection, so we can inject it into our components and services. It also tells MediatR to scan the current assembly for request handlers. The final piece of configuration we're going to do is to add a `using` statement for MediatR in the root _Imports.razor file.

```
@using MediatR;
```

We are now all set to start creating requests and handlers to use with MediatR!

5.3.2 Creating a request and handler to post the form data to the API

We are going to start by creating a request that will contain the data collected by our form. Once this is done, we can create a handler for that request; this will be responsible for posting the data up to the API.

All of our requests are going to live in the BlazingTrails.Shared project—this will allow us to use them in both the API and Client projects. To start, we need to add a reference to MediatR in the Shared project.

```
<PackageReference Include="MediatR" Version="9.0.0" />
```

Now we need to create a new class in the Features > ManageTrails folder called `AddTrailRequest`. The following listing shows the contents of the file.

Listing 5.16   Contents of the AddTrailRequest.cs file

AddTrailRequest is defined as a C# record as opposed to a class. Records are considered preferable for data transfer objects due to their immutability and value type qualities. The record implements the IRequest<T> interface that is used by MediatR when locating a handler. T defines the response type of the request.

```
public record AddTrailRequest(TrailDto Trail) :
    IRequest<AddTrailRequest.Response>
{
    public const string RouteTemplate = "/api/trails";

    public record Response(int TrailId);
}

public class AddTrailRequestValidator :
    AbstractValidator<AddTrailRequest>
{
    public AddTrailRequestValidator()
    {
        RuleFor(x => x.Trail)
            .SetValidator(new TrailValidator());
    }
}
```

This constant defines the address of the API endpoint for the request.

This nested C# record defines the response data for the request.

A validator for the request. This will be executed by the API to make sure the request data is valid.

Specifies the TrailValidator as the validator for the Trail property. This allows us to reuse the validation rules we created earlier.

The first thing to note is that the AddTrailRequest is not a C# class, but a C# record. Records are a new type introduced in C# 9 and are considered the preferable option for DTOs, which is essentially what our request is.

The reason for this is that records can be immutable, meaning once the values of its properties have been set, they can't be changed. If they need to be changed, then a new copy is made with the updated values.

Another advantage of using records is that they use *value-based equality*. Two records are considered equal when all the values of their properties match.

But to me, probably the biggest benefit is how succinct they are. Take the definition of the AddTrailRequest:

```
public record AddTrailRequest(TrailDto Trail)
```

This code is syntactic sugar for the following definition:

```
public record AddTrailRequest
{
    public TrailDto Trail { get; init; }
}
```

I love being able to skip writing all those extra characters! It makes defining requests with large amounts of properties so much more pleasant. You'll have noticed that we also define the response for the request as a nested record.

Moving on from records, `AddTrailRequest` defines a route template as a constant. This will be used later when we create the API endpoint. The benefit is that if we want to change the endpoint's address further down the road, we can do it in a single place.

Finally, we have a validator for the request. This validator is going to be executed by the server when receiving the request to make sure its contents are valid. However, we don't want to duplicate all the great validation rules we created earlier, so as we're using the `TrailDto` type in the request, we can assign the validator we've already created.

Now that we have a request, we need to create a handler for it. We're going to create this in the Client project in the Features > ManageTrails folder. Create a new C# class called `AddTrailHandler.cs`. The following listing shows the code for the handler.

Listing 5.17   AddTrailHandler.cs

```
public class AddTrailHandler :
    IRequestHandler<AddTrailRequest,
    AddTrailRequest.Response>
{
    private readonly HttpClient _httpClient;

    public AddTrailHandler(HttpClient httpClient)
    {
        _httpClient = httpClient;
    }

    public async Task<AddTrailRequest.Response>
    Handle(AddTrailRequest request,
    CancellationToken cancellationToken)
    {
        var response = await _httpClient
            .PostAsJsonAsync(AddTrailRequest.RouteTemplate,
            request, cancellationToken);

        if (response.IsSuccessStatusCode)
        {
            var trailId = await response.Content
                .ReadFromJsonAsync<int>(cancellationToken:
                cancellationToken);
            return new AddTrailRequest.Response(trailId);
        }
        else
        {
            return new AddTrailRequest.Response(-1);
        }
    }
}
```

Request handlers implement the IRequestHandler <TRequest, TResponse> interface. TRequest is the type of request the handler handles. TResponse is the type of the response the handler will return.

An HttpClient is injected and stored in a field to be used to make API calls.

The Handle method is specified by the IRequestHandler interface and is the method called to handle the request by MediatR.

The HttpClient is used to call the API using the route template we defined on the request.

If the request was successful, then the trailId is read from the response and returned using the AddTrailRequest.Response record we previously defined.

If the request failed, a response is returned containing a negative number. This will be used in the calling code to identify a problem.

Request handlers contain only a single method called `Handle`. This method is a requirement of the `IRequestHandler<TRequest, TResponse>` interface. As part of implementing this interface, we need to define the type of `TRequest` and

TResponse. TRequest is the type of request that the handler should process. For us, that type is AddTrailRequest. TResponse is the type that the handler will return to the caller; for us, that is AddTrailRequest.Response.

In the handle method, we use an HttpClient, which is injected via the constructor, to make the API call. You'll notice we're using the route template we defined on the request rather than hardcoding the address.

When the response is returned, we check to see if the request was successful. If it was, then we extract the trailId from the response and return a new AddTrail-Request.Response containing the ID. If it wasn't successful, we still return the response but with a negative ID, which we can use to show error messages on the UI.

To round out our work on the client, we need to hook up our request to the form's submit event. In the AddTrailPage.razor component, we are going to inject MediatR at the top using the inject directive:

```
@inject IMediator Mediator
```

With that in place, we will update the code block of the component. The following listing shows the changes.

Listing 5.18 Updated code block for AddTrailPage.razor

```
private TrailDto _trail = new TrailDto();          This is a new field to track if the
private bool _submitSuccessful;        ◁┘          form was submitted successfully.
private string? _errorMessage;   ◁┐      This is a new field to store an
                                         error message if something went
private async Task SubmitForm()          wrong submitting the form.
{
    var response = await Mediator.Send(         MediatR is used to dispatch the
      ➥new AddTrailRequest(_trail));   ◁┘       AddTrailRequest and await the response.
    if (response.TrailId == -1)                                          ◁
    {
        _errorMessage = "There was a problem saving your trail.";
        _submitSuccessful = false;
        return;                                     Check for a negative TrailId,
    }                                               which indicates an error.

    _trail = new TrailDto();        ◁      A new TrailDto instance is
    _errorMessage = null;                  created, which resets the form
    _submitSuccessful = true;              ready for a new trail to be input.
}
```

First, we've added two new fields that are going to be used to show errors to the user. We'll implement the UI for this in a second.

Inside the SubmitForm method, we're using the Mediator service supplied by MediatR to send the AddTrailRequest—we then await the response. If it has a negative TrailId, we assign an error message and set _submitSuccessful to false. Otherwise, we create a new TrailDto instance, which clears the form ready for another trail to be added.

The final update is to add a small piece of UI to show if the form submitted successfully or not. We're going to add the code shown in the following listing directly above the `EditForm` component.

Listing 5.19   Markup to display success or failure messages

```
@if (_submitSuccessful)                         ◄──────────────────     If submitSuccessful is true,
{                                                                       we show a success alert.
    <div class="alert alert-success" role="alert">
        <svg xmlns="http://www.w3.org/2000/svg" width="18" height="18"
➡fill="currentColor" class="bi bi-check-circle-fill" viewBox="0 0 16 16">
            <path fill-rule="evenodd" d="M16 8A8 8 0 1 1 0 8a8 8 0 0 1 16
➡0zm-3.97-3.03a.75.75 0 0 0-1.08.022L7.477 9.417 5.384 7.323a.75.75 0 0
➡0-1.06 1.06L6.97 11.03a.75.75 0 0 0 1.079-.0213.992-4.99a.75.75 0 0
➡0-.01-1.05z" />
        </svg>
        Your trail has been submitted successfully!
    </div>                                                              However, if submitSuccessful is false
}                                                                       and we have an errorMessage, we
else if (_errorMessage is not null)             ◄─┘                     display an error alert.
{
    <div class="alert alert-danger" role="alert">
        <svg xmlns="http://www.w3.org/2000/svg" width="18" height="18"
➡fill="currentColor" class="bi bi-x-circle-fill" viewBox="0 0 16 16">
            <path fill-rule="evenodd" d="M16 8A8 8 0 1 1 0 8a8 8 0 0 1 16
➡0zM5.354 4.646a.5.5 0 1 0-.708.708L7.293 81-2.647 2.646a.5.5 0 0 0
➡.708.708L8 8.70712.646 2.647a.5.5 0 0 0 .708-.708L8.707 812.647-2.646a.5.5
➡0 0 0-.708-.708L8 7.293 5.354 4.646z" />
        </svg>
        @_errorMessage
    </div>
}
```

The markup we've added will check the `_submitSuccessful` field, and if it's true, it will display a success alert to the user telling them the form was submitted successfully. However, if it's false and the `_errorMessage` field contains some text, then an error alert is shown instead, along with the error message.

That is everything done on the client side. The last task we have is to implement the endpoint, which will receive the request and save the trail into a database.

5.3.3   *Setting up the endpoint*

In the server project, we first need to set up ApiEndpoints. This is straightforward; we just need to add the following NuGet package reference to the server's csproj file:

```
<PackageReference Include="Ardalis.ApiEndpoints" Version="3.1.0" />
```

There is no further configuration required, as the library provides base classes for us to use along with some code analyzers. For the database, we'll be using SQLite with Entity Framework Core. The instructions for the installation and setup of the database can be found in appendix A.

We will continue with our feature folder's theme in the server, so next we create a folder called *Features* in the root with a subfolder called *ManageTrails*. Inside that, we will create a new class called `AddTrailEndpoint.cs` with the code shown in the following listing.

Listing 5.20   AddTrailEndpoints.cs

```
public class AddTrailEndpoint : BaseAsyncEndpoint
    .WithRequest<AddTrailRequest>
    .WithResponse<int>                                 ◁─────────── BaseAsyncEndpoint is
{                                                                   provided by the
    private readonly BlazingTrailsContext _database;                ApiEndpoints library.
                                                                    We use a fluent API to
    public AddTrailEndpoint(BlazingTrailsContext database)          define the request and
    {                                                               the response the
        _database = database;                                       endpoint will handle.
    }

    [HttpPost(AddTrailRequest.RouteTemplate)]          ◁─────────── The route for the endpoint is defined
    public override async Task<ActionResult<int>>                   using the template on the Request.
        HandleAsync(AddTrailRequest request,
        CancellationToken cancellationToken = default)  ◁────────── BaseAsyncEndpoint
    {                                                               provides a single abstract
        var trail = new Trail                                       method we must
        {                                                           override. This method
            Name = request.Trail.Name,                              will be called to handle
            Description = request.Trail.Description,                the incoming request.
            Location = request.Trail.Location,
            TimeInMinutes = request.Trail.TimeInMinutes,
            Length = request.Trail.Length
        };

        await _database.Trails.AddAsync(trail, cancellationToken);

        var routeInstructions = request.Trail.Route
            .Select(x => new RouteInstruction        ◁──────── A collection of RouteInstructions
            {                                                  is created from the incoming
                Stage = x.Stage,                               request. These will be persisted
                Description = x.Description,                   to the database.
                Trail = trail
            });

        await _database.RouteInstructions
            .AddRangeAsync(routeInstructions, cancellationToken);
        await _database.SaveChangesAsync(cancellationToken);  ◁────

        return Ok(trail.Id);   ◁────
    }
}
```

A new Trail instance is created using the data in the request. This is the entity that will be persisted to the database.

The new trail ID is sent back as the response.

After the database entities have been created and populated, they are added to the DbContext, and SaveChanges is called to persist them to the database.

To define an API endpoint, we must inherit from the `BaseAsyncEndpoint` class. This class requires us to define a request and response type. We do this using a fluent

API, which allows us to specify the request type and the response type. These values are used when overriding the `HandleAsync` method, which we'll discuss in a second.

As we're going to be writing to the database, we need to inject an instance of the `BlazingTrailsContext`, which is done in the constructor. We also need to define the route the endpoint will respond to. Once again, this is done using the `Route-Template` defined on the `AddTrailRequest`.

The `HandleAsync` method is where all the work is done. This method takes the request type we specified when inheriting the `BaseAsyncEndpoint` class and returns the response type. Inside the method, we create instances of the database entities `Trail` and `RouteInstruction` using the incoming request. These entities are then added to their relative `DbSets` before `SaveChangesAsync` is called to write them to the database. Finally, the new trail ID is returned using the `Ok()` helper method, which returns a 200 http response code, indicating a success.

At this point, we are all done and we can run the application and test everything out. Figure 5.12 shows the result of a trail being successfully added.

Figure 5.12   The finished form showing a success message after adding a new trail

If all has gone well, you should see your new trail appear in the SQLite database (figure 5.13).

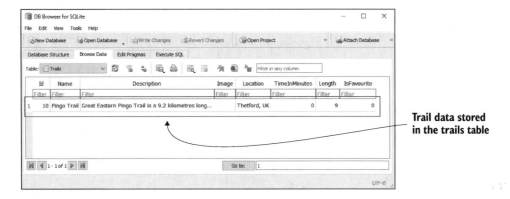

Figure 5.13   The trail added via the form in the SQLite database

At this point, the rest of the application is still using the hardcoded data, so we can't see the new trail in the application yet. Also, you may have spotted that we're missing a couple of pieces of information: the `TimeInMinutes` and the `Image`. We will deal with these issues in the next chapter.

Summary

- The primary advantage of using Blazor form components over traditional HTML forms is validation.
- The `EditForm` component is a drop-in replacement for the HTML form element.
- Blazor ships with component versions of all the standard HTML input controls.
- The `EditForm` requires a model that represents the data the form will collect, as well as a handler for one of the submit events it exposes (`OnSubmit`, `On-ValidSubmit`, `OnInvalidSubmit`).
- Internally, the `EditForm` will construct an `EditContext`, which is the brain of the form and keeps track of the validation state of the model, as well as coordinates validation events.
- To use Blazor's input components, they must be bound to a property on the model passed to the `EditContext`. This is done using the `@bind` directive.
- Blazor ships with a validation component called `DataAnnotations-Validator`, which enables the Data Annotations validation system to be used with models.
- The validation system in Blazor is flexible and extendable, and other validation systems can easily be added by swapping out the validator component.

Forms and validation—
Part 2: Beyond the basics

6

This chapter covers

- Customizing validation CSS class names
- Building custom input components
- Uploading files
- Designing forms to handle adding and editing

In this chapter, we will build on the work we did in chapter 5 by extending our Trail form with some more advanced features. Right now, our form uses some basic styling for validation. However, we're using the Bootstrap CSS framework, which contains much fancier validation styling. Wouldn't it be great if we could take advantage of those classes instead of having to write our own? Well, the good news is we can! And we're going to learn how in the first section of this chapter.

Blazing Trails shows the rough time it takes for a hiker to walk a trail. This is a really helpful feature for users, but currently our form doesn't allow this value to be entered. This is because we store that value as the total time in minutes, even though we display it as hours and minutes. We want the users to be able to enter the time in hours and minutes; they shouldn't have to work out total time in minutes just because that's how the system stores the value. This is a perfect opportunity to implement a custom form component.

Once we're done with custom form components, we'll turn our attention to working with files. The ability to upload files is a common requirement in applications, and Blazing Trails is no different. We need to allow the user to upload a trail image if they choose, and Blazor provides us a component for doing just that. However, this `Input` component doesn't work quite the same as the rest. We'll learn how it differs and how to use it within our form.

Finally, we'll finish up the chapter by modifying our form to allow the editing of existing trails. We'll do this in a way that allows maximum reuse of components but that keeps the code as clean and easy to understand as possible.

6.1 Customizing validation CSS classes

CSS frameworks such as Bootstrap (https://getbootstrap.com), Materialize (https://materializecss.com), or Bulma (https://bulma.io) all have predefined classes for valid and invalid input states. Blazor allows us to use these classes—instead of the default ones it provides—by specifying them in a custom `FieldCssClassProvider`. As we're using Bootstrap in Blazing Trails, let's modify the app to use the classes provided by Bootstrap for valid and invalid inputs.

6.1.1 Creating a FieldCssClassProvider

To do this, we need to create a class derived from `FieldCssClassProvider`. We're going to create this class in a new folder at the root of `BlazingTrails.Client` called `Validation`. The following listing shows the code.

Listing 6.1 BootstrapCssClassProvider.cs

```
public class BootstrapCssClassProvider : FieldCssClassProvider
{
    public override string GetFieldCssClass(EditContext editContext,
    in FieldIdentifier fieldIdentifier)
    {
        var isValid = !editContext
        .GetValidationMessages(fieldIdentifier).Any();

        if (editContext.IsModified(fieldIdentifier))
        {
            return isValid ? " is-valid" : "is-invalid";
        }

        return isValid ? "" : "is-invalid";
    }
}
```

Check if the current field has any validation errors and set isValid appropriately.

The field has been modified. Return custom CSS classes depending on whether the field is valid or not.

The field has not been modified. Return a custom CSS class if the field is invalid but not if it's valid.

When deriving from `FieldCssClassProvider`, we need to override the `Get-FieldCssClass` method. This method takes an `EditContext` and a `FieldIdentifier` that represents the field in the form we're getting CSS classes for. As I mentioned in chapter 5, the `EditContext` is the brain of the form and keeps track of the state of each field in the form. We can use the `GetValidationMessages` method on the `EditContext` to check if there are any validation messages for the current field. If there are, then we know the field is currently not valid and we can set the `isValid` variable accordingly, or vice versa.

Next, we can use the `IsModified` method on the `EditContext` to check if the field has been edited by the user in any way. For a field to be modified, the user must have typed something or changed a selection. Even typing into an empty field and then removing all the characters returning it to its originally empty state would class the field as modified.

When we have a modified field—depending on if it's valid or not—we're going to return either the `is-valid` CSS class or the `is-invalid` CSS class. These classes are part of the Bootstrap framework and will allow us to remove the custom CSS classes we created in the previous chapter.

If the field isn't modified, then we're only going to return a CSS class when the field is invalid. If we returned a valid CSS class at this point, all the fields in the form would show valid styling when it was first loaded before any user input has occurred, as shown in figure 6.1.

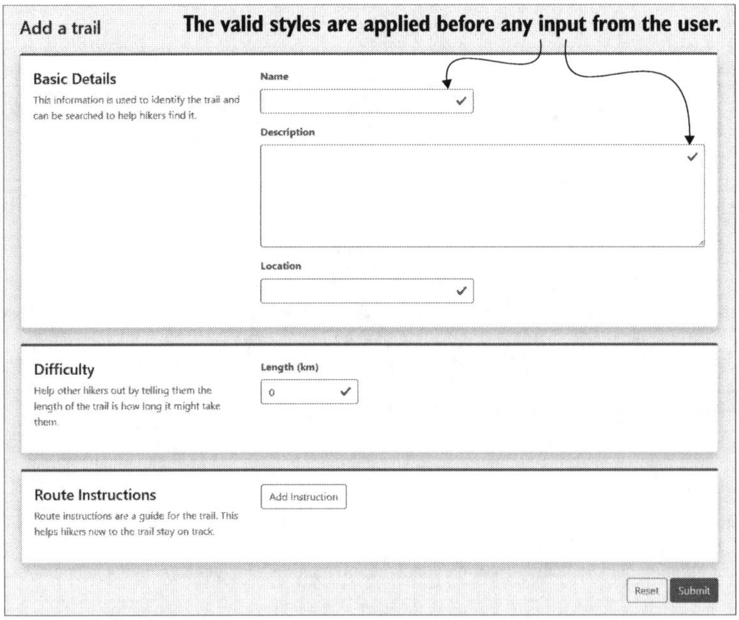

Figure 6.1   Valid styling is shown on all fields as soon as the form is loaded.

As you can see, this would create a bad user experience, as it appears that the form is valid, even when no data has been entered or selected.

6.1.2 Using custom FieldCssClassProviders with EditForm

To use our `BootstrapCssClassProvider` with the `EditForm` component, we need to plug it in. To do this, we use the `EditContext`. When we created our form in chapter 5, we passed a model to the `EditForm` component. Internally, the `EditForm` creates an `EditContext` instance using that model. However, we can create an `EditContext` ourselves and pass that to the `EditForm` component instead of the model.

Depending on what you're doing, this can be especially useful. Having direct access to the `EditContext` allows us to perform actions such as manually triggering validation via the `Validate` method. Or hook onto events such as `OnFieldChanged` or `OnValidationStateChanged`. However, we're going to use it to plug in our custom CSS class provider.

To update our new trail form to use the new `BootstrapCssClassProvider`, we will add the following code.

Listing 6.2 AddTrailPage.razor: Using `BootstrapCssClassProvider`

```
<EditForm EditContext="_editContext"
➥OnValidSubmit="SubmitForm">            ◁──┐  We pass the EditContext instance we
                                            │  create to the EditForm rather than
// other code omitted for brevity          │  passing it to the model directly.

private EditContext _editContext = default!;   ◁──┐  Shows the new private field
                                                   │  for our EditContext instance
protected override void OnInitialized()
{
    _editContext = new EditContext(_trail);    ◁──┐  Creates a new EditContext
    _editContext.SetFieldCssClassProvider(        │  instance for the trail model
    ➥new BootstrapCssClassProvider());   ◁──┐
}                                            │  Configures the EditContext to use
// other code omitted for brevity            │  our new BootstrapCssClassProvider
```

We start by adding a new private field for our `EditContext` instance. We create a new instance of `EditContext` inside the `OnInitialized` life cycle method, passing in the trail model we previously passed directly to the `EditForm`. We then use the `SetField-CssClassProvider` method to plug in our new `BootstrapCssClassProvider`. Finally, we update the opening tag of the `EditForm`, passing our `EditContext` instance rather than passing to the trail model.

> **NOTE** It's important to set either the `EditContext` or `Model` parameter on an `EditForm`. Attempting to set both parameters will result in a run-time error.

At this point, the form is configured to use the custom CSS validation classes. To see the styling in action, run the app and complete a few fields of the form and click Submit. Figure 6.2 shows the new styling.

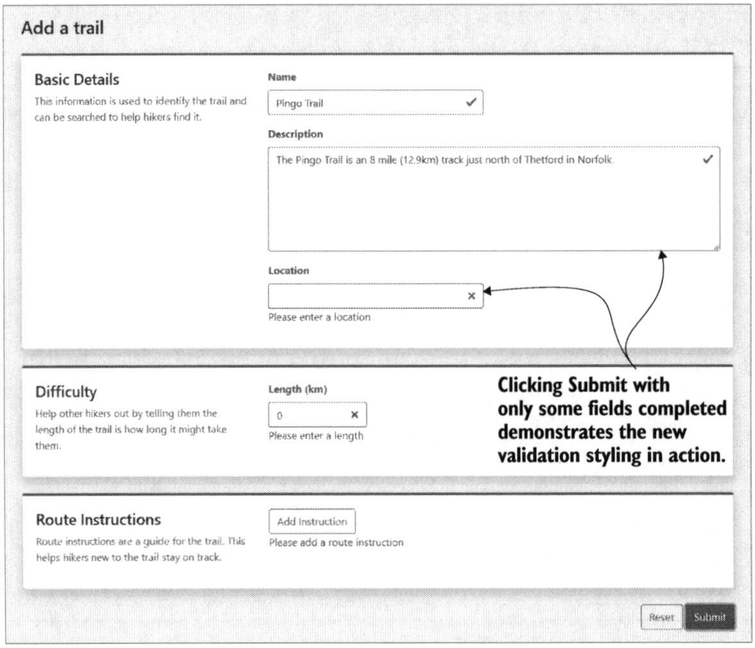

Figure 6.2   The new validation styling using the Bootstrap CSS classes

Before we move on, we just need to tidy up our CSS. We will remove the classes we created in chapter 5 for validation, except the `.validation-message` class, as they're no longer required. Inside the app.css file, in wwwroot > css, make the modifications shown in the following listing.

Listing 6.3   app.css: Removing redundant validation CSS classes

```
input.invalid,
textarea.invalid,
select.invalid {
    border-color: red;
}
```
Remove this CSS class.

```
input.is-valid.modified,
text.is-valid.modified,
select.is-valid.modified {
    border-color: green;
}
```
Remove this CSS class.

The `validation-message` class needs to remain, as it styles the validation message shown under the input. Currently, it's not possible to specify custom CSS classes for the `ValidationMessage` component. The other two sets of styles can be removed. These are the styles that are now being provided by Bootstrap.

6.2   *Building custom input components with InputBase*

While Blazor provides us all the basic input components we need to build a form, at some point we will need something a little more complex—or a little more tailored to our needs. For Blazing Trails, we have such a need.

You may have noticed that the `TrailDto` and `Trail` database entity have a field for recording the time it takes to complete a trail called `TimeInMinutes`. We're currently not exposing this on our form because it wouldn't be a nice experience for the user, as they would have to work out the total number of minutes. It would be much nicer if they could input hours and minutes and the app does the work of converting it. This is a great opportunity for a custom input component.

To help us get started with building a custom input component, the Blazor team has included a base type that is going to do a lot of the heavy lifting for us, `Input-Base<T>`. This type is going to handle the integration with Blazor's `EditContext`. This means that our component will automatically be registered with the validation system and have its state tracked. In fact, all we need to do is provide the UI and an implementation for a method called `TryParseValueFromString`. You can see what the   final component will look like in figure 6.3.

As you can see, the component will render two input elements allowing the user to input the trail walking time in hours and minutes. Internally, the component will take those two values and convert them to a single integer value that will be bound to the form model.

Figure 6.3   The final look of the custom input component we're going to build

6.2.1   *Inheriting from InputBase<T>*

The first thing we need to do is create a new component in our `ManageTrails` feature called `InputTime.razor`. Then we can add the initial code for the component shown in the following listing.

Listing 6.4   InputTime.razor: Initial code

```
@inherits InputBase<int>

<div class="input-time">
    <div>
        <input class="form-control"
               type="number"
               min="0" />
        <label>Hours</label>
    </div>
    <div>
        <input class="form-control"
               type="number"
               min="0"
               max="59" />
```

The inherits directive allows us to specify InputBase<T> as a base class for our component. The type parameter must match the type of the form model property the component will bind to. In our case, that is an int.

This input will record the hours the user enters.

This input will record the minutes the user enters.

```
        <label>Minutes</label>
    </div>
</div>

@code {
    protected override bool TryParseValueFromString(
    ⇒string? value, out int result,
    ⇒out string validationErrorMessage)
        => throw new NotImplementedException();
}
```

> When using InputBase<T>, we must provide an implementation for the **TryParseValueFromString** method. However, with our design, this method won't be called.

We start by inheriting from `InputBase<T>` using the `inherits` directive and setting the type parameter to `int`. The type specified should be the type you want to work with on the form model. Our `TimeInMinutes` property is an `int`:

```
public int TimeInMinutes { get; set; }
```

The markup section of the component declares two regular HTML input elements—one for the hours and one for the minutes. Their type attributes are set to `number`. The browser will use this to stop non-numeric values from being entered by the user. There are also `min` and `max` attributes set to keep the entered values within the correct ranges for hours and minutes.

In the code block, we have provided an implementation for the `TryParseValue-FromString` method. This method must be implemented by any component derived from `InputBase<T>`. Its job is to convert a string value to the type that the component is bound to on the form model. However, depending on how you build a custom input component, this method may not ever get called. This will be the case with our custom component. Let me explain why. The base class provides two properties to update the model value:

- `CurrentValueAsString`
- `CurrentValue`

If we were writing a component that only required a single HTML input element, we could bind that input directly to the `CurrentValueAsString` property. We'd need to use this property, as HTML inputs only work with string values. When a value was entered in the input, it would set `CurrentValueAsString` and Blazor would then call the `TryParseValueFromString` method. This is because Blazor can't reliably convert `CurrentValueAsString` to the type we specified when inheriting from `InputBase<T>`.

However, we have two input elements. We can't bind them both to one property. So, we need to create our own fields to bind them to. We then need to take those individual values and convert them into a single integer value we can update the model with. This is where the second property comes in. `CurrentValue` is a generic property and will adopt the type specified when inheriting `InputBase<T>`. In our case, that would be an `int`. If this property is used to set the model value, then no type conversion is required. Hence the `TryParseValueFromString` method will not be called.

This might sound a bit complex, so let's see it in action. The following listing shows the binding of the inputs and the updating of the model.

Listing 6.5 InputTime.razor: Binding to inputs

```
// Other code omitted for brevity
<input class="form-control" type="number" min="0"
@onchange="SetHourValue" value="@_hours" />
// Other code omitted for brevity

// Other code omitted for brevity
<input class="form-control" type="number" min="0"
max="59" @onchange="SetMinuteValue"
value="@_minutes" />
// Other code omitted for brevity

@code {
    private int _hours;
    private int _minutes;

    // Other code omitted for brevity

    private void SetHourValue(ChangeEventArgs args)
    {
        int.TryParse(args.Value?.ToString(),
        out _hours);
        SetCurrentValue();
    }

    private void SetMinuteValue(ChangeEventArgs args)
    {
        int.TryParse(args.Value?.ToString(),
        out _minutes);
        SetCurrentValue();
    }

    private void SetCurrentValue()
        => CurrentValue = (_hours * 60)
        + _minutes;
}
```

The hour input's value is set using the _hours private field. Whenever that value is changed, the onchange event calls the SetHourValue method.

The minutes input's value is set using the _minutes private field. Whenever that value is changed, the onchange event calls the SetMinuteValue method.

These fields track the current value of each input.

Using the ChangeEventArgs, this method extracts the new value entered by the user and converts it to an integer and sets the _hours field. It then calls SetCurrentValue.

Using the ChangeEventArgs, this method extracts the new value entered by the user and converts it to an integer and setting the _minutes field. It then calls SetCurrentValue.

The _hours and _minutes fields are converted to a total minutes value, and then the CurrentValue property is set to that value.

Until now, when we've bound to HTML inputs, we've used the `bind` directive. However, that method wouldn't be optimal in this scenario. We need to perform some actions every time either the hour or minute values change. While we could use the `bind` directive with a property and do the work inside the `setter` method, that would still require us to have a private backing field.

Instead, we're using fields to set the value of the inputs and then handling the `onchange` event of each one so we can perform some logic. For reference, what we're doing here is what the `bind` directive does under the hood.

Both the `SetHourValue` and `SetMinuteValue` methods do the same thing. They extract the value entered in the input and convert it to an integer value setting either the _hour or _minute field, depending on which method is firing. We must do this conversion, as all HTML inputs work with strings. Once the fields have been set, the `SetCurrentValue` method is called.

The `SetCurrentValue` method works out the total number of minutes based on the values of the _hours and _minutes fields. It then assigns that value to the `CurrentValue` property—this property comes from the base class. By setting this property, all the logic for triggering validation and updating the model value will be run.

The final piece to the component involves loading an existing value—for example, when the component is being used to edit an existing record. For this we will use the `OnParametersSet` life cycle method. The code is shown in the following listing.

Listing 6.6   InputTime.razor: Loading existing values

```
protected override void OnParametersSet()      If the model property bound
{                                              to the component has a value,
    if (CurrentValue > 0)          ◄───┘       CurrentValue will be set.
    {
        _hours = CurrentValue / 60;    Set the values of hours and minutes
        _minutes = CurrentValue % 60;  based on the CurrentValue.
    }
}
```

When the component is used in a form that is editing an existing record, the model property that it is bound to could have a value. If that's the case, the `CurrentValue` property on the base class will hold that value. We can check if it's greater than 0, and if so, we know we have an existing value we need to process. We can then perform the calculations required to set the hours and minutes fields, based on the `Current-Value`. Our component is almost complete; we just need to add some styling.

6.2.2   *Styling the custom component*

To give our new component the right look, we need to add a little CSS. Once again, we'll take advantage of Blazor's CSS isolation feature. Figure 6.4 shows how the component will look when we're done.

Figure 6.4   The labels and inputs displayed in a row once the new styling has been applied

We will add a new SCSS file into the Features > ManageTrails folder called *Input-Time.razor.scss*. We will add the following code into this file.

Listing 6.7 InputTime.razor.scss

```scss
.input-time {
    display: flex;

    div {
        display: flex;
        align-items: center;
        margin-right: 20px;

        input {
            width: 90px;
            margin-right: 10px;
        }

        label {
            margin-bottom: 0;
        }
    }
}
```

Using display: flex on both the container div and the internal div will display all the elements in a row.

Most of the CSS is self-explanatory. The key layout feature we're leveraging is `display: flex`. This is going to make all the inputs and labels display in a row.

The last piece of styling we need to configure is for validation. Another nice feature of using `InputBase` is that it provides us a property called `CssClass` that outputs the correct validation classes based on our field's state. For example, if our field contained an invalid value, based on the classes we've configured in our `Bootstrap-CssClassProvider`, `CssClass` would output the string `"is-invalid"`.

We're going to reference the `CssClass` property in the class attribute on both of our input elements. First, we'll update the hours input:

```
<input class="form-control @CssClass" type="number" min="0"
    @onchange="SetHourValue" value="@_hours" />
```

Then we'll update the minutes input:

```
<input class="form-control @CssClass" type="number" min="0" max="59"
    @onchange="SetMinuteValue" value="@_minutes" />
```

Our custom input component is complete. We can now turn our attention to integrating it in our form.

6.2.3 *Using the custom input component*

We will add our new custom component to the Difficulty section of the form, right under the Length field. The following listing shows the updated code for the Difficulty section of the form.

Listing 6.8 AddTrailPage.razor: Updated Difficulty section

```
<FormFieldSet Width="col-3">
    <label for="trailLength" class="font-weight-bold text-secondary">
    ➥Length (km)</label>
```

```
    <InputNumber @bind-Value="_trail.Length" class="form-control"
     ➥id="trailLength" />
    <ValidationMessage For="@(() => _trail.Length)" />
</FormFieldSet>

<FormFieldSet Width="col-5">
    <label for="trailTime" class="font-weight-bold text-secondary">
    ➥Time</label>
    <InputTime @bind-Value="_trail.TimeInMinutes"
     ➥id="trailTime" />                              ◄
    <ValidationMessage For="@(() => _trail.TimeInMinutes)" />
</FormFieldSet>
```

> The InputTime component is bound to the model property using the same bind-Value syntax as the other input components on the form.

As you can see, the new component is bound to the model property using the same bind-Value syntax that the other input components use. The new component is now integrated into the form, but we still have a few updates to make.

We need to add some validation for the `TimeInMinutes` property to our `Trail-Validator` class. We also need to update the `AddTrailEndpoint` in the API to use the value from the model, as it's currently hardcoded. Let's start with the validation.

If we open the `TrailDto` class in the BlazingTrails.Shared project—under Features > ManageTrails—we can add the following validation rule to the `Trail-Validator` class:

```
RuleFor(x => x.TimeInMinutes).GreaterThan(0).WithMessage("Please enter a
    time");
```

This rule is going to make sure that the user has entered a positive value for the trail time. This can be placed anywhere in the existing list of rules; order doesn't matter.

With the validation updated, we just need to update the endpoint. In the Blazing-Trails.Api project, open the `AddTrailEndpoint` class in Features > ManageTrails. At the start of the `HandleAsync` method where the new trail is being created, we are currently hardcoding the value of the `TimeInMinutes` property to 0:

```
TimeInMinutes = 0
```

This needs to be updated to get the value from the request, just like the other properties:

```
TimeInMinutes = request.Trail.TimeInMinutes
```

With that change, we're done. If we run the application, we can see the new component displayed in the form (figure 6.5).

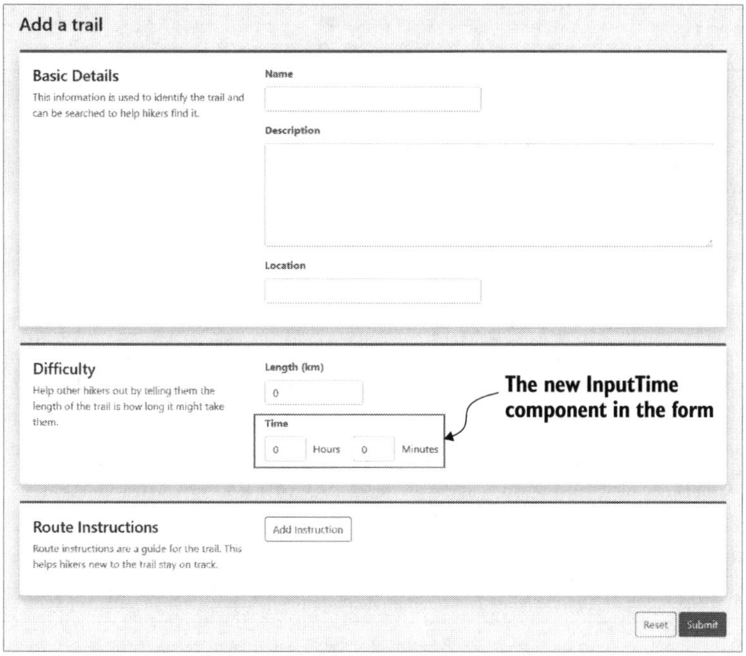

Figure 6.5   The new `InputTime` component displayed in the form

We have successfully created and integrated a custom input component into our form, which enables a much more intuitive experience for the user. The next task we'll tackle is adding the ability for the user to upload an image for a trail.

6.3   Working with files

Just as with other HTML input elements, Blazor provides a component out of the box for uploading files. This component is called `InputFile`. We're going to update our form to use this component, allowing a user to upload an image for their trail—if they choose.

Unfortunately, uploading files isn't as simple as binding the input component to a property on the model. We're going to be changing our form to make two calls to the API. The first is our current call, which uploads the trails details as JSON. The second is going to upload the image—if present—as multipart form data. This happens because there is currently no built-in support in ASP.NET Core for mixing JSON and multipart requests. However, the overhead of the additional request isn't much, and it will only happen if there is an image to upload.

6.3.1   Configuring the InputFile component

We're going to start by adding the `InputFile` component to our form. This is going to be at the end of the Basic Details section, after the location field (see listing 6.9).

Listing 6.9   AddTrailPage.razor: Adding `InputFile` to Basic Details

```
<FormFieldSet>
    <label for="trailImage" class="font-weight-bold text-secondary">
    ➥Image</label>
    <InputFile OnChange="LoadTrailImage" class="form-control-file"
    ➥id="trailImage" accept=".png,.jpg,.jpeg" />
</FormFieldSet>
```

> InputFile doesn't use the bind directive like other input components. Instead, we must handle the OnChange event.

The most important point to notice is that the `InputFile` component doesn't use the `bind` directive as the other input components do. Instead, we must handle the `OnChange` event it exposes. Just as with file uploading in regular HTML forms, we can provide a list of file types we want the user to be able to upload using the `accept` attribute. Under the hood, the `InputFile` component renders an HTML input element with a type of file. The `accept` attribute is passed down to this element when the component renders.

Now that we have the `InputFile` component in place, we need to add the `LoadTrailImage` method to the code block. See the following listing.

Listing 6.10   AddTrailPage.razor: Adding `LoadTrailImage` to code block

```
private IBrowserFile? _trailImage;        ◁── The trailImage field
                                               holds the file data.
// other code omitted for brevity

private void LoadTrailImage(InputFileChangeEventArgs e)   Assigns the selected file
    => _trailImage = e.File;              ◁──────────────  to the trailImage field
```

When the user selects a file, the `OnChange` event will fire and the `LoadTrailImage` method will run. This method uses the `InputFileChangeEventArgs` to assign the selected file to the `trailImage` field so we can access it later, when the form is submitted.

Handling multiple files

In applications that need to allow multiple files to be selected for upload, the `multiple` attribute must be added to the `InputFile` component. This will allow the user to select more than one file in the selection dialog. Once this is in place, some additional functionality on the `InputFileChangeEventArgs` can be used.

The `FileCount` property can be used to check how many files have been selected by the user. To access those files, there is the `GetMultipleFiles` method. This method will return an `IReadOnlyList` of `IBrowserFile`. Each `IBrowserFile` represents a selected file.

By default, `GetMultipleFiles` will return 10 files. If the user has selected more, then the method will throw an exception. However, this limit can be changed by passing in the number of files the method should return.

We now have the basics in place for the user to select an image. We can turn our attention to what happens when the form is submitted.

6.3.2 *Uploading files when the form is submitted*

Currently, when we submit the form, the data entered is packaged into an `AddTrail-Request` and dispatched to the API via MediatR. We're going to extend this logic to check if an image has been selected and make an additional call to upload it.

Starting with the `SubmitForm` method, we're going to update the existing code to the code shown in this listing.

Listing 6.11 AddTrailPage.razor: Updated `SubmitForm` method

```
private async Task SubmitForm()
{
    var response = await Mediator.Send(new AddTrailRequest(_trail));
    if (response.TrailId == -1)
    {
        _errorMessage = "There was a problem saving your trail.";
        _submitSuccessful = false;
        return;
    }

    if (_trailImage is null)          ◁──┐ Checks if a trail image
    {                                      has been selected
        _submitSuccessful = true;
        ResetForm();                  ◁──────────────────┐
        return;
    }
                                                  If no image is selected,
    await ProcessImage(response.TrailId);   ◁──  reset the form.
}                         Call ProcessImage method
                          passes in the trail ID returned
                          from the previous API call.
private void ResetForm()                        ◁────────┘
{
    _trail = new TrailDto();
    _editContext = new EditContext(_trail);
    _editContext.SetFieldCssClassProvider(
    ➥new BootstrapCssClassProvider());
    _trailImage = null;
}
```

The first change is a check to see if a trail image has been selected. If an image hasn't been selected, then we can reset the form as the method did originally. The logic for resetting the form is now in its own method. As we'll see in a second, this is because it will be called in multiple places and refactoring it into its own method will avoid duplication of code.

If a trail has been selected, then we call the `ProcessImage` method. This method takes the trail ID returned from the `AddTrailRequest`. Listing 6.12 shows the code for the `ProcessImage` method.

> **Listing 6.12   AddTrailPage.razor: `ProcessImage` method**

The trail image is uploaded via the **UploadTrailImageRequest**, which takes the trail ID and the image as an **IBrowserFile**.

```
private async Task ProcessImage(int trailId)
{
    var imageUploadResponse = await Mediator
    .Send(new UploadTrailImageRequest(trailId, _trailImage));

    if (string.IsNullOrWhiteSpace(imageUploadResponse.ImageName))
    {
        _errorMessage = "Your trail was saved,
        but there was a problem uploading the image.";
        return;
    }

    _submitSuccessful = true;
    ResetForm();
}
```

If the upload wasn't successful, an error message is shown.

If the upload is successful, the form is reset.

The method first attempts to upload the image. This is done using an `UploadTrail-ImageRequest`, dispatched via MediatR. The request takes the trail ID the image is for, as well as the image to be uploaded.

If there was a problem uploading the image, then an error message is shown to the user. If the image was uploaded successfully, the form is reset and the user will be able to add another trail if they choose.

BUILDING THE REQUEST AND HANDLER

That is all the changes we need to make in the form component. We now need to add the `UploadTrailImageRequest` to BlazingTrails.Shared, a handler for the request in the Client project. The following listing shows the code for the `UploadTrail-ImageRequest` class, which is in the BlazingTrails.Shared project under Features > ManageTrails.

> **Listing 6.13   UploadTrailImageRequest.cs**

```
public record UploadTrailImageRequest(int TrailId, IBrowserFile File) :
IRequest<UploadTrailImageRequest.Response>
{
    public const string RouteTemplate =
    "/api/trails/{trailId}/images";

    public record Response(string ImageName);
}
```

The record is defined with two properties for trailId and the file to be uploaded.

Shows the route template for the request

This is the response that the request will return.

You will notice as we add more requests that their formats are largely uniform. The properties that make up the request are defined using *positional construction*—an awesome feature of C# records.

In this case, we're defining the `TrailId` property and the `File` property using positional construction. The record also defines a route template, which is used in both the endpoint and handler, as well as a response, which defines the data returned from the request.

Now that we have the request in place, we can add a handler for it back in the Client project. This new class will go in the `ManageTrails` feature. The following listing shows the code.

Listing 6.14 UploadTrailImageHandler.cs

```
public class UploadTrailImageHandler :
IRequestHandler<UploadTrailImageRequest, UploadTrailImageRequest.Response>
{
    private readonly HttpClient _httpClient;

    public UploadTrailImageHandler(HttpClient httpClient)
    {
        _httpClient = httpClient;            The IBrowserFile type includes a
    }                                        helper method that allows the
                                             file to be read as a stream.
    public async Task<UploadTrailImageRequest.Response> Handle
    (UploadTrailImageRequest request, CancellationToken cancellationToken)
    {
        var fileContent = request.File
        .OpenReadStream(request.File.Size, cancellationToken);

        using var content = new MultipartFormDataContent();   A MultipartFormDataContent
        content.Add(new StreamContent(fileContent),           type is created, and the file
        "image", request.File.Name);                          is added to it.

        var response = await _httpClient
        .PostAsync(UploadTrailImageRequest.RouteTemplate       The file is posted
        .Replace("{trailId}", request.TrailId.ToString()),     to the API.
        content, cancellationToken);

        if (response.IsSuccessStatusCode)
        {
            var fileName = await
            response.Content.ReadAsStringAsync(
            cancellationToken: cancellationToken);       If the upload was successful,
            return new UploadTrailImageRequest           the API response is
            .Response(fileName);                         deserialized and returned.
        }
        else
        {
            return new UploadTrailImageRequest
            .Response("");          If the upload failed, a response containing
        }                           an empty string is returned.
    }
}
```

We start by reading the selected file into a stream using the `OpenReadStream` method, which is provided by the `IBrowserFile` type. Once we have the file to upload as a stream, we can create a new `MultipartFormDataContent` object and add the file to it.

NOTE While we're including the file's name when adding it to the content, we won't be using it in the API. This is because the filename could be used for malicious purposes and must be considered a security concern. In the API endpoint, we will give the file a new name. We must include a name at this point, however, for the request to be successful.

Once we've constructed the content we want to send to the API, we use the `Http-Client` to post it. As part of doing this, we replace the `{trailId}` placeholder in the route template with the trail ID passed in the request.

If the operation is successful, we deserialize the response and return it using the response type we defined on the request. Otherwise, we return a failed response.

ADDING THE API ENDPOINT

The final piece to the add is the API endpoint. This will go in the API project under Features > ManageTrails. However, before we add it, we need to do a few admin tasks.

First, we will add a package from NuGet to the API project. The package is called *ImageSharp* (https://github.com/SixLabors/ImageSharp). We'll use this package to resize the uploaded image to the correct dimensions for our app.

To install the `ImageSharp` package, add the following package reference to the BlazingTrails.Api.csproj file:

```
<PackageReference Include="SixLabors.ImageSharp" Version="1.0.3" />
```

Second, we'll create a new folder in the root of the API project called *Images*. This is where we'll store all the trail images that are uploaded.

Third, we'll make a small update in the Program.cs file that will enable the API to serve the images in the new Images folder to the Blazor application as static files. After the existing call to `app.UseStaticFiles()`, add the following code:

```
app.UseStaticFiles(new StaticFileOptions()
{
    FileProvider = new
     PhysicalFileProvider(Path.Combine(Directory.GetCurrentDirectory(),
     @"Images")),
    RequestPath = new Microsoft.AspNetCore.Http.PathString("/Images")
});
```

With our admin tasks complete, we can go ahead and add our endpoint. The following listing shows the code for the `UploadTrailImageEndpoint` class.

Listing 6.15   UploadTrailImageEndpoint.cs

```
public class UploadTrailImageEndpoint : BaseAsyncEndpoint
➥.WithRequest<int>.WithResponse<string>

{
    private readonly BlazingTrailsContext _database;

    public UploadTrailImageEndpoint(BlazingTrailsContext database)
    {
```

```
        _database = database;
    }


    [HttpPost(UploadTrailImageRequest.RouteTemplate)]
    public override async Task<ActionResult<string>> HandleAsync([FromRoute]
    ➥int trailId, CancellationToken cancellationToken = default)
    {
        var trail = await _database.Trails
        ➥.SingleOrDefaultAsync(x => x.Id == trailId,          Attempts to load the
        ➥cancellationToken);                                   trail matching the trailId
        if (trail is null)                                     and returns a bad
        {                                                      request if it doesn't exist
            return BadRequest("Trail does not exist.");
        }

        var file = Request.Form.Files[0];
        if (file.Length == 0)                         Using the Request object, attempts to
        {                                             load the file posted in the request and
            return BadRequest("No image found.");     returns a bad request if it can't be found
        }

        var filename = $"{Guid.NewGuid()}.jpg";        ◁──┐ Creates a new filename for
        var saveLocation = Path.Combine(Directory           the uploaded image that is
        ➥.GetCurrentDirectory(), "Images", filename);       safe to use in the application

        var resizeOptions = new ResizeOptions
        {
            Mode = ResizeMode.Pad,
            Size = new Size(640, 426)                  Using ImageSharp, resize the
        };                                             uploaded image to the
                                                       correct dimensions and save
        using var image = Image.Load(file              it to the filesystem.
        ➥.OpenReadStream());
        image.Mutate(x => x.Resize(resizeOptions));
        await image.SaveAsJpegAsync(saveLocation,
        ➥cancellationToken: cancellationToken);

        trail.Image = filename;                     ◁── Update the trail with the location of
        await _database                                 the trail image. This will be used
        ➥.SaveChangesAsync(cancellationToken);          later in the UI to load the image.

        return Ok(trail.Image);
    }
}
```

Specifies the save location for the file ─────▷ (var saveLocation = Path.Combine(Directory)

We start by attempting to load the trail from the database that matches the supplied `trailId`. If that fails, we return a bad request. Next, we attempt to load the submitted image using the `Request` object. This object is available in every endpoint and allows access to all the information regarding the current HTTP request. If no image is found, we return a bad request.

At this point we know we have a valid trail and a valid image. The next task is to create a safe filename and specify where the file should be saved on the server. For our purposes, saving the file to a local folder in the root of the API project is sufficient.

However, you could easily save the files to a blob storage solution in your preferred cloud provider.

Next, we use the ImageSharp library to resize the image to the correct dimensions and save it. Resizing images to the same height and width can be tricky. Depending on their original dimensions, the ratio can get distorted and result in skewed images. This is where libraries such as ImageSharp come in handy. ImageSharp offers a pad mode when resizing images. This allows the uploaded image to keep its original aspect ratio and allows additional padding to be added to either the top and bottom or sides of the image as required.

Finally, we update the trail with the location of the image. In the final section of this chapter, we will update the existing areas of the application to load trails from the API. At this point, we'll use this location to load the trail image in the UI.

TESTING EVERYTHING OUT

We've now built everything we need, and it's time to test our work. If we run the application, we can see the new `InputFile` component displayed in the Basic Details section (figure 6.6).

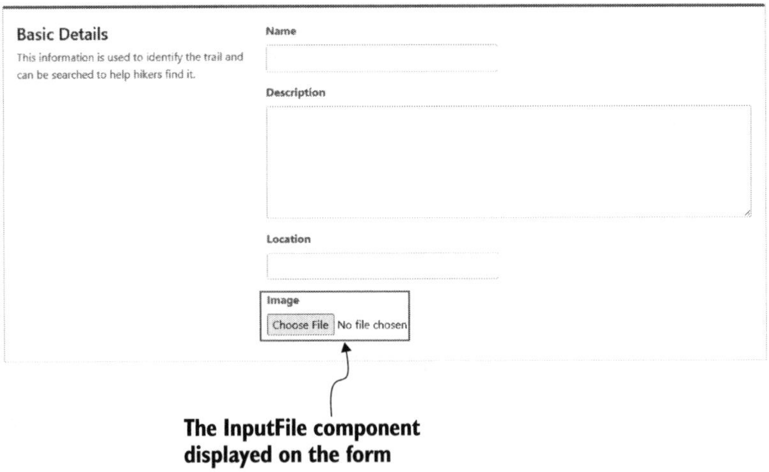

**The InputFile component
displayed on the form**

Figure 6.6   The `InputFile` component displayed on the form

Clicking the Choose File button will open a selection dialogue, as shown in figure 6.7. As we applied an `accept` attribute when we added the `InputFile` to our form, the dialog is showing only files that match the types defined in that attribute.

Once we select an image file and complete the remaining field on the form, we can submit it. If all has gone well, we should see a new image file in the Images folder of the API project. The form should show a success message and be reset, as it was before.

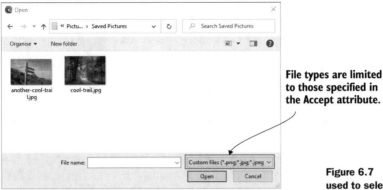

File types are limited
to those specified in
the Accept attribute.

**Figure 6.7 The section dialog
used to select an image to upload**

6.4 *Updating the form to allow editing*

The final piece of work we're going to do is refactor our form so it can handle both adding and editing of trails. To do this, we'll extract the form from `AddTrail⁻` `Page.razor` and make it into a standalone component. We can share it with `AddTrailPage.razor` and a new page we'll add called `EditTrailPage.razor`. We'll also do a bit of reorganization of our ManageTrails feature folder to make things nice and tidy. These changes will also be reflected in the Shared and API projects. Figure 6.8 shows how things will look in the Client project once we're done.

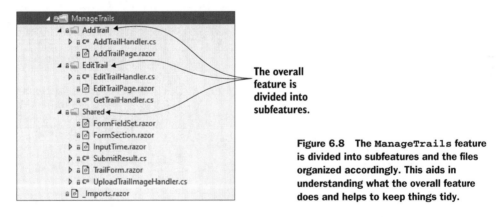

The overall
feature is
divided into
subfeatures.

**Figure 6.8 The `ManageTrails` feature
is divided into subfeatures and the files
organized accordingly. This aids in
understanding what the overall feature
does and helps to keep things tidy.**

As you can see, the overall `ManageTrails` feature has been divided into subfeatures, `AddTrail` and `EditTrail`. There is also a new Shared folder where the trail form and other shared assets sit. Using subfeatures is a great way to aid in the understanding of what the overall feature does. It also stops feature folders from becoming messy.

6.4.1 *Separating the trail form into a standalone component*

The first task we'll tackle is separating out the trail form from the AddTrailPage and make it into its own component, capable of handling both adding and editing. As part of doing this, we'll also start to create the new feature folder structure.

We'll start by creating a new folder called *Shared* in the ManageTrails feature folder of the Client project. In this folder, we will create a new component called Trail-Form.razor. Then we'll move FormFieldSet.razor, FormSection.razor, InputTime.razor, and UploadTrailImageHandler.cs into the Shared folder so they're next to the new TrailForm component we just created. We also need to update the _Imports.razor file to include the new Shared folder by adding the following line:

```
@using BlazingTrails.Client.Features.ManageTrails.Shared
```

Going back to the TrailForm component, we will copy the entire EditForm component from AddTrailPage.razor and paste it into TrailForm.razor. We'll then add some initial code to the code block as shown in this listing.

Listing 6.16   TrailForm.razor: Initial code

```
<EditForm EditContext="_editContext" OnValidSubmit="SubmitForm">

    // Form markup omitted for brevity

</EditForm>

@code {
    private TrailDto _trail = new TrailDto();
    private IBrowserFile? _trailImage;
    private EditContext _editContext = default!;

    [Parameter]
    public Func<TrailDto, IBrowserFile?, Task>
    ➥OnSubmit { get; set; }

    public void ResetForm()
    {
        _trail = new TrailDto();
        _editContext = new EditContext(_trail);
        _editContext.SetFieldCssClassProvider(
        ➥new BootstrapCssClassProvider());
        _trailImage = null;
    }

    protected override void OnInitialized()
    {
        _editContext = new EditContext(_trail);
        _editContext.SetFieldCssClassProvider(
        ➥new BootstrapCssClassProvider());
    }

    private void LoadTrailImage(InputFileChangeEventArgs e)
        => _trailImage = e.File;

    private async Task SubmitForm()
        => await OnSubmit(_trail, _trailImage);

}
```

The OnSubmit parameter defines an event that passes the data entered in the form to the handler specified by the consuming component.

Note that the ResetForm method is public. This will be called by the consuming component to reset the form, if required.

The handler for the EditForm's OnValidSubmit event will invoke the TrailForm's OnSubmit event. This allows the handler to decide how to persist the data from the form.

Some of this code is familiar. The various private fields are lifted straight from the `AddTrailPage` along with the entire `EditForm` component and the `On-Initialized` and `LoadTrailImage` methods. However, there are some new items we need to understand.

We've added a component parameter that defines a component event—`On-Submit`. Farther down the code block we can see how it's triggered. When the `Edit-Form`'s `OnValidSubmit` event is invoked, the `SubmitForm` method is run. This, in turn, calls the `OnSubmit` event passing in the trail data from the form, as well as the image, if one has been selected. It's worth noting here that we're not using the `EventCallback<T>`, which we've used previously. This is because we want to manually control when `StateHasChanged` is called in the handler. More on this later.

The other method we've added is the `ResetForm` method. This method is self-explanatory, but it's important to notice that it is marked as public, rather than private. This is so a component consuming our form can invoke this method and reset the form, when required. More on this in a little bit.

6.4.2 Refactoring AddTrailPage.razor

Now we have the initial logic in place for our form component we can refactor the `AddTrailPage` to use it. But first we'll move `AddTrailPage.razor` and `AddTrail-Handler.cs` into a new folder called *AddTrail*. At this point our ManageTrails feature folder should look like figure 6.9.

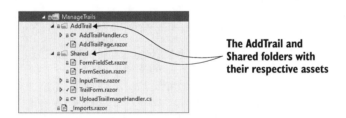

The AddTrail and Shared folders with their respective assets

Figure 6.9   The reorganized ManageTrails feature folder

Now that we have our files in the right place, we will update the markup section of the `AddTrailPage` with the following code.

Listing 6.17   AddTrailPage.razor: Updated markup

```
@page "/add-trail"
@inject IMediator Mediator

<PageTitle>Add Trail - Blazing Trails</PageTitle>

<nav aria-label="breadcrumb">
    <ol class="breadcrumb">
        <li class="breadcrumb-item"><a href="/">Home</a></li>
```

```
                    <li class="breadcrumb-item active" aria-current="page">Add Trail</li>
            </ol>
    </nav>

    <h3 class="mt-5 mb-4">Add a trail</h3>

    @if (_submitSuccessful)
    {
        <div class="alert alert-success" role="alert">
            <svg xmlns="http://www.w3.org/2000/svg" width="18" height="18"
            ➥fill="currentColor" class="bi bi-check-circle-fill" viewBox="0 0 16 16">
                <path fill-rule="evenodd" d="M16 8A8 8 0 1 1 0 8a8 8 0 0 1 16
                ➥0zm-3.97-3.03a.75.75 0 0 0-1.08.022L7.477 9.417 5.384
                ➥7.323a.75.75 0 0 0-1.06 1.06L6.97 11.03a.75.75 0 0 0
                ➥1.079-.0213.992-4.99a.75.75 0 0 0-.01-1.05z" />
            </svg>
            Your trail has been added successfully!
        </div>
    }
    else if (_errorMessage is not null)
    {
        <div class="alert alert-danger" role="alert">
            <svg xmlns="http://www.w3.org/2000/svg" width="18" height="18"
            ➥fill="currentColor" class="bi bi-x-circle-fill" viewBox="0 0 16 16">
                <path fill-rule="evenodd" d="M16 8A8 8 0 1 1 0 8a8 8 0 0 1 16
                ➥0zM5.354 4.646a.5.5 0 1 0-.708.708L7.293 81-2.647 2.646a.5.5
            ➥0 0 0 .708.708L8 8.70712.646 2.647a.5.5 0 0 0 .708-.708L8.707
            ➥812.647-2.646a.5.5 0 0 0-.708-.708L8 7.293 5.354 4.646z" />
            </svg>
            @_errorMessage
        </div>
    }


    <TrailForm @ref="_trailForm" OnSubmit="SubmitNewTrail" />          ⟵
```

> **The original EditForm component is replaced with the new
> TrailForm component. Blazor's @ref directive is used to capture
> a reference to the component. This will be used to invoke the
> ResetForm method. We also provide a OnSubmit handler.**

The code at the top of the markup section is unchanged. However, where the original EditForm component was, only a reference to the new TrailForm component remains. We're using Blazor's @ref directive to capture a reference to the Trail-Form. This is stored in the _trailForm field—which we'll see when we look at the code block. We're also providing a handler for the TrailForm's OnSubmit event.

Before we jump into the code block, we have an opportunity to extract some reusable code out into components. The markup that shows the success and error alerts will also be needed on the edit trail page when we add it a little later. This will save us duplicating a fair amount of code, and if we ever want to update our success and error alerts, we can do it in a single place.

First let's use the code in listing 6.18 to create a new component in the Shared folder called SuccessAlert.razor.

Listing 6.18 SuccessAlert.razor

```
<div class="alert alert-success" role="alert">
    <svg xmlns="http://www.w3.org/2000/svg" width="18" height="18"
    ➥fill="currentColor" class="bi bi-check-circle-fill" viewBox="0 0 16 16">
        <path fill-rule="evenodd" d="M16 8A8 8 0 1 1 0 8a8 8 0 0 1 16
    ➥0zm-3.97-3.03a.75.75 0 0 0-1.08.022L7.477 9.417 5.384 7.323a.75.75 0 0
    ➥0-1.06 1.06L6.97 11.03a.75.75 0 0 0 1.079-.0213.992-4.99a.75.75 0 0
    ➥0-.01-1.05z" />
    </svg>
    @Message
</div>

@code {
    [Parameter, EditorRequired]
    public string Message { get; set; } = default!;
}
```

> The hardcoded success message has been replaced with a parameter to allow the consuming component to provide a success message of its choice.

The component is nice and simple. We've taken the original markup and removed the hardcoded success message and replaced it with a parameter. Now the add and edit trail pages will be able to specify their own unique success messages.

Now let's do the same thing for error markup. We'll add a new component called ErrorAlert.razor and add the following code.

Listing 6.19 ErrorAlert.razor

```
<div class="alert alert-danger" role="alert">
    <svg xmlns="http://www.w3.org/2000/svg" width="18" height="18"
    ➥fill="currentColor" class="bi bi-x-circle-fill" viewBox="0 0 16 16">
        <path fill-rule="evenodd" d="M16 8A8 8 0 1 1 0 8a8 8 0 0 1 16
    ➥0zM5.354 4.646a.5.5 0 1 0-.708.708L7.293 81-2.647 2.646a.5.5 0 0 0
    ➥.708.708L8 8.70712.646 2.647a.5.5 0 0 0 .708-.708L8.707 812.647-2.646a.5.5
    ➥0 0 0-.708-.708L8 7.293 5.354 4.646z" />
    </svg>
    @Message
</div>

@code {
    [Parameter, EditorRequired]
    public string Message { get; set; } = default!;
}
```

> The hardcoded error message success message has been replaced with a parameter to allow the consuming component to provide an error message of its choice.

Just as with the SuccessAlert component, all we've done is copied the markup and replaced the hardcoded message with a parameter.

We can now update the AddTrailPage to use the new components as shown in the following listing.

Listing 6.20 AddTrailPage.razor: Adding the alert components

```
@if (_submitSuccessful)
{
```

```
    <SuccessAlert Message="Your trail has been added
    ➥successfully!" />
}
else if (_errorMessage is not null)
{
    <ErrorAlert Message="@_errorMessage" />
}
```

◀— The previous markup for the success alert has been replaced with the new SuccessAlert component, passing in a custom success message.

◀— The previous markup for the error alert has been replaced with the new ErrorAlert component, passing in a custom error message.

As you can see, this has tidied up the code for the Alert section nicely. Plus, we can reuse the new components when we build the edit trail page. It's a win-win!

With that small refactor out of the way, we can get back to updating the code block for `AddTrailPage.razor`. The updated code block is shown in the following listing.

Listing 6.21   AddTrailPage.razor: Updated code block

```
@code {
    private bool _submitSuccessful;
    private string? _errorMessage;
    private TrailForm _trailForm = default!;

    private async Task SubmitNewTrail(TrailDto trail, IBrowserFile? image)
    {
        var response = await Mediator.Send(new AddTrailRequest(trail));
        if (response.TrailId == -1)
        {
            _submitSuccessful = false;
            _errorMessage = "There was a problem saving your trail.";
            StateHasChanged();
            return;
        }

        if (image is null)
        {
            _submitSuccessful = true;
            _trailForm.ResetForm();
            StateHasChanged();
            return;
        }

        _submitSuccessful = await ProcessImage(response.TrailId, image);
        if (_submitSuccessful)
        {
            _trailForm.ResetForm();
        }

        StateHasChanged();
    }

    private async Task<bool> ProcessImage(int trailId,
    ➥IBrowserFile trailImage)
    {
```

◀— If there was an error saving the trail, manually call StateHasChanged to update the UI with the error message.

◀— If the trail was saved successfully and didn't have an image, reset the TrailForm via the reference captured by the _trailForm field.

◀— Shows a manual call to StateHasChanged to trigger an update of the UI

◀— If we are here, we've attempted to upload a trail image. We trigger a UI update to show the result of that operation.

```
var imageUploadResponse = await Mediator.Send(
➥new UploadTrailImageRequest(trailId, trailImage));

if (string.IsNullOrWhiteSpace(imageUploadResponse.ImageName))
{
    _errorMessage = "Your trail was saved, but there was a
    ➥problem uploading the image.";
    return false;
}

    return true;
    }
}
```

At this point, the add trail page should be working as it did previously. We're now going to add in the edit functionality.

6.4.3 Adding the edit trail feature

Before we start making any changes in the Client project to enable editing, we need to make some changes to the Shared project. There are a few jobs for us to do:

1 We must update the `TrailDto` class—specifically, to handle updating the trail image.
2 We need to update the folder structure so it mirrors the feature folder structure in the Client project.
3 We need to add two new requests for our edit functionality: `EditTrail-Request` and `GetTrailRequest`.

Let's work through each of these items, starting at the top.

UPDATING THE TRAILDTO CLASS

When editing a trail, we will need to be able to display the trail's current image, if it has one. We will also need to give the user the ability to remove the image, update it, or leave it unchanged. To enable these scenarios, we'll update the class with two additional properties and a new enum, as shown in the following listing.

Listing 6.22 **TrailDto.cs: Add new properties and `ImageAction` enum**

```
public class TrailDto
{
    // other properties omitted

    public string? Image { get; set; }          ⟵─ Image holds the filename
                                                    of an existing image.
    public ImageAction ImageAction { get; set; } ⟵┐
}                                                   ImageAction allows us to set what
                                                    operation to perform on the trail
public enum ImageAction    ⟵┐                      image when updating the trail.
{                            Contains the various
    None,                    operations that can be
    Add,                     performed on an image
    Remove
}
```

When we add the edit functionality to the Client project, we need to load the trail to edit from the API. At this point we need to know if the trail has an image. This is where the new `Image` property comes in. If there is an image, this will contain the filename of that image so we can display it to the user.

When the user is modifying a trail with an image, we need to know what operation, if any, we're performing on that image. This is where the second new property and new `enum` come in. If they add or remove the image, we will record that intent using the `ImageAction` property. We can then reference this in our endpoint to understand what to do.

UPDATING THE SHARED PROJECT'S FOLDER STRUCTURE

To keep things organized, we want to make sure we keep the same feature folder structure throughout the solution. Based on our changes in the Client project, we need to add three new folders in the ManageTrails folder:

- AddTrail
- EditTrail
- Shared

Then we can move the existing files into their new homes. The AddTrailRequest.cs file goes in the AddTrail folder and the TrailDto.cs and UploadImageRequest.cs files go in the Shared folder.

ADDING THE NEW EDITTRAILREQUEST AND GETTRAILREQUEST TO THE SHARED PROJECT

While we're in the Shared project, we might as well add the two new requests we need for editing a trail. The first request we're going to add is the `GetTrailRequest`. We'll add this in the new EditTrail folder we just created. The following listing shows the code.

Listing 6.23   GetTrailRequest.cs

```
public record GetTrailRequest(int TrailId) :
    IRequest<GetTrailRequest.Response>
{
    public const string RouteTemplate = "/api/trails/{trailId}";

    public record Response(Trail Trail);
    public record Trail(int Id, string Name, string Location, string? Image,
        int TimeInMinutes, int Length, string Description,
        IEnumerable<RouteInstruction> RouteInstructions);
    public record RouteInstruction(int Id, int Stage, string Description);
}
```

The record contains a single property that holds the ID of the trail to retrieve.

The request returns a response that contains all the information needed by the Trail form.

The `GetTrailRequest` takes an ID for the trail that must be retrieved from the API. It also defines the response for the request. This is a copy of the current data for the requested trail and will be used to populate the trail form.

The other request we need to add is the `EditTrailRequest`. This will be called when the form is submitted once the user has finished editing. Again, this will be added to the EditTrail folder alongside the previous request. The following listing shows the code.

Listing 6.24 EditTrailRequest.cs

```
public record EditTrailRequest(TrailDto Trail) :
➥IRequest<EditTrailRequest.Response>
{
    public const string RouteTemplate = "/api/trails";
    public record Response(bool IsSuccess);
}

public class EditTrailRequestValidator : AbstractValidator<EditTrailRequest>
{
    public EditTrailRequestValidator()
    {
        RuleFor(x => x.Trail).SetValidator(
        ➥new TrailValidator());
    }
}
```

> Shows the edited trail data stored in the Trail property on the record

> To validate the trail, we reuse the TrailValidator that lives with the TrailDto. This ensures we're only using one set of validation rules whether we're adding or editing a trail.

The `EditTrailRequest` takes the edited trail. To make sure that data is valid, we reuse the same `TrailValidator` we used with the `AddTrailRequest`. This ensures we're using the same validation rules whether we're adding or editing a trail.

All the changes for the Shared project are complete. We can now head back into the Client project and build the new edit trail feature.

ADDING THE EDITTRAILPAGE TO THE CLIENT PROJECT

Back in the Client project. Let's start by creating a new folder in the ManageTrails folder called *EditTrail*. In that folder, we're going to add a new component called `EditTrailPage.razor`. The following listing shows the code for the markup section of the new component.

Listing 6.25 EditTrailPage.razor: Markup section

```
@page "/edit-trail/{TrailId:int}"
@inject IMediator Mediator

<PageTitle>Edit Trail - Blazing Trails</PageTitle>

<nav aria-label="breadcrumb">
    <ol class="breadcrumb">
        <li class="breadcrumb-item"><a href="/">Home</a></li>
        <li class="breadcrumb-item active" aria-current="page">
        ➥Edit Trail</li>
    </ol>
</nav>

@if (_isLoading)
{
```

> As we need to load the trail being edited from the API, we're going to show a loading message until the trail is available.

```
    <p>Loading trail...</p>
}
else
{
    <h3 class="mt-5 mb-4">Editing trail: @_trail.Name</h3>

    @if (_submitSuccessful)
    {
        <SuccessAlert
        ➥Message="Your trail has been edited successfully!" />
    }
    else if (_errorMessage is not null)
    {
        <ErrorAlert Message="@_errorMessage" />
    }

    <TrailForm Trail="_trail"
    ➥OnSubmit="SubmitEditTrail" />
}
```

> We reuse the SuccessAlert we created when refactoring the AddTrailPage component.

> We reuse the ErrorAlert we created when refactoring the AddTrailPage component.

> The TrailForm is referenced as in the AddTrailPage. However, this time it also provides a handler for the OnSubmit event. We're also passing in the trail to be edited.

Most of this code is extremely like that of the AddTrailPage component—with the word *Add* swapped for *Edit*. A key difference is the addition of the if statement, which shows a loading message when isLoading is true. As we need to fetch the details of the trail to edit from the API, it is a good practice to show a loading indicator of some kind, just in case the call is slow to return. Once the trail has been loaded, the rest of the markup is displayed, including the TrailForm.

Although we've not implemented this yet—we'll do that once we're done here—we're passing in the trail we want to edit to the TrailForm component. We also supply a handler for the form's OnSubmit event.

Now let's take a look at the code block. We're going to do this in two parts, as there are quite a few things to point out. The following listing shows the first half of the code block.

Listing 6.26   EditTrailPage.razor: Code block part 1

```
private bool _isLoading;
private bool _submitSuccessful;
private string? _errorMessage;
private TrailDto _trail = new TrailDto();

[Parameter] public int TrailId { get; set; }

protected override async Task OnInitializedAsync()
{
    _isLoading = true;

    var response = await Mediator
    ➥.Send(new GetTrailRequest(TrailId));
```

> When the component is initialized, the _isLoading field is set to true.

> The request is then dispatched to the API via MediatR.

```
if (response.Trail is not null)
{
    _trail.Id = TrailId;
    _trail.Name = response.Trail.Name;
    _trail.Description = response.Trail.Description;
    _trail.Location = response.Trail.Location;
    _trail.Image = response.Trail.Image;
    _trail.Length = response.Trail.Length;
    _trail.TimeInMinutes = response.Trail.TimeInMinutes;
    _trail.Route.Clear();
    _trail.Route.AddRange(response.Trail
    ➥.RouteInstructions.Select(ri => new TrailDto.RouteInstruction
    {
        Stage = ri.Stage,
        Description = ri.Description
    }));
}
else
{
    _errorMessage = "There was a problem loading the trail.";
}
_isLoading = false;
}
```

⟵ **If the trail is returned, its details are copied into a local field, which is passed to the TrailForm.**

⟵ **_isLoading is set to false once the trail has been loaded or an error message has been set.**

This part of the code block deals with loading the trail to be edited. When the component is initialized, the _isLoading field is set to true, which causes the loading message to be displayed in the markup. Then the request to loading the trail to be edited is dispatched via MediatR. If a trail is returned, then its details are copied into the _trail field. As we just saw in the markup, this field is passed into the TrailForm component so it can display the trail's current details to the user.

Let's move on to part 2 of the code block. This part is shown in the following listing and covers persisting any updates to the trail.

Listing 6.27 EditTrailPage.razor: Code block part 2

```
private async Task SubmitEditTrail(TrailDto trail, IBrowserFile? image)
{
    var response = await Mediator.Send(new EditTrailRequest(trail));
    if (!response.IsSuccess)
    {
        _submitSuccessful = false;
        _errorMessage =
        ➥"There was a problem saving your trail.";
    }
    else
    {
        _trail.Name = trail.Name;
        _trail.Description = trail.Description;
        _trail.Location = trail.Location;
        _trail.Length = trail.Length;
        _trail.TimeInMinutes = trail.TimeInMinutes;
        _trail.Route.AddRange(trail.Route.Select(ri =>
        ➥new TrailDto.RouteInstruction
```

If there was an error saving the trail, an error message is shown.

Any updates made to the trail instance from the form are applied to the trail.

```
        {
            Stage = ri.Stage,
            Description = ri.Description
        }));

        _submitSuccessful = true;

        if (trail.ImageAction == ImageAction.Add)
        ➥_submitSuccessful = await ProcessImage(trail.Id, image!);
        if (trail.ImageAction == ImageAction.Remove)
        ➥_trail.Image = "";
    }
}

    StateHasChanged();
}

private async Task<bool> ProcessImage(int trailId, IBrowserFile trailImage)
{
    var imageUploadResponse =
    ➥await Mediator.Send(new UploadTrailImageRequest(trailId, trailImage));

    if (string.IsNullOrWhiteSpace(imageUploadResponse.ImageName))
    {
        _errorMessage =
        ➥"Your trail was saved, but there was a problem uploading the image.";
        return false;
    }

    _trail.Image = imageUploadResponse.ImageName;
    return true;
}
```

If the user updated the trail image, ProcessImage is called to upload the new image.

If the user removed the image, the Image property is cleared.

StateHasChanged is called to render any updates to the UI based on image actions.

If a new image was selected, update the local trails Image property with the new filename.

When the user submits the form, the SubmitEditTrail method will be called. The first thing it does is submit the updated trail details to the API via MediatR. The response is then checked and if the request wasn't successful, an error message is displayed to the user.

If the request was successful, then the trail instance is updated with the values of the trail from the form. We do this because when we call StateHasChanged at the end of the method, the form will lose any changes made. This happens because the TrailForm is a child of the EditFormPage and calling StateHasChanged will re-render the EditTrailPage. This also re-renders the TrailForm and provides a fresh copy of any parameters being passed in. As we're passing in the trail from the EditTrailPage, this will overwrite any changes entered by the user.

Once the trail is updated, we indicate that the form was submitted successfully by setting the _submitSuccessful field to true. We do this here, as the Process-Image method could override it if there is a problem uploading a new image.

Next, the ImageAction property is checked to see what should happen next. If an image has been added, then the ProcessImage method is called, which uploads the new image. A key job this method does is set the _trail.Image property to the name of the newly uploaded image. This matters because it allows the newly uploaded image to be displayed on the form once the submit process is complete.

If the `ImageAction` is to remove the image, then the `Image` property is set to an empty string. In the earlier request to update the trail details—which we'll look at in a bit—the physical image will be removed from the server. So, we are just tidying up the UI state with this operation.

Finally, we can trigger a UI update by calling `StateHasChanged`.

UPDATING THE TRAILFORM TO HANDLE EDITING

To handle editing, we need to complete some updates to the `TrailForm` component. We need to add a parameter that allows a trail to be passed in for editing. We also need to add some logic that will handle setting the `ImageAction` value we just talked about.

We'll start by adding the code that will enable a trail to be passed in for editing. The following listing contains the updates.

Listing 6.28   TrailForm.razor: Updates to enable trail editing

```
[Parameter]
public TrailDto? Trail { get; set; }
```
The Trail parameter will allow an existing trail to be passed into the form.

```
protected override void OnParametersSet()
{
    _editContext = new EditContext(_trail);
    _editContext.SetFieldCssClassProvider(new BootstrapCssClassProvider());

    if (Trail != null)
    {
        _trail.Id = Trail.Id;
        _trail.Name = Trail.Name;
        _trail.Description = Trail.Description;
        _trail.Location = Trail.Location;
        _trail.Image = Trail.Image;
        _trail.ImageAction = ImageAction.None;
        _trail.Length = Trail.Length;
        _trail.TimeInMinutes = Trail.TimeInMinutes;

        _trail.Route.Clear();
        _trail.Route.AddRange(Trail.Route.Select(ri =>
        new TrailDto.RouteInstruction
        {
            Stage = ri.Stage,
            Description = ri.Description
        }));
    }
}
```

If we have a Trail, then we're editing. We need to copy the details of the trail to edit to the local _trail field that the form components are bound to.

OnInitialized is replaced with OnParametersSet. This will be called whenever an update happens to the object passed in via the Trail parameter. We need this so we can update or remove the image after the SubmitEditTrail handler in the EditTrailPage runs.

The `Trail` parameter allows the consumer, the `EditTrailPage`, to pass in a trail to be edited. The `OnInitialized` method has been replaced with the `OnParameters-Set` method. As we learned in an earlier chapter, the `OnParametersSet` method will be called whenever a component parameter changes. We need this functionality, so if an image is changed or removed during editing, the updated value—which is set in the `EditTrailPage > SubmitEditTrail` method—can be shown on the form.

Our final job in the `TrailForm` component is to handle setting the `ImageAction` property. In terms of UX, we're going to display the existing trail image, if there is one, and provide a button to remove it (figure 6.10).

If an image exists, it's displayed with a button to allow the user to remove it.

Figure 6.10   When a trail being edited has an image, it will be displayed with an option to remove it.

Once an image has been removed, we'll display the `InputFile` component so the user can select a new image. Let's look at the following code.

Listing 6.29   TrailForm.razor: Updates for editing the trail image

```
// other code omitted
<FormFieldSet Width="col-6">
    <label for="trailImage" class="font-weight-bold text-secondary">
    ⮡Image</label>
    @if (string.IsNullOrWhiteSpace(_trail.Image))
    {
        <InputFile OnChange="LoadTrailImage"                      If the trail doesn't have an image,
        ⮡class="form-control-file" id="trailImage"                render the InputFile component,
        ⮡accept=".png,.jpg,.jpeg" />                              allowing the user to select one.
    }
    else
    {
        <div class="card bg-dark text-white">
            <img src="images/@_trail.Image" />
            <div class="card-img-overlay">                        If the trail has an
                <button class="btn btn-primary btn-sm"            image, display it
                ⮡@onclick="RemoveTrailImage">Remove</button>      along with a button
            </div>                                                to remove it.
        </div>
    }
</FormFieldSet>
// other code omitted
@code {
    // other code omitted
    private void LoadTrailImage(InputFileChangeEventArgs e)
```

```
{
    _trailImage = e.File;
    _trail.ImageAction = ImageAction.Add;          ⟵┐  Set the ImageAction to add
}                                                        │  when an image is selected.

private void RemoveTrailImage()                    ⟵┐  This method is called when the
{                                                        │  Remove Image button is clicked. It
    _trail.Image = null;                                 │  will reset the Image property,
    _trail.ImageAction = ImageAction.Remove;             │  triggering the InputFile component
}                                                        │  to show. It also marks the image to
// other code omitted                                    │  be removed on the server.
}
```

In the markup portion of the code, we're adding a check for an existing image around the `InputFile` component. If no image exists, we continue to display the `InputFile` component, as before. However, if an image exists, we display it along with a button to remove it. The styling for all this is taken care of by Bootstrap. We're using the `card` component markup (https://getbootstrap.com/docs/5.1/components/card/).

Back in the code block, there is a small update to the `LoadTrailImage` method. It now sets the `ImageAction` to `Add` whenever a trail is selected. A new method for removing the trail image has also been added. This is called by the new Remove button we just added in the markup. It clears the `Image` property and sets the `Image-Action` to `Remove`. This results in the UI updating to display the `InputFile` component. The user is then able to select a new image if they choose.

ADDING THE GETTRAILREQUEST AND EDITTRAILREQUEST HANDLERS

Our final job in the Client project is to add the handlers for the `GetTrailRequest` and `EditTrailRequest`. Once these are in place, we can add the API endpoints and we're done!

Both new handlers will live in the ManageTrails > EditTrail feature folder. The following listing shows the `GetTrailHandler`.

Listing 6.30 GetTrailHandler.cs

```
public class GetTrailHandler :
➥IRequestHandler<GetTrailRequest, GetTrailRequest.Response?>
{
    private readonly HttpClient _httpClient;

    public GetTrailHandler(HttpClient httpClient)
    {
        _httpClient = httpClient;
    }

    public async Task<GetTrailRequest.Response?>
    ➥Handle(GetTrailRequest request, CancellationToken cancellationToken)
    {
        try
        {
            return await _httpClient
            ➥.GetFromJsonAsync<GetTrailRequest.Response>(
```

```
        ➥GetTrailRequest.RouteTemplate.Replace("{trailId}",
        ➥request.TrailId.ToString()));      ◁──┐  The placeholder, trailId, in the
    }                                            RouteTemplate is replaced with
    catch (HttpRequestException)                 the ID of the trail to edit before
    {                                            making the HTTP request.
        return default!;
    }
    }
}
```

The handler receives the request from MediatR and makes an HTTP GET request to the API. Before doing this, it replaces the `{trailId}` placeholder in the `Route-Template` with the ID of the trail from the request. Now let's look at the `EditTrail-Handler` in the following listing.

Listing 6.31   EditTrailHandler.cs

```
public class EditTrailHandler :
➥IRequestHandler<EditTrailRequest, EditTrailRequest.Response>
{
    private readonly HttpClient _httpClient;

    public EditTrailHandler(HttpClient httpClient)
    {
        _httpClient = httpClient;
    }

    public async Task<EditTrailRequest.Response>
    ➥Handle(EditTrailRequest request, CancellationToken cancellationToken)
    {
        var response = await _httpClient
        ➥.PutAsJsonAsync(EditTrailRequest.RouteTemplate,
        ➥request, cancellationToken);       ◁──┐  The updated trail details are set
                                                 to the API via a HTTP PUT request.
        if (response.IsSuccessStatusCode)
        {
            return new EditTrailRequest
            ➥.Response(true);              ◁──┐  If the request was successful, a true
        }                                        response is sent back to the caller.
        else
        {
            return new EditTrailRequest.Response(false);
        }
    }
}
```

The handler receives the updated trail details from MediatR and sends them to the API using an HTTP PUT request. Depending on whether that call was successful or not, either `true` or `false` is returned to the caller.

ADDING THE API ENDPOINTS FOR GETTRAILREQUEST AND EDITTRAILREQUEST

We are almost finished! The last step we must take is to update the API. Before we add the new endpoints, we need to update the folder structure to match the Client and

Shared projects. Currently, we have only the ManageTrails folder containing the AddTrailEndpoint.cs and UploadTrailImageEndpoint.cs files. Let's add the subfolders to match the other projects:

- AddTrail
- EditTrail
- Shared

Now we can move the AddTrailEndpoint.cs file into the AddTrail folder. Then we can move the UploadTrailImageEndpoint.cs file into the Shared folder. We're now ready to add the `GetTrailEndpoint` and `EditTrailEndpoint`.

Let's start with the `GetTrailEndpoint`. We'll add that in the new `EditTrail` directory with the following code.

Listing 6.32   GetTrailEndpoint.cs

```
public class GetTrailEndpoint :
BaseAsyncEndpoint.WithRequest<int>.WithResponse<GetTrailRequest.Response>
{
    private readonly BlazingTrailsContext _context;

    public GetTrailEndpoint(BlazingTrailsContext context)
    {
        _context = context;
    }

    [HttpGet(GetTrailRequest.RouteTemplate)]
    public override async Task<ActionResult<GetTrailRequest.Response>>
    HandleAsync(int trailId, CancellationToken cancellationToken = default)
    {
        var trail = await _context.Trails
        .Include(x => x.Route)
        .SingleOrDefaultAsync(x => x.Id == trailId,
        cancellationToken: cancellationToken);     ◁──┐ First, the requested trail is
                                                       │ loaded from the database.
        if (trail is null)
        {
            return BadRequest(
            "Trail could not be found.");     ◁──┐ If the trail can't be found,
        }                                         │ a BadRequest is returned.

        var response = new GetTrailRequest.Response(
        new GetTrailRequest.Trail(trail.Id,
            trail.Name,
            trail.Location,
            trail.Image,
            trail.TimeInMinutes,
            trail.Length,
            trail.Description,
            trail.Route.Select(ri =>
            new GetTrailRequest.RouteInstruction(ri.Id, ri.Stage,
            ri.Description)))));
```

```
        return Ok(response);
    }
}
```

◁—— **If the trail is found, a new GetTrailRequest.Response instance is returned containing the trail's details.**

The endpoint first attempts to load the requested trail from the database. If this fails, then a `BadRequest` is returned by the API. If the trail is loaded successfully, a new `GetTrailRequest.Response` instance is returned by the API, containing the details of the requested trail.

Let's move on and add the `EditTrailEndpoint`. This will also live in the EditTrail folder alongside the `GetTrailEndpoint`. The code is shown in the following listing.

Listing 6.33   EditTrailEndpoint.cs

```
public class EditTrailEndpoint :
➥BaseAsyncEndpoint.WithRequest<EditTrailRequest>.WithResponse<bool>
{
    private readonly BlazingTrailsContext _database;

    public EditTrailEndpoint(BlazingTrailsContext database)
    {
        _database = database;
    }

    [HttpPut(EditTrailRequest.RouteTemplate)]
    public override async Task<ActionResult<bool>>
➥HandleAsync(EditTrailRequest request,
➥CancellationToken cancellationToken = default)
    {
        var trail = await _database.Trails
        ➥.Include(x => x.Route)
        ➥.SingleOrDefaultAsync(x => x.Id == request.Trail.Id,
        ➥cancellationToken: cancellationToken);          ◁—— The trail to edit is loaded from the database.

        if (trail is null)
        {
            return BadRequest("Trail could not be found.");   ◁—— If the trail can't be found, a BadRequest is returned.
        }

        trail.Name = request.Trail.Name;
        trail.Description = request.Trail.Description;
        trail.Location = request.Trail.Location;
        trail.TimeInMinutes = request.Trail
        ➥.TimeInMinutes;
        trail.Length = request.Trail.Length;              Otherwise, the
        trail.Route = request.Trail.Route.Select(         trail is updated
        ➥ri => new RouteInstruction                       with the details
        {                                                 from the request.
            Stage = ri.Stage,
            Description = ri.Description,
            Trail = trail
        }).ToList();
```

```
    if (request.Trail.ImageAction == ImageAction.Remove)
    {
        System.IO.File.Delete(Path.Combine(
        ➥Directory.GetCurrentDirectory(), "Images",
        ➥trail.Image!));
        trail.Image = null;                         ◄───────
    }


    await _database.SaveChangesAsync(cancellationToken);

    return Ok(true);
    }
}
```

If the ImageAction is set to Remove, the physical file is removed from disk and the Image property is set to an empty string.

The endpoint starts by retrieving the trail to edit from the database. If the trail can't be found, then a `BadRequest` is returned. Otherwise, the trail is updated with the details contained in the request. If the `ImageAction` is set to `Remove`, the existing trail image is deleted from the filesystem on the server and the `Image` property is cleared.

We just need to make a small addition to the `UploadTrailImageEndpoint`, and then we're finished. To handle the updating of a trail image, we need to update the code to remove an existing image if one exists. The update is shown in the following listing. Some existing code is shown above and below the new code, to show where it should be inserted.

Listing 6.34 **UploadTrailImageEndpoint.cs**

```
await image.SaveAsJpegAsync(saveLocation, cancellationToken:
    cancellationToken);

if (!string.IsNullOrWhiteSpace(trail.Image))       ◄───────
{
    System.IO.File.Delete(Path.Combine(Directory
    ➥.GetCurrentDirectory(), "Images", trail.Image));  ◄───
}
trail.Image = filename;
await _database.SaveChangesAsync(cancellationToken);
```

Checks if the trail the image belongs to already has an existing image

If the trail has an existing image, remove it from the filesystem.

The new code checks if the trail the new image belongs to already has an image. If it does, then that image is deleted from the filesystem. And we're done! We can now give everything a test to make sure the editing works as expected.

6.4.4 *Testing the edit functionality*

We will have to do a bit of manual intervention to check that our edit logic is functioning correctly. This is because the rest of the site isn't loading trails from the database yet. That functionality is added in appendix B.

First, add a new trail to the application, or if you already have one, then you can use that. Next, we'll open the trails table in the database and find the trail ID. If you're following along and using a SQLite database, you can use a tool called *DB Browser for SQLite* (https://sqlitebrowser.org) to do this.

Once you have the trail ID, go to the running application in your browser and update the URL to `https://localhost:[Port]/edit-trail/[TrailID]`. You will need to add in the port your application is running on, as well as the trail ID. Then press Enter to load the page. If all has gone well, you should be looking at the trail details as shown in figure 6.11.

Figure 6.11   The trail form in update mode displaying data for an existing trail

As you can see, the title of the page is telling us we're updating a trail and what that trail is. Each section of the form is showing the data that was entered originally. At this point, feel free to update any details and ensure they're saved.

Remember, the rest of the app is still using our hardcoded test data. It will need to be updated to use the new API we've built. The work to do that is covered in appendix B; the coming chapters will assume that work has been completed.

Summary

- While Blazor Input components output default validation class names, it is possible to customize them by providing a custom FieldCssClassProvider.
- If using a custom FieldCssClassProvider, it must be registered with the EditContext.
- Blazor provides an out-of-the-box component called InputBase<T> as a starting point for creating custom input components.
- A type parameter must be specified when inheriting from InputBase<T>. When binding model properties to the component, they must match the type parameter.
- When inheriting from InputBase<T> an implementation must be provided for the TryParseValueFromString method; however, it may not be used.
- There are two properties provided by InputBase<T> to update the model value bound to a custom input component: CurrentValueAsString and CurrentValue.
- InputFile is a component included with Blazor for working with files in forms.
- The bind directive isn't used when working with InputFile. Instead, a handler must be provided for the component's OnChange event.
- The OnChange event provides its handler with InputFileChangeEventArgs, which contains the file(s) selected by the user along with the total count of files selected.
- By default, a maximum of 10 files can be selected by the user—selecting more will result in the component throwing an exception. However, the maximum limit value can be modified.
- A selected file is represented as an IBrowserFile, which contains a method called OpenReadStream that allows the file's contents to be read.

Creating more repsable components

7

This chapter covers
- Using templates to define specific regions of UI
- Enhancing templates with generics
- Sharing components using Razor class libraries

Reusability is one of the compelling reasons for using components. They allow us to define chunks of markup and logic that can be reused by simply referencing them in other markup. This is an immensely powerful tool. So far, we've taken advantage of this on several occasions in previous chapters:

- `TrailCard` component
- `FormSection` component
- `FormFieldSet` component
- `SuccessAlert` and `ErrorAlert` components

NOTE If you're following along building the example application, you will need to complete appendix B before starting this chapter.

In this chapter, we're going to take reusability to the next level. We'll learn how to leverage templates and generics to make the ultimate reusable components. To give us a practical example, we'll be enhancing the home page of Blazing Trails with a component that allows the user to toggle the layout between a grid and a table (figure 7.1).

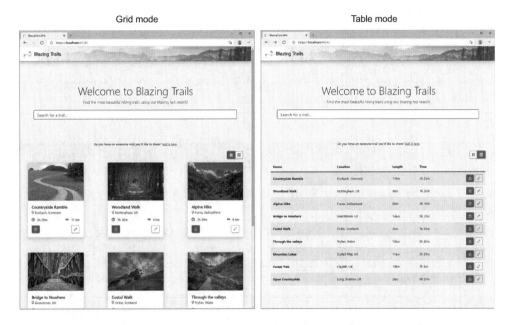

Figure 7.1 The home page of Blazing Trails with the final `ViewSwitcher` component we'll be building during this chapter. The component allows the user to toggle between a grid view and a table view of the available trails.

Once we've built our `ViewSwitcher` component, we'll finish the chapter by learning about Razor class libraries (RCL). RCLs allow us to bundle up any common components and share them across applications. This can be done via a project reference, or RCLs can be packed and shipped via NuGet—just like any other .NET library.

7.1 Defining templates

Templates are a powerful tool when building reusable components. They allow us to specify chunks of markup to be provided by the consumer, which we can then output wherever we wish. We have already used some basic templating when we built the `FormSection` and `FormFieldSet` components in the previous chapters. In those components, we defined a parameter with a type of `RenderFragment` and a name of `ChildContent`:

```
[Parameter] public RenderFragment ChildContent { get; set; }
```

This is a special convention. Defining a parameter with this specific name and type allows us to capture whatever markup has been specified between the start and end tags of the component. However, for our `ViewSwitcher` component, we're going to need something a little more advanced.

The `ViewSwitcher` component allows the user to toggle between a card view and a table view of the available trails. To make this component as reusable as possible, we don't want to hardcode the markup for either the grid or the table view. Instead, we want to define these as templates that allow the consumer of the component to define these areas for themselves.

Let's look at the initial markup for the `ViewSwitcher` component. For now, we will create this component in the Client project under Features > Home > Shared. See the following listing.

Listing 7.1   ViewSwitcher.razor: Initial code

```
<div>
    <div class="mb-3 text-end">
        <div class="btn-group">
            <button @onclick="@(() =>
            _mode = ViewMode.Grid)" title="Grid View" type="button"
            class="btn @(_mode == ViewMode.Grid ? "btn-secondary"
            : "btn-outline-secondary")">
                <i class="bi bi-grid-fill"></i>
            </button>
            <button @onclick="@(() =>
            _mode = ViewMode.Table)" title="Table View" type="button"
            class="btn @(_mode == ViewMode.Table ? "btn-secondary"
            : "btn-outline-secondary")">
                <i class="bi bi-table"></i>
            </button>
        </div>
    </div>

    @if (_mode == ViewMode.Grid)
    {
        @GridTemplate
    }
    else if (_mode == ViewMode.Table)
    {
        @TableTemplate
    }
</div>

@code {
    private ViewMode _mode = ViewMode.Grid;

    [Parameter, EditorRequired]
    public RenderFragment GridTemplate { get; set; }
    = default!;
    [Parameter, EditorRequired]
    public RenderFragment TableTemplate { get; set; }
    = default!;

    private enum ViewMode { Grid, Table }
}
```

The two buttons allow the user to toggle between the two views offered by the component.

Specifies where the markup provided by the consumer for the GridTemplate should be output

Specifies where the markup provided by the consumer for the TableTemplate should be output

Defines the GridTemplate parameter

Defines the TableTemplate parameter

The enum defines the two view modes and avoids using magic strings.

The component starts with some markup that renders two buttons. These buttons allow the user to toggle between the two views offered by the component. To do this, we're setting the value of _mode to either Grid or Table. The _mode field is defined in the code block and defaulted to Grid. The buttons also use a simple expression to apply different CSS classes to highlight which of the modes is currently active.

Depending on which mode is active, the component renders one of two templates defined in the code block, GridTemplate or TableTemplate. A template is just a parameter with a type of RenderFragment.

We're also going to add some styling for the component. We'll add a new file called *ViewSwitcher.razor.scss* and add the following code.

Listing 7.2   ViewSwitcher.razor.scss

```
.grid {                                          ◁─────────────    This class defines the styling for the
    display: grid;                                                 grid view.
    grid-template-columns: repeat(3, 288px);
    grid-column-gap: 123px;
    grid-row-gap: 75px;
}

table {                 ◁─────                This class defines the
    width: 100%;                             styling for the table view.
    margin-bottom: 1rem;
    color: #212529;
    border-collapse: collapse;

    ::deep th, ::deep td {
        padding: .75rem;
        vertical-align: middle;
    }

    ::deep thead tr th {
        border-bottom: 4px solid var(--brand);
        border-top: none;
    }

    ::deep tbody tr:nth-of-type(odd) {
        background-color: rgba(0,0,0,.05);
    }
}
```

That is all we need for now. Let's jump over to HomePage.razor and implement ViewSwitcher. Then we can run the app and see what everything looks like. We're going to replace the current code that renders the grid of trails with the code shown in the following listing.

Listing 7.3   HomePage.razor: Using ViewSwitcher

```
<ViewSwitcher>            │     Defines the markup
    <GridTemplate>      ◁─┘     for the GridTemplate
```

```
        <div class="grid">
            @foreach (var trail in _trails)
            {
                <TrailCard Trail="trail" OnSelected="HandleTrailSelected" />
            }
        </div>
    </GridTemplate>
    <TableTemplate>
        <table class="table table-striped">
            <thead>
                <tr>
                    <th>Name</th>
                    <th>Location</th>
                    <th>Length</th>
                    <th>Time</th>
                    <th></th>
                </tr>
            </thead>
            <tbody>
                @foreach (var trail in _trails)
                {
                    <tr>
                        <th scope="col">@trail.Name</th>
                        <td>@trail.Location</td>
                        <td>@(trail.Length)km</td>
                        <td>@trail.TimeFormatted</td>
                        <td class="text-right">
                            <button @onclick="@(() =>
HandleTrailSelected(trail))" title="View" class="btn btn-primary">
                                <i class="bi bi-binoculars"></i>
                            </button>
                            <button @onclick="@(() => NavManager
.NavigateTo($"/edit-trail/{trail.Id}"))" title="Edit"
class="btn btn-outline-secondary">
                                <i class="bi bi-pencil"></i>
                            </button>
                        </td>
                    </tr>
                }
            </tbody>
        </table>
    </TableTemplate>
</ViewSwitcher>
```

Defines the markup for the TableTemplate

To specify the markup for a particular template, we define child elements that match the name of the parameter. In our case, that is `GridTemplate` and `TableTemplate`. The markup we've defined above for the `GridTemplate` and `TableTemplate` will be output by `ViewSwitcher` where we specified the `@GridTemplate` and `@Table-Template` expressions.

We can now run the app and see what everything looks like. Figure 7.2 shows a side-by-side comparison of the two views.

Figure 7.2 Grid and table views offered by the `ViewSwitcher` component

That's great! We now have the initial version of the component in place. Next, we're going to introduce generics to `ViewSwitcher`.

7.2 Enhancing templates with generics

Currently, our component is working well. It allows us to define the markup for the table and grid views and for the user to toggle between them. However, I think we can improve things a bit. Right now, we must define a lot of markup in the `HomePage` when we're using the component. We're defining a div with a class of `.grid` around a `foreach` block in the grid template. Then for the table template, we're providing the entire markup for the table.

As we know we're going to be displaying a grid or a table, we can bake some of the boilerplate markup into the component. Then when we use the component, we only have to specify the markup and data specific to that usage. To do this, we will introduce generics into our `ViewSwitcher` component. The following listing shows the updated code.

Listing 7.4 ViewSwitcher.razor: Updated to use generics

```
@typeparam TItem
// code omitted
@if (_mode == ViewMode.Grid)
{
    <div class="grid">
        @foreach (var item in Items)
        {
            @GridTemplate(item)
        }
    </div>
}
```

A type parameter is specified using the typeparam directive.

We now only require the header cells to be specified when using the component, rather than all the markup for the head of the table.

```
else if (_mode == ViewMode.Table)
{
    <table>
        <thead>
            <tr>
                @HeaderTemplate
            </tr>
        </thead>
        <tbody>
            @foreach (var item in Items)
            {
                <tr>
                    @RowTemplate(item)
                </tr>
            }
        </tbody>
    </table>
}
// code omitted
@code {
    private ViewMode _mode = ViewMode.Grid;

    [Parameter, EditorRequired]
    public IEnumerable<TItem> Items { get; set; }
    ➥= default!;
    [Parameter, EditorRequired]
    public RenderFragment<TItem> GridTemplate { get;
    ➥set; } = default!;
    [Parameter, EditorRequired]
    public RenderFragment HeaderTemplate { get; set; }
    ➥= default!;
    [Parameter, EditorRequired]
    public RenderFragment<TItem> RowTemplate { get;
    ➥set; } = default!;
    // code omitted
}
```

We now require only the header cells to be specified when using the component, rather than all the markup for the head of the table.

The component now accepts a list of items to be displayed.

Defining RenderFragments with a type parameter allows the consumer to use properties of that type when defining a template.

We start by introducing a type parameter to the component. We do this using the @typeparam directive. Once we do this, we can reference the type parameter when defining our template parameters in the code block. We're now stating that the GridTemplate and RowTemplate will contain items of type TItem. When we invoke these RenderFragments in the markup section, we can pass in an object of type TItem. These items are coming from the new Items parameter we've created. We'll see the benefit of this in more detail in a second, when we update the HomePage, but by defining our template parameters with a type, we'll be able to access properties of that type when defining the template.

Let's go and update the HomePage to work with the changes we've made to ViewSwitcher. The updated code for HomePage.razor is shown in the following listing.

Listing 7.5 HomePage.razor: Replace existing `ViewSwitcher` code

The list of trails is now passed into the ViewSwitcher rather than having to define foreach loops in the templates.

The GridTemplate is now cleaner, as we no longer need to define the grid and a foreach loop.

```
<ViewSwitcher Items="_trails">
    <GridTemplate>
        <TrailCard Trail="context"
        ➥OnSelected="HandleTrailSelected" />
    </GridTemplate>
    <HeaderTemplate>
        <th>Name</th>
        <th>Location</th>
        <th>Length</th>
        <th>Time</th>
        <th></th>
    </HeaderTemplate>
    <RowTemplate>
        <th scope="col">@context.Name</th>
        <td>@context.Location</td>
        <td>@(context.Length)km</td>
        <td>@context.TimeFormatted</td>
        <td class="text-right">
            <button @onclick="@(() =>
            ➥HandleTrailSelected(context))" title="View"
            ➥class="btn btn-primary">
                <i class="bi bi-binoculars"></i>
            </button>
            <button @onclick="@(() =>
            ➥NavManager.NavigateTo($"/edit-trail/{context.Id}"))"
            ➥title="Edit" class="btn btn-outline-secondary">
                <i class="bi bi-pencil"></i>
            </button>
        </td>
    </RowTemplate>
</ViewSwitcher>
```

The header template allows us to define the columns our table needs, but without all the boilerplate we had before.

In the template that uses RenderFragment<T>, we can now access properties of the object through a variable called context. This allows loads of flexibility when building our markup.

The list of trails is now passed into the `ViewSwitcher` via the `Items` parameter. This means we no longer need to worry about defining `foreach` loops in various templates, like before. This has tidied up the `GridTemplate` a lot. We need to define only the markup for an individual item now.

As the `GridTemplate` is defined as `RenderFragment<T>`, we can access any properties of `T` in our template. We access these via a special parameter called `context`. As the `TrailCard` component needs an instance of a `Trail`, we can just pass `context` to the `Trail` parameter. The `RowTemplate` shows accessing properties of `T` to an even greater extent.

The other change we made was to add in a `HeaderTemplate` so we could define the columns of our table without all the extra boilerplate markup we had before. As you can see, we need to define only the individual cells now. This reduces the amount of code we need to write considerably.

This is looking great, but there is one other small improvement we can make to help the readability of our code—the `context` parameter. If we were scanning over a component, we would have to pause for a second to understand what *context* meant in this scenario. In our case, `context` is a `Trail`. Wouldn't it be great if it were just called `trail` instead? I think so. And the great news is, we can name it whatever we like! The following listing shows the `ViewSwitcher` on the `HomePage` with a renamed `context` parameter.

Listing 7.6   HomePage.razor: Rename `context` variable

```
<ViewSwitcher Items="_trails">
    <GridTemplate Context="trail">              ◁──┐
        <TrailCard Trail="trail"
        ➥OnSelected="HandleTrailSelected" />         ◁──────────┐
    </GridTemplate>
    <HeaderTemplate>
        <th>Name</th>
        <th>Location</th>                         The context parameter
        <th>Length</th>                           can be renamed using
        <th>Time</th>                             the Context attribute.
        <th></th>
    </HeaderTemplate>
    <RowTemplate Context="trail">               ◁──┘
        <th scope="col">@trail.Name</th>
        <td>@trail.Location</td>
        <td>@(trail.Length)km</td>
        <td>@trail.TimeFormatted</td>
        <td class="text-right">                      Once renamed, the
            <button @onclick="@(() =>                   new name can be
            ➥HandleTrailSelected(trail))" title="View"   used within the
            ➥class="btn btn-primary">               template to refer
                <i class="bi bi-binoculars"></i>      to the object.
            </button>
            <button @onclick="@(() =>
            ➥NavManager.NavigateTo($"/edit-trail/{trail.Id}"))"
            ➥title="Edit" class="btn btn-outline-secondary">
                <i class="bi bi-pencil"></i>
            </button>
        </td>
    </RowTemplate>
</ViewSwitcher>
```

We can rename the `context` parameter using the `Context` attribute on a template. This is available only when the template is defined as `RenderFragment<T>`. Once renamed, the new name can be used to refer to the object being displayed in the template. As you can see, this has made the code far more readable and easier to understand at a glance.

We can take this one step further. We can rename the `context` parameter at the component level, and all the templates will automatically inherit the name (listing 7.7).

Listing 7.7   HomePage.razor: Rename `context` at the component level

```
<ViewSwitcher Items="_trails" Context="trail">        ⟵─┐  The context parameter is
    <GridTemplate>                                        │  renamed at the component level.
        <TrailCard Trail="trail"
        ➥OnSelected="HandleTrailSelected" />
    </GridTemplate>
    <HeaderTemplate>
        <th>Name</th>
        <th>Location</th>
        <th>Length</th>
        <th>Time</th>
        <th></th>
    </HeaderTemplate>                                        Once renamed,
    <RowTemplate>                                            the new name
        <th scope="col">@trail.Name</th>                     can be used
        <td>@trail.Location</td>                             within the
        <td>@(trail.Length)km</td>                           template to
        <td>@trail.TimeFormatted</td>                        refer to the
        <td class="text-right">                              object.
            <button @onclick="@(() =>
            ➥HandleTrailSelected(trail))" title="View"
            ➥class="btn btn-primary">
                <i class="bi bi-binoculars"></i>
            </button>
            <button @onclick="@(() =>
            ➥NavManager.NavigateTo($"/edit-trail/{trail.Id}"))"
            ➥title="Edit" class="btn btn-outline-secondary">
                <i class="bi bi-pencil"></i>
            </button>
        </td>
    </RowTemplate>
</ViewSwitcher>
```

By renaming the `context` parameter at the component level, we can remove the individual names from each template.

7.3   *Sharing components with Razor class libraries*

In this final section, we're going to cover how we can share components between applications. It could be that you're looking to build up a library of common components you use across all your applications. Or maybe you're looking to open source a cool Blazor component you've created. No matter what your intent, the way to share Blazor components is via a Razor class library (RCL).

RCLs might sound familiar if you've been in the ASP.NET space for a while. They're not new and, historically, have been used to share Razor Pages, as well as models, views, and controllers for MVC applications. But now we can also use them to share Blazor components. Let's add a new RCL to our applications so we can learn how they work.

Using the command line, navigate to the folder that contains the solution file for Blazing Trails. Then run the following commands:

```
dotnet new razorclasslib -o BlazingTrails.ComponentLibrary
dotnet sln add
    BlazingTrails.ComponentLibrary\BlazingTrails.ComponentLibrary.csproj
dotnet add BlazingTrails.Client\BlazingTrails.Client.csproj reference
    BlazingTrails.ComponentLibrary\BlazingTrails.ComponentLibrary.csproj
```

These commands will:

1 Create a new RCL.

2 Add it to the solution.

3 Add a reference to it in the Client project.

You can also do this using Visual Studio or Rider if you prefer.

Once you've run those commands, switch back to your IDE. If it's Visual Studio, it will ask you to reload the solution. You should now see the new project in the solution explorer as shown in figure 7.3.

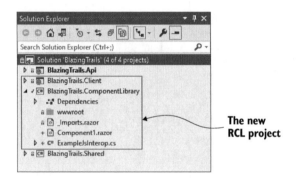

The new
RCL project

**Figure 7.3   The new Razor class
library with its default files**

As with most project types in .NET, the RCL comes with some example files. We don't need these, so you can delete them—except _Imports.razor. It also comes with a directory called *wwwroot*. If we had any static assets to ship with our RCL, such as images, CSS, or JavaScript files, we could add them here and reference them in the host project. But as we don't, go ahead and delete it as well. The RCL should now contain just the _Imports.razor file.

Now that our library is ready, we can move the ViewSwitcher.razor and ViewSwitcher.razor.scss files over from the Client project. Depending on your IDE, it may make copies of the files rather than moving them. If this happens, be sure to delete the originals from the Client project. The last bit of configuration we need to do is add in the same code we did to the Client project to handle building our Sass. First, we need to add a package.json file to the project with the following code.

Listing 7.8   package.json

```
{
  "scripts": {
    "sass": "sass"          ◁──┐  Defines the script that
  },                            └─ will build the Sass files
```

```
"devDependencies": {
  "sass": "1.28.0"
}
}
```

Defines a dev dependency on the Sass package. This is used in the earlier script to build any Sass files.

The package.json file defines a single script that will be called to build the Sass in the project. It also defines the dependency on the Sass package that is used in that script. Now, open the BlazingTrails.ComponentLibrary.csproj file and replace what's there with the following code.

Listing 7.9   BlazingTrails.ComponentLibrary.csproj

```
<Project Sdk="Microsoft.NET.Sdk.Razor">
  <PropertyGroup>
    <TargetFramework>net6.0</TargetFramework>
    <Nullable>enable</Nullable>
    <ImplicitUsings>enable</ImplicitUsings>
    <NpmLastInstall>node_modules/.last-install
    ➥</NpmLastInstall>
  </PropertyGroup>
```

Stores when the NPM install was last run

```
  <ItemGroup>
    <SupportedPlatform Include="browser" />
  </ItemGroup>

  <ItemGroup>
    <PackageReference Include="Microsoft.AspNetCore.Components.Web"
    ➥Version="6.0.0" />
  </ItemGroup>

  <Target Name="CheckForNpm"
  ➥BeforeTargets="RunNpmInstall">
  <Exec Command="npm --version" ContinueOnError="true">
    <Output TaskParameter="ExitCode" PropertyName="ErrorCode" />
  </Exec>
  <Error Condition="'$(ErrorCode)' != '0'"
  ➥Text="NPM is required to build this project." />
  </Target>
```

Checks if the NPM is installed and errors if it's not found

```
  <Target Name="RunNpmInstall"
  ➥BeforeTargets="CompileScopedScss" Inputs="package.json"
  ➥Outputs="$(NpmLastInstall)">
    <Exec Command="npm install" />
    <Touch Files="$(NpmLastInstall)" AlwaysCreate="true" />
  </Target>
```

Runs the NPM install if the package.json has been modified since the last time the NPM install was run

```
  <Target Name="CompileScopedScss"
  ➥BeforeTargets="Compile">
      <ItemGroup>
        <ScopedScssFiles Include="**/*.razor.scss" />
      </ItemGroup>
```

Compiles any SCSS files within the project

Finds all SCSS files in the project

```
    <Exec Command="npm run sass -
    ➥%(ScopedScssFiles.Identity) %(relativedir)%(filename).css" />
  </Target>
</Project>
```

I will skim over this, as we've already covered what this does in chapter 3. But as a quick recap, we've added three tasks that will run when the project is built. The first will check if NPM is installed on the machine and produce an error if it's not found. The second will run NPM install if the package.json has been updated since the last time it was run—say, if we'd updated a package version or added a dependency. The third task calls the script defined in package.json to build the Sass files in the project.

That is all the configuration we need to do in the RCL. We can now switch back to the Client project and add a new using statement to the main _Imports.razor in the root of the project. Add the following line to the file:

```
@using BlazingTrails.ComponentLibrary
```

At this point, we can run a build of the solution and run the application. Everything should be working as it was before.

The eagle-eyed among you may be wondering how the styles for our View-Switcher component are still working. They're now in another project, and we've not added any kind of reference to them. Well, that's because Blazor has already done that for us. Let's understand what's happened.

With the application running, open the browser developer tools and move to the Source tab. I'm using the latest version of Microsoft Edge, so this may be slightly different in other browsers. You should see what's shown in figure 7.4.

Blazor automatically bundles any scoped CSS files in RCLs and makes the bundle available to the host application via a framework-generated folder called _content.

The scoped CSS from RCLs is automatically imported into the main scoped CSS bundle created by the host application.

Figure 7.4 Blazor automatically bundles any scoped CSS from an RCL and makes that bundle available via a framework-generated folder called `_content`. The RCL bundle is then automatically added to the main styles bundle created by the host application.

Any scoped CSS files found in an RCL are automatically bundled up in the same way they are in a Blazor project. This bundle is then exposed through a framework-generated folder called *_content*. The bundle from the RCL is also automatically imported into the main CSS bundle of the host application.

Summary

- Templates are defined by creating parameters with a type of `RenderFragment`.
- Defining a template with the name `ChildContent` will capture all the markup entered between the start and end tags of a component.
- Templates can be generically typed.
- Generically typed templates require an object of type `T` to be passed into them when they are invoked.
- When providing markup for a template that is generically typed, the properties of `T` are available to be used in the markup via a parameter called `context`.
- The `context` parameter can be renamed to aid readability via the `Context` attribute.
- The `context` parameter can be renamed on a specific template or at the component level. If done at the component level, all generic templates in the component inherit the new name.
- Components are shared using a Razor class library.
- Razor class libraries can be packaged and shipped via NuGet, as with other .NET libraries.
- When using scoped CSS in an RCL, it's automatically bundled and included in a host Blazor application.

Integrating with JavaScript libraries

This chapter covers

- Wrapping JavaScript libraries to work with Blazor
- Calling JavaScript functions from C#
- Calling C# methods from JavaScript

While one of the major reasons for choosing Blazor is to write our frontend applications using C# to avoid JavaScript, there are some things that can still only be done using JavaScript. A great example of this is accessing the browser's web storage APIs. It's a common requirement to store data in either local storage or session storage, but both features can be accessed only via JavaScript code. Beyond just needing to use some JavaScript out of necessity, there are also many fantastic, feature-packed JavaScript libraries available that just aren't available in C#. It makes sense to take advantage of these battle-tested libraries and not reinvent the wheel when we don't have to.

The great news for us is that Blazor has some fantastic JavaScript interop APIs. Using these APIs, we can call into JavaScript and also have JavaScript call into our application. This allows us to wrap the interactions with JavaScript in either C# classes or components. Once this is done, the rest of our application just deals with either the C# class or the component and never needs to care about the underlying

JavaScript call. If designed correctly, another benefit is that we can swap the JavaScript library out at any point for another JavaScript library or even a C# library if one becomes available.

In this chapter, we're going to learn about Blazor's JavaScript APIs by implementing a popular JavaScript library called Leaflet (https://leafletjs.com/) into the Blazing Trails application. Leaflet is an open source JavaScript library used for displaying interactive maps. We'll use Leaflet to replace the current route instructions with a map that shows waypoints outlining the route of the trail. Figure 8.1 shows the final map component we'll be building to use on the edit trail form.

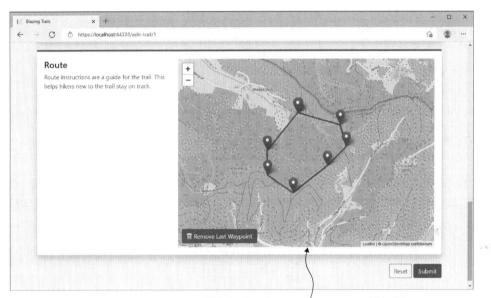

This is what the map component we'll build
in this chapter will look like when we're done.

Figure 8.1 The completed map component that calls the Leaflet JavaScript library to display interactive maps

As you can see, this creates a much nicer UI for mapping out a trail. We'll build the map component in such a way that it can be used for both editing a set of waypoints and displaying a read-only view of them. We can then update the drawer on the home page that shows the trail details with the same map.

8.1 Creating a JavaScript module and accessing it via a component

We're going to create a component called `RouteMap`, which will handle all the interactions with Leaflet. The rest of the application will only deal with this component and be totally ignorant of the fact that JavaScript is being called. As this component is a good candidate for reuse, it makes sense for us to add it to our BlazingTrails.Component-Library project that we added in the last chapter. It can then be easily shared with other applications in the future, if required.

The first step in wrapping Leaflet is to write our own JavaScript code that initializes the library. We'll then call this from our `RouteMap` component. Originally, Blazor's JavaScript interop APIs required that functions be added to the global scope for them to be invoked by an application. While this worked, it's not considered a good practice to pollute the global scope with random functions. There is also an increased risk that the name of your function will collide with another.

Since .NET 5, Blazor has an improved option for working with JavaScript—JavaScript isolation. This method doesn't require functions to be added to the global scope and fits in much better with modern JavaScript best practices. This is the method we will be using to wrap Leaflet.

Another Blazor feature we'll use to build our `Map` component is collocated JavaScript, introduced in .NET 6. This feature allows us to place JavaScript files alongside the components that use them rather than having to place them in a wwwroot folder, as we would with other static assets. I really like this, as it means less jumping between folders and makes understanding the code base a bit easier.

We'll start by adding a new folder to the root of the BlazingTrails.Component-Library project called *Map*. Then we'll add a new JavaScript file inside it called *RouteMap.razor.js* with the code shown in listing 8.1. It's important that the JavaScript file shares the same name as the component that uses it, just with a `.js` extension. Blazor requires this naming convention when using collocated JavaScript files.

Listing 8.1   RouteMap.razor.js

```
export function initialize(hostElement) {
    hostElement.map = L.map(hostElement)
    .setView([51.700, -0.10], 3);

    L.tileLayer('https://{s}.tile.openstreetmap.org/{z}/{x}/{y}.png', {
        attribution: '&copy;
        <a href="https://www.openstreetmap.org/copyright">OpenStreetMap</a>
        contributors',
        maxZoom: 18,
        opacity: .75
    }).addTo(hostElement.map);

    hostElement.waypoints = [];
    hostElement.lines = [];

    hostElement.map.on('click', function (e) {
        let waypoint = L.marker(e.latlng);
        waypoint.addTo(hostElement.map);
        hostElement.waypoints.push(waypoint);
```

The initialize function takes a single parameter that is a reference to the element the map should be rendered in.

Leaflet is initialized on the hostElement.

Adds a layer that displays a copyright message in the bottom right of the map

This hooks up a handler for the click event exposed by the map. When the map is clicked, the handler will add a waypoint and if there is more than one waypoint, add a line connecting them.

```
    let line = L.polyline(hostElement.waypoints.map(m => m.getLatLng()),
➥{ color: 'var(--brand)' }).addTo(hostElement.map);
    hostElement.lines.push(line);
  });
}
```

The `initialize` function takes a single parameter, `hostElement`. This is a reference to the element where Leaflet should render the map. We're going to pass this in from our Blazor component. The function is also marked with the `export` keyword. This is what's going to allow us to take advantage of Blazor's JavaScript isolation feature.

What is JavaScript isolation in Blazor?

A JavaScript module (http://mng.bz/gwg8) is essentially a JavaScript file that exports functions, consts, or anything that makes sense to export. Blazor's JavaScript isolation feature allows JavaScript modules to be loaded on demand rather than be constantly present.

It means that the consuming application doesn't have to add a reference to the JavaScript file. Instead, the framework will download the file if required. This is especially useful when writing Blazor libraries that use JavaScript, as the consumers don't have to add script tags in their host pages. This also means that if a user doesn't access a component that uses the module, then the file will never be downloaded.

The first operation the `initialize` function performs is to render the map on the host element. Next, a layer is added, which contains some copyright information about the map tiles being used. Finally, a handler is added for the map's `onclick` event. This will add a new waypoint wherever the user clicks. Once there is more than one waypoint, it will also draw a line between them.

Now we can turn our attention to creating the `RouteMap` component. Add a new component to the Map folder called `RouteMap.razor` with the following code.

Listing 8.2 RouteMap.razor

```
@using Microsoft.JSInterop
@inject IJSRuntime JSRuntime
@implements IAsyncDisposable

<div class="map-wrapper">
    <div style="height: @(Height); width:@(Width);"
➥@ref="_map"></div>                    ◁─┐ Using the ref directive, an
</div>                                       element reference is captured
                                             that can be passed to JavaScript.
@code {
    private ElementReference _map;
    private IJSObjectReference? _routeMapModule;
```

```
[Parameter] public string Height { get; set; } = "500px";
[Parameter] public string Width { get; set; } = "1000px";

protected override async Task OnAfterRenderAsync(bool firstRender)
{
    if (firstRender)
    {
        _routeMapModule = await JSRuntime.InvokeAsync
        <IJSObjectReference>("import", "./_content/
        BlazingTrails.ComponentLibrary/Map/RouteMap.razor.js");
        await _routeMapModule
        .InvokeVoidAsync("initialize", _map);
    }
}

async ValueTask IAsyncDisposable.DisposeAsync()
{
    if (_routeMapModule is not null)
    {
        await _routeMapModule.DisposeAsync();
    }
}
}
```

The IJSRuntime interface is used to import the routeMap JavaScript module.

The initialize function exported by the routeMap module is called, passing in the element reference where the map should be rendered.

Implements IAsyncDisposable to clean up the module reference when the component is destroyed

The `RouteMap` component defines a small amount of markup, including a div that we're capturing an element reference to. We will pass this reference to our JavaScript function, and Leaflet will render the map inside of it.

We're using the `OnAfterRenderAsync` life cycle method to work with our Java-Script code. It's important to use this method whenever you're working with JavaScript, as it will only ever be called after the component has been rendered and the DOM is in place. As JavaScript code usually operates on the DOM, using an earlier life cycle method may result in errors.

When the component is first rendered, we're using the `IJSRuntime` abstraction to load our `routeMap` module and capture a reference to it. This line of code also serves as the trigger for the "on demand" loading of the JavaScript file for the JavaScript isolation feature. As this code is in a Razor class library, we need to use a special path to reference the physical file. This path is broken down as follows:

```
./content/{project name}/{path to file}
```

In our case, the project name where the file resides is BlazingTrails.Component-Library, and because we're using the collocated JavaScript feature, the last segment is just the path to the file from the root of the project:

```
./_content/BlazingTrails.ComponentLibrary/Map/RouteMap.razor.js
```

Once we've loaded our module, we then call the `initialize` function to render the map. We do this via the `InvokeVoidAsync` method. This method allows us to call into JavaScript functions that don't return a value. There is also another method, `InvokeAsync`, that does allow values to be returned from the JavaScript side.

The final thing we do is a little housekeeping by implementing the `IAsync-Disposable` interface. This allows the reference to the JavaScript module to be disposed of correctly when the component is destroyed.

At this point, we have the initial version of our `RouteMap` component. It can call into our JavaScript module and initialize the Leaflet map in the element we pass it to. We just need to test it out. To do this, we'll implement the new `RouteMap` component in the `TrailForm` component.

8.1.1 Testing out the RouteMap component

Before we can update the `TrailForm` with the new `RouteMap` component, we need to add references to the Leaflet library in the index.html page. We'll add two things—a link to Leaflet's CSS file and a script tag for Leaflet itself.

In the head tag of the wwwroot > index.html file in the Client project, add the following line under the link to the Bootstrap icon's CSS:

```
<link rel="stylesheet" href="https://unpkg.com/leaflet@1.7.1/dist/leaflet.css"
    integrity="sha512-xodZBNTC5n17Xt2atTPuE1HxjVMSvLVW9ocqUKLsCC5CXdbqCmbl
    AshOMAS6/keqq/sMZMZ19scR4PsZChSR7A=="
    crossorigin="" />
```

We can then add the following script tag directly after the blazor.webassembly.js file or the blazor.server.js file if you're using Blazor Server:

```
<script src="https://unpkg.com/leaflet@1.7.1/dist/leaflet.js"
        integrity="sha512-XQoYMqMTK8LvdxXYG3nZ448hOEQiglfqkJs1NOQV44cWnUrBc8
        PkAOcXy20w0vlaXaVUearIOBhiXZ5V3ynxwA=="
        crossorigin=""></script>
```

Now we can add the new `RouteMap` component to the `TrailForm` (Features > ManageTrails > Shared). We'll remove all the code inside of the `Route FormSection` and add a reference to the `RouteMap` component. The resulting section looks like this:

```
<FormSection Title="Route"
            HelpText="Route instructions are a guide for the trail. This
            helps hikers new to the trail stay on track.">
    <RouteMap Width="100%" />
</FormSection>
```

We'll also need to add a `using` statement for the `RouteMap` component. We add this at the top of the `TrailForm` component rather than in an _Imports.razor file, as we only need this temporarily:

```
@using BlazingTrails.ComponentLibrary.Map
```

We can now run the app and check that everything is working correctly. If all has gone to plan, you should see a map rendered in the Route section.

You can interact with the map at this point. Using your mouse, you can click and drag to move around and use the mouse wheel or the Plus and Minus button in the

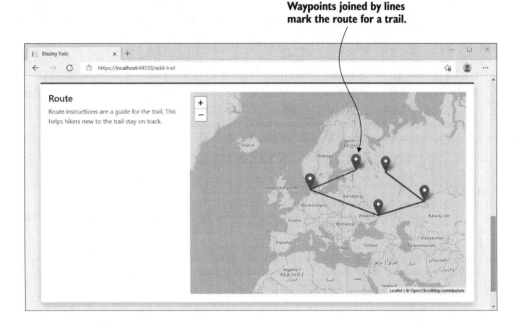

Figure 8.2   **Clicking on the map will drop a waypoint. For each additional waypoint dropped, a line will be drawn, linking them together.**

top left to zoom in and out. You can also click anywhere and drop a waypoint. If you add a second waypoint, you will see a line is drawn between them (figure 8.2).

Now that we've verified that our initial `RouteMap` component works, we will add one additional feature before we move on to the next section: the ability to delete a waypoint.

8.1.2   *Calling JavaScript functions from C# and returning a response*

When we initialized the map, we called into JavaScript using the `InvokeVoidAsync` method, which doesn't require a value to be returned. But what if we wanted to return a value from our JavaScript call? In that case, we can use the `InvokeAsync<T>` method. To learn about this, we will add the ability to delete a waypoint from the map and return a message containing details about the deleted waypoint.

The ability to delete waypoints is very important. As you may have already discovered while testing out the map, it's easy to drop a waypoint in the wrong place or just in error. We will add a button that will allow the user to delete the last waypoint they dropped. Continuing to click the button will continue to delete waypoints until they are all gone.

Back in our JavaScript file, RouteMap.razor.js, we will add a new function called *deleteLastWaypoint*. The code for the function is shown in listing 8.3.

Listing 8.3 RouteMap.razor.js: Delete the last waypoint

```
export function deleteLastWaypoint(hostElement) {
    if (hostElement.waypoints.length > 0) {              ◄──┐  Checks to make sure there
        let lastWaypoint = hostElement.waypoints[            │  are waypoints to be deleted
        hostElement.waypoints.length - 1];
        hostElement.map.removeLayer(lastWaypoint);       ── Removes the last
        hostElement.waypoints.pop();                        waypoint from the map

        if (hostElement.lines.length > 0) {             ◄──┐  Checks to see if there is a line
            let lastLine = hostElement.lines[               │  that needs to be deleted
            hostElement.lines.length - 1];
            lastLine.remove(hostElement.map);            ── Removes the last
            hostElement.lines.pop();                        line from the map

            return `Deleted waypoint at latitude
            ${lastWaypoint.getLatLng().lat}
            longitude ${lastWaypoint.getLatLng().lng}`;
        }
    }
}
```

The function starts by checking if there are waypoints to be deleted. Next, it finds the last waypoint and removes it from the map and from the list of waypoints stored on the `hostElement`. Another check is then performed to see if there is a line that needs to be deleted. This is to make sure we don't end up with line coming from a waypoint and not connecting to anything. Finally, we return a string that includes the latitude and longitude of the waypoint that was deleted.

With the JavaScript in place, we can move back to the `RouteMap` component. We're going to add a button that will trigger our new `delete` function. The following listing shows the new markup and method.

Listing 8.4 RouteMap.razor: Triggering `deleteLastWaypoint`

```
                                        This new div contains the Delete button.
                                        This will be used to position the button
<div class="map-wrapper">               correctly on the map with CSS.
    <div class="controls">           ◄──┘
        <button @onclick="DeleteLastWaypoint"
        class="btn btn-secondary" title="Delete last waypoint"
        type="button">                        The Delete button triggers the
            <i class="bi bi-trash"></i>       DeleteLastWaypoint method.
            Remove Last Waypoint
        </button>
    </div>
    <div style="height: @(Height); width:@(Width);" @ref="_map"></div>
</div>

@code {
    // Other code omitted for brevity
    public async Task DeleteLastWaypoint()
    {
```

```
        if (_routeMapModule is not null)
        {
            var message = await _routeMapModule
            ➥.InvokeAsync<string>("deleteLastWaypoint", _map);
            Console.WriteLine(message);
        }
    }
}
```

The InvokeAsync method executes the deleteLastWaypoint JavaScript function, returning a string.

The string returned from deleteLastWaypoint is output to the browser console.

We start by adding some new markup, which is a div containing the Delete button. The Delete button has an `onclick` event that calls the new `DeleteLastWaypoint` method. This method uses the reference to the `routeMap` JavaScript module to execute the `deleteLastWaypoint` function using the `InvokeAsync<T>` method. We set the type parameter to a string, as that is what we're expecting back from the call. The returned message is then output to the browser console.

Before we test out our new delete feature, we need to add a small bit of CSS to position the button correctly on the map. We will add a new file called *Route-Map.razor.scss* in the Map folder of the ComponentLibrary project. Then add the following code.

Listing 8.5   RouteMap.razor.scss

We set the position property of the main div containing the map as relative. This will allow us to position child elements relative to the parent.

```
.map-wrapper {
    position: relative;

    .controls {
        position: absolute;
        bottom: 10px;
        left: 10px;
        z-index: 1000;
    }
}
```

This is the class for the div containing the Delete button. We set its position property to absolute and then set its position to be in the bottom left corner of the parent.

The CSS is quite simple; we define a class, which is used on the container element for the map. We set its position property to `relative`. This allows us to set the position of any child elements relative to the parent. Then we define a class that is applied to the div containing the Delete button we just created. It will position that element in the bottom left corner of the map, 10 pixels away from the edges. By setting the `z-index` property to 1,000, we ensure that it sits on top of all other elements.

We can now run the application and check our work. Navigating to the add trail form, you should now see a Delete button in the bottom left corner of the map (figure 8.3). Clicking it at this point should do nothing, but if you add a few waypoints and click the button, you should see them being removed. If you open the browser console, you should see messages describing each waypoint that was removed.

New Delete Waypoint button

Message returned from JavaScript displaying in the console

Figure 8.3   The new Delete button is positioned on the map and the message returned
from JavaScript is displayed in the console.

> **NOTE**   If you're using Blazor Server rather than Blazor WebAssembly, you won't
> see the message in the browser console. Instead, it will be in the web server out-
> put. This is displayed either in the Output > Web Server window in Visual Studio
> or at the command prompt if running the app using the .NET CLI.

The RouteMap component is coming along nicely. We can add waypoints, connect
them with a line, and remove them if necessary. However, right now all the data
regarding the waypoints is being held in JavaScript. We need to get access to this information in our C# code so we can save the route into the database when the form is
submitted. That's what we'll tackle next.

8.2   Calling C# methods from JavaScript

When working with either custom JavaScript functions or with JavaScript libraries,
there will come a time when you need to call methods in your Blazor application to
invoke some logic or to retrieve or pass some data. Just as with calling out to Java-
Script, Blazor has built-in APIs that we can leverage from our JavaScript code to call
C#. We're going to use those APIs in Blazing Trails to pass the position of each waypoint dropped on the map back to our RouteMap component. Once we have that
data in our C# code, we can save it along with the rest of the trail data.

In order to call a method on a component from JavaScript, we need to create a reference to that component and pass it into a JavaScript function. Once that reference object is in the function, we can use it to call methods on that component instance. Blazor has a special class for doing this called `DotNetObjectReference<T>`. Let's implement it in our `RouteMap` component. We'll update the `RouteMap` component with the following code.

Listing 8.6   RouteMap.razor: Using `DotNetObjectReference<T>`

```
@implements IDisposable
@code {
    private DotNetObjectReference<RouteMap>        │ This new private field holds the
    ➥_routeMapReference;                            │ reference to the component.
    // Other code omitted for brevity
    protected override async Task OnAfterRenderAsync(bool firstRender)
    {
        if (firstRender)
        {
            _routeMapModule = await JSRuntime
            ➥.InvokeAsync<IJSObjectReference>("import",
            ➥"./_content/BlazingTrails.ComponentLibrary/Map/
            ➥RouteMap.razor.js");
            _routeMapReference =
            ➥DotNetObjectReference.Create(this);

            await _routeMapModule.InvokeVoidAsync("initialize", _map,
    _routeMapReference);
        }
    }

    [JSInvokable]
    public void WaypointAdded(decimal latitude, decimal longitude)
        => Console.WriteLine(
    ➥$"Added Waypoint - Latitude: {latitude},
    ➥Longitude {longitude}");
    // Other code omitted for brevity
    void IDisposable.Dispose()
        => _routeMapReference?.Dispose();
}
```

An object reference is created by calling the Create method and passing it to the instance of the component.

The call to initialize the JavaScript function is updated to pass the reference to the RouteMap component.

The new WaypointAdded method is decorated with the [JSInvokable] attribute, which allows it to be called from JavaScript.

We implement IDisposable so we can properly dispose of the routeMapReference.

Whenever a waypoint is added to the map, the longitude and latitude of the marker will be passed to our component from JavaScript and written to the browser console.

First, we're creating a new private field that will hold the reference to the instance of the `RouteMap` component. We then use the `Create` method of the `DotNetObject-Reference` class to create a reference to the component that we can pass to

JavaScript. Then we add this reference as an additional argument when calling the `initialize` JavaScript function.

Next, we've added a new method called `WaypointAdded`. It'll be called from our JavaScript code whenever a new waypoint is added, passing in its longitude and latitude—which we'll output in the browser console. A key point here is that this method is decorated with the `[JSInvokable]` attribute. This allows the method to be called from JavaScript. Without this attribute, attempting to invoke it from Java-Script will cause an error.

Finally, we implement the `IDisposable` interface so we can correctly dispose of the `_routeMapReference` when the component is destroyed.

With the changes to the `RouteMap` component in place, we can then modify the RouteMap.razor.js file to call the `WaypointAdded` method. The following listing shows the updated code.

Listing 8.7   RouteMap.razor.js: Calling component methods

```
export function initialize(hostElement, routeMapComponent) {
    // Other code omitted for brevity
    hostElement.map.on('click', function (e) {                    The signature of the function is
        let waypoint = L.marker(e.latlng);                        updated to take the reference to
        waypoint.addTo(hostElement.map);                          the route map component.
        hostElement.waypoints.push(waypoint);
        let line = L.polyline(hostElement.waypoints.map(m => m.getLatLng()),
        ⟼{ color: 'var(--brand)' }).addTo(hostElement.map);
        hostElement.lines.push(line);

        routeMapComponent.invokeMethodAsync(
        ⟼'WaypointAdded', e.latlng.lat, e.latlng.lng);
    });                                                           The invokeMethodAsync function is used
}                                                                 on the routeMapComponent object to
                                                                  call the WaypointAdded method.
```

First, we update the signature of the `initialize` function. We're adding an extra parameter, `routeMapComponent`, which holds the reference to the `RouteMap` component instance that called the function. This object gives us access to a function called `invokeMethodAsync`. In our click event handler, we use this to call the `Way-pointAdded` method, passing in the latitude and longitude of the waypoint.

That is everything we need. We can now run the application and check our work (figure 8.4). If all has gone to plan, you should see the latitude and longitude output into the browser console whenever you click to add a waypoint on the map.

Things are looking good! We can now access the data for each waypoint from our C# code. Our next step is to integrate the map component into our form so we can save the waypoints when the form is submitted.

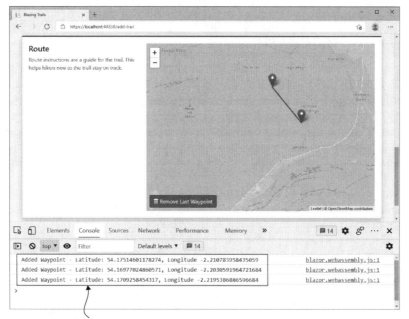

Whenever a new waypoint is added, a message is output
to the console containing its latitude and longitude.

Figure 8.4   The messages that are output to the browser console whenever a new
waypoint is added to the map.

8.3   Integrating the RouteMap component with the TrailForm

We've completed most of the work needed to wrap Leaflet, so now we can focus on
integrating our `RouteMap` component into the `TrailForm`. To do this, we'll wrap it
in a custom form control, which will allow us to apply validation and ultimately save
the waypoint data into the database along with the other details of the trail. The following listing shows the updates.

Listing 8.8   RouteMap.razor: Enhancements for forms integration

```
@code {
    // Other code omitted for brevity
    [Parameter]
    public List<LatLong> Waypoints { get; set; }
    ➥= new List<LatLong>();
    [Parameter]
    public EventCallback<LatLong> OnWaypointAdded
    ➥{ get; set; }
    [Parameter]
    public EventCallback<LatLong> OnWaypointDeleted
    ➥{ get; set; }
```

This new parameter allows
us to pass a list of waypoints
into the component.

This is a new event for when
a waypoint is added.

This is a new event for when
a waypoint is deleted.

```
// Other code omitted for brevity
protected override async Task OnAfterRenderAsync(bool firstRender)
{
    if (firstRender)
    {
        // other code omitted for brevity
        await _routeMapModule
        ➥.InvokeVoidAsync("initialize", _map,
        ➥_routeMapReference, Waypoints);
    }
}

public async Task DeleteLastWaypoint()
{
    if (_routeMapModule is not null)
    {
        var waypoint = await _routeMapModule
        ➥.InvokeAsync<LatLong>("deleteLastWaypoint", _map,
        ➥_routeMapReference);
        await OnWaypointDeleted
        ➥.InvokeAsync(waypoint);
    }
}

[JSInvokable]
public async Task WaypointAdded(decimal latitude,
➥decimal longitude)
    => await OnWaypointAdded
    ➥.InvokeAsync(new LatLong(latitude, longitude));
// Other code omitted for brevity
}
```

The waypoints are passed into the JavaScript function.

The return type for the deleteLastWaypoint function is updated to LatLong.

The OnWaypointDeleted event is triggered rather than writing to the console.

The Updated WaypointAdded method triggers the OnWaypointAdded event.

We added three new component parameters. The first, Waypoints, will allow us to pass in a list of waypoints. We will use this when editing a form to display whatever waypoints already exist. The other two, OnWaypointAdded and OnWaypointDeleted, will allow the consumer of this component to be notified when a waypoint is added or deleted. These new parameters work with a new type called LatLong, which we'll look at in a second. The call to the initialize function has been updated to pass in any existing waypoints. We've also updated the DeleteLastWaypoint method to trigger the new OnWaypointDeleted event. You'll also notice the return type has been changed from string to LatLong—we'll be updating the JavaScript in a second to return an object containing the latitude and longitude of the deleted waypoint. The WaypointAdded method now triggers the OnWaypointAdded event instead of writing to the console.

Let's have a quick look at that LatLong object now. This is a record type, and we need to add it to the ComponentLibrary project alongside the RouteMap component in the Map folder. Create a file called *LatLong.cs* and add the following line to it:

```
public record LatLong(decimal Lat, decimal Lng);
```

This is just a simple DTO and contains no logic. It just holds the coordinates for a way-point. To finish the enhancements to the `RouteMap`, we need to make some updates to the JavaScript. The following listing shows the changes.

Listing 8.9   RouteMap.razor.js: Displayed existing waypoints

```
export function initialize(hostElement,
  routeMapComponent, existingWaypoints) {
    // other code omitted for brevity
    hostElement.waypoints = [];
    hostElement.lines = [];
    if (existingWaypoints && existingWaypoints.length > 0) {
        existingWaypoints.forEach(cord => {
            let waypoint = L.marker(cord);
            waypoint.addTo(hostElement.map);
            hostElement.waypoints.push(waypoint);
            let line = L.polyline(hostElement.waypoints
                .map(m => m.getLatLng()), { color: 'var(--brand)' })
                .addTo(hostElement.map);
            hostElement.lines.push(line);
        });
    }

    if (hostElement.waypoints.length > 0) {
        var waypointsGroup = new L.featureGroup(
            hostElement.waypoints);
        hostElement.map.fitBounds(waypointsGroup
            .getBounds().pad(1));
    }

    // other code omitted for brevity
}

export function deleteLastWaypoint(hostElement) {
    if (hostElement.waypoints.length > 0) {
        // other code omitted for brevity

        return { "Lat": lastWaypoint.getLatLng().lat,
            "Lng": lastWaypoint.getLatLng().lng };
    }
}
```

The function signature has been updated to allow existingWaypoints to be passed in.

If there are any existingWaypoints, we loop over them and create a marker for each one and any lines needed to join the markers.

When there are existingWaypoints, zoom the map so all of the waypoints are visible and the route is centered.

Instead of returning a string, the function now returns an object, which can be deserialized into a LatLong record in C#.

The first change is to add the `existingWaypoints` parameter to the function signature, allowing us to pass in an array of existing waypoints. In the first `if` block, we check to see if we have any existing waypoints. If we do, then we create markers for each of them and any lines needed to join them together. In the second `if` block, if we have existing waypoints, we use the `fitBounds` function from Leaflet to zoom the map so all the waypoints are visible and the route they define is centered in the map. Finally, we've updated what the `deleteLastWaypoint` function returns. It now passes back an object that can be deserialized into the new `LatLong` C# record we previously created.

Now that the `RouteMap` is ready, we can create our custom `Input` component to wrap it and integrate it with the form. We'll be creating this new component in the Shared folder of the `ManageTrails` feature in the Client project. Create a new component called `InputRouteMap.razor` and add the following code.

Listing 8.10   InputRouteMap.razor

```
@using BlazingTrails.ComponentLibrary.Map
@inherits InputBase<List<TrailDto.WaypointDto>>          ◁─┐  Defines the type that the
                                                            component will be able
<div class="@CssClass">                                     to bind to in the form
    <RouteMap Width="100%" OnWaypointAdded="AddWaypoint"
    ➥OnWaypointDeleted="DeleteWaypoint"
    ➥Waypoints="_waypoints" />          ◁─┐  The input component sets up handlers for both
</div>                                      the OnWaypointAdded and OnWaypointDeleted
                                            events and passes in any existing waypoints.
@code {
    private List<LatLong> _waypoints = new List<LatLong>();

    protected override void OnParametersSet()
    {
        if (CurrentValue?.Count > 0)              If there are existing waypoints,
        {                                         convert them to a list of LatLong so
            _waypoints.Clear();                   they can be passed to JavaScript.
            _waypoints.AddRange(CurrentValue
            ➥.Select(x => new LatLong(x.Latitude, x.Longitude)));
        }
    }

    protected override bool TryParseValueFromString(
    ➥string? value, out List<TrailDto.WaypointDto> result,
    ➥out string validationErrorMessage)
=> throw new NotImplementedException();

    private void AddWaypoint(LatLong waypoint)           When a new waypoint
    {                                                    is added, it is added to
        _waypoints.Add(waypoint);                        the collection on the
        CurrentValue?.Add(new TrailDto.WaypointDto(      form model.
        ➥waypoint.Lat, waypoint.Lng));
    }

    private void DeleteWaypoint(LatLong waypoint)        When a new waypoint is
    {                                                    deleted, it is removed
        _waypoints.Remove(waypoint);                     from the collection on
        CurrentValue?.Remove(new TrailDto.WaypointDto(   the form model.
        ➥waypoint.Lat, waypoint.Lng));
    }
}
```

As we're creating a custom form component, we start by inheriting from `InputBase`. We specify that this component will bind to a `List<TrailDto.WaypointDto>`, which we'll set up after this. We then add the `RouteMap` component and handlers for the `OnWaypointAdded` and `OnWaypointDeleted` events, as well as pass in any existing waypoints. Using the `OnParametersSet` method, we check to see if there are any existing waypoints. If there are, we convert them to a list of `LatLong` so they can be passed into the `RouteMap` component.

To finish up, we need to add a bit of styling. Add a new file called *InputRoute-Map.razor.scss* in the Shared folder and add the following CSS class:

```
.is-invalid {
    border: 1px solid #dc3545;
}
```

When the form's validation logic is triggered, this will add a red border to the new `Input` component if the user has failed to add any waypoints to the map (figure 8.5).

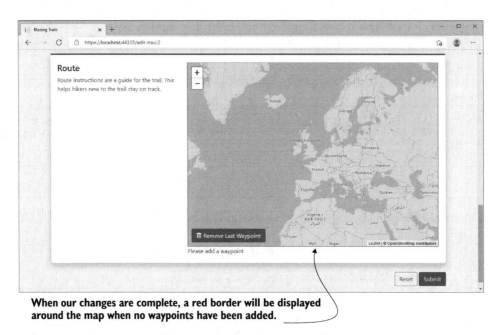

When our changes are complete, a red border will be displayed around the map when no waypoints have been added.

Figure 8.5   Once we complete our changes, a border will be displayed around the map when the user attempts to submit the form without adding any waypoints.

Before we add the new input to the `TrailForm`, we need to update the `TrailDto` class (BlazingTrails.Shared > Features > ManageTrails > Shared). Currently, it expects us to be adding route instructions. We need to update it to work with our new waypoints. We're going to remove the `Route` property as well as the `RouteInstruction` class, then replace them with the following two lines:

```
public List<WaypointDto> Waypoints { get; set; } = new List<WaypointDto>();

public record WaypointDto(decimal Latitude, decimal Longitude);
```

We also need to update the `TrailValidator`. We can remove the two rules for the `Route` property and replace them with the following line:

```
RuleFor(x => x.Waypoints).NotEmpty().WithMessage("Please add a waypoint");
```

We can then remove the `RouteInstructionValidator` class entirely, as it's no longer required.

While we're in the Shared project, we can also update the `GetTrailRequest` (Features > ManageTrails > EditTrail). We need to remove the `RouteInstruction` record and replace it with the following `Waypoint` record:

```
public record Waypoint(decimal Latitude, decimal Longitude);
```

Then we can update the `Trail` record to use the new `Waypoint` record:

```
public record Trail(int Id, string Name, string Location, string Image, int
    TimeInMinutes, int Length, string Description, IEnumerable<Waypoint>
    Waypoints);
```

That's all the changes needed in the Shared project. Let's go and plug in our new input component to the form. Then we can update our API endpoints, and we should be good to go!

In the `TrailForm` component (BlazingTrails.Client > Features > ManageTrails > Shared), we will replace the current reference to the `RouteMap` component with the following two lines:

```
<InputRouteMap @bind-Value="_trail.Waypoints" />
<ValidationMessage For="@(() => _trail.Waypoints)" />
```

Then in the `OnParametersSet` method, we'll remove the two lines that reference the old `Route` property:

```
_trail.Route.Clear();
_trail.Route.AddRange(Trail.Route.Select(ri => new TrailDto.RouteInstruction
{
    Stage = ri.Stage,
    Description = ri.Description
}));
```

Replace them with these two lines, which use the new `Waypoints` property:

```
_trail.Waypoints.Clear();
_trail.Waypoints.AddRange(Trail.Waypoints.Select(wp => new
    TrailDto.WaypointDto(wp.Latitude, wp.Longitude)));
```

The final updates we'll do are in the API. We need to update the `AddTrailEndpoint` and `EditTrailEndpoint` to use the new waypoints. We also need to update the database to store waypoints.

Let's start with the database changes. Under Persistence > Entities, add a new class called `Waypoint` with the following code.

Listing 8.11   Waypoint.cs

```
public class Waypoint                       ◁──┐  Defines the Waypoint
{                                               │  database entity
    public int Id { get; set; }
    public int TrailId { get; set; }
    public decimal Latitude { get; set; }
    public decimal Longitude { get; set; }

    public Trail Trail { get; set; } = default!;
}

public class WaypointConfig :                        │  Shows the database configuration
  IEntityTypeConfiguration<Waypoint>         ◁──┘  settings for the Waypoint entity
{
    public void Configure(EntityTypeBuilder<Waypoint> builder)
    {
        builder.Property(x => x.TrailId).IsRequired();
        builder.Property(x => x.Latitude).IsRequired();
        builder.Property(x => x.Longitude).IsRequired();
    }
}
```

The Waypoint class defines what data will be saved regarding a waypoint. As way-points will always belong to a trail, each waypoint will be saved with a reference to the trail they belong to. The WaypointConfig class specifies some simple rules stating that the three properties—TrailId, Latitude, and Longitude—must not be null at the database level.

We can now delete the old RouteInstruction class, which is in the same folder. Then in the Trail class, we can remove the Route property and replace it with the following:

```
public ICollection<Waypoint> Waypoints { get; set; } = default!;
```

The last update regarding the database is in the BlazingTrailsContext class under Persistence. The following listing shows the updated code.

Listing 8.12   BlazingTrailsContext.cs: Changing to Waypoints

```
public class BlazingTrailsContext : DbContext
{
    public DbSet<Trail> Trails => Set<Trail>();
    public DbSet<Waypoint> Waypoints { get; set; }
      => Set<Waypoint>():                    ◁──┐  Replaces the
                                                 │  RouteInstructions DbSet
    public BlazingTrailsContext(
      DbContextOptions<BlazingTrailsContext> options)
      : base(options) { }

    protected override void OnModelCreating(ModelBuilder modelBuilder)
    {
        base.OnModelCreating(modelBuilder);
        modelBuilder.ApplyConfiguration(new TrailConfig());
```

```
        modelBuilder.ApplyConfiguration(
        ➥new WaypointConfig());        ◄─┐ Replaces the
    }                                     │ RouteInstructionConfig
}
```

The first change removes the old `RouteInstructions` property and replaces it with a new `Waypoints` one. The second change removes the `RouteInstruction` configuration and replaces it with the `Waypoint` configuration. When we create a new Entity Framework (EF) migration in a second, these two changes will translate into instruction to EF to drop the `RouteInstructions` table and create a new `Waypoints` one.

Those are all the database changes we need to do. All that's left is to generate a new migration and apply that to the database. I'm using the Package Manager Console in Visual Studio to do this. With the BlazingTrails.Api project selected, run the following commands:

```
Add-Migration AddWaypoints
Update-Database
```

The first command will create a new migration, which will drop the old `RouteInstructions` table and create a new one for `Waypoints`. The second command will run that migration against the database and apply the changes.

Now that the database is taken care of, we can update our endpoints. We'll start with the `AddTrailEndpoint`. The following listing shows the updated `HandleAsync` method.

Listing 8.13   AddTrailEndpoint.cs: Update to `HandleAsync` method

```
public override async Task<ActionResult<int>> HandleAsync(
➥AddTrailRequest request, CancellationToken cancellationToken = default)
{
    var trail = new Trail
    {
        Name = request.Trail.Name,
        Description = request.Trail.Description,
        Location = request.Trail.Location,
        TimeInMinutes = request.Trail.TimeInMinutes,
        Length = request.Trail.Length,
        Waypoints = request.Trail.Waypoints.Select(
        ➥wp => new Waypoint
        {                                   The waypoints are added
            Latitude = wp.Latitude,         to the trail as part of the
            Longitude = wp.Longitude        object initializer.
        }).ToList()
    };

    await _database.Trails.AddAsync(trail, cancellationToken);
    await _database.SaveChangesAsync(cancellationToken);

    return Ok(trail.Id);
}
```

The `HandleAsync` method has had all traces of the `RouteInstruction` type removed, and we're now adding waypoints as part of the object initializer for the `Trail`. Let's move on to the `EditTrailEndpoint`. The following listing shows the updates.

```
public override async Task<ActionResult<bool>> HandleAsync(
➥EditTrailRequest request, CancellationToken cancellationToken = default)
{
    // other code omitted for brevity
    trail.Name = request.Trail.Name;
    trail.Description = request.Trail.Description;
    trail.Location = request.Trail.Location;
    trail.TimeInMinutes = request.Trail.TimeInMinutes;
    trail.Length = request.Trail.Length;
    trail.Waypoints = request.Trail.Waypoints.Select(
    ➥wp => new Waypoint
    {
        Latitude = wp.Latitude,            Existing waypoints are
        Longitude = wp.Longitude           updated whenever
    }).ToList();                            the trail is changed.
    // other code omitted for brevity
}
```

We've removed the reference to the old `Route` property and replaced it with the new `Waypoints` property. The `GetTrailEndpoint` needs a small update. This is called when we load a trail to be edited and we need to update it to send back the waypoints. We need to replace the line

```
trail.Route.Select(ri => new GetTrailRequest.RouteInstruction(ri.Id,
    ri.Stage, ri.Description)))));
```

with this line:

```
trail.Waypoints.Select(wp => new GetTrailRequest.Waypoint(wp.Latitude,
    wp.Longitude)))));
```

Now we have completed all our updates, and we can run the application to test our work. If all has gone to plan, you will be able to add waypoints to a trail, save the trail, and re-edit it so that the existing waypoints will be displayed.

8.4   *Displaying the RouteMap on the TrailDetails drawer*

The final update we're going to make to the application is to display the map in a read-only mode on the trail details drawer. Figure 8.6 shows what this will look like when we're done.

Before we make any changes to the `TrailDetails` component, we're going to update the `Trail.cs` class (BlazingTrails.Client > Features > Home > Shared). Currently, it doesn't have a property to hold the waypoints of a trail, so we're going to add it now. Place the following code after the last property in the class:

```
public List<LatLong> Waypoints { get; set; } = new List<LatLong>();
```

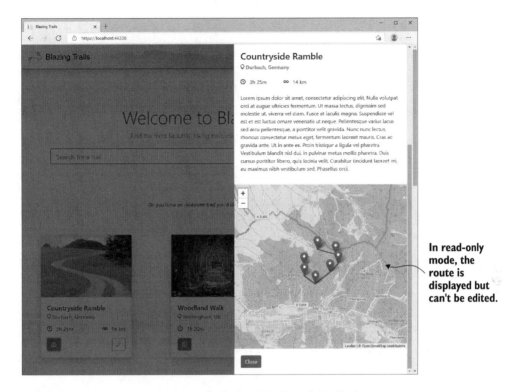

In read-only mode, the route is displayed but can't be edited.

Figure 8.6   The RouteMap component is displayed in the trail details drawer.

Now we'll move on to the RouteMap component. The following listing shows the updates.

Listing 8.15   RouteMap.razor: Change to enable read-only mode

```
<div class="map-wrapper">
    @if (!IsReadOnly)
    {
        <div class="controls">
            <button @onclick="DeleteLastWaypoint" class="btn btn-secondary"
                    title="Delete last waypoint" type="button">
                <i class="bi bi-trash"></i> Remove Last Waypoint
            </button>
        </div>
    }
    <div style="height: @(Height); width:@(Width);" @ref="_map"></div>
</div>

@code {
    // other code omitted for brevity
    [Parameter] public bool IsReadOnly { get; set; }

    protected override async Task OnAfterRenderAsync(bool firstRender)
```

We will only display the Delete Last Waypoint button if the value of IsReadOnly is false.

The new IsReadOnly parameter allows the consumer to decide how they want the map to display.

```
    {
        if (firstRender)
        {
            // other code omitted for brevity
            await _routeMapModule.InvokeVoidAsync(
            "initialize", _map, _routeMapReference, Waypoints,
            IsReadOnly);
        }
    }
    // other code omitted for brevity
}
```

> The value of IsReadOnly is passed to the initialize JavaScript function.

We've added a new component parameter, `IsReadOnly`, to allow the consumer of the component to specify how the map should be displayed. We then use this in the markup to hide the Delete Last Waypoint button based on its value. We also pass it into the `initialize` JavaScript function, which we'll look at next.

With the updates to the `RouteMap` component complete, let's make the necessary updates to the JavaScript code. The following listing shows the changes.

Listing 8.16   RouteMap.razor.js: Updates to allow read-only mode

```
export function initialize(hostElement,
routeMapComponent, existingWaypoints, isReadOnly) {
    // other code omitted for brevity
    if (!isReadOnly) {
        hostElement.map.on('click', function (e) {
            let waypoint = L.marker(e.latlng);
            waypoint.addTo(hostElement.map);
            hostElement.waypoints.push(waypoint);
            let line = L.polyline(hostElement.waypoints
            .map(m => m.getLatLng()), { color: 'var(--brand)' })
            .addTo(hostElement.map);
            hostElement.lines.push(line);

            routeMapComponent.invokeMethodAsync('WaypointAdded',
            e.latlng.lat, e.latlng.lng);
        });
    }
}
```

> The signature is updated to accept the isReadOnly parameter.

> The click handler for the map is wrapped in a check of isReadOnly, and the handler will only be set up if isReadOnly is false.

We first update the function's signature to accept the `isReadOnly` parameter. We then use this new parameter to wrap the click handler with a check. The click handler will only be set up if the value of `isReadOnly` is false. This will stop any waypoints appearing on the map if a user clicks on it when it's in read-only mode.

With read-only mode available on the `RouteMap`, we can add it to the `Trail-Details` component (Features > Home > Shared). Listing 8.17 shows the changes.

Listing 8.17   TrailDetails.razor: Add RouteMap in read-only mode

```
@using BlazingTrails.ComponentLibrary.Map              ◁─────────────

<div class="drawer-wrapper @(_isOpen ? "slide" : "")">
    <div class="drawer-mask"></div>
    <div class="drawer">
        <div class="drawer-content">
            // other code omitted for brevity
            <div>
                @if (_activeTrail.Waypoints.Any())
                {
                    <RouteMap
                      ➥Waypoints="_activeTrail.Waypoints"
                      ➥Width="100%" IsReadOnly="true" />
                }
            </div>
        </div>
        // other code omitted for brevity
    </div>
</div>
```

> We add a new using statement to save having to fully qualify the RouteMap component.

> If the trail has waypoints, we display the RouteMap component passing it the list of waypoints. We also specify that the component renders in read-only mode by setting IsReadOnly to true.

We start by adding a using statement; then we don't have to fully qualify the Route-Map component when we use it in the markup. Next we add a new div, which contains an if statement. That statement checks if the trail is null and that there are waypoints. If these checks pass, the RouteMap component is displayed, passing in the waypoints and setting it to read-only mode by setting IsReadOnly to true.

Now we just need to load the waypoint data when we load the trails on the home page, and we'll be done.

We'll first update the GetTrailsRequest (Features > Home > Shared) in the Shared project. Replace the current Trail record with the following two lines:

```
public record Trail(int Id, string? Name, string Image, string Location, int
    TimeInMinutes, int Length, string Description, List<Waypoint>
    Waypoints);

public record Waypoint(decimal Latitude, decimal Longitude);
```

We've added a new record to represent a waypoint. We've also added a list of waypoints to the Trail record. Now we can update the endpoint in the API to return those waypoints.

Using the GetTrailsEndpoint in BlazingTrails.Api > Features > Home > Shared makes the changes shown in the following listing.

Listing 8.18   GetTrailsEndpoint.cs: Updates to return waypoints

```
[HttpGet(GetTrailsRequest.RouteTemplate)]
public override async Task<ActionResult<GetTrailsRequest.Response>>
➥HandleAsync(int trailId, CancellationToken cancellationToken = default)
{
```

```
var trails = await _context.Trails
➥.Include(x => x.Waypoints)
➥.ToListAsync(cancellationToken);
```
When loading the trails from the database, include the Waypoints data.

```
var response = new GetTrailsRequest.Response(trails.Select(trail => new
➥GetTrailsRequest.Trail(
    trail.Id,
    trail.Name,
    trail.Image,
    trail.Location,
    trail.TimeInMinutes,
    trail.Length,
    trail.Description,
    trail.Waypoints.Select(wp =>
    ➥new GetTrailsRequest.Waypoint(wp.Latitude,
    ➥wp.Longitude)).ToList()
)));
```
Populate the new Waypoints property with the waypoint data from the database.

```
    return Ok(response);
}
```

The first change is to include the waypoint data when retrieving the trails from the database. Once we have that data, we can make the second change when constructing the GetTrailsRequest.Response. We use that data to populate the new Waypoints property we just added.

Finally, back in the BlazingTrails.Client project, we can update the HomePage .razor component (BlazingTrails.Client > Features > Home). In the code block, we're going to populate the Waypoints property we added to the Trail class at the start of this section with the waypoints returned by the GetTrailsEndpoint.

Listing 8.19   HomePage.razor: Populating waypoints

```
protected override async Task OnInitializedAsync()
    {
        // other code omitted
        Id = x.Id,
        Name = x.Name,
        Image = x.Image,
        Description = x.Description,
        Location = x.Location,
        Length = x.Length,
        TimeInMinutes = x.TimeInMinutes,
        Waypoints = x.Waypoints.Select(wp => new
        ➥BlazingTrails.ComponentLibrary.Map.LatLong(
        ➥wp.Latitude, wp.Longitude)).ToList().
        // other code omitted
    }
```
This populates the trail's waypoints, which will be used by the TrailDetails component.

We're done! At this point, we can build the solution and run everything to check out our work (figure 8.7).

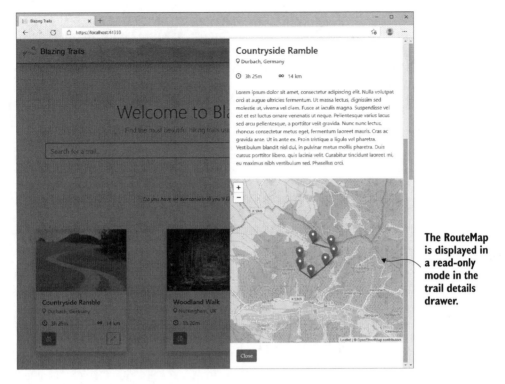

The RouteMap is displayed in a read-only mode in the trail details drawer.

Figure 8.7 The Trail Details pane displaying the `RouteMap` component with various waypoints outlining the route for the trail

Open any trail from the home page you've added waypoints for, and you should see the map being displayed with the relevant waypoints.

Summary

- The Blazor application can make calls into JavaScript via the `IJSRuntime` abstraction.
- `IJSRuntime` can be used to make calls to any JavaScript function in the global scope using the `InvokeAsync` and `InvokeVoidAsync` methods.
- When writing custom JavaScript, instead of adding it to the global scope, a better practice is to use JavaScript modules.
- `IJSRuntime` can be used to load JavaScript modules into C#, where a reference is captured to that module using the `IJSObjectReference` type.
- Functions exported by a module can be executed using the `InvokeAsync` and `InvokeVoidAsync` methods provided by the `IJSObjectReference` interface.
- When using `IJSObjectReference`, it should be disposed of correctly by implementing the `IAsyncDisposable` interface.

- The `DotNetObjectReference<T>` class is used to create references to instances of .NET objects, which can be passed to JavaScript functions.
- Inside JavaScript functions, the `DotNetObjectReference` can be used to call any method on that instance.
- For C# methods to be invokable from JavaScript, they must be decorated with the `[JSInvokable]` attribute.

Securing Blazor applications

9

This chapter covers

- Integrating with an external identity provider
- Displaying UI based on a user's authentication status
- Restricting pages to authorized users
- Authorizing users by role

Having the ability to customize and tailor the user's experience in an application is almost a must-have nowadays. Although it's possible to add a certain measure of customization by storing values in cookies or local storage, often the common approach is to have users create an account and sign in to the application—this is also far more secure.

Once a user is signed in, it opens all kinds of opportunities. In e-commerce sites, such as Amazon, users can view their previous orders, track current ones, and view tailored recommendations of products they might like. On news sites, users can create customized news feeds containing just the information they're interested in seeing.

When allowing users to sign in to an application, there are two processes that must happen:

- *Authentication*—The process of determining if someone is who they claim to be
- *Authorization*—The process of checking if someone has the rights to access a resource

For example, a user can be authenticated (logged in) but not authorized to view a page in an application. This could be because the page is restricted to administrators and the user is not in that role.

In this chapter, we will secure Blazing Trails to allow only users who are logged in to the application to create trails. We will also restrict users to be allowed to edit only their own trails. Finally, we will build on this functionality by adding in *roles*. Roles are a way of grouping users. We will create an administrator role and allow any user in that role to edit any trail in the system.

To enable this functionality, we'll need an identity provider (IdP). An IdP is responsible for storing and managing a user's digital identity. They also offer a way to control access to resources such as APIs, applications, or services. Some large IdPs you would have heard of are Microsoft, Google, Facebook, and Twitter. If you've ever used your credentials from one of these to sign in to a third-party service, you've used an IdP. Figure 9.1 shows an overview of the process.

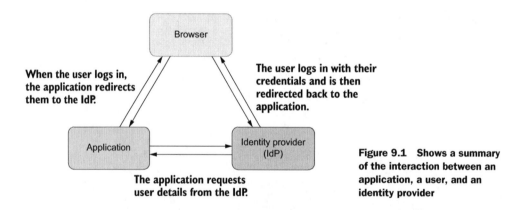

Figure 9.1   **Shows a summary of the interaction between an application, a user, and an identity provider**

Blazor can interoperate with any provider compliant with OpenID Connect (OIDC) (https://openid.net/connect/), and there are many options (identity providers) available for doing this. Here are a few of the more popular providers:

- Duende's IdentityServer
- Azure Active Directory
- Auth0
- Azure Active Directory B2C
- Okta

My personal favorite is Auth0 (https://auth0.com). It's a feature-rich IdP with an easy-to-understand, clear interface. It supports a vast array of login methods, from username and password to passwordless logins—and the best bit is they offer a free account that supports up to 7,000 active users. This is the identity provider we'll be using to enable authentication and authorization in Blazing Trails.

9.1   *Integrating with an identity provider: Auth0*

Gone are the days of rolling your own authentication system. Creating a `Users` table in your database and storing usernames and passwords is no longer acceptable. Having your application be the latest breach on haveibeenpwned.com is not something you want to happen. Authentication and authorization are complex issues, and using an IdP abstracts a large chunk of the complexity—and responsibility—away from us.

When using an IdP, we delegate the sign-up and login process to it. Users are forwarded from our application to the IdP, where they log in. They are then sent back to our application once that process is complete. The specifics of what happens depends on what *flow* (https://auth0.com/docs/authorization/flows) is used.

When using Blazor WebAssembly with Auth0, we use the Authorization Code Flow with Proof of Key for Code Exchange (PKCE). In this flow, the user is sent to Auth0 to log in. When they successfully complete the login, they are returned to the application with an authorization code. Blazor then makes a call to Auth0 with the code and requests an access token and an ID token, which are kept in the browser's session storage. Figure 9.2 visualizes this process.

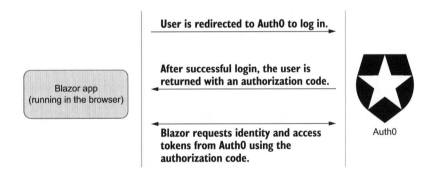

Figure 9.2   This diagram shows the process of logging in to a Blazor WebAssembly application via Auth0 using the Authorization Code Flow with PKCE.

The ID token is used by Blazor to construct a `ClaimsIdentity` for the user. This is an object that represents the user's digital identity for that application. We can then access this information in various ways, which we'll explore later in this chapter. The access token is used when making calls to an API and contains details regarding what the user is allowed to access.

If you're using Blazor Server, the process is a little different. When the user is redirected back from the IdP to the Blazor Server app, an additional request is made to

Auth0 for the user details, which are then saved into a cookie. There are no access tokens or ID tokens in this scenario.

Now that we have a bit of an idea what is happening, let's get on with the integration. If you haven't already, head over to http://auth0.com/signup to create a free account.

9.1.1   *Registering applications with Auth0*

The first thing we need to do is register both our Blazor WebAssembly application and our API with Auth0. From the menu in the Auth0 dashboard (https://manage .auth0.com), select Applications > Applications. Then select Create Application.

We'll register the Blazor app first. In the modal, enter the name as `Blazing Trails Client`. Then select Single Page Web Applications as the application type. Then click Create. After Auth0 creates the application, move to the Settings tab and make a note of the Domain and Client ID—we'll need these a little later. Then scroll down to the Application URIs section and enter the following in the Allowed Callback URLs box:

```
https://localhost:{port}/authentication/login-callback
```

Make sure to replace `{port}` with the port your BlazingTrails.Api project runs from. Just to be clear, that's the port the API project runs from, not the Client project. Once you've done that, scroll to the bottom of the page and click Save Changes.

Now let's register the API. From the main menu on the left, select Applications > APIs. Then click Create API. In the modal, enter the name as `Blazing Trails API`; then for the `Identifier`, enter `https://blazingtrailsapi.com`. The `Identifier` is a unique string that identifies a particular API. If we had multiple APIs, we would need to request access tokens for each one using its identifier. Although the `Identifier` can be any unique string value, Auth0 recommends using a URL. If Blazing Trails were a public site and the API was accessible from https://blazingtrails.com/api, we would use that URL. But since it's not, we will use this fake URL instead. Nothing will ever call this URL, so the fact that it's fake doesn't cause any issues.

Leave the Signing Algorithm as it is, and click Create. At this point, both of our applications have been successfully registered with Auth0.

9.1.2   *Customizing tokens from Auth0*

As part of the login process, ASP.NET Core constructs a type called `ClaimsPrincipal`, which contains an `Identity` property that is of type `ClaimsIdentity`. This represents a user identity for an application. We'll be accessing this in both our Blazor app and our WebAPI over the course of this chapter, when we need to check something about the user's identity. One of the properties we'll be accessing is called `Name`, which we'll do like this: `User.Identity.Name`.

This is going to be automatically populated with the user's email address in our Blazor app, as Blazor uses the ID token to construct the `Identity`, and it contains a claim with the user's email address. However, the access token doesn't contain this claim by default. This means that when we call the API, it won't be able to populate the `User.Identity.Name` property with the user's email. In fact, we wouldn't have access to the user's email at all and we're going to need the user's email to know what trails they own.

> ## What is a claim?
>
> Claims are key-value pairs that represent information about the user issued by an identity provider. There are a set of standard claims defined (http://mng.bz/XZOE), but custom claims can also be added. Examples of standard claims are `given_name`, `family_name`, and website. Claims are used by an application to decide if a user can perform a certain task or access a certain feature. This is known as *claims-based authorization*.
>
> An example of this is an application that restricts access based on age. If the IdP issues a claim that contains the logged-in user's date of birth, then, if the application trusts the issuer, it can accept or reject the user based on the value of that claim.

The good news is that Auth0 allows us to customize the claims that are returned for each token. From the main menu in Auth0, select Auth Pipeline > Rules. Then click the Create button. On the next screen, select the Empty Rule option. This will give us a blank rule that we can use to define the additional claims we want. Name the rule `Customize Tokens`, then add the code in listing 9.1. This code is run by Auth0 whenever a user logs in and will add the name claim to the access token with the value of that claim being the user's email address. Now when we send the access token to the API from Blazor, the API will be able to populate the `User.Identity.Name` property with the user's email address.

Listing 9.1 Customize tokens rule in Auth0

```
function (user, context, callback) {
  const accessTokenClaims = context.accessToken || {};    ⟵ Defines a variable that holds the access tokens claims
  accessTokenClaims['http://schemas.xmlsoap.org/ws/
  ➥2005/05/identity/claims/name'] = user.email;    ⟵ Adds the name claims with the value being the user's email address

  callback(null, user, context);
}
```

That's all the customization we need to do in Auth0 for now. Let's head over to our Blazing Trails solution and finish the setup there.

9.1.3 Configuring Blazor WebAssembly to use Auth0

The first step is to add a new file called *appsettings.json* to the wwwroot directory with the following code:

```
{
  "Auth0": {
    "Authority": "{Domain}",
    "ClientId": "{Client ID}"
  }
}
```

Make sure to replace {Domain} and {Client ID} with the values you noted down when registering the Blazor app with Auth0.

The appsettings.json file

There are various ways to specify application settings in ASP.NET Core (http:// mng.bz/M5o8) and the appsettings.json file is one of them. Different versions of this file can be created to correspond to different deployment environments by creating a file with the naming convention of appsettings.{environment} .json—where {environment} should match the value of the ASPNETCORE_ ENVIRONMENT variable.

As an example, let's say we wanted to use a different tenant in Auth0 for our production environment. We would create an appsettings.production.json file with the same Auth0 block, then change the `Authority` and `ClientId` values to match those of the tenant we wanted to use in production.

Just remember, in Blazor WebAssembly, this file is shipped to the browser in plain text and is easily viewable using the browser's developer tools. Never store any sensitive values or keys in this file.

We then need to install two additional NuGet packages. The Blazor WebAssembly authentication package (`Microsoft.AspNetCore.Components.WebAssembly .Authentication`) and the http extensions package (`Microsoft.Extensions .Http`).

The authentication package provides a set of primitives that help authenticate users and obtain tokens from IdPs to call secured APIs. We'll need this so we can talk to Auth0. The http extensions package will give us access to `IHttpClientFactory`, which we'll need to retrieve named http clients in our code.

Add the following package references next to the existing ones in the Blazing-Trails.Client.csproj file:

```
<PackageReference
    Include="Microsoft.AspNetCore.Components.WebAssembly.Authentication"
    Version="6.0.0" />
<PackageReference Include="Microsoft.Extensions.Http" Version="6.0.0" />
```

Once they're installed, we can open the Program.cs file and add the code shown in the following listing.

Listing 9.2   Program.cs: Adding Auth0 integration

```
public static async Task Main(string[] args)
{
    // other code omitted for brevity

    builder.Services.AddOidcAuthentication(options =>     ⟵┐  Adds support for
    {                                                       │  authentication using
        builder.Configuration.Bind("Auth0",                 │  OIDC-compliant
                                                            ─┘  identity providers
```

```
      ➥options.ProviderOptions);
        options.ProviderOptions.ResponseType = "code";
    });

    await builder.Build().RunAsync();
}
```

**Specifies that the type of
authentication and authorization flow
should be Authorization Code flow**

**Specifies that the configuration for the OIDC provider should
come from the settings we put in the appsettings.json file**

We start by adding the `AddOidcAuthentication` extension method. This sets up and registers all the necessary services in Blazor for integrating with an OIDC-compliant identity provider. We then state that the configuration for the identity provider should be retrieved from the Auth0 section of the appsettings.json we just created. Finally, we specified the authentication and authorization flow to use. For SPA applications, the current recommended flow is Authorization Code Flow with Proof Key for Code Exchange (PKCE).

NOTE More detailed information on Authorization Code Flow with PKCE and other flows can be found on Auth0's docs site (http://mng.bz/aJwX).

With the changes in Program.cs complete, we need to add a script tag to the index.html page in the wwwroot folder. Above the current script tag referencing the `blazor.webassembly.js` script, add the following tag:

```
<script src="_content/
    Microsoft.AspNetCore.Components.WebAssembly.Authentication/
    AuthenticationService.js"></script>
```

This script registers an authentication service that sits in JavaScript. It handles the storage and retrieval of tokens from the browser's session storage. It also manages the sign-in and sign-out operations with the identity provider.

To avoid having to fully qualify the names of auth-specific components, we will add a couple of `using` statements to the main `_Imports.razor` at the root of the project.

```
@using Microsoft.AspNetCore.Authorization
@using Microsoft.AspNetCore.Components.Authorization
@using Microsoft.AspNetCore.Components.WebAssembly.Authentication
```

Next, we will update the router in `App.razor`. The following listing shows the updated code.

Listing 9.3 App.razor: Authentication updates

```
<CascadingAuthenticationState>
    <Router AppAssembly="@typeof(Program).Assembly">
        <Found Context="routeData">
            <AuthorizeRouteView RouteData="@routeData"
            ➥DefaultLayout="@typeof(MainLayout)">
```

**Provides a CascadingParameter
containing the current
authentication state of the user**

**The AuthorizeRouteView
component replaces the existing
RouteView component.**

The Authorizing template is displayed while the user's authentication status is being determined.

```
<Authorizing>
    <p>Determining session state, please wait...</p>
</Authorizing>
<NotAuthorized>
    <h1>Sorry</h1>
    <p>You're not authorized to reach this page.
    ➥You need to log in.</p>
</NotAuthorized>
        </AuthorizeRouteView>
        <FocusOnNavigate RouteData="@routeData" Selector="h1" />
    </Found>
    // other code omitted for brevity
    </Router>
</CascadingAuthenticationState>
```

The NotAuthorized template is displayed when the user isn't authorized to access a page in the application.

The first change is to wrap the `Router` in the `CascadingAuthenticationState` component. This component provides a `CascadingParameter` to all child components—the whole application—which contains the user's current authentication state. Next, we've replaced the default `RouteView` component with the `AuthorizeRouteView` component. This new component can interact with Blazor's authentication system. It will allow us to decorate pages with an `Authorize` attribute that will limit access to only authorized users. The `AuthorizeRouteView` comes with two templates, `Authorizing` and `NotAuthorized`. The `Authorizing` template is shown while Blazor is determining if the user is authorized or not. The `NotAuthorized` template is shown when the user attempts to access a page component they don't have access to.

The final task we need to perform is to add a new page. This page is going to handle the various authentication operations, such as logging in and logging out—it's the callback page we specified during the Auth0 setup. Create a new folder under Features called *Auth*. Then add a new Blazor component called `Authentication.razor`, as shown in the following listing.

Listing 9.4 Authentication.razor

```
@page "/authentication/{action}"
@using Microsoft.Extensions.Configuration

@inject NavigationManager Navigation
@inject IConfiguration Configuration

<RemoteAuthenticatorView Action="@Action">
    <LogOut>
        @{
            var authority =
            ➥(string)Configuration["Auth0:Authority"];
            var clientId =
            ➥(string)Configuration["Auth0:ClientId"];

            Navigation.NavigateTo(
            ➥$"{authority}/v2/logout?client_id={clientId}");
        }
    </LogOut>
```

The page takes an action parameter that is used to determine what operation to perform.

The RemoteAuthenticatorView is responsible for managing the user's authentication status and interacts with Auth0.

By default, Blazor logs the user out on the client but the logout from Auth0 must be handled manually by calling the Auth0 logout endpoint.

```
</RemoteAuthenticatorView>

@code{
    [Parameter] public string? Action { get; set; }
}
```

The Authentication page takes an action parameter that determines what operation it's going to perform—examples are `login` and `logout`. The page contains the `RemoteAuthenticatorView` component. This component's job is to manage the user's authentication status by performing any interactions with Auth0. The login process happens seamlessly, with no additional code required. But the logout process is different. By default, Blazor logs the user out of only the client application; it doesn't terminate the login at the identity provider. This we must perform manually. To do so, we add code to the `LogOut` template. This will be executed when a logout action is requested, and it will redirect the user to Auth0 to complete the logout process.

This is everything we need to integrate Blazor with Auth0. Now let's set up the API.

9.1.4 Configuring ASP.NET Core WebAPI to use Auth0

Just as we did with the Blazor app, we're going to start by adding the Auth0 settings to the appsettings.json file. Add the following section to the file:

```
"Auth0": {
  "Authority": "{Domain}",
  "ApiIdentifier": "{Identifier}"
}
```

Replace `{Domain}` with the same domain you used in the Blazor registration (remember to include `https://`). Also replace `{Identifier}` with the `Identifier` you used when registering the API.

Next, we need to install a new NuGet package, which will allow us to work with access tokens in the API. Add the following package reference to the Blazing-Trails.Api.csproj file.

```
<PackageReference Include="Microsoft.AspNetCore.Authentication.JwtBearer"
    Version="6.0.0" />
```

From here, we can open the Program.cs file and add the following code.

Listing 9.5 Program.cs: Adding authentication services

```
// other code omitted
builder.Services.AddAuthentication(options =>          ◁──┐ This adds various services required
{                                                          │ by authentication services and
    options.DefaultAuthenticateScheme =                    │ allows configuration of options.
    ➥JwtBearerDefaults.AuthenticationScheme;
    options.DefaultChallengeScheme =
    ➥JwtBearerDefaults.AuthenticationScheme;            ┌─ This tells the API to authenticate
}).AddJwtBearer(options =>                            ◁──┘  using JSON Web Tokens (JWTs).
{
```

```
    options.Authority = builder
    ➥.Configuration["Auth0:Authority"];
    options.Audience = builder
    ➥.Configuration["Auth0:ApiIdentifier"];
});
```

> Here we tell the API where it can validate the tokens.

```
var app = builder.Build();
```

First, we call the `AddAuthentication` method. This registers and sets up various services needed for authentication. We can then tell the API to use JSON Web Tokens (JWTs) for authentication by calling the `AddJwtBearer` method. Next, we load the Auth0 configuration from the appsettings.json so the API knows where to validate the tokens that are sent to it.

The final step is to add the authentication and authorization middleware. It's important where these are placed in the file, as order matters here. Add them between the `app.UseRouting()` and `app.MapControllers()` calls:

```
app.UseAuthentication();
app.UseAuthorization();
```

At this point, the API is all set up and ready to go.

9.2 Displaying different UI fragments based on authentication status

The first component we're going to build will provide the links for anonymous users to log in and authenticated users to log out. It will be displayed at the top of each page just under the main header bar—this will give users access to it at all times. We'll put this new component in the Auth feature folder. The following listing shows the code for the new component.

Listing 9.6 LoginStatus.razor

```
@inject NavigationManager Navigation
@inject SignOutSessionStateManager SignOutManager

<div class="container text-right">
    <AuthorizeView>
        <Authorized>
            <div>
                Hello, @context.User.Identity!.Name
                <a href="#" @onclick="BeginSignOut">
                ➥Log out</a>
            </div>
        </Authorized>
        <NotAuthorized>.
            <a href="authentication/login">
            ➥Log in/Sign up</a>
        </NotAuthorized>
    </AuthorizeView>
</div>
```

The AuthorizeView component is used to display UI fragments based on a user's authorization status.

Information about the user can be accessed via the context parameter.

The markup in the Authorized template will be displayed when the user is authorized.

The logout link allows logged-in users to log out of the application.

The markup in the NotAuthorized template is displayed to any unauthorized user.

The login link will redirect the user to the Authentication page component, where they will be forwarded to Auth0 to be authenticated.

```
@code{
    private async Task BeginSignOut(
    ➥MouseEventArgs args)
    {
        await SignOutManager.SetSignOutState();
        Navigation.NavigateTo("authentication/logout");
    }
}
```

**The BeginSignOut method uses the SignOutManager
class to help prevent cross-site request forgery
(CSRF) attacks on the logout endpoint. It sets some
state, which is checked in the logout function of
the Authentication page component before
allowing the user to complete the logout process.**

The `AuthorizeView` component defines two templates, `Authorized` and `Not-Authorized`. Inside the `Authorized` template, we place any markup we want authorized users to see. Inside the `NotAuthorized` template, we place any markup we want to show unauthorized users. The keyword here is *authorized*. Remember: a user can be logged in (*authenticated*) but still not allowed to view content (*authorized*). In this case, authorized just requires a user to be logged in, as we haven't specified any roles or policies the user needs to meet. We'll be covering this a little later when we implement roles.

If we have an authorized user, we display a greeting along with the user's email address. We access this email via a `ClaimsPrincipal`, which contains the user's `ClaimsIdentity`—`User.Identity`. We touched on this earlier: `User.Identity` is populated with information from the claims in the ID token returned from Auth0. By default, Auth0 returns the user's email address as the value for the name claim. Blazor, by default, maps the name claim to the `Name` property on the `User.Identity` object. It's worth noting that, depending on your identity provider and its configuration, different information could be returned in the name claim. It's also possible to tell Blazor which claim to use to populate the `Name` property. This is done in the `Program.Main` method, inside the `AddOidcAuthentication` call:

```
options.UserOptions.NameClaim = ClaimTypes.GivenName;
```

We also render a logout link with an onclick handler defined. Clicking this link triggers the `BeginSignOut` method defined in the code block. This method redirects the user to the logout action of the Authentication page. But before doing that, it uses the `SignOutManager` to safeguard the logout action from cross-site request forgery (CSRF) attacks. It does this by setting some state, which is then checked by the logout action. If this state isn't present when the logout action is executed, then the logout process won't proceed.

When we have an unauthenticated user, in this case an anonymous user, we display a link to log in. This link redirects the user to the login action of the Authentication page. Once there, they are redirected to Auth0 to either enter their email and password or sign up for a new account.

We can now add the `LoginStatus` component to the `Header` component in the Layout feature folder. Then we run the application to check that everything is working. The following listing shows the updated `Header` component.

Listing 9.7   Header.razor: Adding the `AccessControl` component

```
@using BlazingTrails.Client.Features.Auth          ◁──┐  Adds using statement for the
                                                       │  AccessControl component
<nav class="navbar mb-3 shadow">
    <a class="navbar-brand" href="/">
        <img src="/images/logo.png">
    </a>
</nav>
                          ┌─ References the
<LoginStatus />      ◁────┘  AccessControl component
```

We've added a `using` statement to save having to fully qualify the path, then added a reference to the `LoginStatus` component. We can now run the application and check to see that everything is working (figure 9.3).

The Log in/Sign up link is displayed for anonymous users.

Once logged in, the user sees a personalized greeting and Log out link.

Figure 9.3   The sign-in/sign-up link is displayed to anonymous users at the top. Then the customized greeting and logout link is displayed to signed-in users at the bottom.

You should now see the Log in/Sign up link being displayed at the top right of the screen just under the main header. You should be able to follow the link and create an account and sign in.

9.2.1 Updating the Home feature

Because users can now sign up to Blazing Trails and log in and out, we will make some changes regarding what they will see. Up until now, any anonymous user could create or edit a trail. This needs to change. We want only logged-in users to be able to create trails, and we want only the owner of a trail to be able to edit it.

To make this happen, we first need to make a change to our API. We will add a new Owner column to the `Trail` entity so we can store the email address of the user who created it. We can then return the owner data when we get the trails to display on the home page and check it against the currently logged-in user. If they match, we can display the button to edit the trail; otherwise, we won't.

Open Trail.cs in the BlazingTrails.Api > Persistence > Entities folder. Then add the following property to the class:

```
public string Owner { get; set; } = default!;
```

While we're here, we can also update the `TrailConfig` class in the same file. We need to add the following line to make the new `Owner` property required at a database level:

```
builder.Property(x => x.Owner).IsRequired();
```

With those two lines in place, we can create a new migration that will update the trail table in the database. From Visual Studio's package manager console, run the following two commands:

```
Add-Migration AddOwnerToTrail
Update-Database
```

The first command creates a new migration to add an Owner column to the Trails database table. The second command will run that migration to apply the change to the database.

We now have a blank Owner column in our Trails database table. For now, we need to manually add some email addresses to this column. For now, use the email address of an account you've already created in Auth0. Later, we'll update the `Add Trail` feature so this is added automatically when a user creates a trail.

With the database changes complete, we can update the GetTrailsEndpoint (BlazingTrails.Api > Features > Shared). The following listing shows the change.

> **Listing 9.8 GetTrailsEndpoint.cs: Returning the trail owner**

```
// other code omitted for brevity
var response = new GetTrailsRequest.Response(trails.Select(trail =>
new GetTrailsRequest.Trail(
        trail.Id,
        trail.Name,
        trail.Image,
        trail.Location,
        trail.TimeInMinutes,
        trail.Length,
```

```
        trail.Description,
        trail.Owner,
        trail.Waypoints.Select(wp => new GetTrailsRequest.Waypoint(
        ➥wp.Latitude, wp.Longitude)).ToList()
    )));
// other code omitted for brevity
```

The new owner data is added to the response.

You will see an error after this change, as we also need to update GetTrailsRequest.cs. This is in BlazingTrails.Shared > Features > Home > Shared. Update the `Trail` record as follows to include an `Owner` property:

```
public record Trail(int Id, string Name, string? Image, string Location, int
    TimeInMinutes, int Length, string Description, string Owner,
    List<Waypoint> Waypoints);
```

This should remove the error in the endpoint, and the application will compile once again. We can now focus our attention back to our Blazor code. In BlazingTrail.Client > Features > Home > Shared, we will add an `Owner` property to Trail.cs.

```
public string Owner { get; set; } = "";
```

Now we can move up a folder and begin our work on the `HomePage` component. We're going to update the row template and make a small update to the `OnInitialized-Async` method (listing 9.9).

Listing 9.9   HomePage.razor: Adding `AuthorizeView` to `RowTemplate`

```
...
<RowTemplate>
        <th scope="col">@trail.Name</th>
        <td>@trail.Location</td>
        <td>@(trail.Length)km</td>
        <td>@trail.TimeFormatted</td>
        <td class="text-right">
            <AuthorizeView>
                @if (trail.Owner.Equals(
                ➥context.User.Identity?.Name,
                ➥StringComparison.OrdinalIgnoreCase)
                {
                    <button @onclick="@(() =>
                    ➥NavManager.NavigateTo($"/edit-trail/{trail.Id}"))"
                    ➥title="Edit" class="btn btn-outline-secondary">
                        <i class="bi bi-pencil"></i>
                    </button>
                }
            </AuthorizeView>
            <button @onclick="@(() => HandleTrailSelected(trail))"
            ➥title="View" class="btn btn-primary">
                <i class="bi bi-binoculars"></i>
            </button>
        </td>
    </RowTemplate>
// other code omitted
```

The existing Edit button is wrapped in an AuthorizeView component.

If the trail's owner and the logged-in user are the same, we display the Edit button.

```
@code {
// other code omitted
protected override async Task OnInitializedAsync()
{
    // other code omitted for brevity
    _trails = response.Trails.Select(x => new Trail
        {
            Id = x.Id,
            Name = x.Name,
            Image = x.Image,
            Description = x.Description,
            Location = x.Location,
            Length = x.Length,                          The Owner from the API
            TimeInMinutes = x.TimeInMinutes,            response is mapped to the
            Owner = x.Owner,                            Owner on the local Trail class.
            Waypoints = x.Waypoints.Select(wp =>
            ➥new BlazingTrails.ComponentLibrary.Map.LatLong(wp.Latitude,
            ➥wp.Longitude))
            ➥?.ToList() ?? new List<ComponentLibrary.Map.LatLong>();
        });
    // other code omitted
}
// other code omitted
}
```

The existing Edit button is wrapped in an `AuthorizeView` component. This immediately makes the button visible to only logged-in users—but we need a little more. Inside the `AuthorizeView`, we use the `context` variable to compare the current-user email with the email stored in the owner property of the trail. If they match, we display the Edit button. If not, nothing will be displayed. Finally, in the code block, we're mapping the `Owner` information that is returned from the API response to the `Owner` we just added to the local `Trail` class.

While we're on the `HomePage` component, we will make one other change. The call to action at the top of the page needs updating. It contains a link to the `Add Trail` form, which we want to display only to logged-in users. We'll use the `AuthorizeView` component to display different messages depending on whether the user is logged in or not. The following listing shows the update.

Listing 9.10   HomePage.razor: Call to action update

```
// other code omitted for bevity
<AuthorizeView>                          An AuthorizeView component is added, defining
    <Authorized>                         both Authorized and NotAuthorized templates.
        <div class="mb-4">
            <p class="font-italic text-center">Do you have an awesome trail
            ➥you'd like to share? <a href="add-trail">Add it here</a>.</p>
        </div>
    </Authorized>                        When a user is not authorized, they see a modified
    <NotAuthorized>                      call to action prompting them to log in or sign up.
        <div class="mb-4">
            <p class="font-italic text-center">Do you have an awesome trail
```

When a user is authorized, they see the original call to action link.

```
             ➥you'd like to share? Please <a href="authentication/login">
                ➥log in or sign up</a>.</p>
            </div>
          </NotAuthorized>
      </AuthorizeView>
// other code omitted for brevity
```

When logged-in users view the page, they will still see the original call to action, with the link to the add trail form. However, when anonymous users view the page, they will see a modified version of the call to action. It will prompt them to either log in to the application or sign up for an account.

The changes for the HomePage are complete. We now need to make a small update to the SearchPage component before moving on to the TrailCard component. In the SearchPage component, we need to add the same mapping between the owner properties we did on the HomePage. In the OnInitializedAsync method, add the following line to the addTrails variable declaration:

```
Owner = x.Owner
```

Now let's update the TrailCard component. In the TrailCard, we're going to add the same code as we did for the RowTemplate on the home page (see listing 9.11). Just as we did before, we're wrapping the existing button in an AuthorizeView component. We then use the context variable to check the current user's email against the owner of the trail. If they match, the Edit button is displayed.

Listing 9.11   TrailCard.razor: Hiding Edit Trail button from unauthorized users

```
// other code omitted for brevity
<AuthorizeView>                               ◄──────  The existing Edit button is wrapped
        @if (Trail.Owner.Equals(                       in an AuthorizeView component.
        ➥context.User.Identity?.Name,
        ➥StringComparison.OrdinalIgnoreCase))
        {
            <button class="btn btn-outline-secondary mt-3 float-right"
            ➥title="Edit" @onclick="@(() =>
            ➥NavManager.NavigateTo($"/edit-trail/{Trail.Id}"))">
                <i class="bi bi-pencil"></i>
            </button>
        }
      </AuthorizeView>
// other code omitted for brevity
```

If the trail's owner and the logged-in user are the same, we display the Edit button.

We can now run the application and test our work. Starting off without logging in, we should see a view of the home page like that shown in figure 9.4. As you can see, no Edit buttons are visible on the trail cards.

Now, log in with the same user you set the owner property to for any existing trails. You should now see an Edit button available on the trail card (figure 9.5).

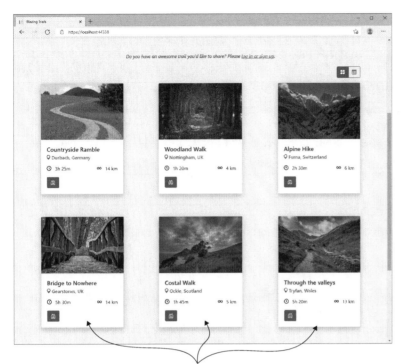

Figure 9.4   The Edit button is no longer displayed on the trail card when a user is logged out.

When logged out, no Edit buttons are visible on the trail cards.

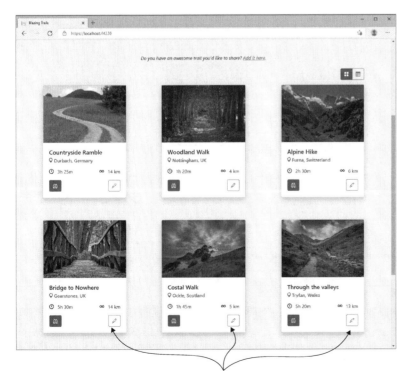

Figure 9.5   The Edit button is displayed once a user logs in to the application.

When logged in, the Edit button is visible on the trail card.

That's some great work. But hiding buttons isn't enough. We also need to protect pages from direct access; a user could easily just type in the address of the Add Trail page. That's what we'll look at next.

9.3   *Prevent unauthorized users accessing a page*

Restricting access to pages is a common requirement when building applications. Blazor uses a similar approach to that of WebAPIs—the `Authorize` attribute. We can use the `@attributes` directive to apply the `[Authorize]` attribute to a page component. This works in tandem with the `AuthorizeRouteView` component in the router to restrict page-level access. We added the `AuthorizeRouteView` earlier in the chapter, but let's try and understand its purpose in a little more detail.

By default, the Router contains a component called `RouteView`. This component's job is to render the requested page based on the URL. The limitation of this component is that it has no awareness of security. This is where the `Authorize-RouteView` component comes in. It's a drop-in replacement for the `RouteView`, and it understands Blazor's security features. Before navigating to a page, it will check that the user is authorized to view that page by checking for the `Authorize` attribute. It will then either load the page or render any markup specified in the `NotAuthorized` template it exposes.

In Blazing Trails, we need to protect our Add and Edit Trail pages from unauthorized users. So far, we've made changes to render the links to only those pages when a user is logged in. However, that won't protect us from a user who knows the direct URL. To protect against this, we need to add the following line of code to each page:

```
@attribute [Authorize]
```

My preferred place to add this is directly below the `@page` attribute. So, for the `EditTrailPage` (BlazingTrails.Client > Features > ManageTrails > EditTrail), it should look like this:

```
@page "/edit-trail/{TrailId:int}"
@attribute [Authorize]
```

And for the `AddTrailPage` (BlazingTrails.Client > Features > ManageTrails > AddTrail), it should look like this:

```
@page "/add-trail"
@attribute [Authorize]
```

That's it! If we run the application now and try to access either page without logging in, we will see the message shown in figure 9.6—which is defined in the `Authorize-RouteView` component's `NotAuthorized` template.

If we then log in to the application, we can navigate to either page as expected. On the surface, it looks like we've done our job. Unauthorized users can no longer load the Edit Trail or Add Trail pages. But what about the server? We added the `Autho-rize` attribute to prevent users typing in a URL and going directly to a restricted

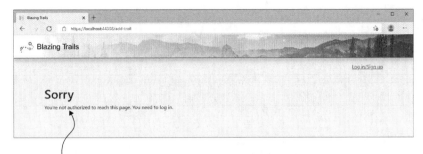

The content of the AuthorizeRouteView's NotAuthorized template
is displayed when attempting to navigate to a restricted page.

Figure 9.6 When trying to access a restricted page as a logged-out user, the
`AuthorizeRouteView` component's `NotAuthorized` template is displayed.

page, but what if a malicious user knows the address of the add trail endpoint and
tries to post directly to that? Currently, we have no protection for this type of attack.

It's important to understand that SPA applications like Blazor WebAssembly can
never be made truly secure. They run on a client machine, which means they are open
to all sorts of tampering and can even be decompiled. Therefore, the API is the only place
we are truly secure. Whatever we do on the client is essentially just cosmetic and is there
to provide a good user experience. Securing the server is the most important thing.

9.3.1 Securing API endpoints

A major part of securing our API involves doing one thing, adding the `[Authorize]`
attribute to all the endpoints that only authorized users should access. These endpoints all reside in the Features > ManageTrails folder.

- `AddTrailEndpoint`
- `EditTrailEndpoint`
- `GetTrailEndpoint`
- `UploadTrailImageEndpoint`

Using the `AddTrailEndpoint` as an example, the following shows what each endpoint should look like once the attribute is added:

```
[Authorize]
[HttpPost(AddTrailRequest.RouteTemplate)]
public override async Task<ActionResult<int>> HandleAsync(AddTrailRequest
    request, CancellationToken cancellationToken = default)
```

We also need to add an additional check into the `GetTrailEndpoint`, `EditTrail-
Endpoint`, and `UploadTrailImageEndpoint` to ensure that the user accessing
those endpoints is also the owner of the trail, as we don't want any logged-in users to
be able to edit any trail. Starting with the `GetTrailEndpoint` (Features > Manage-
Trails > EditTrail), we'll add a check for the owner (see listing 9.12).

Listing 9.12 GetTrailEndpoint.cs: Adding check for owner

```
public override async Task<ActionResult<GetTrailRequest.Response>>
➥HandleAsync(int trailId, CancellationToken cancellationToken = default)
{
    var trail = await _context.Trails.Include(x => x.Waypoints)
    ➥.SingleOrDefaultAsync(x => x.Id == trailId,
    ➥cancellationToken: cancellationToken);

    if (trail is null)
        return BadRequest("Trail could not be found.");

    if (!trail.Owner.Equals(
    ➥HttpContext.User.Identity!.Name,
    ➥StringComparison.OrdinalIgnoreCase))
        return Unauthorized();

    // other code omitted for brevity
}
```

> A check is performed to see if the owner of the trail is the same as the logged-in user.

> If the current user isn't the owner, an Unauthorized response is returned.

We check the trail's owner against the currently logged-in user, and if they don't match, we return an `Unauthorized` response to the client. We can now do the same check in the `EditTrailEndpoint` (see the following listing).

Listing 9.13 EditTrailEndpoint.cs: Adding check for owner

```
public override async Task<ActionResult<bool>> HandleAsync(
➥EditTrailRequest request, CancellationToken cancellationToken = default)
{
    var trail = await _database.Trails.Include(x => x.Waypoints)
    ➥.SingleOrDefaultAsync(x => x.Id == request.Trail.Id,
    ➥cancellationToken: cancellationToken);

    if (trail is null)
        return BadRequest("Trail could not be found.");

    if (!trail.Owner.Equals(
    ➥HttpContext.User.Identity!.Name,
    ➥StringComparison.OrdinalIgnoreCase))
        return Unauthorized();
    // other code omitted for brevity
}
```

> A check is performed to see if the owner of the trail is the same as the logged-in user.

> If the current user isn't the owner, an Unauthorized response is returned.

Last but not least, we can add the check to the `UploadTrailImageEndpoint` (see the following listing).

Listing 9.14 UploadTrailImageEndpoint.cs: Adding check for owner
---

```
public override async Task<ActionResult<string>> HandleAsync(
➥[FromRoute] int trailId, CancellationToken cancellationToken = default)
{
    var trail = await _database.Trails.SingleOrDefaultAsync(
    ➥x => x.Id == trailId, cancellationToken);
```

```
    if (trail is null)
        return BadRequest("Trail does not exist.");

    if (!trail.Owner.Equals(
➥HttpContext.User.Identity!.Name,
➥StringComparison.OrdinalIgnoreCase))
        return Unauthorized();
    // other code omitted for brevity
}
```

> A check is performed to see if the owner of the trail is the same as the logged-in user.

> If the current user isn't the owner, an Unauthorized response is returned.

That is all we need to do to secure our endpoints from a direct attack. We have also enforced our criteria that only trail owners should be able to edit a trail. If we run the application, we can test our work. Log in with a trail owner account and attempt to edit the trail. Unfortunately, we'll see an error (figure 9.7).

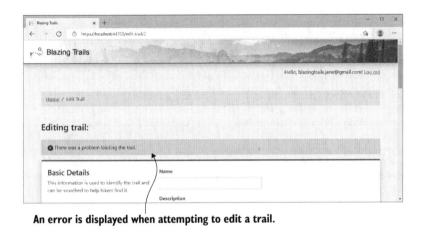

An error is displayed when attempting to edit a trail.

Figure 9.7   When attempting to edit a trail, an error is shown.

If we check in the browser tools, we'll see a more descriptive error:

```
Failed to load resource: the server responded with a status code of 401 ()
```

So, what's happened? Now that we have secured the endpoints on the API, we need to provide the API with something to prove we are who we say we are. Specifically, we need to send an access token whenever we make a call to it from Blazor. Let's look at how we do this next.

9.3.2   Calling secure API endpoints from Blazor

When calling secured endpoints from SPA applications such as Blazor, it is common to include an access token in the request. This access token is issued by an identity provider—in our case Auth0—and it allows the API to verify what we're allowed to access. When we log in via Auth0, our access token is returned to the Blazor app, where it is stored in the browser's session storage.

But how do we get the token from there and into our requests? Well, Blazor comes with a custom message handler called `BaseAddressAuthorizationMessage-Handler` that we can use with the `HttpClient` to include our access token automatically on any request to the API.

> **NOTE** The `BaseAddressAuthorizationMessageHandler` works only when making requests to an API with the same base address as the Blazor application. For example, a Blazor app running from `https://blazingtrails.com` could use the handler if the API resides at `https://blazingtrails.com/api` but not if it resides at `https://blazingtrailsapi.com`. If you have this requirement, you can build your own custom message handler (http://mng.bz/GEdJ).

We configure the handler in the `Program.Main` method. We'll add a named `Http-Client` instance and will configure it to use the `BaseAddressAuthorization-MessageHandler`. The following listing shows the updated `Program.Main` method.

Listing 9.15 Program.cs: Adding secure `HttpClient`

```
// other code omitted for brevity
builder.RootComponents.Add<App>("#app");
builder.RootComponents.Add<HeadContent>("head::after");

builder.Services.AddHttpClient("SecureAPIClient",
    client => client.BaseAddress =
    new Uri(builder.HostEnvironment.BaseAddress))
    .AddHttpMessageHandler
        <BaseAddressAuthorizationMessageHandler>();

builder.Services.AddScoped(sp => new HttpClient {
    BaseAddress = new Uri(builder.HostEnvironment.BaseAddress) });

// other code omitted for brevity
```

> Register a new named HttpClient, called SecureAPIClient, and configure it to use the BaseAddressAuthorization MessageHandler.

We're using the `AddHttpClient` extension method to register a new named `Http-Client` called `SecureAPIClient`. It's configured to use the `BaseAddress-AuthorizationMessageHandler`, so our access token will be included in any request we make with it.

It's important to note that we've kept the original `HttpClient`. In applications like Blazing Trails, which have both secure and nonsecure endpoints, you will need to use the correct client, depending on the endpoint you're calling. This is because the `BaseAddressAuthorizationMessageHandler` will throw an `AccessTokenNot-AvailableException` if it can't find an access token to attach to the request. So, we only want to use the `HttpClient` configured with that handler for requests we know the user will be logged in for, which, for us, are just the requests in the `ManageTrails` feature.

Let's update the request handlers in `ManageTrails` to use the new `SecureAPI-Client`. Starting with the `AddTrailHandler`, update the code to that shown in the following listing.

Listing 9.16   AddTrailHandler.cs: Update to use `SecureAPIClient`

```
public class AddTrailHandler :
    IRequestHandler<AddTrailRequest, AddTrailRequest.Response>
{
    private readonly IHttpClientFactory
    _httpClientFactory;

    public AddTrailHandler(
        IHttpClientFactory httpClientFactory)
    {
        _httpClientFactory = httpClientFactory;
    }

    public async Task<AddTrailRequest.Response> Handle(
        AddTrailRequest request, CancellationToken cancellationToken)
    {
        var client = _httpClientFactory
            .CreateClient("SecureAPIClient");
        var response = await client
            .PostAsJsonAsync(AddTrailRequest.RouteTemplate,
            request, cancellationToken);
        // other code omitted for brevity
    }
}
```

> The constructor now takes an **IHttpClientFactory** instance instead of an **HttpClient**, which is saved to a private field.

> The **IHttpClientFactory** is used to get an instance of the **SecureAPIClient**.

> The **SecureAPIClient** is used to make the API request, allowing the access token to be attached.

We start by updating the constructor to take an `IHttpClientFactory` instead of an `HttpClient`. This is then stored in a private field for use in the `Handle` method. Inside the `Handle` method, we use the `IHttpClientFactory` to create an instance of the `SecureAPIClient`, which we then use to call the API. We can now repeat this process for the `GetTrailHandler`.

Listing 9.17   GetTrailHandler.cs: Update to use `SecureAPIClient`

```
public class GetTrailHandler :
    IRequestHandler<GetTrailRequest, GetTrailRequest.Response?>
{
    private readonly IHttpClientFactory
    _httpClientFactory;

    public GetTrailHandler(
        IHttpClientFactory httpClientFactory)
    {
        _httpClientFactory = httpClientFactory;
    }

    public async Task<GetTrailRequest.Response?> Handle(
        GetTrailRequest request, CancellationToken cancellationToken)
    {
```

> The constructor now takes an **IHttpClientFactory** instance instead of an **HttpClient**, which is saved to a private field.

```
        try
        {
            var client = _httpClientFactory
            .CreateClient("SecureAPIClient");
            return await client
            .GetFromJsonAsync<GetTrailRequest.Response>(
            GetTrailRequest.RouteTemplate.Replace("{trailId}",
            request.TrailId.ToString()));
        }
        catch (HttpRequestException)
        {
            return new GetTrailRequest.Response(null);
        }
    }
}
```

The IHttpClientFactory is used to get an instance of the SecureAPIClient.

The SecureAPIClient is used to make the API request, allowing the access token to be attached.

And we can also update the `EditTrailHander`.

Listing 9.18   EditTrailHandler.cs: Update to use `SecureAPIClient`

```
public class EditTrailHandler :
IRequestHandler<EditTrailRequest, EditTrailRequest.Response>
{
    private readonly IHttpClientFactory
    _httpClientFactory;

    public EditTrailHandler(
    IHttpClientFactory httpClientFactory)
    {
        _httpClientFactory = httpClientFactory;
    }

    public async Task<EditTrailRequest.Response> Handle(
    EditTrailRequest request, CancellationToken cancellationToken)
    {
    var client = _httpClientFactory
    .CreateClient("SecureAPIClient");
    var response = await client
    .PutAsJsonAsync(EditTrailRequest.RouteTemplate,
    request, cancellationToken);
    // other code omitted for brevity
}
```

The constructor now takes an IHttpClientFactory instance instead of an HttpClient, which is saved to a private field.

The IHttpClientFactory is used to get an instance of the SecureAPIClient.

The SecureAPIClient is used to make the API request, allowing the access token to be attached.

Finally, we can update the `UploadTrailImageHandler`.

Listing 9.19   UploadTrailImageHandler.cs: Update to use `SecureAPIClient`

```
public class UploadTrailImageHandler :
IRequestHandler<UploadTrailImageRequest, UploadTrailImageRequest.Response>
{
    private readonly IHttpClientFactory
    _httpClientFactory;

    public UploadTrailImageHandler(
    IHttpClientFactory httpClientFactory)
```

The constructor now takes an IHttpClientFactory instance instead of an HttpClient, which is saved to a private field.

```
{
    _httpClientFactory = httpClientFactory;
}
```

The constructor now takes an
IHttpClientFactory instance instead of an
HttpClient, which is saved to a private field.

```
public async Task<UploadTrailImageRequest.Response> Handle(
    UploadTrailImageRequest request, CancellationToken cancellationToken)
{
    var fileContent = request.File.OpenReadStream(request.File.Size,
        cancellationToken);

    using var content = new MultipartFormDataContent();
    content.Add(new StreamContent(fileContent), "image",
        request.File.Name);

    var client = _httpClientFactory
        .CreateClient("SecureAPIClient");
    var response = await client
        .PostAsync(UploadTrailImageRequest.RouteTemplate
        .Replace("{trailId}", request.TrailId.ToString()),
        content, cancellationToken);
    // other code omitted for brevity
}
}
```

The **IHttpClientFactory** is used to get
an instance of the SecureAPIClient.

The SecureAPIClient is used to
make the API request, allowing
the access token to be attached.

With all the handlers updated, we can now run our application again and check that our changes have been successful. Log in to the application and run through adding a new trail and editing an existing one. Everything should now be working as expected.

9.4   Authorizing users by role

While some applications may need a user to be logged in only to perform actions, often a further level of permissioning is required. One option to enable this is called *roles*. The concept of roles was introduced to ASP.NET (pre-Core) and has been around ever since. How roles are created and managed will depend on the underlying identity provider. For server-based apps, like Blazor Server or Razor Pages, roles may be encoded into a cookie. But for SPA applications, they are usually encoded into the access, and/or ID tokens as a claim—which will be the case for us.

To see how roles work with Blazor, we'll add an Administrator role to Blazing Trails. Users who are in this role will be able to edit any trail in the system, regardless of whether they're the owner or not.

9.4.1   Adding roles in Auth0

Before we make any updates to our Blazor app, we're going to head over to Auth0 and create the administrator role and assign a user to it.

Once you're in the Auth0 dashboard, click the User Management option in the left-hand menu, then select Roles. From there, click the Create button to add a new role (figure 9.8).

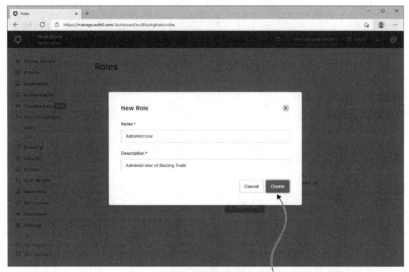

**Enter Administrator for the name and add a
description. Then click Create to add the role.**

Figure 9.8   Adding a new role to Auth0

For the role name, enter `Administrator`. You can then enter a description for the
role; this can be anything you wish. Once you're done, click Create to finish. Auth0
will then create the new role and show the role settings page. From here, select the
Users tab and then click Add Users (figure 9.9).

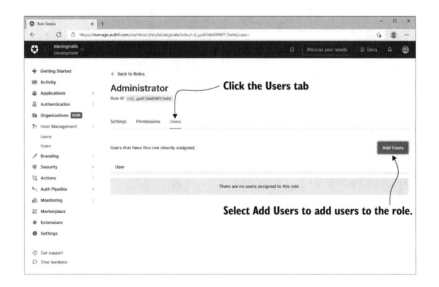

Figure 9.9   Adding users to a role in Auth0

Use the search box to find the user you wish to give the administrator role (you can give it to multiple users if you wish), and then click Assign. The user will then be assigned the role and appear in the list of users.

Now we have the role created and a user assigned. The last thing we need to do in Auth0 is tell it to include roles in the access and ID token it returns when we log in. We're going to update the existing rule we created earlier to include the user's email. This can be found under the Auth Pipeline > Rules menu. Click the `Customize Tokens` rule to edit it. Then update the function with the following code.

Listing 9.20 Customize Token function in Auth0

```
function (user, context, callback) {
  const accessTokenClaims = context.accessToken || {};   Adds a new variable
  const idTokenClaims = context.idToken || {};           for the ID token claims
  const assignedRoles = (context.authorization
  || {}).roles;                                          Gets the roles the
accessTokenClaims['http://schemas.xmlsoap.org/ws/        user is assigned to
  2005/05/identity/claims/name'] = user.email;
  accessTokenClaims['http://schemas.microsoft.com/ws/
  2008/06/identity/claims/role'] = assignedRoles;        Adds the assigned roles to
  idTokenClaims['http://schemas.microsoft.com/ws/        the access tokens claims
  2008/06/identity/claims/role'] = assignedRoles;
                                                          Adds the assigned roles
  callback(null, user, context);                         to the ID tokens claims
}
```

First, we add a new variable to hold the ID tokens claims. Then we create a new variable to hold the roles the user is assigned to. We get these roles via `context .authorization.roles`, which is an array of strings containing the names of the roles the user is assigned to.

Once we have the roles, we can then assign them to each token. To assign the claim, we must pass in a claim name and a value. In this case, the claim name is expressed as a URI, `http://schemas.microsoft.com/ws/2008/06/identity/ claims/role`. Then the value is the list of roles.

Auth0 will now return an array of roles for each user when they log in. Let's head back to our Blazor app, where we can configure it to look for these roles.

9.4.2 Consuming Auth0 roles in Blazor WebAssembly

When the roles are sent from Auth0 in the access and ID tokens, they are sent as a single claim that contains the array of roles the user is in. For example:

```
http://schemas.microsoft.com/ws/2008/06/identity/claims/role:
    ['Administrator', 'SomeOtherRole']
```

However, for Blazor to work with these roles, we need to convert this single claim into a claim per role, like this:

```
http://schemas.microsoft.com/ws/2008/06/identity/claims/role: 'Administrator'
http://schemas.microsoft.com/ws/2008/06/identity/claims/role: 'SomeOtherRole'
```

The obvious question at this point is why not add multiple role claims to the Auth0 tokens so we don't have to do this? Unfortunately, you can't have multiple claims with the same name in a token. Therefore, it's down to the token consumer to handle separating array values. To do this, we will create a custom user factory. We'll create it in the Features > Auth folder. The following listing shows the code for the class.

Listing 9.21   CustomUserFactory.cs

```
public class CustomUserFactory<TAccount> :                          The class inherits from the
    AccountClaimsPrincipalFactory<RemoteUserAccount>      ◁───      AccountClaimsPrincipal-
{                                                                    Factory<T> class.
    public CustomUserFactory(IAccessTokenProviderAccessor accessor)
        : base(accessor) { }

    public override async ValueTask<ClaimsPrincipal>               CreateUserAsync is overridden
        CreateUserAsync(RemoteUserAccount account,                 to apply custom logic when a
        RemoteAuthenticationUserOptions options)       ◁───        user is authenticated.
    {
                                                                   Calling base.CreateUserAsync
        var initialUser = await base.CreateUserAsync(              creates a ClaimsPrincipal
            account, options);                         ◁───        representing the user.

        if (initialUser?.Identity?.IsAuthenticated ?? false)
        {
            var userIdentity = (ClaimsIdentity)initialUser.Identity;

            account.AdditionalProperties
                .TryGetValue(ClaimTypes.Role, out var roleClaimValue);

            if (roleClaimValue is not null                         Checks to make sure the
                && roleClaimValue is JsonElement element           roleClaimValue isn't null
                && element.ValueKind == JsonValueKind.Array)  ◁─   and that it is an array
            {
                userIdentity.RemoveClaim(
                    userIdentity.FindFirst(ClaimTypes.Role));

                var claims = element.EnumerateArray()
                                .Select(x =>
                    new Claim(ClaimTypes.Role, x.ToString()));

                userIdentity.AddClaims(claims);
            }
        }
        return initialUser ?? new ClaimsPrincipal();
    }
}
```

The account.Additional-Properties collection contains the claims for the user and their values in JSON format.

Removes the original role claim with the roles as a string array

Generates a single role claim for each role and adds them to the ClaimsIdentity representing the current user

Our `CustomUserFactory<T>` inherits from the `AccountClaimsPrincipal-Factory<T>` class. This class contains a virtual method we can override called `Create-UserAsync`. This method is called when a user logs into the application, and its job is to create a `ClaimsPrincipal` for the user. You can think of a `ClaimsPrincipal` like a wallet that contains a user's identities. However, while technically it can hold more than one identity, it almost always contains only one.

The first thing we do is call into base.CreateUserAsync(). This method will do all the hard work for us of constructing a ClaimsIdentity for the user—based on the token sent back by Auth0—then bundling it up into a ClaimsPrincipal. This means we can just focus on separating the collection of roles into individual claims.

Next, we get the array of roles using the AdditionalProperties collection of the RemoteUserAccount type. This is a dictionary whose key is the claim name and the value is the claims value in JSON format. Using the TryGetValue method, we can get the value of the role claim. We then perform a check to make sure it's not null and that it's a JSON array.

Once we know we're dealing with an array of roles, we can remove the original role claim from the user's ClaimsIdentity. Then create an individual role claim for each role in the array and add them into the ClaimsIdentity.

We now need to hook up our CustomUserFactory so it will be called whenever a user logs in. This is done in the Program.Main method (as shown in the next listing).

Listing 9.22 Program.cs: Registering the CustomUserFactory

```
// other code omitted for brevity

builder.Services.AddOidcAuthentication(options =>
{
    builder.Configuration.Bind("Auth0", options.ProviderOptions);
    options.ProviderOptions.ResponseType = "code";
}).AddAccountClaimsPrincipalFactory
<CustomUserFactory<RemoteUserAccount>>();      ⟵  Registers the CustomUserFactory
                                                   using the AddAccountClaims-
// other code omitted for brevity                 PrincipalFactory method
```

Registering the CustomUserFactory is quite simple thanks to the AddAccount-ClaimsPrincipalFactory<T> extension method—which is chained onto the AddOidcAuthentication method. Our CustomUserFactory is now registered and will be called whenever a user logs into the app.

9.4.3 Implementing role-based logic

Now that we have Blazor all set up to use the roles provided by Auth0, we can get on with updating our app to allow administrators to edit any trail. We're going to start off in the API and work forward to our Blazor app. We need to update three endpoints in Features > ManageTrails:

- GetTrailEndpoint.cs
- EditTrailEndpoint.cs
- UploadTrailImageEndpoint.cs

We need to make the same change in all three endpoints, so we'll look at GetTrail-Endpoint.cs as an example; then you can repeat the update in the other two endpoints.

We're going to update the existing owner check to also check for the administrator role.

```
if (!trail.Owner.Equals(HttpContext.User.Identity!.Name,
    StringComparison.CurrentCultureIgnoreCase) &&
    !HttpContext.User.IsInRole("Administrator"))
{
    return Unauthorized();
}
```

Users who are in the administrator role will now bypass the unauthorized check. Repeat this change for the `EditTrailEndpoint` and `UploadTrailImage-Endpoint`. Once that is done, we can move over to the Client.

In BlazingTrails.Client, we need to update the `HomePage` component (Features > Home) and the `TrailCard` component (Features > Home > Shared). In both components, we need to update the owner check, just like we did in the API, to show the Edit Trail button when a user is in the administrator role. The following listing shows the update to the `HomePage` component.

Listing 9.23   HomePage.razor: Show Edit button for administrators

```
// other code omitted for brevity

<AuthorizeView>
    @if (trail.Owner.Equals(
    ➥context.User.Identity?.Name,
    ➥StringComparison.OrdinalIgnoreCase)
    ➥|| context.User.IsInRole("Administrator"))    ◁──┐
    {
        <button @onclick="@(() =>
        ➥NavManager.NavigateTo($"/edit-trail/{trail.Id}"))" title="Edit"
        ➥class="btn btn-outline-secondary">
            <i class="bi bi-pencil"></i>
        </button>
    }
</AuthorizeView>

// other code omitted for brevity
```

Using the IsInRole helper method, we can allow users in the administrator role to have access to the Edit Trail button.

Just as we did in the API, we're using the `IsInRole` helper method to check if the currently logged-in user is an administrator. If they are, the Edit Trail button will be shown for them. We can now perform the same update to the `TrailCard` component (as shown in the following listing).

Listing 9.24   TrailCard.razor: Show Edit button for administrators

```
// other code omitted for brevity

<AuthorizeView>
    @if (Trail.Owner.Equals(
    ➥context.User.Identity?.Name,
    ➥StringComparison.OrdinalIgnoreCase)
    ➥|| context.User.IsInRole("Administrator"))    ◁──┐
    {
```

Using the IsInRole helper method, we can allow users in the administrator role to have access to the Edit Trail button.

```
            <button class="btn btn-outline-secondary mt-3 float-right"
        ➥title="Edit" @onclick="@(() =>
        ➥NavManager.NavigateTo($"/edit-trail/{Trail.Id}"))">
                <i class="bi bi-pencil"></i>
            </button>
        }
</AuthorizeView>

// other code omitted for brevity
```

These are all the changes that are needed to allow administrators to edit trails. We can now run the application and test our work. If you log in with the account you assigned to the administrator role, you should see the Edit Trail button displayed for all trails (figure 9.10).

Logged in as a user in the Administrator role

Figure 9.10 When logged in as a user in the administrator role, the Edit Button is present on all trail cards.

As an administrator, you will see an Edit button on all trail cards.

Although we've not needed this functionality in Blazing Trails, it's also good to know that role checks are supported by the AuthorizeView component and the Authorize attribute. So, if you only wanted to show some markup to users in certain roles, you can do that like this:

```
<AuthorizeView Roles="SuperUser">
    <p>This will only be seen by users in the SuperUser role.</p>
</AuthorizeView>
```

```
<AuthorizeView Roles="SuperUser, Administrator">
    <p>This will only be seen by users in the SuperUser or Administrator
    role.</p>
</AuthorizeView>
```

The same goes for restricting access to whole pages. When applying the `Authorize` attribute to a page component, it's possible to specify what roles a user must be in to access that page:

```
@attribute [Authorize(Roles = "SuperUser")]
```

And just like the `AuthorizeView`, you can pass in multiple roles, if you wish:

```
@attribute [Authorize(Roles = "SuperUser, Administrator")]
```

As well as roles, Blazor also supports policies. You can find more information on them on the Microsoft Docs site (http://mng.bz/z4rA).

Summary

- Blazor WebAssembly applications can never be made truly secure, as they run on the client and can't be trusted.
- Blazor WebAssembly applications commonly use token-based authentication.
- Blazor Server apps commonly use cookie-based authentication.
- When signing into a Blazor WebAssembly application via an identity provider, two tokens are returned—an access token and an ID token.
- The ID token contains information about the user's identity, while the access token contains information about what they are allowed to access. However, custom claims can be added to either one.
- The `AuthorizeView` component is used to show different pieces of UI based on the user's authorization status.
- The `AuthorizeRouteView` component replaces the `RouteView` component in the Router to allow access to pages to be restricted using the `[Authorize]` attribute.
- When calling a secure API endpoint from Blazor WebAssembly, the access token must be included as an http header. This is done automatically when using the `BaseAddressAuthorizationMessageHandler` with an `HttpClient`.
- An `HttpClient` configured to use the `BaseAddressAuthorization-` `MessageHandler` can't be used by unauthenticated users, as it will throw an `AccessTokenNotAvailableException`.
- Blazor supports restricting access based on roles or policies.
- A role check can be done in code using the `User.Identity.IsInRole()` method.
- The `AuthorizeView` component supports both roles and policies via its `Roles` and `Policy` parameters.
- The `Authorize` attribute also supports roles and policies via its `Roles` and `Policy` properties.

Managing state 10

This chapter covers

- Persisting application state in memory
- Coordinating state across multiple components
- Organizing application state
- Persisting application state using browser local storage

State management is always a hot topic in SPA applications. But what is *state*? Well, state can be thought of as the sum of all data held by a system at any given point in time. We've already seen lots of examples of state in previous chapters. Anywhere we've created a field or property on a component to store a value is state. Users of an application alter state all the time by performing actions within the system. They might click a button that increments a counter or enter values in a form that trigger validation.

Sometimes user actions might alter state, which has consequences across multiple components. A good example of this is when a user adds an item to their cart on Amazon. The basket automatically updates to show the number of items it's currently holding. This is when *state management* comes into play.

State management techniques offer ways of organizing state and controlling how state changes are propagated through an app. There are a range of options for managing state, from using child events or cascading parameters—as we've used previously in this book—to using advanced patterns such as Flux (https://facebook .github.io/flux/), which was invented by Facebook to manage the state in their client applications. As always in software engineering, the solution you pick will depend on the complexity of the problem you're solving.

In this chapter, we will explore managing state in Blazor using a centralized state store. A state store is just an object that can be injected into any area of the application and allows that component or class to access whatever state we choose to expose. We will cover two options for this state store: the first is a simple in-memory implementation where any state will be lost when the application restarts or the user navigates away. This is useful for handling session state that doesn't need to be persisted across multiple sessions. The second uses the browser's local storage feature to persist state across sessions. This technique is useful when you want to persist state values for a longer period.

10.1   Simple state management using an in-memory store

The simplest way to add state management to a Blazor application is via an in-memory store. This is essentially a class that is going to store some state for the lifetime of the user's session. Once the session ends—which will be when the browser tab or the browser itself is closed—the state will be lost. The state we're going to track is that of the `Add Trail` form.

We all know how frustrating it can be when you're filling out a large form and something happens and everything you've entered is lost. There's quite a lot of information to complete when adding a new trail to Blazing Trails. Wouldn't it be cool if the form could remember what we had entered so if we didn't submit the trail for whatever reason, the information we entered would be there waiting for us when we came back?

Now, for this version of state management, there are limitations. The data is going to be stored in memory, so if the user navigates away from the app or closes the browser, the state will be lost. But we'll look at how we can make state more persistent a little later in the chapter.

10.1.1 Creating and registering a state store

The first task we have is to create a state store. This is a central place where the various pieces of state we want to persist can be saved to and retrieved from. We're going to create a class called `AppState` that will perform this role for us.

To keep things organized, we will create a new folder in the root of BlazingTrails.Client called *State*. In that folder, we will add the new `AppState` class with the code in listing 10.1.

> **Listing 10.1 AppState.cs**

```
public class AppState
{
    private TrailDto _unsavedNewTrail = new();        This will store the
    public TrailDto GetTrail()                         unsaved new trail.
        => _unsavedNewTrail;              Allows the unsaved trail to be retrieved
    public void SaveTrail(TrailDto trail)
        => _unsavedNewTrail = trail;       Allows an unsaved trail to be stored
    public void ClearTrail()              This will be used when the trail is
        => _unsavedNewTrail = new();      submitted to clear the unsaved trail.
}
```

We first define a private field that will store the unsaved trail data. It's important to note that the field is private. Generally, you shouldn't allow state to be altered directly. It should be altered only via defined routes. This allows the propagation of that state change to be handled correctly—but more on this later.

We then have three methods that manipulate the `_unsavedNewTrail` field in some way. The `GetTrail` method allows the retrieval of the unsaved trail data. The `SaveTrail` method allows an unsaved trail to be stored. Finally, the `ClearTrail` method allows the unsaved trail data to be cleared.

Now that we've created our `AppState` class, we need to register it with the services container so we can inject it into any components or classes that need it. We'll head over to Program.cs and add the following line before the `await builder.Build()` `.RunAsync()` line:

```
builder.Services.AddScoped<AppState>();
```

This line will register our `AppState` class as a *scoped* service in our application. If you recall from chapter 2, when we talked about service scopes in Blazor, you'll remember that they behave a little differently than they do in other ASP.NET frameworks. So, when we register this service as scoped, it has the equivalent behavior of a singleton. In fact, we could use singleton. But that wouldn't work for Blazor Server applications in the same way. It would provide one `AppState` instance that would be shared by every user, not an instance per user. By using a scoped service, we're ensuring the same behavior across Blazor WebAssembly and Blazor Server.

10.1.2 Saving data entered on the form to AppState

With our `AppState` class set up, we can turn our attention to how we'll save the unsubmitted `Add Trail` form data. To do this, we'll create a new component that will sit in the form and listen for updates to the form's model. Every time an update occurs, we'll take a copy of the model and store it our `AppState`.

We'll add this new component in the Features > ManageTrails > Shared folder. However, we're not going to add a Razor file this time; instead, we'll add a regular class, because this new component will have no UI element and it never will. Now, we could easily create a regular component without any markup and just add our logic to the code block. But I want to show you an alternative. There's no right or wrong here; it's more about personal preference. Go ahead and add a new class called Form-StateTracker with the following code.

Listing 10.2   FormStateTracker.cs

Here we're injecting the AppState class into the component. Blazor uses property injection, so we decorate the property with the Inject attribute.

To mark a class as a component, we inherit from ComponentBase.

```
public class FormStateTracker : ComponentBase
{
    [Inject]
    public AppState AppState { get; set; }
    [CascadingParameter]
    private EditContext CascadedEditContext
    { get; set; }
    protected override void OnInitialized()
    {
        if (CascadedEditContext is null)
        {
            throw new InvalidOperationException(
            $"{nameof(FormStateTracker)} requires a cascading
            parameter of type {nameof(EditContext)}");
        }
        CascadedEditContext.OnFieldChanged +=
        CascadedEditContext_OnFieldChanged;
    }
    private void CascadedEditContext_OnFieldChanged(
    object sender, FieldChangedEventArgs e)
    {
        var trail = (TrailDto)e.FieldIdentifier.Model;
        if (trail.Id == 0)
        {
            AppState.SaveTrail(trail);
        }
    }
}
```

We capture a reference to the EditContext, which is cascaded from the EditForm component. This will allow us to know when the model is updated and take a copy.

By subscribing to the OnFieldChanged event, we'll be notified every time the model is updated.

A little sanity check to make sure the component is used within an EditForm. If it's used outside of one, the EditContext property will be null and we'd see a meaningful error in the console or logs.

When the OnFieldChanged event fires, we grab a copy of the model.

Only new trails will have an ID of 0, so if this is the case, we save the model to our state store.

To make a component from a regular class, we need to inherit from ComponentBase. This will give us access to the various life cycle methods of a component. Because Blazor uses property injection, we define any services we want injected by adding a property of the correct type and decorating it with the Inject attribute. In this case, it's the AppState we're injecting. Next, we define a cascading parameter of type EditContext. This will be provided for us by the EditForm component. As we learned in chapter 5, the EditContext is the brain of the form, and it gives us the ability to hook into form events and gives us access to the form model.

When the component is initialized, we're performing a check to make sure the EditContext isn't null. This is to make sure the component is inside of an Edit-Form. If the EditContext is null, then a meaningful error message will be displayed. As long as there are no issues, we subscribe to the OnFieldChanged event of the

`EditContext`. This will allow us to be notified every time a new value is entered into the form.

Inside the `OnFieldChanged` event handler, we capture the model and check if the `Id` property is 0. This is to ensure we're only saving new trail data and not a trail being edited. If we have a new trail, we save a copy of the model to our state store.

We can now add the `FormStateTracker` component to the `TrailForm` component. We'll add the following directly under the `FluentValidationValidator`:

```
<FluentValidationValidator />
<FormStateTracker />
```

That takes care of recording the form state, but how will we reload it? To enable that functionality, we're going to make a few more changes to the `TrailForm`. The following listing shows the updated code.

Listing 10.3 TrailForm.razor: Enabling reloading of form state

```
@inject AppState AppState                          ◁——  The AppState is injected
// other code omitted for brevity                        into the component.
@code {
    // other code omitted for brevity
    public void ResetForm()
    {
        AppState.ClearTrail();                  ◁——  When resetting the form, we also call
        // Other code omitted for brevity             the ClearTrail method on AppState.
    }                                                 This will only get called after a new
    protected override void OnParametersSet()         trail has been successfully added.
    {
        if (Trail is not null)              ◁——  If the Trail parameter is populated, it
        {                                         means we're editing a trail, so we
            _trail.Id = Trail.Id;                 populate the form model using that data.
            _trail.Name = Trail.Name;
            _trail.Description = Trail.Description;
            _trail.Location = Trail.Location;
            _trail.Image = Trail.Image;
            _trail.ImageAction = ImageAction.None;
            _trail.Length = Trail.Length;
            _trail.TimeInMinutes = Trail.TimeInMinutes;
            _trail.Waypoints.Clear();
            _trail.Waypoints.AddRange(
            ➥Trail.Waypoints.Select(wp => new TrailDto.WaypointDto(
            ➥wp.Latitude, wp.Longitude)));
        }
        else
        {
            _trail = AppState.GetTrail();       ◁——  When adding a trail, attempt to
        }                                             get an existing trail from AppState.
                                                      If no existing state is present, a
        _editContext = new EditContext(_trail);       new blank model will be returned.
        _editContext.SetFieldCssClassProvider(
        ➥new BootstrapCssClassProvider());
    }
    // other code omitted for brevity
}
```

We start by injecting our `AppState` into the component. Next, we add a call to the `ClearTrail` method on our state store to the `ResetForm` method. This method is called only when a new trail has been successfully added. This makes it an ideal point to remove any state we have stored about that trail, making it ready for the next new trail the user might add.

The last change is to the `OnParametersSet` method. We've given it a bit of a refactor to enable it to load any new trail state stored in `AppState`. We start with a check on the `Trail` parameter. If this has a value, then we're editing a trail and we populate the model with that data. Otherwise, we attempt to get the saved trail data from the state store. If there isn't any state saved, then this method will return a new model that can just be passed straight to the `EditContext`, which makes things quite neat.

That's it for our changes! We've now added the ability to persist any unsaved changes to the `Add Trail` form. You can go ahead and run the application and test the feature. If you head to the `Add Trail` form and enter some data into the form, then navigate back to the home page, and back to the `Add Trail` form, you should see the data you entered still present in the form.

10.2 Improving the AppState design to handle more state

The current design of our `AppState` class works great when we're tracking state for only one feature. But what happens when we want to track various bits of state across the application? Just dumping lots of properties and methods in a single class would become a tangled ball of mud very quickly, and maintenance would be a nightmare. So how can we improve our `AppState` design and make it extendable and maintainable? The answer—multiple state stores.

We're going to extract the current state we've placed in the `AppState` class into a new class called `NewTrailState`. Then we're going to refactor the `AppState` class to reference that new state container. Essentially, we're going to turn the `AppState` class into a hub where we can access any state in the application from one place.

To get started, let's extract the current state into a new container called *NewTrail-State.cs*. The following listing shows the code for the class. This should sit alongside the existing `AppState` class in the State folder.

Listing 10.4   NewTrailState.cs

```
public class NewTrailState
{
    private TrailDto _unsavedNewTrail = new();
    public TrailDto GetTrail()
        => _unsavedNewTrail;
    public void SaveTrail(TrailDto trail)
        => _unsavedNewTrail = trail;
    public void ClearTrail()
        => _unsavedNewTrail = new();
}
```
◁── **The existing property and methods from the AppState class are now here.**

We can now head back to the `AppState` class and make the necessary changes there. The following listing shows the updated code.

Listing 10.5 AppState.cs: Updated to be a state hub

```
public class AppState
{
    public NewTrailState NewTrailState { get; }          Allows access to the
                                                          NewTrailState object
    public AppState()
    {                                                     Initializes the
        NewTrailState = new NewTrailState();              NewTrailState
    }
}
```

The `AppState` now just contains a single property that holds an instance of the Add Trail state. Once again, you'll notice it's read-only. As we mentioned earlier in the chapter, state shouldn't be altered directly but rather through defined routes. In this case, the `AppState` class is going to make sure the `NewTrailState` is initialized correctly.

You can see this design will be much easier to work with as more state is added. Each piece of new state is defined in its own class, then is referenced from the central `AppState`. This means we still only work with a single `AppState` object in our classes and components, but we can hook into any piece of state across the application, if we need to.

Before we move on, we just need to fix a few build errors that resulted from our refactoring. The first fix is in the `FormStateTracker` (Features > ManageTrails > Shared) class. We need to replace the following line in the `OnFieldChanged` handler:

```
AppState.SaveTrail(trail);
```

with this line:

```
AppState.NewTrailState.SaveTrail(trail);
```

The other fixes are in the `TrailForm` component. The first is in the `ResetForm` method. Here we replace

```
AppState.ClearTrail();
```

with

```
AppState.NewTrailState.ClearTrail();
```

The second fix is in the `OnParametersSet` method. We need to replace

```
var newTrail = AppState.GetTrail();
```

with

```
var newTrail = AppState.NewTrailState.GetTrail();
```

With those changes in place, we should now have an application that builds again. You can run it up and check that everything is still working as it was before.

10.3 *Creating persistent state with browser local storage*

So far, we've created a simple state store and had a couple of components write some state and read it out again. In this section, we will implement something a bit more complex. We're going to add a new feature to Blazing Trails that allows users to mark trails as favorites. Figure 10.1 shows what this feature will look like once we're done.

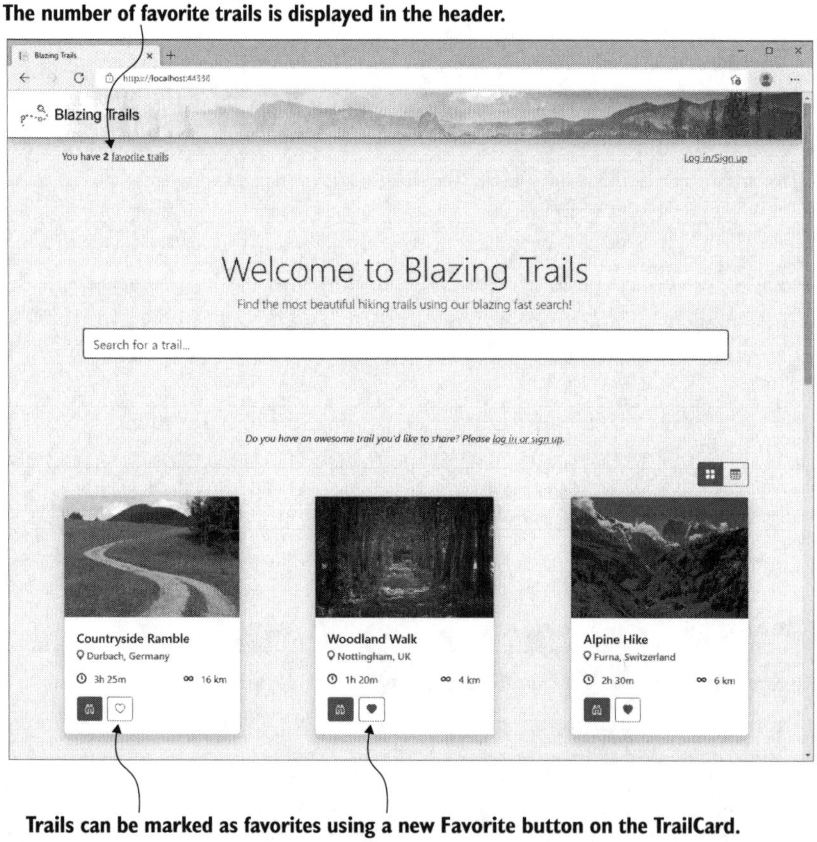

The number of favorite trails is displayed in the header.

Trails can be marked as favorites using a new Favorite button on the TrailCard.

Figure 10.1   The finished home page, which allows users to mark trails as favorites and displays the current number of favorite trails they have.

However, to make this feature as useful as possible, we don't want it to be just for logged-in users; we want anonymous users to be able to take advantage of this as well. In order to achieve this, we will use the browser's local storage system to persist the data. This will allow anonymous user selections to be maintained between visits to the site.

NOTE It's worth noting that the browser's local storage is not limitless. The HTML spec recommends an arbitrary limit of 5 megabytes per origin (https://www.w3.org/TR/webstorage/#disk-space), and this is what all the major browsers support.

We're also going to display the current number of favorite trails the user has in the header; this will need to change in real time as trails are marked/unmarked as favorites.

10.3.1 Defining an additional state store

We start by creating the state store for the new favorite trails feature. This store will be much more complex than our previous one, as it will be responsible for reading and writing to local storage and for triggering an event when the state changes to allow subscribed components to react.

Before we create the new state store, we're going to add a NuGet package to help us work with local storage—`Blazored.LocalStorage`. This is one of my creations and was the first NuGet package I ever published. Normally, to use the browser's local storage, we'd need to use JavaScript interop. By using this NuGet package, we can avoid that and just inject an interface into any component that wants to save or read data from local storage.

Add the following package reference to the BlazingTrails.Client.csproj file:

```
<PackageReference Include="Blazored.LocalStorage" Version="4.1.2" />
```

The only other thing we must do to configure the new package is to add the following line to the `Program.Main` method:

```
builder.Services.AddBlazoredLocalStorage();
```

This will add the necessary services to the services container so we can inject them into our components or classes.

Now let's focus on getting our new state store in place. In the State folder, add a new class called `FavoriteTrailsState` and then add the following code.

Listing 10.6 FavoriteTrailsState.cs

```
public class FavoriteTrailsState
{
    private const string FavouriteTrailsKey = "favoriteTrails";
    private bool _isInitialized;
    private List<Trail> _favoriteTrails = new();
    private readonly ILocalStorageService _localStorageService;
    public IReadOnlyList<Trail> FavoriteTrails =>
    ➥_favoriteTrails.AsReadOnly();
    public event Action? OnChange;
    public FavoriteTrailsState(
    ➥ILocalStorageService localStorageService)
    {
        _localStorageService = localStorageService;
    }
```

The current favorited trails are kept in a private list so they can't be manipulated directly.

The favorite trails are exposed via a read-only list.

The OnChange event allows concerned components to subscribe to changes in the store.

The ILocalStorageService interface is provided by Blazored.LocalStorage and gives us the ability to read and write to the browser's local storage feature.

```
public async Task Initialize()        ◄─┐   This will be called when the
{                                        │   application initially boots in
    if (!_isInitialized)                 │   order to set up the store.
    {
        _favoriteTrails = await _localStorageService
        ➥.GetItemAsync<List<Trail>>(FavouriteTrailsKey)
        ➥?? new List<Trail>();        This adds a trail to the list of favorites and
        _isInitialized = true;        persists a copy of the favorite trails to local
        NotifyStateHasChanged();      storage. Finally, it calls NotifyState-
    }                                 HasChanged, which is responsible for
}                                     triggering the OnChange event.
public async Task AddFavorite(Trail trail)        ◄─
{
    if (_favoriteTrails.Any(_ => _.Id == trail.Id)) return;
    _favoriteTrails.Add(trail);
    await _localStorageService
    ➥.SetItemAsync(FavouriteTrailsKey, _favoriteTrails);
    NotifyStateHasChanged();
}
public async Task RemoveFavorite(Trail trail)   ◄─┐  This method will do the reverse
{                                                 │  of the AddFavorite method. It
    var existingTrail = _favoriteTrails           │  removes the trail from the list
    ➥.SingleOrDefault(_ => _.Id == trail.Id);     │  of favorites and saves the
    if (existingTrail is null) return;            │  update to local storage before
    _favoriteTrails.Remove(existingTrail);        │  calling NotifyStateHasChanged.
    await _localStorageService
    ➥.SetItemAsync(FavouriteTrailsKey, _favoriteTrails);
    NotifyStateHasChanged();
}                                         │  This is a simple helper method we will
public bool IsFavorite(Trail trail)   ◄─┘  use to check if a trail is a favorite.
    => _favoriteTrails.Any(_ => _.Id == trail.Id);
private void NotifyStateHasChanged()      ◄─┐  This method is responsible for
    => OnChange?.Invoke();                   │  raising the OnChange event, which
}                                            │  notifies subscribers that something
                                             │  has changed in the store.
```

Once again, we're storing the state in a private field. Looking at this class, it's more apparent why we don't want to allow the list of favorite trails to be manipulated directly—we need to ensure the OnChange event is raised for every update of the favorites. However, consumers do need access to the list, and we expose it as an IReadOnlyList. The Trail type in both lists is the Trail from the Home feature. However, we'll be moving it to a more appropriate location shortly.

Next, we define an OnChange event, which will allow consumers of our state to subscribe to changes in the store. To make the code a bit tidier, this event will be triggered by a private method called NotifyStateHasChanged, which is at the end of the class. Any method that needs to let consumers know of state changes will call that method, which in turn raises the event.

In the constructor, we're specifying a dependency on the ILocalStorage-Service. This service is provided by Blazored.LocalStorage and will be the interface into the browser's local storage APIs.

Now we come to the first of the public methods, `Initialize`. This method will be called when the application first starts up. Its job is to set up the state store for use. After checking that it's not already initialized, it will attempt to load any existing favorite trails from local storage. After that, it will make the store as initialized and call `NotifyStateHasChanged`.

The `AddFavorite` and `RemoveFavorite` methods do exactly what their names imply. They either add or remove a trail from the list of favorites and then persist the updated list to local storage. Finally, they call `NotifyStateHasChanged` to signal a change has occurred.

Finally, we have the `IsFavorite` method. This is a helper method we will use in a bit to check if a trail is a favorite or not.

Now that we've defined our new state store, we need to add it to the `AppState` class. The following listing shows the updates.

Listing 10.7   AppState.cs: Adding the `FavoriteTrailState`

```
public class AppState
{
    private bool _isInitialized;
    public NewTrailState NewTrailState { get; }
    public FavoriteTrailsState FavoriteTrailsState
    { get; }                                          ◁──────  The new FavoriteTrailsState
                                                               is exposed as a read-only
                                                               property.
    public AppState(
    ILocalStorageService localStorageService)
    {
        NewTrailState = new NewTrailState();          The FavoriteTrailState is
        FavoriteTrailsState =                         newed up passing in the
        new FavoriteTrailsState(localStorageService); ILocalStorageService.
    }
    public async Task Initialize()    ◁──────  The Initialize method gives us
    {                                          a central place to initialize
        if (!_isInitialized)                   any child state stores.
        {
            await FavoriteTrailsState.Initialize();   ◁──────  Here we initialize the
            _isInitialized = true;   ◁─────────────────────   FavoriteTrailsState store.
        }
    }                                We mark the AppState as
}                                    initialized once all child
                                     stores have been initialized.
```

We expose the new `FavoriteTrailsState` via a read-only property as we did for the `NewTrailState`. In the constructor, we're now injecting an instance of the `ILocalStorageService`, which we use when newing up `FavoriteTrailsState`.

Next, we've added a new method called `Initialize`. This method gives us a central place to initialize any child state stores. In our case, we only have one, but in larger applications there could be many. Once the child state store is initialized, we can mark the `AppState` as initialized.

10.3.2 *Adding and removing trails from the favorites list*

In order to add and remove trails from the favorites list, we will add a button to the `Trail-Card` component and to the list view on the home page. When this button is clicked, the trail will either be added or removed from the list of favorites, depending on whether it is currently a favorite or not. Figure 10.2 shows what this button will look like on the `TrailCard`.

We could just add the button and any required logic directly into the `TrailCard` and `HomePage` components directly. But a better option is to create a new component to encapsulate this new functionality. For now, we will add this new button component into the Shared folder in the Home feature. Add a new component called `FavoriteButton.razor` with the following code.

The Favorite button that marks a trail as a favorite

Figure 10.2   The new Favorite button on the `TrailCard` component

Listing 10.8   FavoriteButton.razor

```
@inject AppState AppState
@if (AppState.FavoriteTrailsState.IsFavorite(Trail))
{
    <button class="btn btn-outline-primary ml-1"
    title="Favorite" @onclick="@(() =>
    AppState.FavoriteTrailsState.RemoveFavorite(Trail))">
        <i class="bi bi-heart-fill"></i>
    </button>
}
    else
    {
        <button
        class="btn btn-outline-primary ml-1" title="Favorite"
        @onclick="@(() =>
        AppState.FavoriteTrailsState.AddFavorite(Trail))">
            <i class="bi bi-heart"></i>
        </button>
    }
@code {
    [Parameter, EditorRequired]
    public Trail Trail { get; set; } = default!;
}
```

Which button to render is determined by checking if the trail it represents is a favorite.

If the trail is a favorite, a button with an onclick handler to remove the trail is rendered.

If the trail isn't a favorite, a button with an onclick handler to add the trail is rendered.

We start by injecting the `AppState` into the component. Next, we check if the trail passed to the component is a favorite using the `IsFavorite` method on `Favorite-TrailsState`. If it is, then we render a button with an onclick handler that calls the

RemoveFavorite method on FavoriteTrailsState. Otherwise, we render a button that calls the AddFavorite method.

We can now add our FavoriteButton to the TrailCard and HomePage components. Let's start with the TrailCard.

Directly after the markup for the View button, add the following line:

```
<FavoriteButton Trail="Trail" />
```

Then on the HomePage component, add the same line directly above the existing View button. We can run the app and check that everything is working (figure 10.3).

The Favorite button showing
the trail is not a favorite

The Favorite button showing
the trail is a favorite

Figure 10.3   The Favorite button in its two states

You should be able to click the Favorite button on the different TrailCards and toggle between the two states.

10.3.3   *Displaying the current number of favorite trails*

We're going to add some text to the header component to display the current number of favorite trails a user has. Along with this text, we'll include a link to a new page that will allow the user to browse those trails. This number is going to update in real time whenever they mark/unmark a trail as a favorite. Let's look at the code.

Listing 10.9   Header.razor: Adding current favorite trails

```
@using BlazingTrails.Client.Features.Auth
@inject AppState AppState
```

```
@implements IDisposable
<nav class="navbar mb-3 shadow">
    <a class="navbar-brand" href="/">
        <img src="/images/logo.png">
    </a>
</nav>
<div class="container d-flex justify-content-between">
    <p>You have <span class="font-weight-bold">
    ➥@AppState.FavoriteTrailsState.FavoriteTrails.Count
    ➥</span> <a href="/favorite-trails">favorite trails</a>
    ➥</p>
    <LoginStatus />
</div>
@code {
    protected override void OnInitialized()
        => AppState.FavoriteTrailsState.OnChange
        ➥+= StateHasChanged;
    void IDisposable.Dispose()
        => AppState.FavoriteTrailsState.OnChange
        ➥-= StateHasChanged;
}
```

This new div uses Flexbox to allow the new favorite trails text and the original login component to be positioned on the same line.

The new favorite trails text displays the number of trails pulled from AppState and provides a link to a new favorite trails page, which we'll create shortly.

When the component initializes, it subscribes to the OnChange event exposed by FavoriteTrailsState.

When subscribing to events, it's always best practice to unsubscribe from them using IDisposable.

We start by making a small structural change. We've added a new `div`, which contains the new favorite trails text as well as the login component. This `div` uses some built-in Flexbox styles from Bootstrap to align the two elements on the same line but at opposite ends. Then we've added a new `p` tag that contains the new text as well as the favorite trail count—which is pulled directly from AppState.

In the logic block, when the component initializes, we're subscribing to the `OnChange` event and having it trigger a `StateHasChanged` call. This will allow the component to re-render whenever the `FavoriteTrailsState` is updated and give us that real-time count.

Before we run this, we need to make one small change to the login component (Features > Auth). We need to remove the container class from the root `div` element. The line

```
<div class="container text-right">
```

should change to

```
<div class="text-right">
```

With that change complete, we can test our changes. When you run the app and mark and unmark trails as favorites, you'll notice the count in the new text changes in line with the button clicks.

10.3.4 *Reorganizing and refactoring*

In a second, we will add a new page for displaying the user's favorite trails. But before we add this new page, we need to do some quick reorganizing and refactoring.

The new favorites page will use the `TrailCard` component, as well as the `Trail-Details` and `FavoriteButton`. These components are now needed across multiple features, so we're going to move them into a new folder called *Shared* at the root of the Features folder. The `TrailCard` and `TrailDetails` components both use the `Trail` class, which has been sitting alongside them in the Home > Shared folder. We'll move this class as well.

The last piece of housekeeping we're going to do is create a new component that can be displayed when there are no trails. If you recall, we have already created some markup that does this on the home page. But we need that same code for the new favorites page as well. In the new Features > Shared folder, create a new component called `NoTrails.razor` with the following code.

Listing 10.10   NoTrails.razor

```
<div class="no-trails">
    <svg viewBox="0 0 16 16" class="bi bi-tree" fill="currentColor"
    xmlns="http://www.w3.org/2000/svg">
        <path fill-rule="evenodd" d="M8 0a.5.5 0 0 1 .416.22313 4.5A.5.5
0 0 1 11 5.5h-.09812.022 3.235a.5.5 0 0 1-.424.765h-.19111.638 3.276a.5.5
0 0 1-.447.724h-11a.5.5 0 0 1-.447-.724L3.69 9.5H3.5a.5.5 0 0
1-.424-.765L5.098 5.5H5a.5.5 0 0 1-.416-.77713-4.5A.5.5 0 0 1 8 0zM5.934
4.5H6a.5.5 0 0 1 .424.765L4.402 8.5H4.5a.5.5 0 0 1 .447.724L3.31
12.5h9.3821-1.638-3.276A.5.5 0 0 1 11.5 8.5h.098L9.576 5.265A.5.5 0 0 1
10 4.5h.066L8 1.401 5.934 4.5z" />
        <path d="M7 13.5h2V16H7v-2.5z" />
    </svg>
    <h3 class="text-muted font-weight-light">
        @ChildContent
    </h3>
</div>
@code {
    [Parameter]
    public RenderFragment? ChildContent { get; set; }
}
```

> **This component will replace the markup on the home page, which contains a hyperlink. In order to render the link, we must use a RenderFragment instead of having a simple string parameter.**

The markup for the component is a copy of what is currently rendered on the home page when there are no trails in the system. The one change is that the hardcoded text in the h3 tag has been replaced with the contents of the `ChildContent` parameter. This parameter is a `RenderFragment`, as the message that the home page displays contains a hyperlink. It wouldn't be possible to render this correctly if we used a simple string type for the parameter.

The `NoTrails` component also needs some styling. Let's add a new file called *NoTrails.razor.scss* with the following code.

Listing 10.11   NoTrails.razor.scss

```
.no-trails {
    text-align: center;
```

> **Provides the necessary styles for the no-trails component**

```
        margin-top: 100px;
        svg {
            width: 200px;
            color: #dee2e6;
            margin-bottom: 30px;
        }
    }
}
```

These styles are a lift-and-shift from the styles for the home page component. They set various margins and ensure the SVG (Scalable Vector Graphic) is the correct size and is centered on the page.

At this point we can update the `HomePage` component (Features > Home) to use the new `NoTrails` component. Remove all of the markup in the `else` block of the `_trails.Any()` check. Then add the following code:

```
<NoTrails>
    We currently don't have any trails, <a href="add-trail">why not add
    one?</a>
</NoTrails>
```

We can also delete the HomePage.razor.scss file because the styles it contained are no longer needed. They are now part of the `NoTrails` component.

10.3.5 *Showing favorited trails on the favorite trails page*

With our refactoring complete, we can add the new page, which will display the favorited trails. We've already added a link to this new page in the header text we added. We just need to create it and hook it up to our `AppState` to load the trails.

Let's go ahead and create a new feature folder called *FavoriteTrails* (Features > FavoriteTrails) and add a new component to it called `FavoriteTrailsPage.razor`. The code for this new page is shown in the following listing.

> **Listing 10.12 FavoriteTrailsPage.razor**

```
@page "/favorite-trails"
@inject AppState AppState
@implements IDisposable

<PageTitle>Favorite Trails - Blazing Trails</PageTitle>

<nav aria-label="breadcrumb">
    <ol class="breadcrumb">
        <li class="breadcrumb-item"><a href="/">Home</a></li>
        <li class="breadcrumb-item active" aria-current="page">
        ➡Favorite Trails</li>
    </ol>
</nav>

<h3 class="mt-5 mb-4">Favorite Trails</h3>
```

```
@if (AppState.FavoriteTrailsState.FavoriteTrails.Any())
{
    <TrailDetails Trail="_selectedTrail" />
    <div class="grid">
        @foreach (var trail in AppState.FavoriteTrailsState.FavoriteTrails)
        {
            <TrailCard Trail="trail"
            ➡OnSelected="HandleTrailSelected" />
        }
    </div>
}
else
{
    <NoTrails>
        You don't have any favorite trails :(
    </NoTrails>
}
@code {
    private Trail? _selectedTrail;
    protected override void OnInitialized()
        => AppState.FavoriteTrailsState.OnChange
        ➡+= StateHasChanged;
    private void HandleTrailSelected(Trail trail)
        => _selectedTrail = trail;
    void IDisposable.Dispose()
        => AppState.FavoriteTrailsState.OnChange -= StateHasChanged;
}
```

⟵ **If we have favorite trails, we loop over them and display a TrailCard for each one.**

If there are no favorite trails, we display the NoTrails component.

When the page initializes, it subscribes to the OnChange event of the FavoriteTrailsState. This is so if the user unfavorites a trail on the page, it will trigger a re-render and the page will be updated, removing that trail.

Most of this code should be looking very familiar by now. We check for any favorite trails in `AppState` and then render them using the `TrailCard`. If the user doesn't have any favorites, then we display the new `NoTrails` component, passing in an appropriate message.

Down in the logic block, when the page initializes, we're subscribing to the `OnChange` event. When this event fires, it will call the `StateHasChanged` method and trigger a `re-render` of the page. This covers the scenario where the user chooses to remove one of the trails listed on the page from favorites. Performing this action will trigger the `OnChange` event in the state store and, in turn, cause the page to `re-render`, removing the trail.

At this point, we can go ahead and run the app and test the new page out. Mark a few trails as favorites from the home page and then click the link in the header to view the new page (figure 10.4).

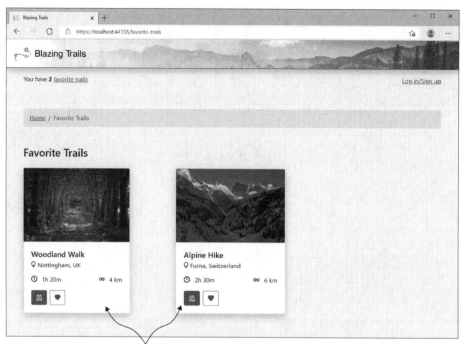

The Favorite Trails page displaying the two trails marked as favorites

Figure 10.4   The new favorites page displaying favorited trails

If all has gone to plan you should see the trails you favorited. You should also be able to unfavorite them and see them disappear from the page.

10.3.6   *Initializing AppState*

You might have noticed while `testing` the changes we've made that hard-refreshing the app (clicking the Refresh button in the browser or pressing F5) loses the state. In fact, the favorited trails are being persisted to the browser's local storage; we're just not reloading them when the app boots up. Let's fix this.

We're going to call the `Initialize` method on the `AppState` in the `App` component, which lives in the root of the Client project. The following listing shows the updates to `App.razor`.

Listing 10.13   App.razor: Initializing `AppState` on app startup

```
@inject AppState AppState
// other code omitted for brevity
@code {
    protected override async Task OnAfterRenderAsync(bool firstRender)
    {
        if (firstRender)
        {
```

```
        await AppState.Initialize();
    }
  }
}
```

On the first render of the App
component, we initialize the AppState.

We've overridden the `OnAfterRenderAsync` life cycle method and used its `first-Render` parameter to ensure we only attempt to initialize the `AppState` once. As we're using Blazor WebAssembly, we could technically use the `OnInitializedAsync` life cycle method instead. However, that wouldn't be compatible with Blazor Server.

Now that we are initializing the `AppState`, we can run the application to test things. If you already had trails favorited, you should see they are now showing immediately when the app boots up. If you didn't, favorite a few trails and perform a hard refresh and you should see they now show when the app restarts.

Summary

- State is the sum of all data held by a system at any given point in time.
- Users manipulate state in an application by performing actions within the system, such as clicking buttons and entering text.
- Managing state can range from simple communication between a parent and child component to full-blown patterns such as Flux.
- A simple in-memory state store can be achieved by using a scoped class that is injected via DI wherever it's needed.
- State values shouldn't be mutated directly; they should be mutated only through methods so propagation of the state change can be handled correctly.
- Splitting related state into individual stores that are accessed via a single parent store is a good way to keep large volumes of state maintainable.
- The browser's local storage feature can be used to persist state values across user sessions.

Testing your
Blazor application

This chapter covers

- Creating a bUnit test project
- Writing tests that verify rendered markup
- Mocking authentication and authorization in tests
- Testing components that use JavaScript interop

Testing is a very important aspect of writing applications. When we have good tests in place, we can produce higher quality applications, faster—Blazor applications are no exception. When it comes to testing Blazor apps, the three most common programmatic testing options are:

- Unit testing
- Integration testing
- End-to-end testing

Unit testing is the lowest level of testing we can utilize. When writing these types of tests, we focus on testing the smallest piece of functionality we can—such as a single method in a class. Due to this, these types of tests are extremely fast—individual tests run in milliseconds—which is handy, as we tend to write more unit tests than any other type. There are several frameworks available to help write unit tests. The three most common are xUnit (https://xunit.net), NUnit (https://nunit.org), and MSTest (http://mng.bz/2nea).

Integration testing is a level up from unit testing. In these tests, we combine several components of the system and test them together, checking that they integrate with each other correctly. These types of tests tend to use the same frameworks as unit tests, but as they are testing more complex scenarios, they can take longer to run than unit tests. An example of integration testing is a test that checks when data is posted to an API endpoint and saves it into the database.

End-to-end testing (E2E testing) is yet another level higher. These types of tests aim to exercise the entire system end to end, hence their name. When writing these tests for web applications, special frameworks are used to operate a *headless browser*. A headless browser is essentially a regular browser running without its UI. It is controlled programmatically, usually via the command line.

Using a headless browser allows the application to be rendered as it would be for a real user. Tests are written that perform the same actions as a user might, such as clicking buttons and navigating between pages. Due to this level of complexity, these tests are the slowest to run. It is common for E2E tests to take several seconds to execute, if not longer, depending on the complexity of the test. A good tool for writing E2E tests is Playwright (https://playwright.dev/). Using Blazing Trails, an example E2E test would be checking that when the View button on the trail card was clicked, the Trail Details drawer opened and displayed the correct trails information—testing the full stack of the application from UI to database.

In this chapter, we will learn how to write tests using a library called *bUnit*. bUnit has been written specifically to help test Blazor components and has many interesting features that we'll explore. We can use bUnit to write unit tests that test individual methods on our components. But we can also use it to write integration tests that check to ensure several components are working together.

We'll start by introducing bUnit and some of its key features. Then we'll cover adding a bUnit test project to the Blazing Trails application. Once our test project is up and running, we'll start adding tests and exploring how bUnit's various features can help us do that efficiently.

11.1   Introducing bUnit

bUnit is a testing library specifically designed for Blazor. It was created and is maintained by Egil Hansen—a Microsoft MVP. It's also supported by the .NET Foundation. The library sits on top of existing testing frameworks such as xUnit, NUnit, and MSTest, which run the tests in the same fashion as a regular unit test. This is an important point to understand, as unlike other UI-testing frameworks, bUnit doesn't require a browser. This means that tests written with bUnit are extremely fast, executing in milliseconds compared to seconds in traditional browser-based UI tests. Some of the key features of bUnit are:

- Interacting and inspecting components under test
- Injecting services or passing parameters and cascading values into components under test
- Having built-in *test doubles* for `IJSRuntime`, authentication and authorization services, and `HttpClient`
- Triggering event handlers in components
- Verifying outcomes using a semantic HTML comparison

What is a test double?

Test double is a generic term used to describe an object that replaces a production object in a test scenario.

Test doubles can take many different forms, such as *a fake*. Fakes are objects that have working implementations tailored for testing. The Blazored LocalStorage test extensions provide a fake for the browser's local storage feature, which stores data in memory instead of calling into the browser's APIs. This allows tests to be performed on the code without the need for a physical browser.

Other examples of test doubles are:

- Mocks
- Stubs
- Dummies

For further reading on test doubles, I recommend this post by Martin Fowler: https://martinfowler.com/bliki/TestDouble.html.

Another interesting feature of bUnit is the ability to write tests using either .cs files or .razor files. When using the .cs file approach, tests look identical to standard unit tests for regular C# classes. However, when using .razor files, we can write markup directly into the test code, which makes writing tests much easier. This is the approach we'll be using in this chapter—more details on this later.

For a complete breakdown of all the features bUnit offers, as well as the official documentation, I encourage you to check out https://bunit.dev.

11.2   Adding a bUnit test project

Before we can start writing any bUnit tests for Blazing Trails, we need to set up a test project in the solution. There are two options for this:

- Installing and using the bUnit project template
- Manually installing the bUnit components in a regular test project

By far the simplest option when you don't already have an existing test project is option 1. This is what we'll cover in this section. However, if you have a solution with an existing test project that you would like to add bUnit to, the bUnit documentation covers the steps needed to do that: http://mng.bz/aJoX.

To install the bUnit project template, we can run the following .NET CLI command:

```
dotnet new --install bunit.template
```

This will install the latest version of the bUnit project template. It's also possible to pass a specific template version to the command:

```
dotnet new --install bunit.template::1.3.42
```

Now that we have the bUnit project template installed, we can then create a new project with it. Navigate to the folder that contains the BlazingTrails.sln file and then run the following command:

```
dotnet new bunit -o BlazingTrails.Tests
```

This will create a new folder called *BlazingTrails.Tests* and will create all the necessary project files within it. While we're here, we can also add the test project to the solution using this command:

```
dotnet sln add BlazingTrails.Tests/BlazingTrails.Tests.csproj
```

We can now switch back over to Visual Studio. If you already have the solution open, you will be prompted to reload it. Otherwise, open the solution, and you should now see the new test project in the Solution Explorer (figure 11.1).

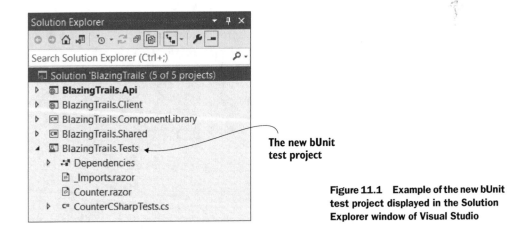

The new bUnit test project

Figure 11.1   Example of the new bUnit test project displayed in the Solution Explorer window of Visual Studio

The template has two example files that we need to remove: Counter.razor and CounterCSharpTests.cs. We will then create a new folder called *Client*. This folder will house any tests we write for components in the BlazingTrails.Client project. We'll also

create a ComponentLibrary folder. This will hold any tests for the BlazingTrails
.ComponentLibrary project.

At this point, the test project is ready to go, but we're going to perform a few additional steps. First, we'll install a package called *AutoFixture* (https://github.com/Auto-Fixture/AutoFixture). AutoFixture is useful when writing tests, as it can generate fake test data. This helps make the setup or arrange phase of our tests much simpler, as we don't have to spend loads of time newing up objects and assigning dummy data to each property.

We will also add a package called `Blazored.LocalStorage.TestExtensions`. This provides us with an in-memory implementation of `LocalStorage` that allows us to test code that uses the Blazored LocalStorage library.

Let's add the following package references to the BlazingTrails.Tests project file:

```
<PackageReference Include="AutoFixture" Version="4.17.0" />
<PackageReference Include="Blazored.LocalStorage.TestExtensions"
    Version="4.1.5" />
```

The next step is to add some using statements to the root _Imports.razor file. These are going to help us a little later when writing our tests. Open the file and add the following lines:

```
@using Microsoft.AspNetCore.Components.Authorization
@using Microsoft.AspNetCore.Components.Forms
@using Microsoft.Extensions.DependencyInjection
@using AutoFixture
@using Bunit.JSInterop.InvocationHandlers
@using MediatR
@using BlazingTrails.Client.State
@using BlazingTrails.Client.Features.Shared
```

All that's left for us to do is add a couple of references to the projects that contain the components we're going to test. These are the `BlazingTrails.Client` and `BlazingTrails.ComponentLibrary`. You can do this using either the .NET CLI or Visual Studio.

For Visual Studio, complete the following steps:

1 Right-click on Dependencies under the BlazingTrails.Tests project.
2 Select `Add Project Reference...`
3 Select both the BlazingTrails.Client and BlazingTrails.ComponentLibrary projects.
4 Click OK to add the references.

From the .NET CLI, navigate to the BlazingTrails.Tests folder and run the following commands:

```
dotnet add reference ../BlazingTrails.Client
dotnet add reference ../BlazingTrails.ComponentLibrary
```

At this point, the new bUnit test project is all set up and ready for us to start writing some tests!

11.3 Testing components with bUnit

We can now focus on writing tests that verify the functionality of some of the components in Blazing Trails. We're not going to write tests that cover all the components in the application; instead, we'll focus on testing select components that cover the most common testing scenarios:

- Testing rendered markup
- Triggering event handlers in tests
- Testing components that use authentication and authorization
- Testing components that make JavaScript interop calls
- Testing multiple components

As I mentioned earlier in the chapter, we'll be writing our tests in .razor files. This is a highlight feature of bUnit and offers us a major advantage over writing our tests in .cs files—the ability to use *templated Razor delegates*. Templated Razor delegates allow us to write markup directly into our C# test code with IntelliSense! Let's look at a quick example to understand the advantage. We'll pretend we have a greeting component that outputs a simple message (see the following listing).

Listing 11.1 Example Greeter component

```
<h1>Hey! @Name. Testing with bUnit is awesome.</h1>

@code
{
    [Parameter]
    public string Name { get; set; }
}
```

The following listing shows what a simple test for that component looks like in a .cs file.

Listing 11.2 Example bUnit test written in a .cs file

```
[Fact]
public void RendersGreeting()
{
    var cut = RenderComponent<Greeter>(
    ➥parameters => parameters.Add(p => p.Name, "Robyn"));

    cut.MarkupMatches(
    ➥"<h1>Hey! Robyn. Testing with bUnit is awesome.</h1>");
}
```

> The RenderComponent method renders the component under test (cut), and we pass in any parameter values needed.

> Markup is verified using a string literal of the expected output.

The `RenderComponent` method is used to specify which component we want to test. We can also pass in the value for the `Name` parameter using `ComponentParameter-CollectionBuilder<TComponent>`. Finally, we verify the expected markup using a string literal. Now let's look at that same test in a .razor file.

Listing 11.3   Example bUnit test written in a .razor file

```
@code
{
    [Fact]
    public void RendersGreeting()
    {
        var cut = Render(@<Greeter Name="Robyn" />);
        cut.MarkupMatches(
    ➥@<h1>Hey! Robyn. Testing with bUnit is awesome.</h1>);
    }
}
```

The @ symbol marks the start of a templated Razor delegate, allowing markup to be written inside C# code.

The expected output is defined as HTML, not a string literal.

This time we're using templated Razor delegates to define the component under test as well as the expected output. We start a templated Razor delegate by using the @ symbol. From there we can type arbitrary markup. The markup can even span multiple lines if required.

Hopefully you can see the benefit of writing tests using this method. The code is easier to read at a glance, and we avoid the use of string literals. The fact that we also get IntelliSense with this method is a bonus.

11.3.1 *Testing rendered markup*

The first tests we're going to write are probably the simplest type we can perform—testing rendered markup. The component we're to test is the `FavoriteButton` component that we added in chapter 10. Let's dive into the test code, and then we'll break it all down to see what's going on.

First, we add a new folder for these tests. We'll mimic the folder structure of the project in order to make tests easy to find. Let's start by creating a Features folder in the Client folder; then we can add a Shared folder inside that.

Inside the new Shared folder, we add a new component called `FavoriteButton-Tests.razor`. Then we can add the following code.

Listing 11.4   FavoriteButtonTests.razor

```
@inherits TestContext
@code
{
    private readonly Fixture _fixture = new();

    public FavoriteButtonTests()
    {
```

Inheriting from the bUnit TestContext gives us access to the features of bUnit.

The Fixture class is from AutoFixture, and we use it to create test data in the tests.

This registers the various services needed to provide an in-memory local storage implementation that can be used for testing.

As the FavoriteButton relies on AppState, we need to add it to the test context's service container so it can be injected into the component.

```
            this.AddBlazoredLocalStorage();
            this.Services.AddScoped<AppState>();
    }

    [Fact]
    public void RendersAddFavoriteButton_When_TrailIsNotFavorited()
    {
        // Arrange
        var testTrail = _fixture.Create<Trail>();

        // Act
        var cut = Render(
            @<FavoriteButton Trail="testTrail" />);

        // Assert
        cut.MarkupMatches(
            @<button class="btn btn-outline-primary ml-1"
            title="Favorite">
                <i class="bi bi-heart"></i>
            </button>
        );
    }
}
```

The fixture instance is used to create a Trail instance with dummy data.

bUnit provides the Render method, which allows us to create an instance of the component we want to test.

Using the MarkupMatches method, we can verify the markup produced from the rendered component.

We first inherit from the `TestContext` base class provided by bUnit. This base class provides all the bUnit functionality from creating and rendering components under test to verifying the markup they produce.

Then we have the `_fixture` field. This stores an instance of the `Fixture` class, provided by AutoFixture. We use this to generate test data in our tests. We could new this up in each test, but by doing it once here, it helps keep our test code clean by avoiding repetition.

Next comes the constructor. The constructor is a great place to add setup code required for each test within the file. In this case, we're configuring the `service` container. As the `FavoriteButton` requires an instance of the `AppState` class to be injected, we must set up the required services so bUnit can inject them when it renders the component being tested. First, we're calling the `AddBlazoredLocalStorage` extension method provided by the `Blazored.LocalStorage.TestExtensions` package we installed earlier. This package was specifically designed to provide test doubles of the Blazored LocalStorage services in bUnit tests. This extension method registers those test doubles, which provide an in-memory implementation of LocalStorage. We need this, as the `AppState` class uses Blazored LocalStorage. The next line sets up the `AppState` as a scoped service in the container, just as we did in the Blazing-Trails.Client project.

On to the first test. The test is set up to use the *arrange, act, assert (AAA) pattern*. This is a widely used testing pattern across the industry. It arranges a test into three steps:

1 *Arrange*—Creates or configures any objects that are used in the execution of the test

2 *Act*—Invokes the component or method under test

3 *Assert*—Verifies that the action of the component or method being tested produces the desired result

In our arrange phase, we're creating the test data—an instance of the `Trail` class—by using the `_fixture.Create<T>` method. In the act phase, we render the component under test, the `FavoriteButton`, using the `Render` method provided by bUnit's `TestContext` class. This returns us an `IRenderedFragment`, which we can use in the assert phase to check the markup that was produced.

bUnit's `MarkupMatches` method uses *semantic markup verification* to confirm if the component has rendered the expected markup. Here we're using the templated Razor delegate syntax to define what we expect the final markup to be. If the expected markup matches what the component rendered, the test will pass.

Semantic markup verification

A common issue when writing UI tests that verify markup is fragile tests—tests that break when something as simple as the order of attributes on an element changes or extra whitespace is added or removed. bUnit's `MarkupMatches` method uses semantic comparison of markup when verifying output. This means that a change in the order of attributes or insignificant whitespace will not break a test.

For example, if we had a component that outputted the following markup, we could write a test that verified this:

```
<button type="button" title="A button">A Button</button>
```

By using bUnit's `MarkupMatches` method, if the output from the component changed to

```
<button title="A button" type="button">A Button    </button>
```

then the test would still pass, as the output is still semantically the same. The order change of the attributes and the additional whitespace in the button text would still produce the same visually rendered output in a browser.

This is only the tip of the iceberg when it comes to bUnit's semantic comparisons. You can also do all the following when verifying markup:

- Ignore attributes
- Ignore entire elements
- Perform case-insensitive comparisons
- Use regex during comparison
- Configure whitespace handling

If you want to dive deeper into these features of bUnit, I would recommend reading the documentation on the semantic HTML comparison found at https://bunit.dev/docs/verification/semantic-html-comparison.

Now we have our first test in place testing that our `FavoriteButton` renders correctly when the trail is not a favorite. Let's add an additional test to check for the inverse condition. It's always a good practice when writing tests to check all potential conditions. The following listing shows the code for the new test.

Listing 11.5 FavoriteButtonTests.razor: `FavoriteButton` render test

```
[Fact]
public async Task RendersRemoveFavoriteButton_When_TrailIsFavorited()
{
    // Arrange
    var testTrail = _fixture.Create<Trail>();

    var appState = this.Services.GetService<AppState>();   ◁── Retrieves the AppState
    await appState.FavoriteTrailsState                           instance from the
    ⟹.AddFavorite(testTrail);          ◁──┐ Adds the testTrail to the list   services container
                                          └ of favorites in AppState
    // Act
    var cut = Render(@<FavoriteButton Trail="testTrail" />);

    // Assert
    cut.MarkupMatches(
        @<button class="btn btn-outline-primary ml-1"
        ⟹title="Favorite">             Verifies that the desired
            <i class="bi bi-heart-fill"></i>   markup is produced
        </button>
    );
}
```

As you can see, most of this test is the same as the previous one. The key difference is in the arrange phase, where we are setting up the conditions for the test. First, we capture a reference to the `AppState` instance in the `services` container. Then we add the `testTrail` to the list of favorites so when `AppState` is injected into the `FavoriteButton`, the trail will be in the list of favorites and trigger the desired functionality.

In the assert phase, we've once again used the `MarkupMatches` method to verify that the correct markup is produced.

11.3.2 Triggering event handlers

A common need when testing components is to trigger events. Probably the most common example of this is triggering a button click. The `FavoriteButton` component we're testing should add or remove the trail it represents from `AppState` when the button it renders is clicked. Let's write a couple of tests to explore how we trigger these types of events with bUnit.

The first test we'll write will make the trail a favorite. The second will remove it as a favorite. Listing 11.6 shows the code.

Listing 11.6   FavoriteButtonTests.razor: Testing add/remove trail

```
[Fact]
public void AddTrailToFavorites_When_TrailIsNotAFavorite()
{
    // Arrange
    var testTrail = _fixture.Create<Trail>();
    var cut = Render(
      @<FavoriteButton Trail="testTrail" />);
    var button = cut.Find("button");

    //Act
    button.Click();

    // Assert
    var appState = this.Services.GetService<AppState>();
    Assert.True(
      appState.FavoriteTrailsState.IsFavorite(testTrail));
}

[Fact]
public async Task RemoveTrailFromFavorites_When_TrailIsFavorite()
{
    // Arrange
    var testTrail = _fixture.Create<Trail>();
    var appState = this.Services.GetService<AppState>();
    await appState.FavoriteTrailsState
      .AddFavorite(testTrail);
    var cut = Render(@<FavoriteButton Trail="testTrail" />);
    var button = cut.Find("button");

    //Act
    button.Click();

    // Assert
    Assert.False(appState.FavoriteTrailsState.IsFavorite(testTrail));
}
```

The rendering of the component is now part of the arrange phase.

Once the component is rendered, we can use the Find method to capture a reference to the button element in its markup.

Instructs bUnit to execute the button's click event

We assert that the trail has been added to the list of favorites in AppState.

The testTrail is added to the list of favorites during the arrange phase so we can check the inverse condition.

For these tests, you can see that we have moved the rendering of the Favorite-Button to the arrange phase. This is because the rendering of the component is no longer the trigger for the functionality we're testing. We need to render the component and then search its markup for the button element it produces. We do this using the Find method. This method takes a CSS selector as an argument and returns the first element that matches the selector. There is also a FindAll method that does the same thing but returns a list of matching elements.

Once we have a reference to the button rendered by the component, we can mimic a user click by calling the Click method. When calling this method, bUnit will make sure the handler for this event is executed on the component and perform any re-rendering.

Finally, we can assert that the desired state has been achieved. We do this by checking that the trail is now a favorite using the IsFavorite method on AppState. We could also check that the component re-rendered with different markup, but we already have the first two tests verifying that behavior. Also, I find it's best to keep to one logical assertion per test so it's clear what is being tested.

The second test is essentially a mirror of the first but with some additional setup so the trail starts as a favorite and can be removed by the click event.

11.3.3 *Faking authentication and authorization*

Now that we have mastered the fundamentals of writing bUnit tests, let's move on to something a little more advanced—testing components requiring authentication and authorization. This is always a tricky subject with testing, but bUnit has built-in functionality that makes it a breeze.

To learn about this type of testing, we're going to write some tests for the `Trail-Card` component. This component renders an Edit button when the logged-in user is the owner of the trail. It also renders the Edit button when the logged-in user is in the administrator role. We'll write a test for each of these scenarios. Let's create these new tests in a Razor file called *TrailCardTests.razor*. This can be added to the same Shared folder as the FavoriteButtonTests.razor file. The following listing shows the initial setup code and first test.

Listing 11.7 TrailCardTests.razor

```
@inherits TestContext

@code
{
    private readonly TestAuthorizationContext       Allows the TestAuthorizationContext
    ➥_authContext;                              ◁─── to be shared across multiple tests
    private readonly Fixture _fixture = new();

    public TrailCardTests()
    {
        this.AddBlazoredLocalStorage();             Adds and sets up the
        this.Services.AddScoped<AppState>();        necessary auth services and
        _authContext = this.AddTestAuthorization();  ◁─── infrastructure for testing
    }

    [Fact]
    public void RendersEditButton_When_UserIsAuthorized()
    {
        // Arrange                                 To save repeating the username in
        var authorizedUser = "Test User";      ◁─── multiple strings, we create it as a variable.
        _authContext.SetAuthorized(authorizedUser);
        var testTrail = _fixture.Create<Trail>();
        testTrail.Owner = authorizedUser;      ◁─── The owner of the trail is set equal to
                                                    the username of the authorized user.
        // Act
        var cut = Render(@<TrailCard Trail="testTrail" />);

        // Assert
```

Sets up authorized user with the given username in the test context

```
        var editButton = cut.Find(
    ➥ "button[title=\"Edit\"]");              │ The Find method is used
                                              ◄─┘ to retrieve the Edit button.
        Assert.NotNull(editButton);          ◄─┐ Verifies that the Edit button is
    }                                           │ present in the rendered markup
}
```

The first new element introduced in this test file is the _authContext field. This holds a reference to a TestAuthorizationContext, which is set up in the constructor. We use this to set up the desired auth conditions for each test. Essentially, the TestAuthorizationContext is a set of test doubles for Blazor's authentication and authorization system.

Inside the arrange phase of the test, we create a variable with the username of the authorized user we want to set up. We can then reference this variable instead of using multiple string literals with the same value. Next, we instruct the Test-AuthorizationContext to set up an authorized user with the given username. We then set the trail owner property to the name of the authorized user.

Once the component has been rendered, we find the Edit button in the markup of the component and assert that it exists.

Now on to the next test. This time we're going to check that an authorized user in the administrator role can also see the Edit button. The following listing shows the new test.

Listing 11.8   TrailCardTests.razor: Testing role-based auth

```
[Fact]
public void RendersEditButton_When_UserIsAdmin()
{
    // Arrange
    var authorizedUser = "Admin User";
    _authContext.SetAuthorized(authorizedUser);    │ This time we specify the role the
    _authContext.SetRoles("Administrator");       ◄─┘ authorized user should belong to.
    var testTrail = _fixture.Create<Trail>();      ◄─┐ Notice we don't set the
                                                      │ owner of the trail equal
    // Act                                            │ to the username of the
    var cut = Render(@<TrailCard Trail="testTrail" />); │ authenticated user.

    // Assert
    var editButton = cut.Find("button[title=\"Edit\"]");
    Assert.NotNull(editButton);
}
```

This test is very similar to the previous one. The key difference is the call to _auth-Context.SetRoles. Here we specify that the user is in the administrator role. You'll also notice that we don't set the Owner property on the test trail instance. This will be given a random string value by AutoFixture consisting of the name of the property and a random GUID. So, it couldn't match that of the authorizedUser variable. We then render the component and assert that the Edit button exists as we did in the previous test.

As you can see, bUnit's features for testing components relying on auth conditions is very straightforward and results in simple, easy-to-understand tests. If you need to set policies or arbitrary claims in your tests, bUnit has you covered here as well. You can use the `SetPolicies` and `SetClaims` methods on the `TestAuthorization-Context` to configure either of these scenarios, or both!

11.3.4 Emulating JavaScript interactions

Writing tests for components that interact with JavaScript poses an interesting problem. bUnit is not running in a browser context; therefore there is no JavaScript run time to interact with. So how do we test components requiring JavaScript interop? The answer—we fake it.

bUnit ships with its own implementation of the `IJSRuntime` interface. This implementation has two modes:

- *Strict mode*—Requires a test to set up all expected JavaScript calls explicitly. Any call not set up will throw an exception.
- *Loose mode*—Returns the default value from any JavaScript invocation without needing to set up the call ahead of time

It's worth noting that the bUnit implementation of `IJSRuntime` is active by default in tests and is set to use `strict` mode.

To see this in action, we're going to write some tests for the `RouteMap` component in the BlazingTrails.ComponentLibrary project. We'll start by adding some new folders to the test project. At the root of the project, add a folder called *ComponentLibrary*; then add a folder inside that called *Map*. Once that is done, we can add our test file, RouteMapTests.razor, to the Map folder. Now go ahead and add the following code to the new test file.

Listing 11.9 RouteMapTests.razor

```
@using BlazingTrails.ComponentLibrary.Map
@inherits TestContext

@code {
    private BunitJSModuleInterop _routeMapModule;
    private JSRuntimeInvocationHandler _routeMapModuleInitializeInvocation;

    public RouteMapTests()
    {
        _routeMapModule = JSInterop.SetupModule();       ⟵  Sets up the call that imports
        _routeMapModuleInitializeInvocation =                the routeMap JavaScript
        ➥_routeMapModule.SetupVoid("initialize", _ => true)  module for all tests in the file
        ➥.SetVoidResult();      ⟵  Sets up the call to the
    }                               initialize function on
                                    the routeMap module
    [Fact]
    public void InitializesMap_When_ComponentFirstRenders()
    {
```

```
// Arrange / Act
var cut = Render(@<RouteMap />);

// Assert
_routeMapModuleInitializeInvocation
    .VerifyInvoke("initialize", calledTimes: 1);
    }
}
```

◁── **As there is no test-specific setup needed, the Arrange and Act step are collapsed into one.**

◁── **The call to the initialize function is verified, including that it happened only once.**

In the constructor, we start by setting up the call the `RouteMap` component makes to import the `routeMap` JavaScript module when it first renders. We do this using the `SetupModule` method. As the `RouteMap` component imports only one module, we're using the parameterless overload of `SetupModule`. This will match any call in the component under test that attempts to import a module. However, if we were importing more than one module in the component under test, we might choose to use another overload that requires the path of the module being imported to be specified. That way we could set up an expected invocation for each module call to make sure they are all imported.

Next, we set up the call to the `initialize` function on the `routeMap` module. This is a void call and doesn't return a value, so we use the `SetupVoid` method. As with the `SetupModule` method, we could use its parameterless overload to match any `InvokeVoidAsync` call within the component being tested—the `RouteMap` component has only one anyway. But as we've already seen that approach, it's worth seeing how the more explicit option works.

In this case, we're specifying the name of the function being called, and then we use a lambda, which returns `true` to indicate that the function can be called with any arguments. The most explicit setup we could do is to specify the name of the function and the exact arguments it is invoked with. But this is useful only in scenarios where multiple calls are made to the same function with different values and you need to verify each variation.

Finally, we chain a call to the `SetVoidResult` method. By default, bUnit's JavaScript run-time implementation will return an incomplete task from `InvokeVoidAsync` calls, which the component under test will await until a call to `SetVoidResult` is made. By chaining it to the setup, we ensure it is called immediately.

Note the chained call to `SetVoidResult`. bUnit will return an incomplete task from any `InvokeVoidAsync` call, which the component will await until `SetVoidResult` is called. By chaining this method call here, we ensure that the task will be completed as soon as the JavaScript call is made.

Now we move on to the test. The test checks that the JavaScript elements of the map are initialized when the component first renders. There is no test-specific setup required here, so we've collapsed the arrange and act step into one and just rendered the `RouteMap` component. In the assert phase, we're verifying that a call was made to the `initialize` function and that it was called only once.

Let's move on and write a second test. This one is going to confirm that a JavaScript interop call is made when the Delete Last Waypoint button is clicked. The following listing shows the code.

Listing 11.10 RouteMapTests.razor: Testing JavaScript calls

```
[Fact]
public void
    CallsDeleteLastWaypointFunction_When_DeleteLastWaypointButtonClicked()
{
    // Arrange
    var latLongResult = new LatLong(1m, 2m);
    var plannedInvocation = _routeMapModule
    .Setup<LatLong>("deleteLastWaypoint", _ => true)
    .SetResult(latLongResult);
    var cut = Render(@<RouteMap />);
    var deleteWaypointButton = cut.Find(
    "button[title=\"Delete last waypoint\"]");

    // Act
    deleteWaypointButton.Click();

    // Assert
    plannedInvocation.VerifyInvoke("deleteLastWaypoint", calledTimes: 1);
}
```

This is a dummy result to be returned from the JavaScript interop call.

Sets up the expected JavaScript invocation to return the dummy latLongResult

In this test, we're checking for a JavaScript invocation that expects a return value. When clicking the Delete Last Waypoint button, the component expects the JavaScript call to return an object containing the latitude and longitude of the waypoint being removed. To set this up, we use the Setup<T> method—the type parameter is the type we're expecting back in the call. Again, we're using an overload that requires us to specify the name of the function being called, but we're using the lambda to state that we don't care about the arguments it's called with. We're chaining the SetResult method this time and passing in the latLongResult to be returned to the component when it invokes the call.

As we've done in previous tests, we're rendering the component, finding the Delete button, and executing its click event. We then verify that the deleteLast-Waypoint function was called once.

11.3.5 Testing multiple components

The final test we're going to write will test multiple components working together. We'll be using the HomePage component as our example this time. We will check that when the View Trail button is clicked on a TrailCard, the TrailDetails component is rendered and displays the details of the correct trail. As part of these tests, we'll also see how we can stub out MediatR calls.

We'll start by creating the folder structure and then the stub for the MediatR call made by the HomePage component. Inside the Client > Features folder in the test project, create a new folder called *Home*. Then add a new C# class called `Get-TrailsHandler.cs`. Next, add the following code.

Listing 11.11 GetTrailsHandler.cs

```
public class GetTrailsHandler : IRequestHandler<GetTrailsRequest,
    GetTrailsRequest.Response>
{
    public async Task<GetTrailsRequest.Response> Handle(
    ➥GetTrailsRequest request, CancellationToken cancellationToken)
    {
        var fixture = new Fixture();
        var dummyTrails = fixture
    ➥.CreateMany<GetTrailsRequest.Trail>();

        return new GetTrailsRequest.Response(dummyTrails);
    }
}
```

AutoFixture is used to create a list of dummy trails to return.

We've created a handler that is almost identical to the production one in the Client project. The key difference is it doesn't talk to the API. Instead, it uses AutoFixture to generate some dummy data that can be returned to the component being tested. This is an example of a test stub.

With the test stub in place, we can move on to creating our test file. In the same folder, add a file called *HomePageTests.razor* with the following code.

Listing 11.12 HomePageTests.razor

```
@using BlazingTrails.Client.Features.Home
@inherits TestContext

@code {
    public HomePageTests()
    {
        this.AddBlazoredLocalStorage();
        this.AddTestAuthorization();
        this.Services.AddScoped<AppState>();
        this.Services.AddMediatR(
    ➥typeof(HomePageTests).Assembly);
    }

    [Fact]
    public void RendersTrailDetails_When_TrailSelected()
    {
        // Arrange
        JSInterop.Mode = JSRuntimeMode.Loose;
        var cut = Render(@<HomePage />);
        var trailCards =
    ➥cut.FindComponents<TrailCard>();
        var viewButton = trailCards[0].Find(
    ➥"button[title=\"View\"]");

        // Act
        viewButton.Click();
```

Sets up MediatR to use the test stub by having it scan the test project assembly for handlers

The TrailDetails component renders the RouteMap component, which makes JS interop calls, so we need to set the JSInterop mode to Loose; otherwise we would need to set up every call.

The FindComponents method allows us to retrieve all instances of the specified component within the rendered component. We can then find the View button on the first TrailCard instance and trigger its click event to render the TrailDetails component.

```
// Assert
var trailDetails = cut.FindComponent<TrailDetails>();

var isOpen = trailDetails.Find(
➥"div.drawer-wrapper.slide");
Assert.NotNull(isOpen);

Assert.Equal(trailCards[0].Instance.Trail.Name,
➥trailDetails.Instance.Trail.Name);
    }
}
```

The first assert verifies that the drawer is open by checking that the slide class has been applied.

The second assert verifies that the Trail.Name on the TrailDetails component matches that of the trail whose View button was clicked.

We've seen most of the code in the constructor before; the only new item is the call to `AddMediatR`. Here we're telling MediatR to scan the test project's assembly for any handlers. This will register our stub handler so it will be called when the `HomePage` component is rendered.

The first step inside the test method is to set the `JSInterop` mode to `Loose`. This is because the `TrailDetails` component contains the `RouteMap` component, which makes JavaScript interop calls. Without setting the mode to `Loose`, we'd need to set up each of the calls it makes, and they're not relevant in this test.

After rendering the `HomePage`, we use the `FindComponents` method to retrieve all instances of the `TrailCard` component rendered within the `HomePage`. We then take the first `TrailCard`, find its View button, and execute its click event.

Finally, we use the `FindComponent` method to retrieve the `TrailDetails` component. Once we have that, we assert that it is open by checking the presence of the slide CSS class. This class is applied only when the drawer is open. Then we ensure that it has the correct trail data by checking the trail name against the name of the trail whose View button was clicked.

Summary

- There are three different types of automated testing we can use to test Blazor applications: unit tests, integration tests, and end-to-end tests.
- Unit tests check a small piece of logic in isolation, such as a method in a class.
- Integration tests are a level higher than unit tests, testing multiple components of a system together.
- End-to-end tests are a level above integrations tests and test a whole system from UI to database.
- bUnit is a testing library designed specifically to test Blazor components.
- bUnit can be used to write both unit tests and integration tests.
- bUnit works with the three most common testing frameworks: xUnit, NUnit, and MSTest.
- bUnit tests can be written in with .cs or .razor files.

- Writing bUnit tests in .razor files is preferred, as we can use the templated Razor delegate syntax to write markup directly into the C# test code.
- bUnit comes with test doubles for `IJSRuntime`, `HttpClient`, and authentication and authorization services.

appendix A
Adding an ASP.NET
Core backend to a Blazor
WebAssembly app

In this appendix, I'll cover the steps required to add an ASP.NET Core backend to an existing Blazor WebAssembly application. The backend will be made up of an ASP.NET Core Web API, a .NET class library, and an SQLite database. It's worth pointing out that if you're starting a new project, then there is a template included that contains this exact setup, minus the database. It's called the Blazor WebAssembly ASP.NET Core hosted template (covered in chapter 2). So, if you're starting fresh, I would recommend using that and avoid the manual steps presented in this appendix.

> **NOTE** We'll be working on the Blazing Trails application from its state at the end of chapter 4. If you're building along with the chapters in this book, you'll need to complete this appendix before working through chapter 5.

A.1 Adding an ASP.NET Core Web API

We'll start by adding the Web API project first. Figure A.1 shows the starting point for our solution.

We're going to add a new Web API project called *BlazingTrails.Api*. When adding a new project to an existing solution, I prefer to do so from the command line using the .NET CLI. I find it a bit quicker than clicking through the menus in Visual Studio or in other IDEs—but use the method that works best for you.

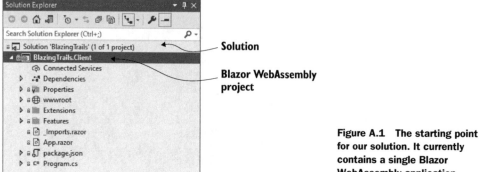

Figure A.1   **The starting point for our solution. It currently contains a single Blazor WebAssembly application.**

Navigate to the folder containing the solution file and then execute the following command:

```
dotnet new webapi -n BlazingTrails.Api
```

With this command, we're asking the CLI to create a new Web API project with the name *BlazingTrails.Api*. After a second or two, the project will be created. To add the new project to the existing solution, we then run this command:

```
dotnet sln add BlazingTrails.Api\BlazingTrails.Api.csproj
```

You should see a message stating that the project has been added to the solution. At this point, you can open the solution in Visual Studio, or reload it if it was already open. You should see the new API project in the solution explorer (figure A.2).

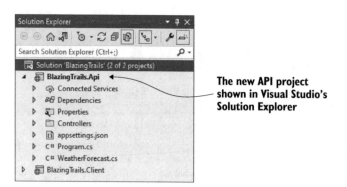

Figure A.2   **The new API project is now part of the existing solution.**

We have now successfully added our API project to the solution. Next, we need to clear out some of the boilerplate code included by the template, then configure it to work with our Blazor app. By the time we're done, the BlazingTrails.Api project will be the startup project for the solution and will serve the Blazor WebAssembly application.

A.1.1   Removing boilerplate from the new API project

A new ASP.NET Core Web API comes with an example controller called `Weather-ForecastController` and a `WeatherForecast` class. These are handy examples to have when first learning to build Web APIs, but they're not of any use to us. So, the first thing we will do is delete the `WeatherForecast` class from the root of the project and delete the entire Controllers folder, along with the `WeatherForecastController` inside it.

New APIs also come with Swagger installed. Swagger is a fantastic tool for documenting APIs, and depending on what you want from your API project, you might want to leave this in place; however, the API we're configuring is purely for our Blazor app, so we're going to remove it. There are three steps to doing this.

1 Remove the Swagger NuGet package from the project (Swashbuckle.AspNet-Core).
2 Remove the Swagger services and middleware from Program.cs.
3 Remove the `launchUrl` property from the launchSettings.json file in the Properties folder.

After completing those steps, all traces of Swagger will be removed from the project and we can focus on configuring it for our Blazor app.

A.1.2   Configuring the API

Now that we have a clean project to work from, we can start to configure it for our needs. To start, we're going to reference a NuGet package that allows us to configure the API to serve the Blazor application. In the csproj file, add the following package reference. Alternatively, the package can be added using the NuGet package manager GUI in Visual Studio:

```
<PackageReference Include="Microsoft.AspNetCore.Components.WebAssembly.Server"
    Version="6.0.0" />
```

This package contains middleware that is going to enable the API project to serve the Blazor WebAssembly application. With that in place, we can head over to the Program.cs file to make some modifications. Replace the code in the file with that shown in the following listing.

Listing A.1   Program.cs: Configuration to serve the Blazor app

```
var builder = WebApplication.CreateBuilder(args);

// Add services to the container.

builder.Services.AddControllers();

var app = builder.Build();

// Configure the HTTP request pipeline.
if (app.Environment.IsDevelopment())
{
```

```
        app.UseWebAssemblyDebugging();          ◄─┐  This middleware enables the debugging
    }                                              │  of Blazor WebAssembly code.

    app.UseHttpsRedirection();
                                          ┌─ This middleware enables the API
    app.UseBlazorFrameworkFiles();    ◄───┘  to serve the Blazor application.
    app.UseStaticFiles();       ◄─┐  This middleware enables static
                                   │  files to be served by the API.
    app.UseRouting();

    app.MapControllers();
    app.MapFallbackToFile("index.html");    ◄─┐  If a request doesn't match to a controller, serve
                                              │  the index.html file from the Blazor project.
    app.Run();
```

The key points to note in the changes are the addition of the `UseWebAssembly-Debugging` middleware. This allows us to still debug our Blazor WebAssembly code once we switch to using the API as the startup project.

Next, we've added the `UseBlazorFrameworkFiles()` and `UseStaticFiles()` middleware. Together, these allow the API to serve the Blazor application files. After all, a Blazor WebAssembly application, once compiled, is just a set of static files.

The other change to note is the addition of the `MapFallbackToFile` endpoint. This instructs the API to route any requests that don't match one of its endpoints to the Blazor application so it can try and handle it.

We're going to jump back over the to the launchSettings.json file next. In here, we'll add in a couple of lines, as shown in the next listing.

Listing A.2 Configuring launchSettings.json for debugging

```
"profiles": {
  "IIS Express": {
    "commandName": "IISExpress",
    "launchBrowser": true,
    "inspectUri": "{wsProtocol}://{url.hostname}:
      ➥{url.port}/_framework/debug/ws-proxy?
      ➥browser={browserInspectUri}",
    "environmentVariables": {
      "ASPNETCORE_ENVIRONMENT": "Development"
    }
  },
  "BlazingTrails.Api": {
    "commandName": "Project",
    "dotnetRunMessages": "true",
    "launchBrowser": true,
    "inspectUri": "{wsProtocol}://{url.hostname}:
      ➥{url.port}/_framework/debug/ws-proxy?
      ➥browser={browserInspectUri}",
    "applicationUrl": "https://localhost:5001;http://localhost:5000",
    "environmentVariables": {
      "ASPNETCORE_ENVIRONMENT": "Development"
    }
  }
}
```

The inspectUri property enables Blazor WebAssembly debugging in Visual Studio, Visual Studio for macOS, and Visual Studio Code.

The lines we've just added enable Blazor WebAssembly debugging in the Visual Studio family of IDEs and text editors. Currently, this feature isn't supported on other IDEs such as JetBrains Rider.

The `inspectUri` enables Visual Studio to recognize that it is running a Blazor WebAssembly app. It will then attempt to connect the script debugging infrastructure to Blazor's debugging proxy. You may notice that the value for the `inspectUri` has a few placeholders in it; these will be substituted by the framework during the debugging session and don't require any manual configuration.

The final piece of configuration we need to do is add a project reference from the BlazingTrails.Api project to the BlazingTrails.Web project, shown in figure A.3.

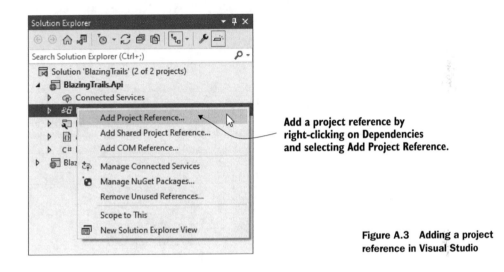

Add a project reference by right-clicking on Dependencies and selecting Add Project Reference.

Figure A.3   Adding a project reference in Visual Studio

Under the API project, right-click Dependencies and select Add Project Reference from the context menu. This will open the Reference Manager (figure A.4).

Select the BlazingTrails.Client project to establish the dependency. Then click OK.

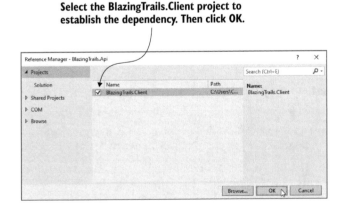

Figure A.4   The Reference Manager is used to configure project dependencies and other references such as DLLs.

In the Reference Manager, check the box next to the BlazingTrails.Client project and then click OK. This will configure the dependency.

Before we run the solution, we just need to set the API project as the startup project. To do this, right-click on the API project and select Set as Startup Project from the context menu. We can now run the application. If everything has gone well, we should see the Blazor application shown in figure A.5.

Note the application is running from the port of the API project.

Figure A.5   The running Blazor application being served by the new API project

If you check out the URL in the address bar, you'll see that the application is now running using the API project's port and not the Client project's port, as it was previously.

A.2   *Adding a .NET class library to share code between client and API*

With the API project in place and configured to serve the Blazor application, we're now going to add in a .NET class library. This library will be used to share code between the Client and API projects—one of the major advantages to building full-stack ASP.NET applications with Blazor.

We'll use the .NET CLI to create the project, just as we did with the API. Starting from the folder containing the solution file, we run the following command to generate the new project:

```
dotnet new classlib -n BlazingTrails.Shared
```

This will generate a new .NET class library called *BlazingTrails.Shared* and will put the files for it in a directory with the same name. We can then add it to the solution with the `sln add` command:

```
dotnet sln add BlazingTrails.Shared\BlazingTrails.Shared.csproj
```

At this point, if you swap back to Visual Studio, you should see the new project in the solution explorer (figure A.6). You may be prompted to reload the solution if it was open while you were running the CLI commands.

To access any shared code from either the Client or API projects, we need to set up project references between them and the Shared project. We do this the same way as we did earlier. Starting with the API project, right-click on the Dependencies node and select Add Project Reference... to bring up the Reference Manager dialog box (figure A.7).

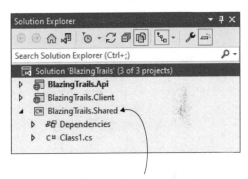

The new Shared project shown in Visual Studio's Solution Explorer

Figure A.6   The new Shared project is now part of the existing solution.

Check the box next to BlazingTrails.Shared to create the project reference. Then click OK.

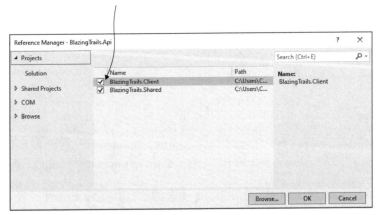

Figure A.7   Adding a project reference via the Reference Manager in Visual Studio

From the dialog box, check the box next to the BlazingTrails.Shared project and then click OK. This will create the project reference. We can then repeat this process for the Client project.

The final step for us to do is remove the Class1.cs file that is generated as part of the project. This is an empty class file and doesn't contain anything of any value. At this point, you should have an empty Shared project containing no files.

A.3   Setting up an SQLite database in the API

In this final section, we're going to complete the setup of our backend by configuring an SQLite database in the API project. I've chosen to use SQLite for this book, as it's a portable database that works cross-platform. You could easily swap this out for a database of your choice, be that SQL Server, MySQL, or whatever you prefer. To interact with the database, we'll use Entity Framework Core (http://mng.bz/aJKx), a popular object-relational mapper (ORM) from Microsoft.

First, we're going to create a new folder in the BlazingTrails.Api project called *Persistence*. This folder is going to contain all the infrastructure needed for the data layer of the application (figure A.8).

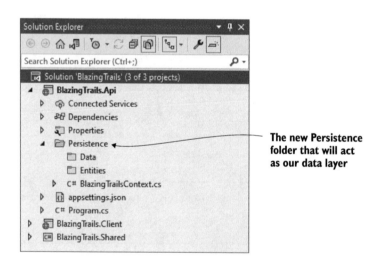

The new Persistence folder that will act as our data layer

Figure A.8   The new Persistence folder in the API project

Inside this folder, we create two more folders, *Data* and *Entities*. Finally, we will add a new class to the root of the Persistence folder called `BlazingTrailsContext.cs`.

We also need to add some NuGet packages. The following package references can be added directly to the BlazingTrails.Api.csproj file; alternatively, the packages can be added via the NuGet package manager GUI in Visual Studio:

```
<PackageReference
    Include="Microsoft.AspNetCore.Diagnostics.EntityFrameworkCore"
    Version="6.0.0" />
```

```
<PackageReference Include="Microsoft.EntityFrameworkCore.Tools"
    PrivateAssets="all" Version="6.0.0" />
<PackageReference Include="Microsoft.EntityFrameworkCore.Sqlite"
    Version="6.0.0" />
```

These commands will install Entity Framework Core, the EF Core SQLite provider, as well as some tooling to help us generate and manage migrations later on.

A.3.1   Configuring the initial entities for the system

Before we can do any work with the context, we need to create the initial entities for our system. We will create two entities called *Trail* and *RouteInstruction*. These are just going to be POCOs (Plain Old CLR Object), which represent the information we want to save to the database for each type.

Inside the Entities folder, create a class called `Trail.cs` and add in the following code.

Listing A.3   Trail.cs: `Trail` class

```
public class Trail
{
    public int Id { get; set; }
    public string Name { get; set; } = default!;
    public string Description { get; set; } = default!;
    public string? Image { get; set; }
    public string Location { get; set; } = default!;
    public int TimeInMinutes { get; set; }
    public int Length { get; set; }

    public ICollection<RouteInstruction> Route
    ➥{ get; set; } = default!         ◁──┐
}
```

> Route is a navigation property and will help create a one-to-many relationship between a Trail and RouteInstructions. Here we're saying a Trail has many RouteInstructions.

As you can see, there isn't a lot to this class; it just defines the properties that make up a trail. The only thing worth pointing out is the Route collection at the bottom. This is a navigation property and will help create a one-to-many relationship between a `Trail` and `RouteInstructions`. In the case of a `Trail`, we're saying that it can have many `RouteInstructions`.

Let's create a new class for `RouteInstruction` next. The code is shown in the following listing.

Listing A.4   RouteInstruction.cs: `RouteInstruction` class

```
public class RouteInstruction
{
    public int Id { get; set; }
    public int TrailId { get; set; }
    public int Stage { get; set; }
    public string Description { get; set; } = default!;

    public Trail Trail { get; set; } = default!;     ◁──┐
}
```

> Trail creates the other side of the one-to-many relationship. This states that each RouteInstruction can have one Trail.

In the code for `RouteInstruction`, we can see the other side of the one-to-many relationship being created. It states that a `RouteInstruction` can have only one `Trail`.

> **NOTE** This relationship is being created by convention, but you can also configure this relationship manually if you wish. That is out of scope for this book, but I would recommend checking out the Microsoft Docs site (http://mng.bz/XZYl), or picking up a copy of *Entity Framework Core in Action* by Jon Smith (http://mng.bz/yv97) to learn more.

Now that we have the initial entities created, we need to configure them for use with Entity Framework. This configuration will allow us to specify whether a property should be nullable in the database, or whether it should have a character limit, things like that. This can be achieved in a couple of ways.

The first is to use data attributes. These are used directly on the entity, and each property is decorated with attributes that tell Entity Framework how that column should be configured in the database table. For example, to make the `Name` property of the `Trail` class not nullable in the database, we use the following data attribute:

```
[Required]
public string Name { get; set; }
```

You can configure everything from field validations to the name of the column it maps to or even the table name. If you're interested in using this method for configuration, I would suggest reading the official docs page on the topic (http://mng.bz/M5gE).

The second way to configure an entity is to use a configuration class. I prefer this method, as I'm not a fan of data attributes. I also use DDD (domain-driven design) in a lot of my professional projects, and my domain entities shouldn't be cluttered with persistence concerns. With this method, all the configuration is done in a separate class, and the entity is ignorant of any of it.

In the case of small projects like Blazing Trails or in CRUD (create, read, update, delete) systems where DDD isn't being used, I lean toward keeping the configuration class in the same file as the entity. This makes updating it easier, and if the system grew more complex over time, I could easily refactor the configuration class out into its own file and move the entity to a domain project with very few issues.

We'll start by configuring the `Trail` entity first. Inside the Trail.cs file, we will add an additional class. This will go inside the namespace but outside the existing class. The code is shown in the following listing.

Listing A.5 Trail.cs: `TrailConfig` class

IEntityTypeConfiguration<T> allows us to specify the configuration for the entity defined as T.

IEntityType-Configuration<T> defines the Configure method; in here, rules can be specified for each property on the model.

```
public class TrailConfig : IEntityTypeConfiguration<Trail>
{
    public void Configure(EntityTypeBuilder<Trail> builder)
    {
        builder.Property(x => x.Name).IsRequired();
```

```
            builder.Property(x => x.Description).IsRequired();
            builder.Property(x => x.Location).IsRequired();
            builder.Property(x => x.TimeInMinutes).IsRequired();
            builder.Property(x => x.Length).IsRequired();
    }
}
```

To create a configuration file, we need to inherit from the `IEntityTypeConfiguration<T>` interface—T being the entity we want to configure. This interface requires us to implement a single method called `Configure`. In the `Configure` method, rules can be specified for each property on the entity. In the case of the code in listing A.5, all the properties, except `IsFavourite`, are being marked as required.

Now let's do the same for the `RouteInstruction` entity. Just as before, we'll add a new configuration class to the existing file. The code is shown in the following listing.

Listing A.6   RouteInstruction.cs: `RouteInstructionConfig` class

```
public class RouteInstructionConfig :
➥IEntityTypeConfiguration<RouteInstruction>     ◁───
{
    public void Configure(EntityTypeBuilder<RouteInstruction> builder)
    {
        builder.Property(x => x.TrailId).IsRequired();    ◁───
        builder.Property(x => x.Stage).IsRequired();
        builder.Property(x => x.Description).IsRequired();
    }
}
```

IEntityTypeConfiguration<T> allows us to specify the configuration for the entity defined as T.

IEntityTypeConfiguration<T> defines the Configure method; in here, rules can be specified for each property on the model.

As with the `Trail` configuration, we're implementing the `IEntityTypeConfiguration<T>` interface. In the `Configure` method, we're then specifying the rules we need. Once again, we're just setting a few of the properties as required.

A.3.2   Setting up the database context

With our entities set up and configured, we can turn our attention to the database context, `BlazingTrailsContext`. The database context is a combination of the Repository pattern and the Unit of Work pattern. In it, we essentially define collections of our entities using properties with a type of `DbSet<T>`. We can then inject it into our application and use it to access and modify data in the database. The following listing shows the updated code for the `BlazingTrailsContext` class.

Listing A.7   BlazingTrailsContext.cs

The DbContext class provides all the base functionality for the context. All database contexts must inherit from this class.

```
public class BlazingTrailsContext : DbContext     ◁───
{
    public DbSet<Trail> Trails => Set<Trail>();
    public DbSet<RouteInstruction> RouteInstructions =>
     Set<RouteInstruction>();
```

Each entity is represented as a collection with the type DbSet<T>. These are essentially repositories.

```
public BlazingTrailsContext(DbContextOptions<BlazingTrailsContext>
options) : base(options) { }

protected override void OnModelCreating(ModelBuilder modelBuilder)
{
    base.OnModelCreating(modelBuilder);

    modelBuilder.ApplyConfiguration(
        new TrailConfig());
    modelBuilder.ApplyConfiguration(
        new RouteInstructionConfig());
}
}
```

> By overriding the **OnModelCreating** method, we can hook up the entity configuration classes we created in the previous section.

To start, our context must inherit from the DbContext class. This class provides all the plumbing to interact with the database. Next, we need to define the collections of our entities. These are essentially repositories and provide a way for us to interact with the tables containing the entity data in the database.

The other thing to note in this class is the application of the entity configuration we created in the previous section. This is done by overriding the OnModelCreating method. In this method, we apply each configuration using the ModelBuilder object.

A.3.3   Connection strings and service configuration

The last step of configuration is to add a connection string to the appsettings.json file and add the required services to the service container. In the appsettings.json file, add the following just inside the final closing bracket:

```
"ConnectionStrings": {
  "BlazingTrailsContext": "DataSource=Persistence/Data/blazingtrails.db"
}
```

This will be used by Entity Framework to locate the database when attempting to save or retrieve data. It will also be used when first creating the database to know where to create it in the file system.

With the connection string set up, we just need to register the Entity Framework services with the services container in Program.cs. To do that, we need to call the AddDbContext<T>() method on the builder.Services property, as shown in the following code:

```
builder.Services.AddDbContext<BlazingTrailsContext>(options =>
    options.UseSqlite(builder.Configuration.GetConnectionString("BlazingTrai
    lsContext")));
builder.Services.AddControllers();
```

This method requires us to pass the type of context we're registering and specify which type of database we're using, along with the connection string we will use to connect to it. At this point, everything is configured and we're ready to generate our first migration and create the initial database.

A.3.4   Creating the first migration and creating the database

With the configuration done, we can now create the initial migration for our application. A migration contains two methods called Up and Down. The Up method contains the desired state of the database based on new changes. The Down method contains the instruction on how to reverse the Up method in case we need to revert the migration.

To create a migration, we can either use the Entity Framework Core tools, which are command-line based (https://docs.microsoft.com/en-us/ef/core/cli/dotnet), or we can use the Package Manager Console, if using Visual Studio on Windows. As I'm on Visual Studio, I will use the Package Manager. If you don't currently have this window open, you can open it by going to the main menu > View > Other Windows > Package Manager Console.

To create a migration, I will use the following command in the Package Manager Console, making sure that the default project is set to BlazingTrails.Api:

```
Add-Migration InitialEntities -o Persistence/Data/Migrations
```

After specifying the command name, Add-Migration, we then give the migration a name. I recommend using camel case to make this readable. Then we specify the output location for the migrations to be a folder called *Migrations* in the Persistence > Data location. Running the command will trigger a build of the application, and after a few seconds, the migration should be shown. Figure A.9 shows the new files and folders created in the API project.

Once the Add-Migration command has been run, a new Migrations folder is created, containing the new migration and a model snapshot, which Entity Framework autogenerates.

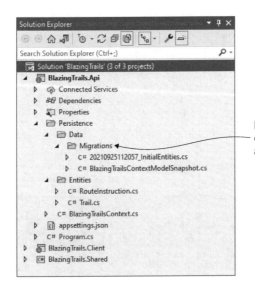

Running the Add-Migration command has created a new database migration.

Figure A.9   The new Migrations folder contains the initial migration.

Now that the migration is in place, we can create the initial database. To do this, we run the `Update-Database` command in the Package Manager Console. This will take the code in the migration we just created and generate a new database that contains two tables, Trails and RouteInstructions. If all goes as expected, then you should see the database appear in the Solution Explorer, as shown in figure A.10.

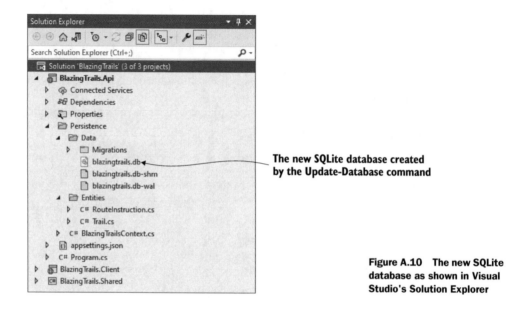

The new SQLite database created by the Update-Database command

Figure A.10   The new SQLite database as shown in Visual Studio's Solution Explorer

At this point, the backend of Blazing Trails is all ready to go! We've got a new API, and we've got a new database configured where we can store the trail data going forward.

appendix B
Updating existing areas to use the API

In this appendix, I'll take you through the steps needed to update the Home and Search features of Blazing Trails to load trail data from the new API created in chapter 5.

> **NOTE** We'll be working on the Blazing Trails application from its state at the end of chapter 6. If you're building along with the chapters in this book, you'll need to complete this appendix before moving on to chapter 7.

As part of this, we'll also add in a link to the home page to allow users to add new trails to the application. Then we'll update the `TrailCard` and `TrailDetails` components to load images from the API. Plus, we'll add a link on the `TrailCard` to allow users to update an existing trail.

B.1 Creating a new API endpoint that returns all trails

Currently, the `HomePage` and `SearchPage` components load trail data from a local file called *trail-data.json*, which is in the Web project's wwwroot folder. While this has been a quick and easy way to get some functionality built, we've now outgrown it. With the work completed in chapter 5 to add a new API to the solution, we now need those pages to get their trails from that API.

We will start in the Shared project and create a feature folder called *Home*. Inside that new folder, we'll create another folder called *Shared*. Inside this folder, we will add a new class called `GetTrailsRequest.cs` with the code in listing B.1.

Listing B.1   GetTrailsRequest.cs

```
public record GetTrailsRequest : IRequest<GetTrailsRequest.Response>
{
    public const string RouteTemplate = "/api/trails";

    public record Trail(int Id, string Name, string? Image,
    ➥string Location, int TimeInMinutes, int Length, string Description);
    public record Response(IEnumerable<Trail> Trails);                    ◄──┐
}
```
**The response of the request is a
collection of Trail records.**

The structure of requests should be looking quite familiar by now. We have the
RouteTemplate and then the response the request returns.

Moving on to the API project, let's create the new endpoint. We'll start by creating
the folder structure. Add a Home folder containing a folder called *Shared*. Inside the
Shared folder, create a class called GetTrailsEndpoint.cs using the following
code.

Listing B.2   GetTrailsEndpoint.cs

```
public class GetTrailsEndpoint : BaseAsyncEndpoint
.WithRequest<int>
.WithResponse<GetTrailsRequest.Response>
{
    private readonly BlazingTrailsContext _context;

    public GetTrailsEndpoint(BlazingTrailsContext context)
    {
        _context = context;
    }

    [HttpGet(GetTrailsRequest.RouteTemplate)]
    public override async
    ➥Task<ActionResult<GetTrailsRequest.Response>>
    ➥HandleAsync(int trailId, CancellationToken cancellationToken
    ➥= default)
    {
        var trails = await _context.Trails
        ➥.Include(x => x.Route)                    │ All trails are retrieved
        ➥.ToListAsync(cancellationToken);    ◄──┘ from the database.

        var response = new GetTrailsRequest
        ➥.Response(trails.Select(trail => new GetTrailsRequest.Trail(
            trail.Id,
            trail.Name,
            trail.Image,
            trail.Location,
            trail.TimeInMinutes,
            trail.Length,
            trail.Description          │ The response is created
        )));                     ◄──┘ from the list of trails.
```

```
        return Ok(response);
    }
}
```

Essentially, the endpoint loads the trails from the database, then creates the response. Notice that we're not including the route instructions, as they are not needed when displaying trail details on the home or search pages.

That is all the work we need to do in the Shared and API projects. We can now turn our attention to the Web project.

B.2 Updating the Home feature to load trail data from the API

Now that we have our new endpoint, we're going to update various components in the Home feature to load trail data from our new API endpoint. But before we do that, we could do with tidying up the feature folder a little.

Currently, there are a lot of files in the Home feature. This isn't a problem if they all belong there—but that isn't the case here. There is a subfeature that we created in chapter 4 that allows users to search for trails. By identifying subfeatures and moving them to their own folders, we can keep larger features organized and easy to navigate. Figure B.1 shows the current structure of the Home folder on the left and the reorganized structure on the right.

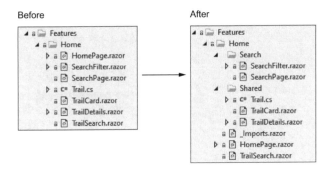

Figure B.1 The Home feature folder is reorganized using subfeatures to keep it tidy.

As you can see, the new structure clearly defines the Search subfeature. It also allows us to declare shared items. These are components, classes, or any other type of file for that matter, that are shared across the main feature and its subfeatures.

We'll start by creating the new Search folder, then move SearchFilter.razor and SearchPage.razor into it. Then we'll add the Shared folder, moving the Trail-Card.razor, TrailDetails.razor, and Trail.cs files into it.

By adding those subfolders, we've introduced extra namespaces. This is because, by default, Blazor components will use the folder structure they reside in to generate their namespace. This will cause some build errors. So, we're going to add a new component called _Imports.razor to the root of the Home folder with the following two lines:

```
@using BlazingTrails.Shared.Features.Home.Shared
@using BlazingTrails.Client.Features.Home.Shared
```

This will make the two namespaces above accessible to all the components and classes inside the Home folder. The first namespace is where the GetTrailsRequest class lives in the BlazingTrails.Shared project. The second namespace is the new Shared folder we just created in the BlazingTrails.Client project.

B.2.1   Adding the GetTrailsHandler class

Now that we've done some housekeeping, we can create the handler for the GetTrailsRequest. The handler will be added to the new Shared folder we just created. The code for the handler is shown in the following listing.

Listing B.3   GetTrailsHandler.cs

```
public class GetTrailsHandler :
    IRequestHandler<GetTrailsRequest, GetTrailsRequest.Response?>
{
    private readonly HttpClient _httpClient;

    public GetTrailsHandler(HttpClient httpClient)
    {
        _httpClient = httpClient;
    }

    public async Task<GetTrailsRequest.Response?>
        Handle(GetTrailsRequest request, CancellationToken cancellationToken)
    {
        try
        {
            return await _httpClient
                .GetFromJsonAsync<GetTrailsRequest.Response>(
                GetTrailsRequest.RouteTemplate);
        }
        catch (HttpRequestException)
        {
            return default!;
        }
    }
}
```

The request is made to the API. If successful, the response is deserialized and returned to the caller.

If the API returns a nonsuccess response code, a null response is returned to the caller.

The handler makes a call to the API, and if a success response is returned, the payload is automatically deserialized and returned to the caller. However, if a nonsuccess code is returned, an HttpRequestException is thrown. This is caught in the catch block, and a null response is returned to the caller.

B.2.2 Updating HomePage.razor and SearchPage.razor to use GetTrailRequest via MediatR

With the `GetTrailsHandler` in place, we can update the Home and Search pages to get trails from the API. To do this, we'll update them to dispatch a `GetTrails-Request` via MediatR. We'll start by updating HomePage.razor, as shown in the following listing.

Listing B.4 HomePage.razor: Update to use MediatR

```
@inject IMediator Mediator              ⟵─┐ Adds the injection
                                           │ of IMediator
// Code omitted for brevity

@code {
    // Code omitted for brevity

    protected override async Task OnInitializedAsync()
    {
        try
        {                                                    Dispatches the
            var response = await Mediator                    GetTrailsRequest
            ➥ .Send(new GetTrailsRequest());      ⟵──        using Mediator
            _trails = response.Trails.Select(x => new Trail
            {
                Id = x.Id,
                Name = x.Name,
                Image = x.Image,
                Description = x.Description,
                Location = x.Location,
                Length = x.Length,
                TimeInMinutes = x.TimeInMinutes
            });
        }
        catch (HttpRequestException ex)
        {
            Console.WriteLine($"There was a problem loading trail data:
            ➥ {ex.Message}");
        }
    }

    // Code omitted for brevity
}
```

We start by removing the injection of the `HttpClient`; we no longer need this, as we'll be dispatching our request using MediatR. We then inject an instance of IMediator into the component.

Down in the code block, we replace the existing `OnInitializedAsync` method. In this version, we dispatch the `GetTrailsRequest` via MediatR. We then use projection to transform the data in the response into the format we require in the component.

As we are now loading trails from the API, we should cover the scenario where there could be no trails to display. Currently, the home page would just be blank if there were no trails. Figure B.2 shows what the home page will look like once we've made our changes.

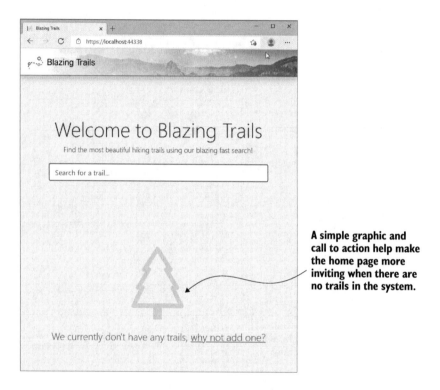

A simple graphic and call to action help make the home page more inviting when there are no trails in the system.

Figure B.2   The call-to-action section, which is displayed when the application has no existing trails

To achieve this, we're going to make an update to the markup section of the Home-Page component. The update is shown in the following listing.

Listing B.5   HomePage.razor: Displaying call to action when there are no trails

```
// Code omitted for brevity
@if (_trails.Any())                          Checks to see if
{                                            there are any trails
    <div class="mb-4">
        <p class="font-italic text-center">Do you have      This new link to add a trail is
        ➥an awesome trail you'd like to share?              shown at the top of the grid
        ➥<a href="add-trail">Add it here</a>.</p>           displaying existing trails.
    </div>
```

```
    <div class="grid">
        @foreach (var trail in _trails)
        {
            <TrailCard Trail="trail" OnSelected="HandleTrailSelected" />
        }
    </div>
}
else
{
    <div class="no-trails">
        <svg viewBox="0 0 16 16" class="bi bi-tree" fill="currentColor"
          xmlns="http://www.w3.org/2000/svg">
            <path fill-rule="evenodd" d="M8 0a.5.5 0 0 1 .416.22313
  4.5A.5.5 0 0 1 11 5.5h-.09812.022 3.235a.5.5 0 0 1-.424.765h-.19111.638
  3.276a.5.5 0 0 1-.447.724h-11a.5.5 0 0 1-.447-.724L3.69 9.5H3.5a.5.5 0
  0 1-.424-.765L5.098 5.5H5a.5.5 0 0 1-.416-.77713-4.5A.5.5 0 0 1 8
  0zM5.934 4.5H6a.5.5 0 0 1 .424.765L4.402 8.5H4.5a.5.5 0 0 1 .447.724L3.31
  12.5h9.3821-1.638-3.276A.5.5 0 0 1 11.5 8.5h.098L9.576 5.265A.5.5 0 0
  1 10 4.5h.066L8 1.401 5.934 4.5z" />
            <path d="M7 13.5h2V16H7v-2.5z" />
        </svg>
        <h3 class="text-muted font-weight-light">
          We currently don't have any trails,
          <a href="add-trail">why not add one?</a></h3>     ◁─┐  This is the call to
    </div>                                                      │  action to add a trail.
}
// Code omitted for brevity
```

We start by adding a check to see if there are any trails to display. If there are, we reuse the original code for displaying the trails—with an additional link to allow users to add new trails.

If no trails are present, then we display an SVG, which is the tree outline we saw in figure B.2. Feel free to replace this with whatever image you prefer. Underneath the SVG is a call to action prompting the user to add a new trail.

To finish things off, we will add a couple of styles to the home page. To do this, we need to add a new SCSS file to the Home feature folder called *HomePage.razor.scss*. Then we can add the following code.

Listing B.6   HomePage.razor.scss

```
.no-trails {                    ◁─┐  This is applied to the container
    text-align: center;            │  of the call-to-action markup.
    margin-top: 100px;

    svg {                       ◁─┐  Shows the styling
        width: 200px;              │  for the SVG image
        color: #dee2e6;
        margin-bottom: 30px;
    }
}
```

The two classes apply some basic styling to the new call-to-action markup. The `no-trails` class center aligns the content and adds a top margin. The `svg` class sets the width of the SVG, as well as its color and bottom margin.

Now that the `HomePage` is updated, let's update the `SearchPage`. The updates are shown in the following listing.

Listing B.7 SearchPage.razor: Update to use MediatR

```
@inject HttpClient Http                          ← Removes the HttpClient injection from the file
@inject IMediator Mediator        ← Adds the injection of IMediator
// Code omitted for brevity
@code {
    // Code omitted for brevity
    protected override async Task OnInitializedAsync()
    {
        try
        {
            var response = await Mediator
            .Send(new GetTrailsRequest());          ← Dispatches the GetTrailsRequest using Mediator
            var allTrails = response.Trails.Select(x => new Trail
            {
                Id = x.Id,
                Name = x.Name,
                Image = x.Image,
                Description = x.Description,
                Location = x.Location,
                Length = x.Length,
                TimeInMinutes = x.TimeInMinutes
            });

            _searchResults = allTrails.Where(x => x.Name
.Contains(SearchTerm, StringComparison.CurrentCultureIgnoreCase)
                                || x.Location
.Contains(SearchTerm, StringComparison.CurrentCultureIgnoreCase));
            _cachedSearchResults = _searchResults;

            UpdateFilters();
        }
        catch (HttpRequestException ex)
        {
            Console.WriteLine($"There was a problem loading trail data:
            {ex.Message}");
        }
    }
    // Code omitted for brevity
}
```

We're performing the exact same changes here as we just did in the `HomePage` component. First, we remove the `HttpClient` and instead inject an instance of `IMediator`. Then we update the code block to dispatch the `GetTrailsRequest` using MediatR. Finally, we use projection to transform the trails returned from the API into the form we need for the component.

B.2.3 Updating TrailCard.razor and TrailDetails.razor

The final update we need to make is to the `TrailCard` and `TrailDetails` components. They both display the trail image, but they need to be updated to load the image from the images folder exposed by the API project.

As trail images are optional, we'll also add in a check. If the trail doesn't have an image, we're going to display a placeholder image using a free service from placeholder.com. This service allows us to dynamically generate an image at the correct size by using a specially formatted URL. For example, the following URL generates a 400 by 200 pixel image in jpg format:

```
https://via.placeholder.com/400x200.jpg
```

Services like this can be very useful when prototyping, in early stage development, or for scenarios like ours where we need a default image when one isn't provided. When we're done, any trail without an image will display the image shown in figure B.3.

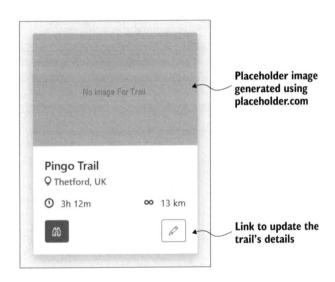

Placeholder image generated using placeholder.com

Link to update the trail's details

Figure B.3   Updates to the TrailCard component

As you can also see from figure B.3, we'll add in a new button that will link to the Edit Trail page we created in chapter 6. This will allow users to update an existing trail.

Let's get started. We'll tackle the `TrailCard` first. It currently displays the trail image using this code:

```
<img src="@Trail?.Image" />
```

We're going to update this line to the following:

```
<img src="@(!string.IsNullOrWhiteSpace(Trail.Image) ? $"images/{Trail.Image}"
    : "https://via.placeholder.com/286x190.jpg?text=No+Image+For+Trail")"
    class="card-img-top">
```

This new code starts by checking if the trail has an image associated with it. If it does, then we output the string `images/{filename}`. However, if the trail doesn't have an image, we output a string that is the URL to load our placeholder image. We'll also use an additional feature of placeholder.com that allows us to specify a message to be displayed in the image. In this case we're adding the text `No Image for Trail`.

Now we can add the new update button. We're going to need the `Navigation-Manager` so we can use its `NavigateTo` method when the button is clicked to programmatically navigate to the Edit Trail page. So, let's inject that at the top of the component:

```
@inject NavigationManager NavManager
```

Then we can add the following line of code directly underneath the existing View button.

```
<button class="btn btn-outline-secondary float-right" title="Edit"
    @onclick="@(() => NavManager.NavigateTo($"/edit-trail/
    {Trail.Id}"))">Update</button>
```

When the button is clicked, the user will navigate to the Edit Trail page. We're passing the ID of the trail we wish to edit using a route parameter.

That's it for the `TrailCard` component. We can now update the `TrailDetails` component. The only thing we need to change here is how the image is loaded. Just like the `TrailCard`, the `TrailDetails` is currently loading the trail image using the following code:

```
<img src="@_activeTrail.Image" />
```

And we can update it to use the same code as we used in the `TrailCard`:

```
<img src="@(!string.IsNullOrWhiteSpace(_activeTrail.Image) ? $"images/
    {_activeTrail.Image}" : "https://via.placeholder.com/
    286x190.jpg?text=No+Image+For+Trail")" class="card-img-top">
```

With that, our updates are complete. All that is left to do is remove the old test data from the Trails folder inside wwwroot. The whole Trails directory can be deleted along with everything inside it.

index

Symbols

@attributes directive 238
@bind directive 89, 116–117
@code block 41–43
@implements directive 60
@inherits directive 37
@layout directive 37
@onclick event 69
@page attribute 238
@page directive 32, 39, 88
@ref directive 162
@typeparam directive 186
#blazor-error-ui .dismiss class 33
#blazor-error-ui class 33

A

AAA (arrange, act, assert)
    pattern 279
AbstractValidator<T> class 124
accept attribute 152, 158
AccountClaimsPrincipalFactory
    class 248
Actiontype 69
Add Trail feature 233
Add-Migration command 303
AddAccountClaimsPrincipal-
    Factory extension
    method 249
AddAuthentication method 230
AddBlazoredLocalStorage
    extension method 279
AddDbContext() method 302
AddFavorite method 263, 265

AddHttpClient extension
    method 242
AdditionalAssemblies
    parameter 86
AddJwtBearer method 230
AddOidcAuthentication
    method 227, 231, 249
AddTrail subfeature 159
AddTrailEndpoint 150, 239
AddTrailEndpoint.cs class 137
AddTrailHandler.cs class 134
AddTrailPage.razor 112, 135,
    161–165
AddTrailRequest type 135
addTrails variable
    declaration 236
Administrator role 245
AdminLayout 37
AOT (ahead-of-time) mode 9
API endpoints
    adding 156–158
    calling secure endpoints from
        Blazor 241–245
    for GetTrailRequest and
        EditTrailRequest 174–177
    returning all trails 305–307
    securing 239–241
    setting up 136–139
APIs (application programming
    interfaces)
    ASP.NET Core Web API
    291–296
        configuring 293–296
        removing boilerplate from
            new API project 293
    posting form data to 132–136

SQLite database in 298–304
    configuring initial entities
        for system 299–301
    connection strings and ser-
        vice configuration 302
    creating first migration and
        creating database
        303–304
    setting up database
        context 301–302
    updating existing areas to
        use 305–314
    creating new API endpoint
        that returns all
        trails 305–307
    updating Home feature to
        load trail data from
        API 307–314
App component 28–30, 85, 270
app.MapControllers()
    method 230
App.razor 29–30
app.UseRouting() method 230
AppAssembly parameter 86
AppState
    improving design 258–260
    initializing 270–271
    saving data entered on form
        to 255–258
aria attribute 127
arrange, act, assert (AAA)
    pattern 279
ASP.NET Core 291–304
    adding .NET class library to
        share code between client
        and API 296–298

ASP.NET Core *(continued)*
adding ASP.NET Core Web
API 291–296
setting up SQLite database in
API 298–304
ASP.NET Core Web API 291–296
configuring API 293–296
configuring to use Auth0
identity provider 229–230
removing boilerplate from
new API project 293
ASPNETCORE_ENVIRON-
MENT variable 226
async lifecycle method 58–60
Auth0 identity provider 223–230
adding roles in 245–247
configuring ASP.NET Core
WebAPI to use 229–230
configuring Blazor Web-
Assembly to use 225–229
consuming roles in Blazor
WebAssembly 247–249
customizing tokens
from 224–225
registering applications
with 224
authentication
displaying different UI fragments based on status
230–238
faking 283–285
Authentication.razor 228
authorization 245–252
adding roles in Auth0
245–247
consuming Auth0 roles in
Blazor WebAssembly
247–249
faking 283–285
implementing role-based
logic 249–252
preventing unauthorized
users access to pages
238–245
calling secure API end-
points from Blazor
241–245
securing API
endpoints 239–241
Authorize attribute 228, 238,
251–252
authorized keyword 231
Authorized template 231
authorizedUser variable 284

AuthorizeRouteView
component 228, 238–239
AuthorizeView component 231,
235–236, 251
Authorizing template 228
AutoFixture package 276

B

base.CreateUserAsync()
method 249
BaseAddressAuthorization-
MessageHandler
handler 242
BaseAsyncEndpoint class
137–138
BeginSignOut method 231
bind directive 90, 118, 147, 152
Blazing Trails application 18–48
building and running 24–25
components of 25–30
App.razor 29–30
Index.html 25–26
Program.cs 27–29
wwwroot folder and
_Imports.razor 30
securing 221–252
authorizing users by
role 245–252
displaying different UI fragments based on authen-
tication status 230–238
integrating with identity
provider 223–230
prevent unauthorized users
accessing page 238–245
setting up 19–24
Blazor WebAssembly tem-
plate configurations
20–21
creating application 21–24
testing with bUnit 272–290
adding bUnit test
project 274–277
overview 273–274
testing components with
bUnit 277–289
writing components 30–48
Blazing Trails home
page 38–48
defining layout 36–38
organizing files using feature folders 31–34
setting up styling 34–36

BlazingTrails.Shared class
library 297
BlazingTrailsContext class 212,
298, 301
Blazor 1–17
adding MediatR to 132
as platform for building UIs
with C# 5–17
Blazor Server 11–16
Blazor WebAssembly 7–11
hosting models 6, 16–17
calling secure API endpoints
from 241–245
choosing, reasons for 2–3
components 3–5
anatomy of 4–5
benefits of component-
based UI 4
defined 3–4
Fluent Validation, configuring for 125–130
router 85–87
Blazor Hybrid 16
Blazor Server 11–16
benefits and tradeoffs 15–16
calculating UI updates 13–14
performance 14–15
Blazor WebAssembly 7–11,
291–304
adding .NET class library to
share code between client
and API 296–298
adding ASP.NET Core Web
API 291–296
configuring API 293–296
removing boilerplate from
new API project 293
benefits and tradeoffs 10–11
calculating UI updates 9–10
configuring to use Auth0
identity provider 225–229
consuming Auth0 roles
in 247–249
setting up SQLite database in
API 298–304
configuring initial entities
for system 299–301
connection strings and service configuration 302
creating first migration and
creating database
303–304
setting up database
context 301–302
template configurations
20–21
blazor.webassembly.js script 227

Blazored.LocalStorage.Test-
Extensions package 276
Body parameter 36–37
boilerplate code, removing 293
browser local storage, persistent
state with 260–271
adding and removing trails
from favorites list 264–265
defining additional state
store 261–263
displaying current number of
favorite trails 265–266
initializing AppState 270–271
reorganizing and
refactoring 266–268
showing favorited trails on
favorite trails page 268–270
Build method 29
builder.RootComponents.Add
method 28
builder.Services property 302
bUnit testing 272–290
adding test project 274–277
overview 273–274
testing components with
277–289
emulating JavaScript
interactions 285–287
faking authentication and
authorization 283–285
testing multiple
components 287–289
testing rendered
markup 278–281
triggering event
handlers 281–283

C

C# 5–17
Blazor Server 11–16
benefits and tradeoffs
15–16
calculating UI updates
13–14
performance 14–15
Blazor WebAssembly 7–11
benefits and tradeoffs
10–11
calculating UI updates 9–10
calling JavaScript functions
and returning
response 200–203
calling methods from
JavaScript 203–205

hosting models 16–17
Blazor Hybrid 16
Mobile Blazor Bindings
16–17
overview 6
card component markup 173
.card-brand class 115
CascadingAuthenticationState
component 228
child components 62–71
passing data to parent 68–71
passing values from parent
to 64–68
TrailDetails
component 64–66
updating HomePage
component 67–68
ChildContent parameter 115,
267
claims-based authorization 225
ClaimsIdentity type 224
ClaimsPrincipal type 224
ClearSearchFilter method 103
ClearTrail method 255, 258
Click method 282
client-side routing 85–89
Blazor's router 85–87
page components 88–89
code security 11, 15
code sharing 3, 11
col class 118
CompileScopedCSS 81
component parameters 62
ComponentBase class 56, 60
components 3–5, 25–30, 49–83
anatomy of Blazor 4–5
App.razor 29–30
benefits of component-based
UI 4
Blazing Trails application,
writing 30–48
Blazing Trails home
page 38–48
defining layout 36–38
organizing files using feature folders 31–34
setting up styling 34–36
creating JavaScript module
and accessing via 195–203
calling JavaScript functions
from C# and returning
response 200–203
testing out RouteMap
component 199–200
defined 3–4

forms 110–122
basic EditForm
configuration 112–115
collecting data with input
components 115–120
creating inputs on
demand 120–122
creating model 111–112
handling multiple routes with
single 96–101
Index.html 25–26
life cycle methods 54–62
Dispose method 60–62
first render 57–58
with async 58–60
page components 88–89
Program.cs 27–29
reusing 180–193
Razor class libraries 189–192
templates 181–189
structuring 51–54
partial class 52–54
single file 51–52
styling 71–82
global styling 72–73
scoped styling 73–76
using CSS
preprocessors 76–82
testing with bUnit 277–289
emulating JavaScript
interactions 285–287
faking authentication and
authorization 283–285
testing multiple
components 287–289
testing rendered
markup 278–281
triggering event
handlers 281–283
working with parent and child
components 62–71
passing data from child to
parent 68–71
passing values from parent
to child 64–68
wwwroot folder and
_Imports.razor 30
Configure method 29, 301
ConfigureServices method 29
connection strings 302
Context attribute 188
context parameter 187–189
context variable 235
Counter.razor project
template 4

Create method 204
CSRF (cross-site request forgery)
attacks 231
CSS classes 141–144
creating
FieldCssClassProvider
141–143
using custom FieldCssClass-
Providers with
EditForm 143–144
CSS preprocessors 76–82
CSS variables 36
CssClass property 149
CurrentValue property 146, 148
CurrentValueAsString
property 146
Customize Tokens rule 247

D

data
collecting with input
components 115–120
passing between pages using
route parameters 92–96
passing from child to parent
components 68–71
saving data entered on form
to AppState 255–258
submitting to server 130–139
adding MediatR to Blazor
project 132
creating request and han-
dler to post form data to
API 132–136
setting up endpoint
136–139
Data folder 298
data transfer objects (DTOs) 3
DataAnnotationsValidator
component 111, 123
DB Browser for SQLite tool 178
DbContext class 302
DDD (domain-driven
design) 300
delete function 201
deleteLastWaypoint
function 200, 202, 208, 287
DeleteLastWaypoint
method 202, 207
Dependencies node 297
DI (dependency injection) 28
display: flex layout feature 149
Dispose method 60–62
div element 266

domain-driven design
(DDD) 300
dotnet build command 24
dotnet restore command 24
dotnet run command 24
dotnet watch command 24
DotNetObjectReference
class 204
DotNetObjectReference<T>
class 204
Down method 303
.drawer class 66, 75–76
.drawer-wrapper.slide > .drawer
class 66
DTOs (data transfer objects) 3

E

E2E testing (end-to-end
testing) 273
edit trail feature 165–177
adding API endpoints for
GetTrailRequest and
EditTrailRequest 174–177
adding EditTrailPage to client
project 167–171
adding GetTrailRequest and
EditTrailRequest
handlers 173–174
adding new EditTrailRequest
and GetTrailRequest to
shared project 166–167
updating shared project's
folder structure 166
updating TrailDto class
165–166
updating TrailForm to handle
editing 171–173
EditContext instance 143
EditForm component 108,
111–115, 125–126, 136,
143–144, 160–162, 256
EditForm tag 116, 126
EditForm's OnValidSubmit
event 161
editing forms 159–178
adding edit trail feature
165–177
adding API endpoints for
GetTrailRequest and
EditTrailRequest
174–177
adding EditTrailPage to client project 167–171
adding GetTrailRequest and

EditTrailRequest
handlers 173–174
adding new EditTrailRe-
quest and GetTrailRe-
quest to shared
project 166–167
updating shared project's
folder structure 166
updating TrailDto
class 165–166
updating TrailForm to handle editing 171–173
refactoring AddTrailPage
.razor 161–165
separating trail form into
standalone
component 159–161
testing edit functionality
177–178
EditorRequired attribute 46, 65
EditTrail subfeature 159
EditTrailEndpoint
endpoint 239–240, 249
EditTrailPage 167–171
EditTrailPage > SubmitEditTrail
method 172
EditTrailPage.razor 167
EditTrailRequest
adding handlers 173–174
adding to shared project
166–167
API endpoints for 174–177
EF (Entity Framework) 213
end-to-end testing (E2E
testing) 273
Entities folder 298
Entity Framework Core in Action
(Smith) 300
ErrorAlert component 163, 180
existingWaypoints
parameter 208
export keyword 197

F

faking authentication and
authorization 283–285
Fast load time 15
favorite trails page
adding and removing trails
from 264–265
displaying current number of
favorite trails 265–266
showing favorited trails
on 268–270

FavoriteButton component 264, 267, 278, 281
FavoriteButtonTests.razor component 278
FavoriteTrailsPage.razor component 268
FavoriteTrailsState class 261
feature folders 31–34
Features project 33
FieldCssClassProvider
    creating 141–143
    using with EditForm 143–144
File property 154
FileCount property 152
files 151–158
    configuring InputFile component 151–153
    uploading when form is submitted 153–158
        adding API endpoint 156–158
        building request and handler 154–156
        testing everything out 158
FilterSearchResults method 102
Find method 282
FindAll method 282
FindComponent method 289
FindComponents method 289
firstRender parameter 271
fitBounds function 208
Fixture class 279
fixture.Createmethod 280
flows 223
Fluent Validation
    configuring Blazor to use 125–130
    configuring validation rules with 123–125
FluentValidationsValidator component 126
For parameter 127
form submit event 110
FormFieldSet component 118, 180–181
FormFieldSet.razor component 118
forms 108–179
    building custom input components with InputBase 145–151
        inheriting from InputBase 145–148
        styling custom component 148–149

using custom input component 149–151
    customizing validation CSS classes 141–144
        creating FieldCssClassProvider 1 41–143
        using custom FieldCssClass-Providers with EditForm 143–144
    submitting data to server 130–139
        adding MediatR to Blazor project 132
        creating request and handler to post form data to API 132–136
        setting up endpoint 136–139
    super-charging with components 110–122
        basic EditForm configuration 112–115
        collecting data with input components 115–120
        creating inputs on demand 120–122
        creating model 111–112
    updating to allow editing 159–178
        adding edit trail feature 165–177
        refactoring AddTrailPage.razor 161–165
        separating trail form into standalone component 159–161
        testing edit functionality 177–178
    validating model 123–130
        configuring Blazor to use Fluent Validation 125–130
        configuring validation rules with Fluent Validation 123–125
    working with files 151–158
        configuring InputFile component 151–153
        uploading when form is submitted 153–158
FormSection component 115, 117, 180–181
FormStateTracker class 256, 259

FormStateTracker component 257

G

generics 185–189
GetFieldCssClass method 142
GetFromJsonAsync method 42, 44
GetMultipleFiles method 152
GetTrail method 255
GetTrailEndpoint endpoint 239, 249
GetTrailRequest
    adding handlers 173–174
    adding to shared project 166–167
    API endpoints for 174–177
    updating HomePage.razor and SearchPage.razor to use 309–312
GetTrailRequest.Response 176
GetTrailsEndpoint.cs class 306
GetTrailsHandler class 308
GetTrailsRequest class 305, 308
GetUriWithQueryParameters method 102–103
GetValidationMessages method 142
global styling
    overview 72–73
    scoped styling and 75–76

H

Handle method 134, 243
HandleAsync method 138, 150, 213–214
Handler method 69
handlers
    adding GetTrailRequest and EditTrailRequest 173–174
    creating to post form data to API 132–136
    triggering event 281–283
    uploading files 154–156
HandleTrailSelected method 71
head element 28, 36
Header component 38–39, 232
headless browser 273
HeadOutlet component 28
HelpText parameter 115
Home feature 262
    loading trail data from API 307–314

Home feature *(continued)*
adding GetTrailsHandler class 308
HomePage.razor and SearchPage.razor to use GetTrailRequest via MediatR 309–312
TrailCard.razor and Trail-Details.razor 313–314
updating 233–238
Home folder 33, 305
HomePage component 52, 63, 68, 70, 90, 234–235, 250, 264–265, 268, 287, 289, 305, 310, 312
updating 67–68
writing components for 38–48
HomePage.razor 33, 218, 309–312
HomePage.razor.scss SCSS file 311
hosted mode 20
hostElement parameter 197
hosting models 16–17
Blazor Hybrid 16
Mobile Blazor Bindings 16–17
overview 6
HttpClient instance 242
HttpRequestException type 42

I

IAsyncDisposable interface 61, 199
IBrowserFile type 155
id attribute 26
Id property 257
identity provider 223–230
configuring ASP.NET Core WebAPI to use Auth0 229–230
configuring Blazor WebAssembly to use Auth0 225–229
customizing tokens from Auth0 224–225
registering applications with Auth0 224
IDisposable interface 60–61, 205
IdP (identity provider) 222
IEntityTypeConfiguration interface 301
IEnumerable private field type 42

if statement 44, 168, 217
IJSRuntime 198, 285
Image property 166, 171, 173, 177
ImageAction property 166, 170, 172
Images folder 34
ImageSharp package 156
_Imports.razor 30, 308
_Imports.razor component 112
in-memory store 254–258
creating and registering state store 254–255
saving data entered on form to AppState 255–258
Index.html 25–26
inheriting from InputBase 145–148
inherits directive 146
initialize function 197–198, 205, 207, 216, 286
Initialize method 263, 270
Inject attribute 41, 135, 256
input components
collecting data with 115–120
customizing with InputBase 145–151
inheriting from InputBase 145–148
styling custom component 148–149
using custom input component 149–151
InputFile component 151–153, 158, 172–173
InputNumber component 120
InputRouteMap.razor component 209
inputs, on demand 120–122
InputText component 116, 120–121
InputTextArea component 116, 120
InputTime component 145, 151
:int route constraint 97
int type parameter 146
integration testing 273
invalid class 127–128
InvokeAsync method 198
InvokeAsync<T> method 200, 202
InvokeMethodAsync function 205
InvokeVoidAsync method 198, 200, 286

is-invalid CSS class 142
is-valid CSS class 142
IsFavorite method 263–264, 282
IsInRole helper method 250
IsModified method 142
IsReadOnly parameter 216
isValid variable 142
Items parameter 186–187

J

JavaScript 194–220
calling C# methods from 203–205
creating module and accessing via component 195–203
calling JavaScript functions from C# and returning response 200–203
testing out RouteMap component 199–200
displaying RouteMap on Trail-Details drawer 214–219
integrating RouteMap component with TrailForm 206–214
testing with bUnit 285–287
JSInterop mode 289
JWTs (JSON Web Tokens) 230

K

keydown event 69

L

latency 15
Latitude property 212
LatLong object 207
LatLong type 207
launchUrl property 293
layout 36–38
Layout folder 33
LayoutComponentBase class 37
Length property 129
life cycle methods 54–62
Dispose method 60–62
first render 57–58
with async 58–60
Lifecycle component 58
Lifecycle.razor component 58
Load time 11
LoadTrailImage method 152, 161, 173
LocationChanged event 87

LoginStatus component 232
LogOut template 229
Longitude property 212
loose mode 285

M

Main method 28–29
MainLayout component 33, 37–38
ManageTrails feature 145, 155, 159, 209, 242
Map component 196
MapFallbackToFile endpoint 294
MarkupMatches method 280–281
MAUI (.NET Multi-platform App UI framework) 6
max attribute 146
MaxLength route parameter 96
MaxTime parameter 103
MaxTime property 103
Mediator service 135
MediatR 132, 309–312
migration, creating first 303–304
Migrations folder 303
min attribute 146
mixins 76
Mobile Blazor Bindings 16–17
Model parameter 143
ModelBuilder object 302
modified class 128
MultipartFormDataContent object 155
multiple attribute 152
MVVM (model-view-viewmodel) 3

N

Name parameter 278
Name property 124–125, 224, 231, 300
NavigateTo method 314
NavigationManager JavaScript service 86
NavigationManager.NavigateTo method 89, 98, 103
nesting 76
.NET class library 296–298
.NET Ecosystem 2
.NET Multi-platform App UI framework (MAUI) 6
NewTrailState class 258

no-trails class 312
NotAuthorized template 228, 231, 238–239
NotEmpty() method 125
NotFound template 87, 92
NotifyStateHasChanged private method 262
NoTrails component 267–269
npm —version command 81
NPM (Node package manager) 77
npm install command 82
NpmLastInstall property 81
NRTs (nullable references types) 43
null forgiving operator (!) 47

O

-o switch 23
OIDC (OpenID Connect) 222
Ok() helper method 138
OnAfterRender method 42, 57–58
OnAfterRenderAsync method 198, 271
OnChange event 90, 147, 152, 262, 266, 269
onclick event 197, 202
OnFieldChanged event 143, 257
OnFieldChanged handler 259
OnInitialized method 57, 161, 171
OnInitializedAsync method 42, 57–59, 100, 143, 234, 236, 271, 309
oninput event 90
OnInvalidSubmit event 111, 113
OnModelCreating method 302
OnParametersSet method 42, 57, 59, 65, 100, 104, 148, 171, 210–211, 258–259
OnParametersSetAsync method 57
OnSelected event 63, 71
OnSubmit component event 161
OnSubmit event 111, 113, 161, 168
OnValidationStateChanged event 143
OnValidSubmit event 111, 113
OnWaypointAdded event 207, 210

OnWaypointAdded parameter 207
OnWaypointDeleted event 207, 210
OnWaypointDeleted parameter 207
OpenID Connect (OIDC) 222
OpenReadStream method 155
Owner property 233–234, 284

P

page components 86, 88–89
page directive 5, 86
pages
    navigating between programmatically 89–92
    passing data between pages using route parameters 92–96
    preventing unauthorized users access to 238–245
        calling secure API endpoints from Blazor 241–245
        securing API endpoints 239–241
PageTitle component 45
Parameter attribute 46, 65, 103
parameters 4, 46
parent components 62–71
    passing data from child to 68–71
    passing values to child 64–68
        TrailDetails component 64–66
        updating HomePage component 67–68
partial class format 52–54
partial keyword 52
Persistence project 298
persistent state with browser local storage 260–271
    adding and removing trails from favorites list 264–265
    defining additional state store 261–263
    displaying current number of favorite trails 265–266
    initializing AppState 270–271
    reorganizing and refactoring 266–268
    showing favorited trails on favorite trails page 268–270

PKCE (Proof of Key for Code Exchange) 223
POCOs (Plain Old CLR Object) 299
positional construction 154
PostAsJsonAsync extension method 42
ProcessImage method 153, 170
Program class 27–29
Program.Main method 28–29, 132, 231, 242, 249, 261
programmatic navigation 89–92
PropertyGroup section 81
PutAsJsonAsync extension method 42

Q

query strings 101–107
    retrieving values using SupplyParameterFrom-Query 103–107
    setting values 101–103

R

RCLs (Razor class libraries) 189–192
refactoring
    AddTrailPage.razor 161–165
    persistent state with browser local storage 266–268
registering
    applications 224
    state store 254–255
RegisterValidatorsFrom-Assembly configuration option 124
RemoteAuthenticatorView component 229
RemoteUserAccount type 249
RemoveFavorite method 263, 265
Render method 280
RenderComponent method 278
rendering
    first 57–58
    testing rendered markup 278–281
Request object 157
requests
    creating to post form data to API 132–136
    uploading files 154–156
required text property 123

ResetForm method 161, 258–259
reusing components 180–193
    Razor class libraries 189–192
    templates
        defined 181–185
        enhancing with generics 185–189
Rider third-party IDE 2
roles 222, 245
routable components 5, 86
Route collection 125, 130
route constraint 96
Route list 121–122
Route property 122, 210–212, 214
RouteInstruction class 39, 112, 210, 212
RouteInstruction entity 299, 301
RouteInstruction nested class 125
RouteInstruction type 214
RouteInstructions property 213
RouteInstructions table 213
RouteInstructionValidator class 211
RouteMap component 195–199, 201, 203–205, 285–286, 289
    displaying on TrailDetails drawer 214–219
    integrating with TrailForm 206–214
    testing out 199–200
routeMap JavaScript module 202, 286
routeMap module 198, 286
RouteMap.razor component 197
Router component 29–30, 37, 85–86
RouteView component 228, 238
routing 84–107
    client-side routing 85–89
        Blazor's router 85–87
        page components 88–89
    handling multiple routes with single component 96–101
    navigating between pages programmatically 89–92
    passing data between pages using route parameters 92–96
    working with query strings 101–107

retrieving values using SupplyParameterFrom-Query 103–107
setting values 101–103
RuleFor method 124
RunNpmInstall 81

S

Sass (syntactically awesome style sheets) 73
SaveTrail method 255
Scoped lifetime 28
scoped service 255
scoped styling 73–76
SearchFilter component 97–99, 101, 103, 106
SearchForTrail method 89–90
SearchPage component 88, 93, 96, 98, 100, 236, 305, 309–312
SearchPage's MaxLength parameter 103
SearchPage's route template 92
SearchTerm route parameter 93
securing Blazor
    applications 221–252
    authorizing users by role 245–252
        adding roles in Auth0 245–247
        consuming Auth0 roles in Blazor WebAssembly 247–249
        implementing role-based logic 249–252
    displaying different UI fragments based on authentication status 230–238
    integrating with identity provider 223–230
        configuring ASP.NET Core WebAPI to use Auth0 229–230
        configuring Blazor Web-Assembly to use Auth0 225–229
        customizing tokens from Auth0 224–225
        registering applications with Auth0 224
    prevent unauthorized users accessing page 238–245
    calling secure API end-points from Blazor 241–245

securing API
endpoints 239–241
semantic markup
verification 280
servers 130–139
adding MediatR to Blazor
project 132
creating request and handler
to post form data to
API 132–136
setting up endpoint 136–139
service configuration, SQLite
database 302
service container 279, 281
SetClaims method 285
SetCurrentValue method 148
SetFieldCssClassProvider
method 143
SetHourValue method 148
SetMinuteValue method 148
SetParametersAsync method 65
SetPolicies method 285
SetResult method 287
setter method 147
SetupModule method 286
Setup<T> method 287
SetupVoid method 286
SetVoidResult method 286
Shared folder 305–306
shared project
adding EditTrailRequest and
GetTrailRequest to
166–167
updating folder structure 166
single file format 51–52
Singleton lifetime 28
.slide class 67
sln add command 297
Smith, Jon 300
SQLite database 298–304
configuring initial entities for
system 299–301
connection strings and service
configuration 302
creating first migration and
creating database 303–304
setting up database
context 301–302
standalone mode 20
Startup class 29
state 50
state management 253–271
creating persistent state with
browser local storage
260–271

adding and removing trails
from favorites list
264–265
defining additional state
store 261–263
displaying current number
of favorite trails
265–266
initializing AppState
270–271
reorganizing and
refactoring 266–268
showing favorited trails on
favorite trails page
268–270
improving AppState
design 258–260
using in-memory store
254–258
creating and registering
state store 254–255
saving data entered on form
to AppState 255–258
StateHasChanged method 266,
269
strict mode 285
structuring components 51–54
partial class 52–54
single file 51–52
styling components 71–82
global styling 72–73
InputBase component
148–149
scoped styling 73–76
using CSS preprocessors
76–82
writing components for
34–36
submit events 113, 135
submit handler 113
SubmitEditTrail method 170
SubmitForm method 135, 153,
161
SuccessAlert component 163,
180
SupplyParameterFromQuery
attribute 101, 103–107
svg class 312
syntactically awesome style
sheets (Sass) 73
System.Text.Json library 42

T

Target element 81
template parameters 92

templated Razor delegates 277
templates
Blazor WebAssembly
configurations 20–21
defined 181–185
enhancing with generics
185–189
test doubles 274
TestContext class 279–280
testing with bUnit 272–290
adding bUnit test
project 274–277
components 277–289
emulating JavaScript
interactions 285–287
faking authentication and
authorization 283–285
testing multiple
components 287–289
testing rendered
markup 278–281
triggering event
handlers 281–283
overview 273–274
TimeInMinutes property 146,
150
TItem type 186
Title parameter 115
tokens, customizing 224–225
Trail class 39, 212, 218, 235, 267,
280, 300
Trail entity 233, 299–300
Trail parameter 46, 171, 187,
258
Trail record 211, 217, 234
Trail type 262
trail-data.json JSON file 40, 305
Trail.cs class 214, 299
_trail.Image property 170
TrailCard component 39, 46–47,
51, 63, 68, 180, 187, 236,
250, 264–265, 267, 283, 289,
305, 313–314
TrailConfig class 233
TrailDetails component 63–68,
71, 73–76, 95, 214, 216, 267,
287, 289, 305, 313–314
TrailDetails drawer 214–219
TrailDetails.razor 313–314
TrailDetails.razor.css
stylesheet 73
TrailDto class 111, 124, 150,
165–166, 210
TrailDto instance 135
TrailDto model 123

TrailDto type 134
TrailForm
  integrating RouteMap compo-
    nent with 206–214
  updating to handle
    editing 171–173
TrailForm component 160, 162,
  168–169, 171–172, 199, 211,
  257, 259
TrailForm's OnSubmit
  event 162
{trailId} placeholder 156, 174
TrailId property 154, 212
TrailSearch component 89–91
TrailValidator class 125, 127,
  150
TrailValidator constructor 125
transform: translateX
  properties 66
Transient lifetime 28
translateX CSS function 67
TResponse type 135
triggering event handlers
  281–283
TryGetValue method 249
TryParseValueFromString
  method 145–147

U

UI updates
  Blazor Server 13–14
  Blazor WebAssembly 9–10
Unauthorized response 240
unit testing 272
Up method 303
Update-Database command 304
UpdateFilters method 103–104
uploading files 153–158
  adding API endpoint 156–158

building request and
  handler 154–156
testing everything out 158
UploadTrailImageEndpoint
  endpoint 239–240, 249
UploadTrailImageRequest
  class 154
UseBlazorFrameworkFiles()
  middleware 294
User.Identity object 231
User.Identity.Name
  property 224–225
Users table 223
using statement 30, 33, 126,
  132, 199, 227, 232

V

valid class 128–129
Validate method 143
validation 123–130
  configuring Blazor to use Flu-
    ent Validation 125–130
  configuring validation rules
    with Fluent Validation
    123–125
  customizing CSS classes
    141–144
    creating FieldCssClass-
      Provider 141–143
    using custom FieldCssClass-
      Providers with
      EditForm 143–144
.validation-message class 144
validation-message class 128,
  144
ValidationMessage
  component 123, 126–127,
  129–130, 144

ValidationSummary
  component 123
validator class 128
Value parameter 117
Value property 118
value-based equality 133
variables 76
ViewSwitcher component
  181–182, 185, 192
VS Code (Visual Studio Code) 2

W

watch command 81
Waypoint class 211–212
Waypoint record 211
WaypointAdded function 205
WaypointAdded method 205,
  207
WaypointConfig class 212
Waypoints parameter 207
Waypoints property 211, 214,
  218
WeatherForecast class 293
WeatherForecastController
  example controller 293
WithMessage() method 125
writing components 30–48
  Blazing Trails home page
    38–48
  defining layout 36–38
  organizing files using feature
    folders 31–34
  setting up styling 34–36
wwwroot folder 30

Z

z-index property 202